Learning the Basics of New Testament Greek

Learning the Basics of New Testament Greek

Formerly Titled:
A Basic Grammar of New Testament Greek

George Aristotle Hadjiantoniou

Edited and Revised by
James H. Gee

AMG
PUBLISHERS
Chattanooga, TN 37422

Learning the Basics of New Testament Greek
(Revised Edition)

ISBN: 0-89957-800-4

Printed in the United States of America.
03 02 01 00 99 98 –R– 6 5 4 3 2 1

To My Wife

Acknowledgements

This edition of George Hadjiantoniou's Greek grammar has gone through a major revision process since the original printing in 1985. Much of this revision work has been done by Dr. James H. Gee, a volunteer editor here at AMG Publishers, with the assistance of Dr. Dennis Wisdom, a long-time professor of New Testament Greek. Dr. Gee is a brilliant Greek scholar and professor, and without his dedication and tireless effort, this revised edition would not have been possible. Other valuable staff members and volunteers have had a hand in this project, and we at AMG Publishers are grateful for them. These people include: Anne Arnett, Dr. Warren Baker, Tony Cortman, Symeon Ioannidis, and Rick Steele, Jr.

Although Dr. Hadjiantoniou and these fine scholars have labored meticulously to make this work free from error, they are not infallible. If you should find a mistake, please let us know.

NOTE: All parenthetical references such as **(3 § 6, i)** should be interpreted in the following order:

(lesson number § paragraph number, roman numeral subpoint)

–THE EDITORS

George Aristotle Hadjiantoniou

Dr. Hadjiantoniou was born in Smyrna, Asia Minor, in 1904. He graduated from law school at the University of Athens, Greece, and practiced law for ten years. A radical change occurred in George's life occasioned by a persecution against believers in northern Greece. Ten Christians were being tried in criminal court, in accordance with the second article of the Greek Constitution, that to this day forbids proselytism. However, these believers were not proselytizing, but simply witnessing to their new-found experience of the new birth in Christ.

Under these circumstances, Dr. Hadjiantoniou was called upon to defend these ten believers. Witnessing the joy these believers demonstrated for the privelege of suffering for Christ gave the lawyer the determination to preach for One who can give such joy in persecution.

After the trial's successful conclusion, he closed his law office and sought ministerial training at the Theological College of Cambridge University in England, and then furthered his studies at the University of Edinburgh, where he earned his Ph.D. specializing in church history.

Dr. Hadjiantoniou pastored churches in England, Greece, and Canada; wrote more than twenty-five books in Greek, some of which have been translated into English, French, or African languages. Some of his best known titles include: *The Historical Introduction to the Old Testament*, *Introduction to the New Testament*, *The Gospel Opened*, *The Twelve*, *The Seven Churches of Revelation*, and *Beyond the Grave*. He was also of major assistance to AMG Publishers in the publication of several word-study reference works, including *The Complete Word Study New Testament*.

Dr. Hadjiantoniou died at his home in Edmonton on Dec. 3, 1995. He is survived by his wife, Helen, and a son.

James H. Gee

Dr. James H. Gee (known to friends and family as Jim) first came to AMG International in 1985 while attending a local missionary conference. At this conference Jim, who lost his beloved wife to a long illness, met Mrs. Gertrude Okken, who had lost her husband, John, in 1983. Jim and Gertrude were married the following year and lived for a short time in Oklahoma where Jim was a freight line supervisor. In 1987, Jim retired and they moved to Chattanooga to work as volunteers for AMG International.

Jim has worked in the purchasing department and also in the Editorial Division of AMG Publishers. He has many talents, but his special love is the study of New Testament Greek. In addition to the hours Jim spent in the revision process of George Hadjiantoniou's Greek grammar he has contributed his time and efforts to such works as *The Complete Word Study New Testament* and *The Complete Word Study Dictionary, New Testament.* During his time in Chattanooga, Jim has taught at the Chattanooga Bible Institute and Covington Theological Seminary in nearby Rossville, Georgia.

Contents

Preface

A few words are probably needed to explain the appearance of still another textbook on New Testament Greek Grammar. The following factors, out of my own teaching experience, contributed to the decision of writing this book.

First is the desire to make the study of Koine Greek as simple as possible for the student by avoiding certain correct, but–in my opinion–unnecessary complications, which tend to add more burdens on the student, such as the "primary" and "secondary" tenses and their respective endings, the "variable vowel," etc.

Another factor is the awareness of the need for a methodical presentation of the material. The aim of this book is to cover the ground in a fuller way than the average textbook does. In order to achieve this, the material of the various units is dealt with in a more exhaustive way, and a richer vocabulary was introduced. A comprehensive vocabulary is provided in the back of the textbook.

From the earliest stages the student is placed in direct contact with the New Testament text (a) by supplying quotations from the NT in illustrating various rules, and (b) by using extensively parts of the text of the New Testament in the exercises, so that the student should be familiarized to a certain extent with the Greek New Testament before he actually starts using it.

A final factor leading to the writing of this book is my classroom experience that it can no longer be taken for granted that the student who takes up the study of the New Testament Greek grammar knows his English grammar. In order to avoid the ensuing confusion and delay in the study, each unit begins with a few introductory remarks about the nature and operation of this unit in all languages.

Preface

In writing this book I am greatly indebted to Blass-Debrunner's *A Greek Grammar of the New Testament and other Early Christian Literature*, A. T. Robertson's *A Grammar of the Greek New Testament in the Light of Historical Research* and Grimm-Thayer's classical work *Greek-English Lexicon of the New Testament*, as well as to E. G. Jay's *New Testament Greek–An Introductory Grammar*; B. Metzger's *Lexical Aids for students of New Testament Greek*, C. F. D. Moule's *An Idiom-Book of New Testament Greek*, and M. Zerwick's *Biblical Greek*.

I wish to acknowledge gratefully the valuable help very generously given me by my friend, Rev. Richard Darling, through his practical advice, and to thank Mrs. Paige Harrison for transforming my poor scribbling into the clear typed pages of the final manuscript.

G. A. H.

Lesson One

The "Koine" Greek ● *The Alphabet* ● *Vowels*
Diphthongs ● *Consonants* ● *Syllables*
Punctuation

1. The Koine Greek Language. The language in which the books of the New Testament were written is known as the "Koine" Greek. This language owes its name and, to some extent, its existence as well, to the conquests of Alexander the Great. Originally there were several Greek dialects, each of them specifically connected with some particular geographical area. Most important of these were the Attic, Ionic, Doric and Aeolic dialects. Eventually the Attic became the literary language of Greece.

Since Alexander the Great recruited the men for his army from all parts of the Greek world, a dialect gradually formed which, having the Attic as a basis, served as a common means of communication among all men of the army, and later among the merchants who followed the army into the conquered lands. The new language was the "Koine" language which means "common"; i.e., common to all Greek-speaking people. Later "Koine" acquired a broader meaning. This brings us to a second name of the language of the New Testament: "Hellenistic period" Greek.

The aim of the ambitious young conqueror was to bring all lands within the borders of his empire under the influence of the Greek civilization; in other words, to "hellenize" them. The Greek word for Greece itself is **Hellas**, and the term used to describe the process of fusing Greek and Oriental cultures is to **hellenize**. Therefore this period of history is known as the "Hellenistic" period. One of the effects of the hellenizing policy of Alexander was to make the new Greek dialect "Koine" in a wider sense, in that it became the common language of the whole Mediterranean world. Although the "Hellenistic period" lasted from the death of Alexander in 323 B.C. to the establishment of the Roman Empire in 30 B.C., the "Koine" survived approximately until the middle of the sixth century of our era, to be succeeded by another, the "Byzantine" form of the Greek language.

The main characteristic feature of the "Koine" is a consistent tendency to simplification through the dropping of many of the formulas of the older Greek dialects. However, the new dialect retained to a large degree the great flexibility of the Greek language.

2. Before we can begin the study of the language, or even of its alphabet, we must deal with the problem of pronunciation. There are two pronunciation "styles" of New Testament Greek: (1) the Erasmian pronunciation which has its origin in the work of the 16th century Dutch scholar Desiderius Erasmus, and (2) the Modern Greek pronunciation.

Whatever the pronunciation of the Greek language in classical times may have been, there can be little doubt that so far as the "Koine" of the Alexandrian period is concerned the Erasmian pronunciation presents serious flaws. The papyri–a collection of private letters, business correspondence, etc., which have been unearthed in Egypt since the 1870s–are written in the "Koine" Greek, and bear witness to the fact that most, if not all, vowels and diphthongs had during that period, not the phonetic value which the Erasmian pronunciation ascribes to them, but the one which they have in spoken Modern Greek. One should beware of being dogmatic with regard to this matter, but at the present time it is quite safe to assert that the Modern Greek pronunciation is in many respects much closer to that of the "Koine" period than the Erasmian one.

However, the Erasmian pronunciation is still in use in American and European colleges and seminaries. In order, therefore, to spare students unnecessary confusion, the Erasmian pronunciation is presented in paragraphs 3 and 4 of this lesson, to be followed in paragraphs 5 and 6 by the one the author of this book considers as more correct. Remember that, unlike Latin, Greek is not a "dead" language; it is still spoken. And it should be at least a matter of interest for the student that he be acquainted with the way the language in which the New Testament was written is still being spoken today.

3. The Alphabet. The Greek alphabet consists of the following twenty-four letters:

Capital letters	Small letters	Name of the letter	Erasmian Pronunciation
Α	α	alpha	a as in father
Β	β	beta	b as in ball
Γ	γ	gamma	g (hard) as in gag
Δ	δ	delta	d as in debt
Ε	ε	epsilon	e as in egg
Ζ	ζ	zeta	z as in daze
Η	η	eta	ee (long) a as in see
Θ	θ	theta	th (hard) as in thug
Ι	ι	yota	i in police or fit
Κ	κ	kappa	k as in keep
Λ	λ	lambda	l as in led
Μ	μ	mu	m as in man
Ν	ν	nu	n as in net
Ξ	ξ	xi	x as in lax
Ο	ο	omicron	o (short) as in omit
Π	π	pi	p as in peg
Ρ	ϱ	rho	r as in run
Σ	σ, ς	sigma	s as in sit
Τ	τ	tau	t as in ten
Υ	υ	upsilon	u as in unity
Φ	φ	phi	ph as in graphic
Χ	χ	khi	kh as in (German ch in Ach)
Ψ	ψ	psi	ps as in tops
Ω	ω	omega	o (long) as in note

The letter sigma has two forms (σ, ς), the latter being used only at the end of a word. In the NT text sentences begin with a small letter. The use of capitals is confined to proper names.

4. Vowels and Diphthongs. Of the above letters the following seven are vowels: **α, ε, η, ι, ο, υ, ω,** the remaining seventeen are consonants.

Of the vowels, **η** and **ω** are always long; **ε** and **ο** are always short; **α**, **ι**, and **υ** are sometimes long, sometimes short. These are called "dichrons."

A diphthong is the fusion of two vowel sounds into one. Therefore a diphthong forms one syllable. Four diphthongs are formed through the addition of **ι** to another vowel: **αι**, **ει**, **οι**, **υι** and four are formed through the addition of **υ**: **αυ**, **ευ**, **ηυ**, **ου**. These diphthongs are pronounced (in Erasmian) as follows:

αι,	ai, as in fire.	αυ,	ou, as in house.
ει,	ei, as in nail.	ευ,	eu, as in feud.
οι,	oi, as in toil.	ηυ,	eu, as in feud.
υι,	we, as in week.	ου,	ou, as in good.

Three particular diphthongs are formed by the letters **α**, **η**, **ω** having the **ι** subscript: **ᾳ**, **ῃ**, **ῳ**. The subscript makes no difference to the pronunciation of these vowels.

All diphthongs are long with the exception of **αι** and **οι** at the end of a word.

Two dots placed above the second vowel **αϊ** (for example the proper name Isaiah: **᾽Ησαΐας**), of one of the above combinations indicate that this is not a diphthong and should not be treated or pronounced as such **᾽Ησαΐας** has four syllables rather than three. This sign is called "diaeresis."

5. Modern Greek pronunciation of the alphabet. Following is the alphabet in the Modern Greek pronunciation of the letters, including that of their names.

Letter	Name of the letter		Pronunciation
α	ἄλφα	(ahl-phah)	ah, as in car.
β	βῆτα	(vee-tah)	v, as in van.
γ	γάμμα	(ghah-mah)	gh, pronounced like the English "y" as in "yet" when followed by "eh" or "ee" sounds; like "gh" when followed by other sounds,

			for which there is actually no corresponding English sound. One should try to pronounce it much deeper from the throat than the English "g" in the word "go."
δ	δέλτα	(dhehl-tah)	dh. as in that.
ε	ἔψιλον	(ehps-ee-lone)	eh, as in get.
ζ	ζῆτα	(zee-tah)	z, as in zero.
η	ἦτα	(ee-tah)	ee, as in see.
θ	θῆτα	(thee-tah)	th, as in third.
ι	ἰῶτα	(yoh-tah)	ee, as in see.
κ	κάππα	(kah-pah)	k, pronounced like "keep" when followed by "eh" or "ee" sounds; like "cup" when followed by other sounds.
λ	λάμβδα	(lahm-dhah)	l, as in lamp.
μ	μῦ	(mee)	m, as in man.
ν	νῦ	(nee)	n, as in now.
ξ	ξῖ	(ksee)	x, as in excellent.
ο	ὄμικρον	(oh-mee-krone)	oh, as in obey.
π	πῖ	(pee)	p, as in part.
ρ	ρῶ	(roh)	r, as in rose. (roll the tongue, like the Scottish "r.")
σ, ς	σῖγμα	(seegh-mah)	s, as in sun. (contrary to the English usage, σ is not pronounced as "z" when found between two vowels.)
τ	ταῦ	(tahf)	t, as in top.
υ	ὔψιλον	(eeps-ee-lone)	ee, as in see.
φ	φῖ	(phee)	ph, as in fall.

χ	χῖ	(khee)	kh, pronounced in a softer way when followed by "eh" or "ee" sounds; in a harder way, deeper from the throat, when followed by other vowel sounds or consonants–in both cases in a harder way than the English "h." In Modern Greek it is pronounced as in Erasmian: χείρ–hand, χήρα–widow
ψ	ψῖ	(psee)	ps, as in hips.
ω	ὠμέγα	(oh-meh-ghah)	oh, as in obey.

Other than for the letters ἔψιλον and ἦτα, the fact that the vowel is long or short does not affect its pronunciation in Modern Greek. In Koine Greek there was probably no difference in pronunciation so far as the qualty of the sound is concerned, either. However, there was probably a difference in the length of time speaking the sound, just as in the English pronunciation of an unaccented syllable or an accented syllable of a word. Thus ὄμικρον (lit.: small o) was probably pronounced like the "oh" in our word *phonetics*, and ὠμέγα (lit.: great O) was probably pronounced like the "oh" in our word *phone*. This would explain the reason for the accentuation rules which will be covered in Lesson 2.

6. According to the Modern Greek pronunciation the diphthongs have the following phonetic value:

αι	like **ε**	as in get.
ει	like **η**	as in see.
οι	like **η**	as in see.
υι	like **η**	as in see.
ου	like **oo**	as in book.

According to the Modern Greek pronunciation diphthongs or two vowel sounds fused into one really don't exist as to sound. They are pronounced like or as single vowels. Even in Erasmian the **ου** is not a true diphthong sound.

In the diphthongs **αυ**, **ευ**, **ηυ**, the second vowel is pronounced: as an "f" when followed by the consonants θ, κ, ξ, π, σ, τ, φ, χ, ψ; and as a "v" when followed by a vowel or the consonants β, γ, δ, ζ, λ, μ, ν, ϱ.

Thus: **αυ** is pronounced either "ahf" or "ahv,"
ευ is pronounced either "ehf" or "ehn,"
ηυ is pronounced either "eef" or "eev."

ωϋ is not a diphthong and the two vowels are pronouned separately. Μωϋσῆς

7. Consonants. Nine of the consonants are classified as follows:

	Labials	Dentals	Gutturals
Hard	**π**	**τ**	**κ**
Soft	**β**	**δ**	**γ**
Aspirate	**φ**	**θ**	**χ**

Two of the consonants **μ** and **ν** are *nasals* and two others **λ** and **ϱ** are *liquids.*

The consonant **γ** when followed by another **γ** or **κ** produces the sound "ng" as in "anger," and when followed by **χ** produces the sound "nh" as in "manhood."

8. Syllables. A word has as many syllables as it has vowels or diphthongs. For practical purposes we are interested only in the last three syllables of a word, *ultima* (the last one), *penult* and *antepenult.* For example ἀπό–στο–λος, ἀπό–(antepenult) στο–(penult) λος (ultima), The importance of these syllables appears in the matter of the accents. A syllable is considered long or short depending on the vowel or diphthong it contains, not the consonant.

A word is divided into syllables as follows:

(i) The consonant precedes the vowel: κα - λός.

(ii) When two or more consonants precede a vowel as a consonant cluster, if the consonant cluster can be used to start a Greek word, they go together at the beginning of the syllable. Thus: Χϱι - στός, but λαμ - βά - νω.

(iii) No syllable can begin with more than one of the same consonant: θά - λασ - σα.

9. Punctuation. The punctuation marks are the following:

(i) The full-stop period (.) and the comma (,) are the same as in English.

(ii) The semicolon is the same as the full-stop written a little higher up (˙).

(iii).The Greek question mark is the same as the English semicolon (;).

EXERCISES

I.

Pronounce the following words:

δωϱον, γϱαφη, ημεϱα, σωτηϱ, αιμα, εχει, πιστος, πϱοφητης, παϱα, σοφια, εκκλησια, ονομα, εθνος, πιστευω, τυφλος, εγγιζω, σταυϱος, καλοις, αγαθος, ακουω, νεκϱους, εσχατῳ, ευϱισκομεν, κϱινετε, ιεϱεις, πϱωτος, βασιλευς, νυν, παιδιον, αγιος, αγαπωμεν, αφιημι, ουδε, ακολουθειτε, εμπϱοσθεν, νικωσι, υποκϱιτης, φιλος, εχθϱος, ϱηματα, αναγγελλω, παϱακαλουσι.

II.

Pronounce the the following sentences:

1. ο Χϱιστος ηλθεν εις τον κοσμον ινα σωσῃ τους αμαϱτωλους.
2. δια της χαϱιτος του κυϱιου εγενομεθα τεκνα του θεου.
3. οι αποστολοι διδασκουσι την αληθειαν.
4. ακουομεν τους λογους της αιωνιου ζωης.
5. ημεις αγαπωμεν τον Χϱιστον οτι αυτος πϱωτος ηγαπησεν υμας.

Lesson Two

Breathings ● *Accents* ● *Elision*

1. Breathings. Every word beginning with a vowel or diphthong takes a breathing mark over that vowel or diphthong. A diphthong takes the breathing mark on the second of its component vowels (**υἱ**).

There are two breathings: the *smooth* (ʼ) which is the most common and the *rough* (ʽ). The breathing mark, smooth or rough, makes no difference in the pronunciation of the vowel or diphthong. It should be noted that in the Erasmian pronunciation a rough breathing is pronounced like the English "**h.**" It is not easy to form a general rule as to which words take the smooth breathing and which the rough. The student will have to memorize them. There are, however, three special rules:

(i) The vowel **υ** at the beginning of a word always takes the rough breathing. If the **υ** is part of the diphthong **υι** it passes the rough breathing to the **ι** (υἱός).

(ii) The article (**ὁ**, **οἱ**, the), if it consists of a vowel or diphthong, always takes the rough breathing .

(iii) The **ϱ**, although it is a consonant, takes the rough breathing if it is the initial letter of a word, (ῥῆμα).

2. Accents. As a rule each word takes an accent mark. There are two exceptions to this rule: (i) words which have no accent; (ii) words which under certain circumstances receive two accent marks. These two exceptions will be dealt with in their proper place. There are three accent marks: *acute* (**ά**), *circumflex* (**ῆ**), and *grave* (**τὸ**).

3. The accent can only be placed on one of the last three syllables of a word. In the case of a diphthong the accent is placed on the second of its component vowels. When an initial syllable takes both a breathing and an accent, the breathing is placed in front of the acute or the grave, and beneath the circumflex: ἄνθρωπος, οἶνος.

4. On which of the three syllables (antepenult, penult, ultima; see **1 § 8**) should the accent be placed? No all-inclusive rules can be formed. However:

(i) *This general rule applying to all words.* The accent cannot be placed on the antepenult if the ultima is long.

(ii) *This special rule applying to the noun.* As will be explained in a later lesson, the noun is inflected and has five cases, the first of which is the nominative. It is the nominative which sets the pattern: in the remaining four cases the accent must be retained on the same syllable as in the nominative, provided rule (i) permits it. Thus: ἀπό–στο–λος, ἀπο–στό–λου, ἀπό–στο–λον.

(iii) *This special rule applying to the verb.* The accent is placed as far away from the ultima as possible, in accordance with rule (i). Thus: λαμβάνω, ἐλάμβανον.

5. Which of the three accents should be used in each particular case? The following are the basic rules.

(i) The acute (´) can be placed on any of the last three syllables; the circumflex (~) only on the last two; and the grave (`) only on the ultima.

General Rules of Accent

Antepenult	Penult	Ultima	Accent
´	´	´	Acute
	~	~	Circumflex
		`	Grave
	´ if accented	LONG	Acute
	~ LONG if accented	SHORT	Circumflex
		LONG ´ or ~	Acute or Circumflex
	if word follows without punctuation	Acute changes to Grave	

Verb Accent

Antepenult	Penult	Ultima
´		SHORT
	´	LONG

(ii) A short syllable can never receive the circumflex.

(iii) If the penult is long and is to be accented, it must receive the acute if the ultima is long; the circumflex, if the ultima is short.

(iv) The grave accent is used only in place of the acute on the ultima of words which are not immediately followed by a punctuation mark.

6. Elision. A small number of words accented on the ultima and ending in a vowel drop the vowel (if the following word begins with a vowel), and replace it by an "apostrophe," a sign like the light breathing. Example: παρά: the **ά** if followed by αὐτοῦ is dropped, making it παρ᾽ αὐτοῦ.

EXERCISE

Correct the mistakes in the following words and state what mistake or mistakes were made in each word:

λ͂ογος, πρόφητης, πρώτος, δαιμ͂ονιον, πλοίον, στρατιῶτης, ὀν͂ομα, εἶδον, τελῶνης, τελώναι, κῆρυσσεις, πῖνεις, οἶκος, οἶκοι, ἔργον, ἑτοιμᾶζω, ἁμᾶρτανω, χὰρις, ἆνθρωποις, βαῖνω, δούλος, δοῦλοις.

Lesson Three

Parts of Speech ● *Parsing* ● *The Verb: Present Active Indicative*
The Conjunction: καί

1. Parts of Speech. Each word in a sentence has a given role to fulfill; accordingly the words are classified into various groups. These are called "parts of speech." Such parts of speech are the verb, the noun, the adjective, the conjunction, the article, the pronoun, etc. Each of these is governed by its own set of rules.

2. Parsing. Parsing is the process whereby a given word is (i) grammatically identified with one of these groups, and (ii) analyzed by having its distinctive features (parts) singled out within the framework of the particular part of speech with which it has been identified.

3. The Verb. Of all the parts of speech we begin our study with the verb because of the vital role it plays in a sentence. The verb is the pivot around which the other parts of the sentence revolve. A sentence without a verb is incomplete.

4. Transitive and Intransitive Verbs. A verb may express an action or a state of being. If the action expressed by the verb exercises an influence on persons or things other than the subject, the verb is called *transitive;* if no such influence is indicated by the verb, it is called *intransitive.*

5. The person or thing which is the recipient of the impact of the action indicated by the transitive verb is called the *direct object* of the verb. Besides the direct object a verb may have an *indirect object* which indicates the person or thing *to* or *for whom* the action denoted by the verb is performed; e.g., "Christ brought the sinners life"–"life" is the direct object, "the sinners," the indirect object of the verb.

6. Distinctive Features of the Verb. We can single out five distinct features of the verb: voice, mood, tense, person, number.

(i) *Tense.* The tense expresses, in general, the time element; i.e., the time at which the action indicated by the verb takes place: (a) in the present, the past, or the future; (b) in the duration of the action; (c) in relation to the time some other action takes place; (d) whether at the time of writing an action is viewed as completed.

(ii) *Voice.* In most languages the verb functions in two voices, the active and the passive. In Greek there is an additional voice, the middle.

In the active voice the subject of the verb is the one which exercises a certain activity; e.g., "I buy the boat." In the passive voice the subject is the recipient of the effects of the activity indicated by the verb; e.g., "The boat is bought by me." It is difficult to formulate a clear-cut and all-embracing account of the functions of the middle voice. At this stage it is sufficient for the student to note that in this voice the subject exercises the activity indicated by the verb with special reference to itself; e.g., "I buy the boat for myself."

(iii) *Mood.* The mood indicates the particular duties entrusted to the verb to fulfill; i.e., make a simple statement of fact or question, give a command, express a wish, etc. There are six moods: indicative, subjunctive, imperative, participle, infinitive, and optative (very rarely used in the NT). **Technically, however, the participle and the infinitive are not finite moods**. A finite verb is a verb which has tense, voice, mood, person and number.

(iv) *Person.* Person identifies the subject–the one performing the action or being affected by it–as either the person speaking, "myself," the person spoken to, "yourself," or the person spoken about, "himself," designated respectively as first person, second person, or third person.

(v) *Number.* If only one person or thing is involved, as the subject, in the action indicated by the verb, the singular number is used; if more than one, the plural.

7. Stem and Ending. For the present, we may consider the verb as basically composed of two parts. The part which remains solid and basically unchanged through all moods, voices, etc., is the *stem;* the part which is appended to the stem and varies according to voice, mood, etc., is the *ending*. It is necessary to grasp the importance of the "endings" in New Testament Greek. In English, the subject is singled out by means of the personal pronoun which precedes the verb (unless the subject is expressed by a noun), while the verb itself remains for the most part unchanged: "I write, you write, they write." But this is not so in Koine Greek. Greek relies on the ending in order to single out the subject; the personal pronoun is rarely used, except for purposes of emphasis.

8. It is necessary, therefore, to break down the verb into its two component parts. The vocabulary of this lesson contains certain verbs in the present tense, active voice, indicative mood, and 1st person singular. All of these have **ω** as their last letter; this is the ending. So, in order to find the stem of a verb we eliminate the **ω** from the 1st person singular indicative active. As we proceed in our study, we shall find that there are certain groups of verbs to which this method cannot be applied. At the present stage, however, we shall content ourselves with verbs which follow this simple method.

9. The endings of the present active indicative are:

	Singular	**Plural**
1st person	–ω	–ομεν
2nd person	–εις	–ετε
3rd person	–ει	–ουσι (ν)

The Greek word λύω (I loose) is a word used in most grammars to learn the Greek verb system. The stem λύ + the appropriate ending results in the following:

λύ+ω=	λύω	λύομεν
	λύεις	λύετε
	λύει	λύουσι(ν)

The **ν** in parenthesis is called "movable **ν**" and is usually added only when the following word begins with a vowel, or at the end of a sentence.

10. In English we have two Presents: "I write" and "I am writing." No such distinction exists in Greek.

11. In present-day English there is no visible distinction between the 2nd person in the singular and that person in the plural. Such visible distinction exists in Greek. Therefore, in order to avoid confusion it may be advisable for the student to translate a singular verb in the exercises by using the archaic "thou . . . est."

12. In English the question is usually formed with the aid of the auxiliary verbs "to do" and "to be": "Do I write?" and "Am I being loosed?" In Greek the question is formed by merely adding the question mark (;) at the end of the sentence.

13. The Conjunction. A conjunction is a word which links together two or more words within a sentence or two or more sentences. The most common of these is καί: *and.* This particular conjunction also renders certain other services in a sentence; these will be dealt with in Lesson 6.

VOCABULARY

ἀκούω:	I hear (takes accusative or genitive object.)
βαπτίζω:	I baptize
βλέπω:	I see, I watch, I beware of
γινώσκω:	I know
γράφω:	I write
διδάσκω:	I teach.
ἐγείρω:	I raise.
ἔχω:	I have
καί:	and, even, also
λαμβάνω:	I take, I receive
λέγω:	I say
λύω:	I loose, I destroy
μανθάνω:	I learn
σῴζω:	I save
φέρω:	I carry, I bring

EXERCISES

I.

Translate into English and parse by person and number.
Example: λύει, "he loosed (3rd sing.)."

μανθάνεις, βλέπομεν, γράφετε, γινώσκεις, ἐγείρομεν καὶ φέρομεν, σῴζουσι, διδάσκομεν, λέγουσι καὶ ἀκούετε, διδάσκεις καὶ μανθάνομεν, μανθάνουσι, ἔχετε, λύουσι, φέρεις, λέγετε, γράφουσι, μανθάνεις καὶ γινώσκεις, λαμβάνομεν καὶ ἔχομεν, βαπτίζεις.

II.

Translate into Greek:

He says, thou learnest, we are teaching, do they say? they have, you loose, thou savest, we see, they know, are you baptizing? We write, knowest thou? I am teaching and you are learning, dost thou write? He is teaching and baptizing, he carries, they are learning, thou destroyest, I receive and he has, art thou teaching and saving? I say and thou hearest, he is writing and knowing, we hear and you write.

Lesson Four

The Noun • *Nouns of the Second Declension*
The Indefinite Article

1. Distinctive Features of the Noun. Four distinct features of the noun can be singled out: case, gender, number and declension.

(i) *Case.* There are five cases, each of them determining the special role assigned to the noun or nouns in the sentence:

Nominative. The noun in this case serves as the subject of the verb.

Genitive. The most common, but by no means exclusive, duty of this case is to express "*possession.*" In English this is usually done by means of the preposition "of"; e.g. "the house of the king." In Greek "of the king" is expressed by putting the noun "king" in the genitive.

Dative. The chief role of this case is to indicate the indirect object of the verb. In English this is expressed by using the prepositions "to" or "for"; e.g. "I give the book to the student." In Greek "to the student" is expressed by putting the noun "student" in the dative.

Accusative. This case is usually used to indicate the direct object of the verb, although, a small number of verbs have their direct object in the genitive or the dative.

Vocative. This case is used in addressing someone. Some further uses of the various cases will be dealt with in a later lesson.

(ii) *Gender.* There are three genders: masculine, feminine and neuter.

(iii) *Number.* There are two numbers: singular and plural. The verb must agree in number with the noun which serves as the subject in the sentence. There is one exception: if the subject is a neuter noun in the plural, the verb can be either in the singular or in the plural.

(iv) There are three *declensions*. In each of them the noun is inflected in a different way; i.e. in each of them the cases have, as a rule, different endings.

2. Stem and Ending. Like the verb, the noun consists of two component parts: the *stem* which remains basically unchanged in all cases and both numbers, and the *ending* which varies in the two numbers and the cases–not necessarily in all of them. In order to find the stem of a noun we employ the method of elimination already familiar to us from the study of the verb. The application of this process to the noun presents certain peculiarities in the nouns of the third declension.

3. It is of great importance that the student should grasp a basic difference between the Greek sentence structure and the English sentence structure. In English, word order is very important as an indicator of sentence function. For example, in English the subject is usually placed before the verb and the object after it. If this order is reversed, especially when the verb is in the 3rd person singular or plural, the meaning of the sentence is radically changed. In the sentence "an apostle teaches a slave" "apostle" is the subject of the verb and "slave" is its object. If the order of the words is reversed, "a slave teaches an apostle," the sentence acquires a totally different meaning. In Greek it is not the order of the words in a sentence, but (in addition to the ending of the verb, as already indicated: **3 § 7**) the particular case of each noun which indicates the subject and object, direct or indirect, respectively. In the above example "ἀπόστολος διδάσκει δοῦλον" the reversal of the words in the sentence: "δοῦλον διδάσκει ἀπόστολος" does not affect in the least the meaning. The nominative of the noun which follows the verb and the accusative of that which precedes it clearly indicate the subject and the object of the verb. It is not unusual in Greek to have the direct or even the indirect object precede the verb. A sentence can also be constructed, and quite often is in the NT text, by placing the verb first: "διδάσκει ἀπόστολος δοῦλον."

In view of this flexibility of the Greek language, the student in translating a sentence should, first of all, locate the verb or verbs; he should then search for a noun (or an adjective, pronoun or participle) in the nominative in order to single out the subject of the verb; then proceed to search for a noun etc. in the accusative, which normally will indicate the direct object; and finally he should determine whether there is an indirect object indicated by a dative.

(Notice that the English in some sentences in the "English to Greek" exercises is very awkward. This is done deliberately to help the student get used to the differences in Greek style and English style. Follow the English word order–awkward though it may be–and you will end up with good Greek.

4. Nouns of the Second Declension. We shall start the study of the noun with the nouns of the second declension for two reasons: (i) this declension is the easiest for the beginner; (ii) it covers a larger number of NT words than the first. This declension includes nouns of all three genders, but the largest number are masculine.

5. Endings. Masculine and feminine nouns have identical endings in all cases of both numbers; gender is determined by the article or adjective modifiers. The endings of the second declension are as follows:

	Masculine and Feminine		**Neuter**	
	Singular	**Plural**	**Singular**	**Plural**
Nom.	–ος	–οι	–ον	–α
Gen.	–ου	–ων	–ου	–ων
Dat.	–ῳ	–οις	–ῳ	–οις
Acc.	–ον	–ους	–ον	–α
Voc.	–ε	–οι	–ον	–α

Here are examples of the conjugation of second declension nouns in all three genders:

	Masculine	**Feminine**	**Neuter**
		Singular	
Nom.	ἀπόστολος	ὁδός	τέκνον
Gen.	ἀποστόλου	ὁδοῦ	τέκνου
Dat.	ἀποστόλῳ	ὁδῷ	τέκνῳ
Acc.	ἀπόστολον	ὁδόν	τέκνον
Voc.	ἀπόστολε	ὁδέ	τέκνον

Plural

Nom.	ἀπόστολοι	ὁδοί	τέκνα
Gen.	ἀποστόλων	ὁδῶν	τέκνων
Dat.	ἀποστόλοις	ὁδοῖς	τέκνοις
Acc.	ἀποστόλους	ὁδούς	τέκνα
Voc.	ἀπόστολοι	ὁδοί	τέκνα

Notice in the above paradigms the application of the rules of the accent, both the one general rule and the special one for the noun.

6. Whenever a noun of the second declension has the accent on the ultima, the genitive and the dative of both numbers will take the circumflex (~). All others take the acute or grave.

7. The Indefinite Article. Although Greek does have a definite article, "the," it does not have an indefinite article, "a, an." Until you learn other reasons for a noun not having a definite article, assume that any noun without a definite article is indefinite, and use the indefinite article, *a, an*, in translation of any singular noun. Thus: ἀπόστολος, *an apostle*; ἀπόστολοι, *apostles*.

8. Neuter Plural Subjects. One exception to the general rule outlined at the beginning of this lesson (**§ 1, iii**) that singular nouns must take singular verbs, and plural nouns must take plural verbs: Neuter Plural nouns are frequently considered as collective nouns, and, therefore, take a singular verb about 60% of the time. For example: "ἀκούει τὰ τέκνα τοὺς λόγους," or "*The children hear the words.*" Since neuter plural nouns do take a plural verb about 40% of the time, you can expect to see either the singular or plural verb given with neuter plural subjects in the Greek-English exercises. But for the sake of consistency, and to help you get used to expecting a singular verb when you see a neuter plural noun, please use a singular verb with all neuter plural nouns when you are translating in the English-to-Greek exercises.

VOCABULARY

Although we have not yet been introduced to the definite article, you need to know the gender of a Greek noun, when you learn it. For this reason the proper definite article is given following the nouns in the vocabulary, in the nominative singular–masc. ὁ, fem. ἡ, neut. τό.

ἄγγελος, ὁ:	messenger, angel
ἀδελφός, ὁ:	brother
ἄνθρωπος, ὁ:	man (not in distinction to woman, but "human being")
ἀπόστολος, ὁ:	apostle
διδάσκαλος, ὁ:	teacher
δοῦλος, ὁ:	slave
δῶρον, τὸ:	gift
θεός, ὁ:	God
ἱερόν, τὸ:	temple: the whole building or complex of buildings including the sacred courts (Matt. 24:1).
κόσμος, ὁ:	world
κύριος, ὁ:	Lord, master
λόγος, ὁ:	word
ναός, ὁ:	temple: in a more limited sense than ἱερόν, esp. the inner sanctuary (Luke 1:9), or our body as a temple of God
ὁδός, ἡ:	road, way.
τέκνον, τὸ:	child (in relation to the parent).
Χριστός, ὁ:	Christ.

EXERCISES

I.

Translate into English:

1. Χριστὸς σῴζει κόσμον. 2. τέκνα διδασκάλων βλέπουσι κύριον. 3. δούλους ἀδελφῶν διδάσκομεν. 4. γινώσκεις δῶρον θεοῦ καὶ

ὁδὸν Χριστοῦ; 5. ἄνθρωποι κόσμου ἱερὰ λύουσιν. 6. λόγους ἀνθρώπων καὶ ἀγγέλων μανθάνετε. 7. ὁδὸν θεοῦ ἀπόστολοι διδάσκουσιν. 8. τέκνα δούλων διδάσκαλοι βαπτίζουσιν; 9. ἀδελφοῖς γράφετε λόγους Χριστοῦ. 10. τέκνα διδασκάλου δῶρα ναῷ φέρει. 11. δοῦλοι ἀδελφῶν ἀγγέλους βλέπουσι καὶ ἀκούουσιν. 12. γινώσκουσιν ὁδὸν κόσμου τέκνα ἀποστόλων. 13. ἀνθρώπους ἄγγελοι θεοῦ ἐγείρουσιν. 14. λόγους διδασκάλων ἀκούουσιν ἀδελφοὶ καὶ διδάσκουσιν δούλους. 15. ἀποστόλοις καὶ ἀδελφοῖς δοῦλοι κυρίου φέρουσι δῶρα. 16. γινώσκετε ὁδὸν θεοῦ; 17. τέκνα ἀνθρώπων διδασκάλους ἀκούει.

II.

Remember to use a singular verb for any neuter plural subjects in the English-Greek exercises. (see § 8).
Translate into Greek:

1. Children of brethren are learning words. 2. Art thou destroying a temple? 3. We bring slaves to a master. 4. You see angels of God. 5. Apostles say words of Christ to men of a world. 6. We are writing to brethren. 7. Slave, dost thou know ways of angels? 8. Does (the) Lord save? 9. Apostles are baptizing children of teachers. 10. Teachers are saying words and a slave is writing. 11. Do apostles raise children of slaves? 12. To a master a teacher brings gifts. 13. Are you baptizing slaves of a temple? 14. Words of God men are writing to brothers. 15. A master of slaves has brothers. 16. To temples we bring children of apostles. 17. Brother, God is saving masters and an apostle is baptizing slaves.

Lesson Five

The Noun ● *Nouns of the First Declension.*
The Definite Article.

1. Nouns of the First Declension. The first declension contains only masculine and feminine nouns, the majority of them being feminine. Nouns of both genders have identical endings in the plural.

2. Feminine Noun. Feminine nouns of the first declension are separated into three groups. The plural forms of each group are the same, while the singular endings used with each group depend on the next to the last letter of the stem. If the stem ends in a vowel or **ϱ**, the endings will use an **α** in all the singulars. If the stem ends in **λ**, **ξ**, **σ**, or **ψ**, the **α** will lengthen to **η** in the genitive and dative singular. If the stem ends in any other consonant, the **α** lengthens to **η** in all the singular forms.

3. The endings of the feminine noun of this declension are as follows:

	First Group	**Second Group**	**Third Group**	**All Groups**
		Singular		**Plural**
Nom.	–α	–α	–η	–αι
Gen.	–ας	–ης	–ης	–ων
Dat.	–ᾳ	–ῃ	–ῃ	–αις
Acc.	–αν	–αν	–ην	–ας
Voc.	–α	–α	–η	–αι

So we actually have three groups of feminine nouns of the first declension. Here are examples of all three:

	Singular		
Nom.	ἐκκλησία	γλῶσσα	προσευχή
Gen.	ἐκκλησίας	γλώσσης	προσευχῆς
Dat.	ἐκκλησίᾳ	γλώσσῃ	προσευχῇ
Acc.	ἐκκλησίαν	γλῶσσαν	προσευχήν
Voc.	ἐκκλησία	γλῶσσα	προσευχή

	Plural		
Nom.	ἐκκλησίαι	γλῶσσαι	προσευχαί
Gen.	ἐκκλησιῶν	γλωσσῶν	προσευχῶν
Dat.	ἐκκλησίαις	γλώσσαις	προσευχαῖς
Acc.	ἐκκλησίας	γλώσσας	προσευχάς
Voc.	ἐκκλησίαι	γλῶσσαι	προσευχαί

4. The nouns which turn the **α** into **η** in the genitive and dative singular have the **α** in the ultima short in all cases of the singular. Most of the nouns which retain the **α** in all cases of the singular have the **α** in the ultima long in all cases of the singular and in the accusative of the plural. Some of the most significant words which do not are ἀλήθεια: *truth,* μετάνοια: *repentance,* ἀσθένεια: *weakness, disease,* εὐσέβεια: *godliness, reverence,* πρόνοια: *providence*; that is why these words can have the accent on the antepenult in the nominative, accusative and vocative singular. In all other cases the **α** is long.

5. Masculine Nouns. The endings most masculine nouns of this declension are as follows:

	Singular	Plural
Nom.	–ης	–αι
Gen.	–ου	–ων
Dat.	–ῃ	–αις
Acc.	–ην	–ας
Voc.	–α	–αι

Notice that the endings in the dative and accusative singular and in all cases of the plural are identical with those of the feminine noun of the **η** group.

6. The following is an example of the masculine noun of this declension:

	Singular	Plural
Nom.	τελώνης	τελῶναι
Gen.	τελώνου	τελωνῶν
Dat.	τελώνῃ	τελώναις
Acc.	τελώνην	τελώνας
Voc.	τελῶνα	τελῶναι

The **α** in the ultima of the vocative singular is short.

7. There is a small number of masculine nouns which have–**ας** as the ending of the nominative singular. Most of these are proper names. Nouns of this group are declined on the pattern of the–**ης** group, the only exception being that **α** is taking the place of **η** in the endings of the singular. If the stem of these nouns ends in a vowel or **ϱ**, the ending of the genitive is **ου**: Μεσσίας –**ου** otherwise the ending of this case is **α**: Σατανᾶς—**ᾶ**.

8. Rules of Accent. Notice that every genitive plural noun in the first declension, whether masculine or feminine, has a circumflex on the ultima, no matter where the accent is for the nominative singular. This is not a violation of the noun rule of accenting given in Lesson **2 § 4**, ii. The original **α** of the stem has contracted with the **ω** of the ending according to rules we will learn later Thus, βασιλεία, βασιλειῶν.

9. Just as in the nouns of the second declension (**4 § 6**), if a noun in the first declension is accented on the ultima, the accent in the genitive and dative of both numbers is the circumflex: κϱιτής (nom. sg.), κϱιτοῦ (gen. sg.), κϱιτῇ (dat. sg.), κϱιτῶν (gen. pl.) κϱιταῖς (dat. pl.).

10. The Definite Article. The role of the definite article is largely the same as that of the English article "the." However, in many places, the Greek article should not be translated into English; to do so would alter the intended meaning. For example, in Greek, proper names usually take the article. Also, abstract nouns which are sometimes capitalized in English, such as Truth, or Love, will usually take the article in Greek. Thus, ὁ Σατανᾶς, "*Satan*" (rather than '*the Satan*,'; ἡ εἰϱήνη, "*peace*" (rather than "*the peace*".) Other differences between the Greek article and the English article will be dealt with at a later stage of our study.

11. The Greek article has three genders and is declined, and it must agree in case, gender, and number with the noun, adjective, pronoun, or participle which it accompanies.

12. The masculine and neuter article present a striking similarity to the endings of the masculine and neuter nouns of the second declension, and the feminine article is very similar to the endings of the feminine noun of the first declension of the–**η** group, with the following three points of difference:

(i) The masculine article drops the final **ς** in the nominative singular.

(ii) The neuter article drops the final **ν** in the nominative and accusative singular.

(iii) The consonant **τ** is prefixed to the above-mentioned endings in all cases and both numbers in the neuter article, and in all cases with the exception of the nominative in both numbers in the masculine and feminine article.

13. The masculine and feminine article in the nominative of both numbers takes the rough breathing.

14. Following the pattern of the nouns of the first and second declensions the article in all three genders takes the circumflex in the genitive and dative in both numbers.

15. The article has no vocative. In its place we often have the exclamation **ὦ**.

16. The article is declined as follows:

	Singular			**Plural**		
	M.	**F.**	**N.**	**M.**	**F.**	**N.**
Nom.	ὁ	ἡ	τό	οἱ	αἱ	τά
Gen.	τοῦ	τῆς	τοῦ	τῶν	τῶν	τῶν
Dat.	τῷ	τῇ	τῷ	τοῖς	ταῖς	τοῖς
Acc.	τόν	τήν	τό	τούς	τάς	τά

17. The form of the article remains unchanged in accompanying nouns of any of the three declensions. Be careful not to be misled by the ending of the noun etc. which follows it. Thus: οἱ προφῆται, αἱ ὁδοί.

VOCABULARY

ἀλήθεια, ἡ:	truth
ἁμαρτία, ἡ:	sin
βασιλεία, ἡ:	kingdom
γλῶσσα, ἡ:	tongue, language
δόξα, ἡ:	glory
εἰρήνη, ἡ:	peace
ἐκκλησία, ἡ:	church
ἐντολή, ἡ:	commandment
ἐπιστολή, ἡ	letter
ζωή, ἡ:	life
ἡμέρα, ἡ:	day
καρδία, ἡ:	heart
μαθητής, ὁ:	disciple
Μεσσίας, ὁ:	Messiah
παραβολή, ἡ:	parable
προσευχή, ἡ:	prayer
προφήτης, ὁ:	prophet
Σατανᾶς, ὁ:	Satan
τελώνης, ὁ:	tax-collector
φωνή, ἡ:	voice
ὦ	O (particle of direct address with vocative)

EXERCISES

Translate into English:

I.

1. οἱ διδάσκαλοι διδάσκουσι καὶ οἱ μαθηταὶ μανθάνουσι λόγους ἀληθείας. 2. ἀκούει τὰς προσευχὰς τῶν τελωνῶν ὁ θεός. 3. τὰ τέκνα τῶν προφητῶν βλέπουσι τὴν ἁμαρτίαν τοῦ κόσμου. 4. γράφετε ταῖς ἐκκλησίαις ἐπιστολὰς εἰρήνης; 5. τῆς φωνῆς τῶν

ἀγγέλων ἀκούουσιν αἱ καρδίαι τῶν τέκνων τῆς βασιλείας. 6. αἱ ἐκκλησίαι ἔχουσι τὰς ἐντολὰς τοῦ θεοῦ καὶ γινώσκουσι τὴν δόξαν τῆς ἡμέρας τοῦ κυρίου. 7. βλέπουσιν οἱ προφῆται καὶ οἱ ἀπόστολοι τὴν ἁμαρτίαν τῆς καρδίας τῶν ἀδελφῶν. 8. τὰς ἐντολὰς ἀκούετε καὶ τοὺς λόγους τῆς ζωῆς. 9. παραβολὰς λέγει ὁ ἀπόστολος καὶ τὰ τέκνα τῶν τελωνῶν μανθάνουσι τὴν ὁδὸν τῆς ζωῆς. 10. τὰ δῶρα τῆς εἰρήνης φέρει τοῖς μαθηταῖς ὁ κύριος. 11. γινώσκει τὰ τέκνα τῆς βασιλείας τὴν φωνὴν τοῦ Μεσσίου. 12. ἀκούουσιν οἱ δοῦλοι τῆς ἐκκλησίας τὴν ἐντολὴν τῆς ἀληθείας. 13. γινώσκετε τὴν ἡμέραν τῆς δόξης τῆς ἐκκλησίας; 14. ὁ θεὸς βλέπει τὴν καρδίαν καὶ ἀκούει τὰς προσευχὰς τῶν ἀδελφῶν. 15. τοὺς τελώνας σῴζει ὁ κύριος. 16. ταῖς ἐκκλησίαις ἐπιστολὰς εἰρήνης γράφουσιν οἱ προφῆται. 17. οἱ ἄγγελοι βλέπουσι τὸν θεόν. 18. γινώσκεις, ὦ τελῶνα, τὴν ἐντολὴν τῆς ζωῆς; 19. τοῖς ἀνθρώποις τοῦ κόσμου ἡ γλῶσσα τῶν ἀποστόλων καὶ τῶν προφητῶν λέγει τὰς παραβολὰς τῆς ἀληθείας. 20. τὴν ἀλήθειαν τῆς ἐκκλησίας ἀκούουσιν οἱ δοῦλοι τῆς ἁμαρτίας καὶ βλέπουσι τὴν δόξαν τῆς βασιλείας.

Translate into Greek:

II.

Note: Watch carefully in this exercise and subsequent exercises for those places where English differs from Greek usage concerning the article. Even though there may not be an article in the English, you may need to supply one in the Greek.

1. The children of the churches know the commandments of life. 2. The disciples of the prophets and of the apostles hear the words of truth and glory. 3. Do the hearts of the tax-collectors know peace? 4. We hear the words of the tongues of the angels. 5. The brothers are receiving the commandments of the day of the kingdom. 6. Dost thou hear the voice of the Messiah? 7. The heart of the disciples has the life of Christ. 8. The Lord of peace saves the slaves of sin. 9. You know the parables of the kingdom of God. 10. We hear the voices of the tax-collectors. 11. The teacher hears the prayers of the brothers and knows the hearts of the men. 12. The word of the Lord saves the world of sin. 13. The messengers are bringing to the churches the letters of the

prophets and the apostles. 14. The teachers of the churches are baptizing the children of the men. 15. To the prophets and the apostles the Lord is saying the words of life and peace. 16. The days of the teachers and of the disciples have peace. 17. Do the children of the tax-collectors know the way of life? 18. The masters and the slaves are learning the tongue (language) of the glory of God. 19. The men are bringing the children of the disciples to the ways of truth. 20. The prayer brings peace to the hearts of the children of God.

Lesson Six

The Negative:

οὐ . . . μή ● μέν . . . δέ ● οὐδέ ● καί . . . καί.

1. The Negative. In Greek negation is usually expressed by the word **οὐ** placed in front of the word to be negated. If the negation concerns a verb, **οὐ** is used in the indicative and **μή** in all other moods. If **οὐ** precedes a word beginning with a vowel or diphthong, it becomes **οὐκ**, and if that vowel has the rough breathing, it becomes **οὐχ**. There are, however, a few departures from this last rule in the NT text.

2. If **οὐ** stands alone and is accented **οὔ**, it means "No."

3. A more emphatic negation is expressed by the word **οὐχί** or by using both the above negatives **οὐ** and **μή** with the aorist subjunctive and less frequently with the future indicative (cf. John 6:35).

4. μέν . . . δέ. These two words are used together, as a rule, to introduce a contrast like our expression *"on the one hand . . . on the other hand."* In many cases, however, it is advisable to leave **μέν** untranslated and proceed to render **δέ** as *"but"* (in a rather weaker sense than ἀλλά) or "*and.*" These two words may be used together with an article or pronoun in the sense of "*some . . . others*" (E.g., see Matt. 13:8; Eph. 4:11). Both of these words are *postpositive;* i.e., they can never stand at the beginning of a clause.

5. When the article is followed by **δέ**, it takes on the meaning of the third person of the personal pronoun (to be dealt with in Lesson 12) and is to be translated "*and* (but) *he/she.*" Thus: ὁ δὲ λέγει: "*and* (but) *he says.*" This usage is quite common in the NT text.

6. οὐδέ. The negative **οὐ** linked together with **δέ** produces the word οὐδέ which, depending on the context, may mean "*and not,*" "*not* *even.*" Thus, οὐδὲ οἱ τελῶναι λέγουσι: "*not even the tax collectors say.*" This word used twice in a sentence has the meaning "*neither . . . nor.*"

7. καὶ . . . καί. The opposite service is rendered by καί used twice in a sentence having the meaning "*both . . . and.*"

8. A single **καὶ** can have the meaning of "*even*" or "*also.*" Thus: καὶ οἱ δοῦλοι γράφουσιν: "*even the slaves* (or: the slaves also) *are writing.*"

VOCABULARY

ἀγάπη, ἡ:	love
ἀλλά:	but (This is one of the words which is affected by elision, ἀλλ'. See **2 § 6**)
ἄρτος, ὁ:	bread; pl. loaves
βάλλω:	I cast, I throw
γραφή, ἡ:	writing, Scripture
δέ	and, but, now, then
δοξάζω:	I glorify
ἐπαγγελία, ἡ:	promise
ἔργον, τό:	work
ἐσθίω:	I eat
εὑρίσκω:	I find
θάνατος, ὁ:	death
κηρύσσω:	I proclaim, I preach
κρίνω:	I judge
λίθος, ὁ:	stone
μέν	on the one hand . . . on the other hand, indeed.
μή	not, no
οἶκος, ὁ:	house
οὐ, οὐκ, οὐχ	not
οὐδέ	and not, not even
πέμπω:	I send
πρόσωπον, τό:	face
ψυχή, ἡ:	soul, life
ὥρα, ἡ:	hour

EXERCISES

Translate into English:

I.

1. οἱ μαθηταὶ τῶν προφητῶν πέμπουσι ταῖς ἐκκλησίαις τὰς γραφὰς τῆς ἀγάπης. 2. οὐδὲ προσευχὴν λέγετε, οὐδὲ τὸν κύριον δοξάζετε. 3. οἱ μὲν εὑρίσκουσι θάνατον, οἱ δὲ τὸ πρόσωπον τοῦ Χριστοῦ βλέπουσιν. 4. οὐ κρίνει ἀλλὰ σῴζει τοὺς ἀνθρώπους ὁ κύριος. 5. καὶ τοῖς ἀδελφοῖς καὶ τοῖς δούλοις κηρύσσομεν τὴν ἐπαγγελίαν τῆς ζωῆς. 6. ἐσθίετε τὸν ἄρτον, ἀλλ᾽ οὐ δοξάζετε τὸν θεόν. 7. οὐδὲ τὴν ὥραν τοῦ θανάτου γινώσκει ἡ ψυχὴ τοῦ μαθητοῦ. 8. τὰ μὲν ἔργα τῆς βασιλείας γινώσκετε, εἰρήνην δὲ οὐκ ἔχετε. 9. καὶ τὰ τέκνα τῶν διδασκάλων καὶ τὰ τέκνα τῶν τελωνῶν βάλλουσι λίθους. 10. οὐ τοῦ κόσμου τὸν οἶκον βλέπομεν ἀλλὰ τοῦ θεοῦ. 11. γινώσκομεν τὰς γραφὰς καὶ τῶν προφητῶν καὶ τῶν ἀποστόλων. 12. οἱ μαθηταὶ οὐχ εὑρίσκουσιν τὴν δόξαν τοῦ κόσμου ἀλλὰ τὴν εἰρήνην τοῦ θεοῦ. 13. καὶ τοῖς τελώναις κηρύσσετε τὴν δόξαν τῆς βασιλείας. 14. οἱ μὲν ἀπόστολοι διδάσκουσιν, οἱ δὲ δοῦλοι τῶν ἐκκλησιῶν μανθάνουσι τὰς ἐντολάς. 15. οὐδὲ τὰς γλώσσας ἀνθρώπων οὐδὲ τὰς γλώσσας ἀγγέλων ἀκούετε. 16. καὶ τὴν ἀλήθειαν τῶν γραφῶν γινώσκετε καὶ τὴν ζωὴν τοῦ θεοῦ ἔχετε. 17. οὐκ ἄνθρωπος ἀλλ᾽ ὁ θεὸς ἀκούει τὰς προσευχὰς τῶν τέκνων τῶν μαθητῶν. 18. κρίνει ὁ θεὸς οὐ τὸ πρόσωπον ἀλλὰ τὴν καρδίαν τῶν ἀνθρώπων. 19. οἱ μὲν ἐσθίουσιν ἄρτον, οἱ δὲ γινώσκουσι τὰς ἐπαγγελίας τοῦ κυρίου. 20. ὁ δὲ πέμπει ταῖς ἐκκλησίαις οὐ λίθους ἀλλὰ δῶρα. 21. οὐδὲ ἡ ψυχὴ εὑρίσκει αγάπην. 22. τὸν κύριον τῶν ἀγγέλων δοξάζει τὰ ἔργα τῶν μαθητῶν. 23. καὶ οἱ ἄνθρωποι τοῦ θεοῦ βάλλουσι λίθους; 24. οὐδὲ οἱ ἄγγελοι οὐδὲ οἱ ἀπόστολοι ἀλλ᾽ ὁ Χριστὸς σῴζει τὸν κόσμον. 25. ἡ ὁδὸς τῶν διδασκάλων καὶ τῶν προφητῶν ἔχει εἰρήνην.

Translate into Greek:

II.

1. Knowest thou the peace of God? 2. Neither the commandments of the church you know, nor do you glorify the Lord. 3. The slaves of the

tax collectors both find the way of life and see the face of Christ. 4. We are preaching the way and the truth and the life; the prophets also preach. 5. The works of sin bring death. 6. We are eating not stones but bread. 7. Even the children of the house of God write letters of peace and say promises of life to the churches. 8. We are finding the hour of the glory of the kingdom. 9. The disciples of the apostles and of the prophets do not judge the men of the world, but they send the Scriptures to the houses of sin. 10. Dost thou hear the voice of love? 11. Neither love dost thou have nor the face of the Messiah dost thou see. 12. The slaves of the temple bring gifts of love both to the teachers and to the disciples. 13. Even the children of the prophets and of the apostles are teaching the way of life to the tax-collectors. 14. The apostle teaches, but (he) also learns. 15. Even the tax-collectors do the prophets baptize. 16. Some know the temple, but others glorify the Lord of the temple. 17. And he says to the men both the commandments and the promises of God. 18. Dost thou have the bread of life? 19. Both the truth of the kingdom do you teach and gifts of love you receive. 20. You are casting stones, but you do not destroy the temple of God.

Lesson Seven

The Adjective:
Adjectives of the First and Second Declensions

1. The Adjective. An adjective is a word joined to a noun in order to supply information about certain qualities of the person or thing denoted by that noun.

2. Like the noun and the article, the adjective is declined, and, like the article, it must agree with the noun it qualifies in case, gender, and number.

3. Attributive and Predicative Adjective. An adjective can be used in two different ways. Let us consider of "the faithful disciple." Not all disciples are necessarily faithful, and of a number of disciples we may want to single out the one who is faithful. This way of using the adjective is called the *attributive* use. But speaking of a certain disciple already known to us we may want to make a further statement about him: "this disciple *is* faithful." This is the *predicative* use of the adjective.

4. In the above example the auxiliary verb "is" made all the difference. In Greek this auxiliary verb is not necessarily used but is always implied when an adjective is used in the predicative sense. In absence of this auxiliary verb, the distinction between an attributive and a predicative adjective is made in the following way:

(i) The attributive adjective always immediately follows the article.

(ii) The predicative adjective never immediately follows the article.

Thus, in "ὁ ἀγαθὸς ἀπόστολος" the adjective ἀγαθὸς immediately follows the article and is, therefore, attributive–the meaning of the phrase being "*the good apostle.*" In "ὁ ἀπόστολος ἀγαθός" the adjective does not immediately follow the article and is, therefore, predicative, the meaning of the sentence being "*the apostle is good.*"

5. Both the attributive and the predicative adjective can be used in two different ways without doing violence to the above rule:

Attributive:

(i) ὁ ἀγαθὸς ἀπόστολος
(ii) ὁ ἀπόστολος ὁ ἀγαθός

In both cases the adjective immediately follows the article, although in (ii) the article is used twice.

Predicative:

(i) ὁ ἀπόστολος ἀγαθός
(ii) ἀγαθὸς ὁ ἀπόστολος

Construction (ii) is especially used when we wish to put more emphasis on the adjective: "*good is the apostle.*"

6. What happens when there is no article? ἀπόστολος ἀγαθὸς may mean *either "a good apostle" or "an apostle is good."* In such cases the context should help to define whether the adjective is used in the attributive or the predicative sense. It is when the context does not render conclusive assistance that a real problem arises for the translator of the NT text. For example, 2 Tim. 3:16 can be interpreted either as "all Scripture is God-breathed and profitable. . . ," or "all God-breathed Scripture is also profitable. . . ."

7. Adjective Used as a Noun. Sometimes an adjective preceded by the article is not accompanied by a noun. In such cases the adjective is treated as if itself were a noun. Thus, οἱ ἀγαθοὶ means "*the good people.*" This usage of the adjective is not uncommon in English; e.g., "the Society for the protection of the blind."

8. Adjectives of the First and Second Declensions: Like the noun, an adjective may belong to any one of the three declensions. However there is quite a large group of adjectives, in which the masculine and neuter follow the pattern of the second declension, while the feminine follows that of the first.

9. Adjectives with the stem ending in a vowel or **ρ** are declined in the feminine gender like the noun of the first–**α** class, while those with the stem ending in a consonant other than **ρ** are declined like the noun of the–**η** class. Thus, δίκαιος, δικαία, δίκαιον, but ἀγαθός, ἀγαθή, ἀγαθόν.

10. There is a smaller group of adjectives which form all three genders on the pattern of the second declension. See the vocabulary and footnote describing the listing of them. To this class belong all compound adjectives which are formed:

(i) Through the prefixing to an adjective or some other word

(a) a preposition: περίλυπος, **ον** (*greatly grieved*)

(b) the privative **α** (**αν** if it precedes a vowel)–corresponding to the English **"un"**: ἄπιστος, ον (*unfaithful*).

(c) an adverb: e.g. **εὐ**: εὐάρεστος, **ον** (*well pleased*).

(ii) Through the suffixing of the ending–ιος or–ιμος to a noun: αἰώνιος (*eternal*), ὠφέλιμος (*useful*). The very common adjective ἁμαρτωλὸς and a very few others also belong to this class.

11. The only divergence in the declension of the adjective from that of the noun is that the feminine adjective does not drop the accent to the ultima in the genitive plural, as the noun of the first declension does. Thus, τῶν δικαίων βασιλειῶν.

VOCABULARY

ἀγαθός, ή, όν:	good
ἀγαπητός, ή, όν:	beloved
ἅγιος, ἁγία, ον:	holy, saint
* ἄδικος, ον :	unrighteousness, unjust
*αἰώνιος, ον:	eternal, everlasting
ἄλλος, η, ο:	another, with the article: the other (Notice the absence of final ν, the neuter is irregular).

*ἁμαρτωλός, όν:	sinful, sinner
*ἄπιστος, ον:	unfaithful, unbelieving, unbeliever
γάρ:	for–in the sense of giving a cause for–(postpositive)
δίκαιος, α, ον:	righteous, just
ἔσχατος, η, ον:	last
καθαρός, ά, όν:	clean
καινός, ή, όν:	new (chiefly in respect of quality as distinguished from the outworn)
καλός, ή, όν:	good, beautiful
μακάριος, α, ον:	blessed
μικρός, ά, όν:	small
νεκρός, ά, όν:	dead
νέος, α, ον:	new (chiefly in respect of time)
πιστός, ή, όν:	faithful, believer
πονηρός, ά, όν:	evil, wicked, bad
πρῶτος, η, ον:	first

(*When you see only two forms for an adjective, assume that the first form is the personal form, covering both masculine and feminine, and the second form is the impersonal form for the neuter; see **§ 10**).

EXERCISES

I.

Translate into English:

1. τοῖς ἁγίοις μαθηταῖς ἄλλην ἐπιστολὴν πέμπουσιν οἱ ἀγαθοὶ διδάσκαλοι. 2. οἱ πρῶτοι ἔσχατοι καὶ οἱ ἔσχατοι πρῶτοι. 3. οὐχ αἱ ἄπιστοι αλλ᾽ αἱ πισταὶ ἀκούουσι γλώσσας ἀγγέλων. 4. μακάριοι οἱ πιστοί, ἔχουσι γὰρ ζωὴν αἰώνιον. 5. οἱ μὲν ἀδελφοὶ ἀγαθοί, οἱ δὲ τελῶναι πονηροί. 6. οὐ τοῖς δικαίοις ἀλλὰ τοῖς ἀδίκοις κηρύσσομεν τὰς ἀγαθὰς καὶ αἰωνίους ἐπαγγελίας. 7. βλέπει ὁ κύριος τὰ πονηρὰ ἔργα τῶν ἁμαρτωλῶν. 8. μακάριαι αἱ ἀγαθαί, γινώσκουσι γὰρ τὴν αἰώνιον δόξαν. 9. ἁμαρτωλὸς ὁ κόσμος, ἡ δὲ ἐκκλησία ἁγία. 10. ἡ ἄδικος καρδία νεκρά. 11. ἀγαπητοὶ οἱ πιστοὶ

μαθηταί, καρδίαν γὰρ καθαρὰν ἔχουσιν. 12. ἀγγέλων φωναὶ καλαί. 13. τοὺς τελώνας τοὺς πονηροὺς κρίνουσιν οἱ δίκαιοι προφῆται. 14. νεκροὶ οἱ ἄπιστοι. 15. οἱ μὲν ἄδικοι εὑρίσκουσι θάνατον, οἱ δὲ δίκαιοι λαμβάνουσι ζωὴν αἰώνιον. 16. τοῖς μαθηταῖς τῆς μικρᾶς ἐκκλησίας τὴν καινὴν ἐντολὴν τῆς ἀγάπης κηρύσσουσιν οἱ ἀπόστολοι οἱ ἅγιοι. 17. μακάρια τὰ τέκνα τῆς βασιλείας, μανθάνουσι γὰρ ἀγαθά. 18. ἀγαθοὶ καὶ δίκαιοι οἱ πιστοί. 19. οὐδὲ τὰς γραφὰς γινώσκουσιν οὐδὲ τὰς αἰωνίους ἐπαγγελίας ἀκούουσιν οἱ πονηροὶ τελῶναι. 20. πονηρὰ λέγει τὰ τέκνα τῶν ἀπίστων. 21. καὶ τοὺς νεκροὺς ὁ κύριος ἐγείρει. 22. καὶ ταῖς πισταῖς καὶ ταῖς ἀπίστοις κηρύσσουσιν οἱ νέοι διδάσκαλοι καινὰς ἐντολάς. 23. ἄλλας παραβολὰς γράφουσιν οἱ κύριοι τοῖς δούλοις. 24. ἀγαθὸς ὁ κύριος, σῴζει γὰρ τοὺς ἁμαρτωλούς. 25. τῇ ἐκκλησίᾳ τῇ ἐσχάτῃ τὰς καινὰς γραφὰς πέμπουσιν οἱ μακάριοι προφῆται.

II.

Translate into Greek:

1. The life of the believers is eternal. 2. The other disciples are writing another commandment to the last church. 3. Blessed are the good brethren, but the unrighteous are evil. 4. Both to the faithful ones (fem.) and to the unfaithful (fem.) you proclaim words of life eternal. 5. Even the evil hearts find the truth of the promises of God. 6. Blessed are the children of the first church, for they see the faces of the holy prophets. (The student should notice that a sentence like this is composed of two smaller ones, in each of which the rule governing the "postpositive" words is to be applied). 7. The last day judges both the believers and the unbelievers. 8. Neither the unrighteous ones nor the unbelievers hear the good and beloved voice. 9. Blessed are the small churches for they see the face of the Lord. 10. The believers both learn the Holy Scriptures and see the glory of the eternal kingdom. 11. The teachers bring good gifts to the temple, the disciples also are bringing. 12. We are hearing the beloved slave of the Lord, for he says good (things; neuter). 13. Eternal and good are the promises of the Messiah. 14. God hears even the tax-collectors' prayers. 15. Not the prophets but the Lord do the believers glorify. 16. Other new commandments do the apostles send to the last disciples. 17. Small but clean are the new

houses of the other slaves. 18. Some are teaching the believers; others are baptizing the disciples. 19. The good (ones) both carry gifts to the first temple and glorify the Lord. 20. Dost thou learn the truth and have peace? 21. The evil (ones) do not have the eternal life.

Lesson Eight

The Verb: Imperfect Active Indicative
The Conjunction ὅτι.

1. Imperfect Active Indicative. As already stated (**3 § 6, i**), one of the services which the tenses of the verb render is to denote the time at which the action indicated by the verb is taking place. We have, so far, studied the tense which deals with the present. Now we shall occupy ourselves with the tenses which deal with the past. Of such tenses there are four. In this lesson we shall confine ourselves to one of these: the imperfect.

2. The difference between the imperfect and the other three tenses stems from the fact that a certain action can have taken place in a continuous way or once for all. This difference is clearly shown in the sentences "I was writing a letter; I used to write letters" and "I wrote, or have written a letter."

3. The imperfect is used to denote a continuous or habitual action in the past. Because of its protracted nature the action in the imperfect is best represented by a line and is, therefore, called "linear," while the action in the remaining three tenses of the past is best represented by a simple dot and is called "punctiliar." A clear example of the difference between the imperfect and the other three tenses is offered in the account of the miraculous feeding of the five thousand in Mark 6:41 and Luke 9:16, where three verbs in the indicative are used: εὐλόγησεν "*he blessed,*" κατέκλασεν "*broke,*" and ἐδίδου "*was giving.*" The first two verbs are in the aorist because the "blessing" and the "breaking" of the loaves were instantaneous actions, while the verb denoting the "giving away" of the bread is in the imperfect because it describes an action of some continuous duration.

4. The imperfect is also used in the NT to denote an action that was attempted but not actually performed. This is known as the "Tendential Imperfect" (denoting that which one intends to do). Thus, ὁ δὲ διεκώλυεν αὐτὸν: "*but he was trying to prevent him*" (Matt. 3:14; cf. also Luke 4:42; Acts 7:26, etc.).

5. The imperfect is found only in the indicative.

6. The imperfect active is conjugated by adding the endings of this tense to the stem (**λυ**), already known from the present. These are:

Singular	**Plural**
–ον	–ομεν
–ες	–ετε
–ε(ν)	–ον

Here is the imperfect active indicative of λύω

ἔλυον	ἐλύομεν
ἔλυες	ἐλύετε
ἔλυε (ν)	ἔλυον

7. Augment. In all tenses denoting an action in the past, besides the adding of the endings *after* the stem, something is added *in front* of it. Thus, in the imperfect, the aorist and the pluperfect is called an "augment." The augment is an exclusive feature of the indicative, and consists:

(i) For verbs beginning with a consonant, in adding the vowel **ε** in front of the stem. This is the "syllabic" augment. Thus, γράφω, **ἔ**–γραφον.

(ii) For verbs beginning with a vowel, in lengthening the vowel. This is the "temporal" augment. The lengthening takes place as follows:

α is turned into **η**; e.g.	ἀκούω becomes ἤκουον.
ε is turned into **η**	ἐγείρω – ἤγειρον (Exception: ἔχω - εἶχον).
ο is turned into **ω**	ὀφείλω – ὤφειλον

The vowels **ι** and **υ** become long, but this makes no difference in the written form of these two vowels.

(iii) For verbs beginning with a diphthong in the lengthening of its component vowels, as follows:

αι is turned into **ῃ**
ει is turned into **ῃ**
οι is turned into **ῳ**
αυ is turned into **ηυ**
ευ is turned into **ηυ** (Frequently remains unchanged.)

If the initial vowel of the stem has the rough breathing mark, this is retained in the augment.

Confusion may be caused by the fact that in the "temporal" augment both the **α** and the **ε** are being lengthened to **η**. This makes it impossible for one to determine whether the **η** of the imperfect or the aorist is the result of the lengthening of an **α** or an **ε** in the present tense. The student should first of all conclude that he is dealing with an imperfect or an aorist through the aid of the ending. Then he should look up in a lexicon all verbs beginning with an **α** or **ε** plus the two or three letters which follow the temporal augment. The list of verbs thus compiled will be very short, and usually, one verb form will fit completely, especially when context is also considered. For example, ἤκουον, must be either ἀκούω or ἐκουω by form, and only the first one is used in the Greek New Testament.

8. Rule of the Accent. The rule which governs the accent of the verb (**2 § 4, iii**) retains its force here. Thus in the imperfect of ἀκούω the accent is transferred to the antepenult: ἤκουον, because, the ultima being now short, the general rule of the accent (**2 § 4, i**) does not stand in the way of the application of the special rule.

9. ὅτι. This conjunction is used to render one of two services:

(i) To denote direct or indirect quotations. It is translated as a direct quotation simply with quotation marks or as an indirect quotation with the word "that" (See **18 § 9**); e.g. "λέγει ὅτι βαπτίζει: *he says that he baptizes,*" but **ὅτι** is not postpositive.

(ii) To denote the cause of a certain action or state. In this sense it is similar to γάρ in meaning, but not in function. ὅτι is a subordinating conjunction and always introduces subordinating clauses that must be connected with a main clause. For example, John 6:2: "And a great crowd was following Him, because they were beholding the miracles which he was doing upon the sick." γάϱ, on the other hand, is a coordinating conjunction linking its clause with what goes before by presenting the cause or explanation for the preceding context. γάϱ always introduces independent clauses which can stand alone, and is usually best translated with the word "for" in the old English sense, as in John 3:16.

10. Ἰησοῦς. The Greek declension of the Hebrew names *Jesus* is a modification of the second declension patttern. Notice that, without the articles, there is no way to distinguish the genitive form from the dative form, and that both resemble the vocative form.

N. ὁ Ἰησοῦς
G. τοῦ Ἰησοῦ
D. τῷ Ἰησοῦ
A. τὸν Ἰησοῦν
V. Ἰησοῦ

VOCABULARY

ἁγιάζω:	I sanctify
ἀνοίγω:	I open
δεικνύω:	I show
ἐλέγχω:	I reprove, I rebuke, I convict
εὐαγγέλιον, τό:	gospel
θύϱα, ἡ:	door
Ἰησοῦς, ὁ:	Jesus
καθαϱίζω:	I cleanse
κλαίω:	I weep, I cry
κλείω:	I close
λεπϱός, ὁ:	leper
νηστεύω:	I fast
νῦν:	now (adverb)
οὐκέτι:	no longer (adverb)

πρεσβύτερος, ὁ:	elder, older; as a designation of an office
σάββατον, τό:	Sabbath
σκανδαλίζω:	I offend, I cause one to stumble
συναγωγή, ἡ:	synagogue
ταπεινός, ή, όν:	humble
τότε:	then (adverb)
υἱός, ὁ:	son
φίλος, η, ον:	friend, friendly
χαίρω:	I rejoice

EXERCISES

I.

Translate into English:

1. τότε μὲν οἱ πρεσβύτεροι τῆς συναγωγῆς ἐδίδασκον, νῦν δὲ οὐκέτι διδάσκουσιν. 2. ἐσκανδάλιζες τοὺς ταπεινοὺς μαθητάς, οὐ γὰρ ἡγίαζες τὴν ἡμέραν τοῦ σαββάτου. 3. τὰ μὲν τέκνα τῆς ἐκκλησίας ἐνήστευον, οἱ δὲ τελῶναι ἤσθιον ἄρτον. 4. καὶ λεπροὺς ἐκαθάριζε καὶ ἁμαρτωλοὺς ἤλεγχεν ὁ Ἰησοῦς. 5. ὁ φίλος τῶν ἁμαρτωλῶν ἐδείκνυε τοῖς ταπεινοῖς τὴν ὁδὸν τῆς ζωῆς. 6. οὐκ ἠλέγχετε τοὺς ἁμαρτωλούς. 7. οὐδὲ τὰς ἐντολὰς τοῦ εὐαγγελίου ἐμανθάνετε, οὐδὲ τὴν ἐπαγγελίαν εὑρίσκετε. 8. οἱ πιστοὶ πρεσβύτεροι ἔκλειον τὴν θύραν τῆς ἐκκλησίας τοῖς πονηροῖς. 9. ὁ μὲν διδάσκαλος ἐκήρυσσε τὰς παραβολὰς τῆς βασιλείας, οἱ δὲ φίλοι ἐμάνθανον τὰς ἐπαγγελίας τοῦ θεοῦ. 10. ἔλεγεν ὁ ἀγαπητὸς ἀδελφὸς ὅτι οὐκ ἔκρινεν ὁ υἱὸς τοῦ ἀνθρώπου ἀλλ᾽ ἔσῳζε καὶ ἐκαθάριζε τοὺς ἀδίκους. 11. οἱ μὲν πιστοὶ ἔχαιρον ὅτι ἤκουον τὰς μακαρίας ἐπαγγελίας τοῦ εὐαγγελίου, οἱ δὲ ἄπιστοι ἔκλαιον. 12. καὶ τελώνας εὕρισκεν ὁ φίλος τῶν ἁμαρτωλῶν. 13. οὐκ ἐκρίνετε τοὺς ἀπίστους, ἀλλ᾽ ἠνοίγετε τοῖς δούλοις τὴν θύραν τῆς βασιλείας. 14. οἱ μὲν ἔγραφον ἐπιστολὰς ταῖς ἁγίαις ἐκκλησίαις, οἱ δὲ ἔπεμπον ἀγαθὰ δῶρα τοῖς ἀγαπητοῖς μαθηταῖς. 15. ἐφέρομεν τὰ τέκνα τῶν ἄλλων προφητῶν τῷ Μεσσίᾳ. 16. οὐχ εὑρίσκομεν εἰρήνην ὅτι οἱ

μαθηταὶ οὐκ ἔλεγον ταῖς ἀπίστοις τὰς ἐντολὰς τοῦ Ἰησοῦ. 17. τότε μὲν ἐγίνωσκες τὴν γλῶσσαν τῆς ἀληθείας ὅτι εἶχες ἀγάπην, νῦν δὲ οὐδὲ τὴν ἀλήθειαν γινώσκεις οὐδὲ ἀγάπην ἔχεις. 18. καὶ τὰ τέκνα τοῦ πονηροῦ ἤκουον τὰς παραβολὰς τῆς αἰωνίου ζωῆς, ἀλλ᾽ οὐκ ἔβλεπον τὸ πρόσωπον τοῦ κυρίου τῆς ζωῆς. 19. οὐκ ἐσκανδάλιζες τοὺς ἀδελφούς, ἀλλ᾽ ἔπεμπες ταῖς ἐκκλησίαις ἐπιστολὰς ἀγάπης. 20. οὐκ ἐγίνωσκες τὰ ἔργα τοῦ θανάτου, εὕρισκες γὰρ τὰ δῶρα τῆς αἰωνίου βασιλείας. 21. καὶ κυρίοις καὶ δούλοις ἐκηρύσσομεν τὸ εὐαγγέλιον, ἤγειρε γὰρ ὁ κύριος τοὺς νεκρούς.

II.

Translate into Greek:

1. Wast thou showing to the humble ones the elders of the synagogue? 2. You were having peace, because you were fasting. 3. Even the sinful tax-collectors were sanctifying the day of the Lord. 4. Then the teacher was showing and the disciples were finding the way, but now he no longer shows. 5. The unrighteous prophets were causing the brethren to stumble, for they were eating the loaves of the children. 6. Jesus Christ was both cleansing the hearts of the believers and was reproving the sinners. 7. Were the disciples of the apostles and of the prophets raising the dead ones? 8. Thou wast (you were) no longer seeing the face of the Lord, because thou wast offending the beloved disciples. 9. The elders of the small churches were judging the children of (the) sin. 10. Were you sending to the slaves of the temple the Scriptures of the eternal promises? 11. Then the children of the elders of the other synagogues were glorifying God, for they were learning the commandments. 12. New parables of the kingdom the prophets were teaching. 13. The evil tax-collectors were not finding the door of the eternal life because they were not knowing the way. 14. Neither the house of the Lord wast thou cleansing nor wast thou fasting. 15. No longer were you preaching the gospel of peace and the believers were weeping. 16. The other disciples were eating the bread of the brothers, but the prophets were fasting. 17. The Son of Man was opening the house of God both to the faithful ones (fem.) and to the unfaithful (fem.). 18. The angels were showing to the men the glory of the day of

the Lord. 19. The teachers were writing words of truth, but they were not teaching the holy Scriptures. 20. Thou wast both teaching and learning.

Lesson Nine

The Preposition • *Prepositions with One and Two Cases*

1. The Preposition. A preposition is a word which is placed before a noun or pronoun and indicates the relationship which exists between the person or thing denoted by that noun or pronoun and some other word in the sentence. For example, "the pen is on the table"; the preposition "on" links the two nouns "pen" and "table" by showing the particular relationship which exists between them. There is a good number of prepositions disclosing a variety of relationships existing between nouns or pronouns in a sentence.

2. In Greek one particular preposition may have more than one meaning. This is determined by the case (genitive, dative or accusative) in which the noun or pronoun which follows that preposition is to be found. In this respect there are three groups of prepositions: those preceding a noun or pronoun which can be found,

(i) only in one of the above-mentioned cases;
(ii) in any of two cases; and,
(iii) in any of all three cases. In this lesson we shall deal with the first two of the above groups. It should be noted that the meanings of the prepositions given below are the main ones. However, certain of them are found in a few places of the New Testament text with other meanings.

3. Prepositions with One Case.

(i) Only with the genitive:

ἀντί: instead of (Luke 11:11); in exchange of (Rom. 12:17).

ἀπό: from, away from (of person, thing or place: Mark 12:34): of time (Matt. 27:45).

ἐκ : (ἐξ if the following word begins with a vowel): out of (Matt. 28:2).

πρό: before (of place: Acts 14:13; of time: John 11:55).

(ii) Only with the dative:

ἐν: in (of place: Luke 7:37; of time: Matt. 3:1), on (of time, as on the eighth day [Luke 1:59]). ἐν is also used to indicate the instrument through which an action is accomplished (Luke 11:19, 20).

σύν: with (Gal. 1:2).

(iii) Only with the accusative:

ἀνά: in, among (preceding μέσον [*midst*]: Matt. 13:25); in a distributive sense (preceding numerals). For example, ἀνὰ δύο; two by two: Luke 10:1

εἰς: into (Matt. 8:23). εἰς is occasionally used with the meaning of ἐν (Matt. 2:23).

4. Prepositions with Two Cases.

διά (with gen.): through, throughout, of place (Mark. 9:30); of time (Luke 5:5); of the instrument through which something is done (Matt. 18:7).

διά (with acc.): on account of, because of (John 20:19); for the sake of (Mark 2:27).

κατά (with gen.): down from (Mark 5:13); against (Mark 9:40).

κατά (with acc.): according to (1 Cor. 15:3); throughout (Luke 9:6); towards (Luke 10:33); used distributively: every (Acts 13:27).

μετά (with gen.): with (Matt. 16:27).

μετά (with acc.): after (Luke 15:13).

περί (with gen.) about, concerning (Mark 12:26).

περί (with acc.): around (Luke 13:8).

πρός (with dat.): near, at (Only six times in NT: John 18:16).

πρός (with acc.): to, towards (Distinguish it from εἰς: into; Mark 6:51); with (Matt. 13:56).

ὑπέρ (with gen.): in behalf of, instead of, in favor of (Matt. 5:44); in place of (Phile. 1:13).

ὑπέρ (with acc.): above (Matt. 10:24).

ὑπό (with gen.): by, indicating the agent of a passive voice verb, for example, baptized by him (Mark 1:5).

ὑπό (with acc.): under (Mark. 4:21).

5. Elision. Whenever a preposition ending in a vowel is followed by a word beginning with a vowel, elision takes place: the vowel of the preposition drops off and is replaced by an apostrophe. Thus, ἀπό, (ἀπ', Matt. 7:23); ἐπί (ἐπ', Matt. 3:16); κατά (κατ', Matt. 1:20); μετά (μετ', Matt. 2:3). This rule does not apply to the prepositions περί and πρό. If the vowel of the following word has the rough breathing, the **π** of ἀπό and ἐπί is turned into **φ** (ἀφ', ἐφ') and the **τ** of ἀντί, κατά and μετά is turned into **θ**: ἀντί, (ἀνθ', Luke 1:20; 12:3) κατά (καθ', Matt. 5:11; 12:25) and μετά (μεθ', Matt. 1:23; 17:1).

6. Prepositions and the Article. For the Greeks, certain words were thought of as definite when used with prepositions, not needing an article. This is especially true of words marking geographical locations or time indicators. For example, "παρὰ ποταμὸν: *by the river.*" (Acts 16:13); "ἐν ἀρχῇ . . . *in the beginning* . . ." (John 1:1). If your instinct tells you to put an English article in your translation exercises, or to leave out a Greek Article, use parentheses to indicate your guess.

VOCABULARY

ἀγρός, ὁ:	field
ἄγω:	I lead
βιβλίον, τό:	book
δένδρον, τό:	tree
ἐγγίζω:	I approach, I draw near (usually with dat.)
ἔρημος, ἡ:	desert
ἑτοιμάζω:	I prepare
ἐχθρός, ά, όν:	enemy
Ἰουδαῖος, ὁ:	Jew
καρπός, ὁ:	fruit
μένω:	I remain, I abide
μόνος, η, ον:	alone, only
ὀλίγος η, ον:	little; pl. few

πάσχω:	I suffer
πίπτω:	I fall
πλοῖον, τό:	ship, boat
σπείρω:	I sow
φεύγω:	I flee
φόβος, ὁ:	fear

EXERCISES

I.

Translate into English:

1. σὺν τοῖς ἁμαρτωλοῖς τελώναις ἤσθιον ἐν τοῖς οἴκοις οἱ πιστοὶ μαθηταὶ τοῦ κυρίου. 2. οἱ μὲν πρὸ τοῦ ἱεροῦ, οἱ δὲ ἐν ταῖς συναγωγαῖς διδάσκουσιν. 3. οὐχ ὑπὲρ τῶν φίλων, ἀλλ᾽ ὑπὲρ τῶν ἐχθρῶν ἔπασχεν ὁ Ἰησοῦς. 4. διὰ τῆς ἐρήμου διὰ τὸν φόβον τῶν Ἰουδαίων ἔπεμπε τὰ τέκνα τῶν προφητῶν ὁ πρεσβύτερος. 5. ἐν τῇ ἡμέρᾳ τῆς προσευχῆς εἴχετε εἰρήνην κατὰ τὸν λόγον τοῦ κυρίου. 6. οὐ λίθον ἀντὶ ἄρτου ἐλαμβάνετε. 7. μένομεν μετὰ τῶν ἀδελφῶν ἐν τῷ οἴκῳ τοῦ κυρίου. 8. ὀλίγους μὲν καλοὺς δὲ καρποὺς ἐλαμβάνομεν ἀπὸ τῶν δένδρων τοῦ μικροῦ ἀγροῦ. 9. καθ᾽ ἡμέραν ἐδίδασκεν ὁ Ἰησοῦς ἐν τῷ ἱερῷ. 10. μετὰ τοὺς προφήτας τοὺς ἀποστόλους μετὰ τῶν ἄλλων μαθητῶν ἔπεμπεν ὁ κύριος πρὸς τὰς ἐκκλησίας. 11. καὶ τῶν ἐχθρῶν τὰ τέκνα ἤγομεν ἐκ τῆς συναγωγῆς εἰς τὴν ἐκκλησίαν. 12. ἐμένετε ἐν τῇ ἀληθείᾳ καὶ ἐχαίρομεν. 13. οἱ ἄλλοι προφῆται ἐλάμβανον ἐν τῷ οἴκῳ τοὺς ἄρτους ἀπὸ τῶν δούλων. 14. διὰ τὴν ἁμαρτίαν τοῦ κόσμου ἔπασχε μόνος ὁ υἱὸς τοῦ θεοῦ. 15. μετὰ ταῦτα ἔφευγον οἱ ἀδελφοὶ ἀπὸ τοῦ ἱεροῦ καὶ ἔφερον δῶρα πρὸς τοὺς προφήτας. 16. περὶ τῆς βασιλείας τοῦ θεοῦ ἐν τῇ ἡμέρᾳ τοῦ σαββάτου ἐδίδασκον οἱ νέοι προφῆται ἐν ταῖς συναγωγαῖς. 17. ἐκ τοῦ οἴκου τῆς ἁμαρτίας καὶ πρὸς τὸν διδάσκαλον ἦγον τοὺς τελώνας οἱ υἱοὶ τῶν προφητῶν. 18. οὐδὲ ὁ μαθητὴς ὑπὲρ τὸν διδάσκαλον, οὐδὲ ὁ δοῦλος ὑπὲρ τὸν κύριον. 19. οἱ τελῶναι σὺν τοῖς ἄλλοις ἁμαρτωλοῖς ἔλεγον λόγους πονηροὺς κατὰ τῶν ἀγαπητῶν ἀδελφῶν ἐν τῇ ἡμέρᾳ τοῦ κυρίου. 20. καὶ ἄλλους ἤγειρεν ἐκ τοῦ

θανάτου ὁ κύριος. 21. οὐ πρὸ τοῦ οἴκου ἀλλ' ἐν τῷ ἀγρῷ ἔσπειρον οἱ δοῦλοι οἱ ἀγαθοί. 22. οἱ μὲν ἦγον τοὺς ἀδελφοὺς πρὸς τὴν συναγωγήν, οἱ δὲ ἔβαλλον λίθους κατὰ τῶν ἀποστόλων. 23. διὰ τῶν ἁγίων γραφῶν ἐμανθάνομεν τὴν ἀλήθειαν κατὰ τὴν ἐντολὴν τῶν προφητῶν. 24. μετὰ τὴν ὥραν τῆς προσευχῆς ἠσθίομεν ἄρτον μετὰ τῶν φίλων ἐν τῷ οἴκῳ τοῦ διδασκάλου. 25. ὀλίγοι τελῶναι ἐνήστευον πρὸ τῆς ἡμέρας τοῦ κυρίου.

II.

Translate into Greek:

1. Dost thou send the children of the synagogue into the church? 2. Because of the love of Christ the apostles write letters of peace to the churches. 3. The Lord of glory was suffering alone instead of the sinners. 4. Not about the first law but about the last days you were preaching. 5. Do you hear tongues of angels from heaven? 6. With the brethren we were glorifying the Lord in the holy day. 7. The faithful disciples were sowing the words of the gospel into the hearts of the humble ones. 8. Dost thou raise the dead ones out of death? 9. According to the word of God the teachers were writing against the unbelievers and in favor of the righteous ones. 10. Neither the prophets nor the apostles do we see above the Lord Jesus. 11. Because of the truth a few tax-collectors were glorifying the Lord on the day of joy. 12. The prophets were sending the faithful disciples out of the house into the ships according to the commandment of the Scriptures. 13. Before the day of the Sabbath we used to receive gifts from the righteous prophets. 14. On account of the promises of the gospel after the parables you were writing the commandments in the holy book. 15. The sons of the kingdom were abiding in Christ with the beloved brothers and were having peace and joy in the heart. 16. We were hearing before the synagogue good words concerning the last days. 17. Instead of the children you were leading the brothers into the house of prayer. 18. On the Lord's day the prophets with the elders were fasting. 19. In favor of the disciples the teacher was saying good (things) to the Jews. 20. Through the cross of Christ we have the eternal life according to the promise of the holy Scriptures.

Lesson Ten

The Preposition: Prepositions with Three Cases
The Verb: Present Indicative of the Verb εἰμί
Proclitics and Enclitics ● *The English Preparatary "There"*

1. Prepositions with Three Cases. There are two prepositions which precede nouns or pronouns in any of three cases: ἐπί and παρά.

ἐπί (with gen.): upon (Matt. 9:2); in the time of (Luke. 3:2).
(with dat.): upon (Matt. 14:8); indicates the authority on which an act is done (Luke 5:5);
at–indicates the basis (Luke 4:22).
(with acc.): indicates motion upon or towards (Matt. 22:9) or against (Matt. 24:7); during (Acts 13:31).

παρά (with gen.): indicates motion from, seeking or taking from–always of persons (John 5:34; 17:8).
(with dat.): beside, nearby (John 19:25).
(with acc.): at, beside, along (Acts 16:13); contrary to (Rom. 16:17).

2. Present Indicative of the verb εἰμί. One of the most common verbs in any language is the verb "to be." In Greek this verb is irregular. In the present indicative it is declined as follows:

εἰμί	I am	ἐσμέν	we are
εἶ	thou art	ἐστέ	you are
ἐστί (ν)	he, she, it is	εἰσί (ν)	they are

3. The Verb εἰμί Does Not Take an Object. The reason for this will be better understood if we remind ourselves that, when dealing with the adjective, we observed that in the predicative adjective the verb "to be" is implied. Thus, in ὁ μαθητὴς ἀγαθὸς the verb "is" is implied between μαθητὴς and ἀγαθὸς. But the verb: in *the disciple is good*, is not always or necessarily implied; usually it is written: ὁ μαθητὴς ἐστὶν ἀγαθός. So, the noun, adjective, etc., which qualifies the verb εἰμί *is not the object* of the verb, but a *predicate* renamer or describer of the subject, because this verb does not indicate any action on the part of the subject, but makes a statement about certain qualities, states, or conditions of it. Therefore, it is not an object in the sentence.

4. The verb εἰμί is not the only verb which does not express an action on the part of the subject. The verb γίνομαι (*I become)*, and others, also take a predicate nominative. In all such cases we must be careful to put the noun, etc. which follows the verb in the same case as the subject.

5. When two nouns are linked as subject and predicate nominative with the verb εἰμί stated or implied, one with the article and the other without one, the one with the article is to be translated as the subject, regardless of which one come first. Thus in John 1:1, "καὶ θεὸς ἦν ὁ λόγος," does not say that God was the Word, but that "*the Word was God* (by nature)." Check a good textbook on Doctrines for the full significance of the fact that the article is used with the word *God* in the first part of the verse, "καὶ ὁ λόγος ἦν πρὸς τὸν θεόν . . . *and the word was with God*," but not with the word *God* in the last part of the verse as cited above. Again, John 4:24, πνεῦμα ὁ θεός, cannot be translated "Spirit is God, but only as "*God is a Spirit.*"

6. Proclitics and Enclitics. There are two groups of words which form exceptions to the rule of the accent (**2 § 2**). These are the "proclitics" and the "enclitics."

7. Proclitics. The proclitics are the words which under normal conditions take no accent. The principal proclitics are:

(i) The masculine (ὁ, οἱ) and feminine (ἡ, αἱ) articles in the nominative of both numbers.

(ii) The prepositions εἰς, ἐκ, ἐν.

(iii) The negative οὐ.

(iv) The words εἰ *(if)*, ὡς *(as)*.

8. Enclitics. The enclitics are the words which are so closely linked with the word which precedes them that, under certain conditions, either lose entirely their accent or have it transferred to the preceding word. The enclitics are:

(i) The verbs εἰμί and φημί in the present indicative, with the exception of the second person singular (εἶ; see **10 § 2**).

(ii) The personal pronoun in the genitive, dative and accusative in the first singular ("unemphatic") and in the second person singular: μου, μοι, με, σου, σοι, σε.

(iii) The indefinite pronoun τις.

(iv) The conjunction τε, the adverbs πόθεν, ποτέ, ποῦ, πῶς, and one or two other words rarely found in the NT text.

9. The rules governing enclitics have been introduced for euphonic reasons; in essence, an enclitic should be read as if it were part of the preceding word. Thus:

(i) All enclitics of one syllable lose their accent or transfer it to the preceding word, e.g., ὁ θεός μου: *"my God."*

(ii) An enclitic of two syllables retains its accent only if the preceding word has an acute accent on the penult, e.g., ἡ θύρα ἐστὶν: *"it is the door."*

(iii) If the word preceding an enclitic has an acute accent on the ultima in its lexical form, it will keep the acute accent even though it is now followed by another word before punctuation, e.g., ὁδός τις: *"a certain way"* (cf. **2 § 4, 5**).

(iv) If the word preceding an enclitic has a circumflex on the penult or an acute on the antepenult, it receives the accent of the enclitic as a second accent in the form of an acute on the ultima, e.g., ὁ οἶκός μου: *"my house"*; διδάσκαλοί ἐσμεν: *"we are teachers."*

(v) If the word preceding an enclitic is a proclitic, it receives the accent of the enclitic in the form of an acute, e.g., ἔκ τινος: *"out of someone."*

(vi) When two or more enclitics are found in a row, the enclitic which comes first takes the accent of the one which follows, and so on, in the form of an acute on the ultima, and the last enclitic remains unaccented, e.g., δοῦλοί μού εἰσιν: *"they are my slaves."*

10. The 3rd person singular of the verb εἰμί in the present indicative does not lose its accent, but has it on the penult (ἔστι[ν]) when:

(i) It means "to exist" (Heb. 11:6).
(ii) It occurs after οὐκ and certain other words (Matt. 28:6).

11. The English Preparatory "There." In English the word "there" is placed in front of a verb not in a locative sense but in a preparatory way, in order to indicate that the subject in the sentence will follow the verb. This usage is especially common with the verb "to be" (cf. Matt. 16:28 "There are [be] some standing here, who [which . . ."]). This "preparatory there" is not used in Greek. Matthew 16:28 literally reads, "Some of the ones standing here are, who . . ."

VOCABULARY

ἀκάθαρτος, ον:	unclean
ἀληθινός, ή, όν:	true
διάβολος, ὁ:	devil
διώκω:	I pursue, I persecute
ἕτερος, α, ον:	another, different
θησαυρός, ὁ:	treasure
καθαρός, ά, όν:	clean
κρύπτω:	I hide
οἶνος, ὁ:	wine
ὅλος, η, ον:	whole. This adjective presents a peculiarity in that it retains the attributive sense although it never occurs in the attributive position in the NT, i.e., it immediately follows the article (Matt. 16:26, etc.).
οὐρανός, ὁ:	heaven, sky (frequently occurs in the plural with a singular translation)
πίνω:	I drink
πιστεύω:	I believe (usually takes its object in the dative. Can also be followed by εἰς and the accusative, thus acquiring a stronger

meaning: I trust. However, this distinction is not consistently applied in the NT text.).

σοφία, ἡ:	wisdom
σταυρός, ὁ:	cross
τόπος, ὁ:	place
τυφλός, ή, όν:	blind
ὑπομονή, ἡ:	patience

EXERCISES

I.

Translate into English:

1. οἱ προφῆταί εἰσι πιστοί, καὶ τοὺς λόγους τῆς αἰωνίου ζωῆς κηρύσσουσιν. 2. διὰ τὴν ἀγάπην τῆς βασιλείας ἔμενον μεθ' ὑπομονῆς αἱ πισταὶ παρὰ τῷ σταυρῷ τοῦ Ἰησοῦ. 3. οὐ παρὰ τὴν ὁδὸν ἀλλ' ἐν τῷ ἀγρῷ εὕρισκες τὸν θησαυρόν. 4. κατὰ τὴν καινὴν ἐντολὴν πὶνομεν οἶνον νέον. 5. ἀκάθαρτοί ἐσμεν ὅτι ἐν τῇ ἡμέρᾳ τοῦ σαββάτου ἠσθίομεν ἄρτον παρὰ τὴν ἐντολήν. 6. οὐχ ὑπὲρ καθαρᾶς ἀλλ' ὑπὲρ ἀκαθάρτου ἐκκλησίας ἔλεγε προσευχὴν σὺν τοῖς μαθηταῖς ὁ προφήτης. 7. παρὰ τῶν ἀποστόλων ἐλαμβάνομεν τὰς ἁγίας γραφάς. 8. ἡ σοφία ἐστὶ καλή, καὶ ἔχει ἀγάπην πρὸς τοὺς ἀδελφούς. 9. οἱ τυφλοὶ προφῆται ἄγουσι φίλους ἐπὶ φίλους. 10. ἀπὸ τῶν ἡμερῶν τῶν ἀγαθῶν διδασκάλων οὐκέτι δοξάζετε τὸν θεὸν ἐν τῇ συναγωγῇ. 11. ζωὴ ἐν ταῖς καρδίαις τῶν πιστῶν ἐστιν ὁ λόγος τοῦ θεοῦ. 12. οὐκ ἀπ' ἀνθρώπων ἀλλὰ παρὰ τοῦ θεοῦ ἐλαμβάνομεν τὴν ἀληθινὴν σοφίαν. 13 ἅγιοι οὔκ ἐστε, καὶ ἐδιώκετε τοὺς πρεσβυτέρους τῆς ἑτέρας ἐκκλησίας διὰ τὴν ἀλήθειαν. 14. θάνατον ἑτοιμάζει τῇ ψυχῇ τοῦ ἀπίστου ἡ ἁμαρτία κατὰ τὰς γραφάς. 15. καθ' ὅλην τὴν ἡμέραν ἐμένομεν παρὰ τοῖς ἀδελφοῖς καὶ ἐλαμβάνομεν παρ' αὐτῶν δῶρα τοῦ οὐρανοῦ. 16. ἐβλέπομεν τοὺς ἀγγέλους καὶ ἐξ ὅλης τῆς ψυχῆς ἐδοξάζομεν τὸν θεὸν διὰ τὰς ἐπαγγελίας τοῦ εὐαγγελίου. 17. μετὰ τοὺς διδασκάλους καὶ οἱ μαθηταὶ μετὰ χαρᾶς καὶ ἀγάπης ἐκήρυσσον ἑτέροις ἀνθρώποις

περὶ τῆς βασιλείας τῶν οὐρανῶν. 18. διὰ τὸ ἔργον τοῦ σταυροῦ καθαρός εἰμί, καὶ μένω παρὰ τῷ ἱερῷ. 19. οὐ μόνον σὺν ὀλίγαις καθαραῖς καὶ πισταῖς ἀλλὰ καὶ σὺν ταῖς ἀκαθάρτοις καὶ ἀπίστοις ἤσθιον ἄρτον καὶ ἔπινον οἶνον οἱ μαθηταὶ διὰ τὴν ἀγάπην τοῦ θεοῦ. 20. ἅγιος εἶ, ὦ θεέ, καὶ παρὰ τῶν ἁμαρτωλῶν λαμβάνεις δῶρα.

II.

Translate into Greek:

For the best pratice in accenting enclitics in this exercise, use the verb εἰμί whenever you can, and follow word order as closely as you can in those sentences using εἰμί.

1. An apostle am I, not from men nor through man, but through Jesus Christ. 2. Dost thou abide upon the promises of the holy Scriptures? 3. Alone are a few disciples in another house on account of the fear of the Jews. 4. You believe (trust) in Jesus Christ and you find peace and the pure wisdom. 5. Faithful we are and we were remaining with patience beside the house of prayer. 6. On the authority of the word of the Lord the good prophets were closing the door of the synagogue on the day of the Sabbath both to the clean and to the unclean (women). 7. Contrary to the commandment of the gospel he was leading the believers into the desert. 8. We were offending both friends and enemies because after the hour of prayer we were eating bread and were drinking wine with sinners and tax-collectors. 9. The brothers of the apostles are blind and they were fasting beside the road. 10. The sinners were fleeing away from the face of the elders on account of the words of the holy Scriptures. 11. Not in behalf of a few righteous ones but in behalf of the whole church through the work of the cross the Lord is preparing a place in the heavens. 12. Dost thou abide along the door of the small clean church? 13. Even from the dead (ones) the prophet was raising men on the authority of the word of the Lord. 14. Because of the truth of the gospel the unbelievers are persecuting the other sons of the kingdom also. 15. Beloved are the teachers of the last church and they are preaching concerning the gospel of peace. 16. We were seeing the prophet beside the enemies of the cross. 17. Thou wast suffering, O

Christ, in behalf of the whole church. 18. You are sinners and you do not find peace in the words of the Holy Scriptures. 19. In the whole world contrary to the promises of the unbelievers thou dost not find the true wisdom. 20. Both peace and glory the whole church was receiving from God, for it was believing upon (lit., into) Jesus Christ.

Lesson Eleven

The Verb ● *Compound Verbs*
Present and Imperfect Indicative Active

1. The Compound Verbs. The prepositions we have dealt with in the last two lessons can also be prefixed to a verb and thus form a *compound verb.* The same function is performed by prepositions in the English language; thus "over-burden," "under-stand," "with-draw." Compound verbs are very common in the New Testament.

2. The examples of English prepositions as parts of a compound verb cited above make it clear that a preposition can affect the original verb in a variety of ways. In NT Greek a preposition as part of a compound verb:

(i) May intensify the meaning of the original verb. Thus, γινώσκω *(I know),* ἐπιγινώσκω (*I know thoroughly* [A striking example can be found in 1 Cor. 13:12]).

(ii) May complete the meaning of the original verb. Thus, ἄγω *(I lead),* ἀπάγω *(I lead) away.* The meaning of the verb is further expanded when more than one preposition is used in the construction of the new verb: λείπω *(I leave),* καταλείπω *(I leave behind),* ἐγκαταλείπω *(I abandon* or *I desert).* The completed meaning of the verb can, as a rule, be gathered from the meaning of the particular preposition used for the construction of the compound verb.

(iii) May produce an entirely new meaning. Thus, γινώσκω: *I know,* ἀναγινώσκω: *I read.*

(iv) May produce no discernible difference in meaning. Thus λαμβάνω, and παραλαμβάνω both mean essentially, *(I receive).*

3. The preposition which has been used to form the compound verb often has to be repeated in the sentence. Thus, ἐκβάλλω ἐκ τοῦ οἴκου: *"I cast out of the house."*

4. When the original verb begins with a vowel and the preposition ends in a vowel elision takes place. This rule does not apply to the prepositions περί and πρό. The preposition ἐκ before the original verb beginning with a vowel and before the augment of the imperfect and the aorist becomes ἐξ (**9 § 3, 5**).

5. The **ν** of the prepositions ἐν and σύν:

(i) Before a labial consonant (**π**, **β**, **φ**) as the initial letter of the original verb is turned into **μ**. e.g., συμφωνέω *(I agree with).* ἐμβλέπω *(I look at).*

(ii) Before a guttural (**κ**, **γ**, **χ**) is turned into **γ**. e.g, συγχαίρω, I rejoice with.

(iii) Before **λ** (**ν**) is turned into **λ**. e.g, συλλαμβάνω, (*I sieze*).

(iv) Before **ζ** or **σ** (only in the case of σύν) is dropped.

6. Compounds Verbs in the Present and Imperfect Indicative. The compound verb is conjugated in these two tenses in exactly the same way as the original verb. The augment in the imperfect and the aorist is prefixed to the stem of the original verb and after the preposition. Thus, προσφέρω, προσέφερον. The rule which governs the accent of the verb (**2 § 4, iii**) is applied here also. However, the accent cannot be placed farther back than the augment, i.e., it cannot be placed on the preposition. Thus, συνάγω—συνῆγον.

VOCABULARY

ἀναβαίνω:	I go up
ἀναβλέπω:	I look up, I recover my sight
ἀναγινώσκω:	I read
ἀπάγω:	I lead away
ἀποθνῄσκω	I die
ἀποκτείνω:	I kill
ἀπολύω:	I release, I loose

ἀποστέλλω:	I send (Usually on a mission, in distinction with the more general πέμπω)
βαίνω:	I go (In the NT only as part of a compound verb)
βιβλίον, τό:	book
δαιμόνιον, τό:	demon, evil spirit
ἐγκαταλείπω:	I forsake (Notice the two prepositions; stronger meaning than καταλείπω)
ἐκβάλλω:	I cast out, I throw out
ἐπιγινώσκω:	I know thoroughly
ἐπιστρέφω:	I return
καταβαίνω:	I go down
κατακρίνω:	I condemn
καταλείπω:	I leave behind, I forsake
λείπω:	I lack, I need, I leave in the sense of abandon
παραλαμβάνω:	I receive
προσφέρω:	I bring to, I offer
σταυρός, ὁ:	cross
συλλαμβάνω:	I seize, I conceive (of a woman)
συνάγω:	I gather together
ὑπακούω:	I obey (with dat.)
ὑποστρέφω:	I return

EXERCISES

I.

Translate into English:

1. ἐν ταῖς ἡμέραις τῶν προφητῶν καὶ οἱ δοῦλοι ἀνέβαινον εἰς τὸ ἱερὸν καὶ προσέφερον δῶρα πρὸς τὸν κύριον. 2. οὐδὲ τὰς γραφὰς ἀναγινώσκεις οὐδὲ ταῖς ἐντολαῖς τοῦ κυρίου ὑπακούεις. 3. ὅτι οἱ δοῦλοί ἐστι πονηροί, συνελάμβανον τοὺς προφήτας. 4. οὐ κατέκρινεν ὁ Ἰησοῦς τὸν κόσμον, ἀλλ᾽ ἀπέθνησκεν ἐπὶ τοῦ σταυροῦ καὶ προσέφερε ζωὴν αἰώνιον τοῖς ἁμαρτωλοῖς. 5. οὐκ

ἐγκατελείπετε τοὺς λόγους τῆς ἀληθείας, ἀλλ᾽ ἐξεβάλλετε ἐκ τῆς ἐκκλησίας τοὺς ἀπίστους. 6. ἐπὶ τῷ λόγῳ τοῦ πιστοῦ μαθητοῦ καὶ οἱ τυφλοὶ ἀνέβλεπον. 7. οὐ τὰς πιστὰς ἀλλὰ τὰς ἀπίστους ἀπήγετε πρὸς τοὺς πρεσβυτέρους. 8. καὶ οἴκους καὶ ἀγροὺς κατέλειπες διὰ τὴν βασιλείαν τῶν οὐρανῶν, ἐπεγίνωσκες γὰρ τὰς γραφάς. 9. πιστοί ἐστε, καὶ οὐκ ἀπ᾽ ἀνθρώπων παρελαμβάνετε τὰς καινὰς ἐπαγγελίας. 10. κατὰ τὴν ὥραν τῆς προσευχῆς κατὰ τὴν ἐντολὴν τοῦ θεοῦ ἀνεβαίνομεν σὺν τοῖς ἀδελφοῖς εἰς τὸ ἱερόν. 11. μετὰ ταῦτα ὅλη ἡ ἐκκλησία ὑπήκουε τῷ ἀποστόλῳ. 12. μετὰ τοὺς προφήτας τὸν υἱὸν ἀπέστελλεν ὁ θεὸς εἰς τὸν κόσμον. 13. οὐκ ἀπ᾽ ἀνθρώπων ἀλλ᾽ ἀπὸ τοῦ κυρίου παρελαμβάνομεν τὰς ἀληθινὰς ἐντολὰς τοῦ εὐαγγελίου. 14. οἱ προφῆται σὺν τοῖς πρεσβυτέροις ἀνεγίνωσκον ἐν τῷ βιβλίῳ περὶ τῆς βασιλείας τοῦ οὐρανοῦ καὶ ἐξέβαλλον δαιμόνια. 15. οἱ μαθηταὶ κατέλειπον τὸ πλοῖον καὶ ἐπέστρεφον εἰς τὸν οἶκον τοῦ διδασκάλου. 16. ὀλίγοι τελῶναι ἀπέλυον τοὺς δούλους καὶ προσέφερον δῶρα πρὸς τοὺς διδασκάλους. 17. καὶ οἱ ἄγγελοι τοῦ οὐρανοῦ ἔχαιρον ὅτι οἱ υἱοὶ τῶν ἄλλων προφητῶν οὐκ ἐγκατέλειπον τὰς ἐντολὰς τῆς ἀληθείας. 18. διὰ τὸν φόβον τῶν Ἰουδαίων οἱ ἀπόστολοι συνῆγον τοὺς μαθητὰς ἐν ἑτέρῳ τόπῳ 19. ἡ ψυχὴ τοῦ ἁμαρτωλοῦ καταβαίνει εἰς τὴν ὁδὸν τοῦ θανάτου. 20. ἐν τῷ κόσμῳ ὅλῳ καὶ τυφλοὶ ἀνέβλεπον καὶ ἁμαρτωλοὶ ἐπεγίνωσκον τὰς ἐπαγγελίας τῆς βασιλείας. 21. οἱ μὲν ἀποστέλλουσι τὰ τέκνα πρὸς τοὺς φίλους, οἱ δὲ ὑποστρέφουσι πρὸς τὸ ἱερόν. 22. οὐκ ἀπέθνῃσκες ἐν τῇ ἁμαρτίᾳ, ἀλλ᾽ ὑπήκουες τῇ φωνῇ τοῦ κυρίου καὶ συνῆγες τὸν καρπὸν τῆς ζωῆς. 23. εἴχετε εἰρήνην ἐν τῇ ἐκκλησίᾳ, ἐξέβαλλε γὰρ ὁ κύριος τὸν φόβον ἐκ τῆς καρδίας τῶν πιστῶν. 24. ἐν τῇ μικρᾷ συναγωγῇ ἀκούομεν μὲν τῆς φωνῆς ἀνθρώπων, ὑπακούομεν δὲ τῷ κυρίῳ. 25. διὰ τὴν ἀγάπην τοῦ κυρίου οἱ πιστοὶ μαθηταὶ κατέβαινον καὶ εἰς τοὺς οἴκους τῶν ἀδίκων.

II.

Translate into Greek:

1. Readest thou in the Scriptures the words of eternal life? 2. Not the righteous (fem.) but the humble ones (fem.) receive from God the promises of the blessed kingdom. 3. A few disciples were not going

down into another house, but were offering prayers on behalf of the whole church. 4. The masters are righteous, and they release the slaves. 5. The humble disciples were going up alone into the temple. 6. The small children of the elders return to the house and find treasures of love. 7. The sinners were killing the Lord of glory on the cross. 8. God does not forsake the humble ones in the ways of sin. 9. Not a stone but the bread of life eternal the church offers to unclean tax-collectors. 10. On the authority of the commandment of the evil elders the slaves were killing the teachers of the synagogue and were returning to the houses. 11. The blind brothers of the beloved prophet were recovering (their) sight. 12. Not from the angels of the heaven but from the teachers of the whole church you were receiving the fruit of patience. 13. In the days of the apostles the other teachers used to offer the books of wisdom even to the unclean ones. 14. Holy art thou and thou wast casting out demons on the authority of the commandment of the Messiah. 15. Even the tax-collectors were obeying the elders of the other synagogue on account of the glory of the kingdom. 16. Both the masters and the slaves used to know thoroughly the truth concerning the work of the cross. 17. Some used to leave behind the children and go up into the temple and were offering good gifts, but others were going down to the fields and were gathering together fruits. 18. Were you returning into the way of life and were you obeying the voice of the truth? 19. The children of the devil were killing the sons of the kingdom beside (at) the door of the temple. 20. A few small churches were receiving good letters and were reading the words of the true wisdom. 21. Neither a prophet nor an apostle but the Lord of glory was dying upon the cross instead of the sinners of the whole world. 22. We know thoroughly the commandments of God for through the whole day we were reading the holy Scriptures.

Lesson Twelve

The Pronoun • *The Personal Pronoun*

1. The Pronoun. As its name suggests, a pronoun is a word which is used in the place of a noun. This is a convenient working definition, but is not absolutely correct because, as a matter of fact, some of the pronouns do not take the place of a noun, while others seem to have been assigned the role of an adjective. However, this definition will do for the needs of the present study.

2. The word whose place is taken by the pronoun is called its "antecedent." In the sentence "We love God and worship Him," "Him" is the pronoun which has been used instead of repeating the noun "God," the antecedent. There are several kinds of pronouns: personal, demonstrative, relative, possessive, reflexive, reciprocal, interrogative, and indefinite.

3. The Personal Pronoun. The personal pronoun is found in three persons, and the third person in three genders exactly as in English: I, thou, he–she–it.

4. The personal pronoun is declined like a noun or adjective, but has no vocative case. The third person personal pronoun must agree with its antecedent in gender and number, but not always in case. In putting the pronoun in the right gender the student must take care not to be misled by the gender of the antecedent in English, which may not be the same as that of the Greek noun; e.g. "I received a letter and I read it"; the pronoun "it" is in the neuter gender, but its antecedent "letter" in Greek (ἐπιστολὴ) is a feminine noun, and the pronoun should therefore be not αὐτό but αὐτήν.

5. The student will notice the affinity between the 1st and 2nd persons in their declension, their endings in the plural being identical in all cases. In the 3rd person the masculine and neuter have second declension endings (the **ν** in the nominative and accusative singular of the neuter being dropped), and the feminine has first declension of the –**η** group endings.

6. It may be useful to repeat at this point what we have already observed when dealing with the verb. In English, if a noun is not present, the personal pronoun is always placed before the verb in order to indicate its subject; in Greek it is not necessary to do so because that service is rendered by the ending of the verb. However, the personal pronoun is placed before the verb when it is desirable to put an emphasis on the subject. Thus διδάσκω *(I teach)*, but ἐγὼ διδάσκω *(I myself teach* or *it is I who teaches)*. Such an emphasis is especially necessary when there is an explicit contrast or parallelism between the subjects of two verbs. Thus, "ἐγώ εἰμὶ δοῦλος, σὺ δὲ εἶ ὁ κύριος" *(I am a slave, but thou art the master)*.

7. The personal pronoun is declined as follows:

First Person			**Second Person**	
		Singular		
N. ἐγώ		I	σύ	thou
G. ἐμοῦ	or μου	of me, my	σοῦ σου	of thee, yours
D. ἐμοί	or μοι	to or for me	σοί σοι	to or for thee
A. ἐμέ	or με	me	σέ σε	thee
		Plural		
N. ἡμεῖς		we	ὑμεῖς	you
G. ἡμῶν		of us, ours	ὑμῶν	of you, yours
D. ἡμῖν		to or for us	ὑμῖν	to or for you
A. ἡμᾶς		us	ὑμᾶς	you

Third Person

Singular

Masculine		**Feminine**		**Neuter**	
N. αὐτός	he	αὐτή	she	αὐτό	it
G. αὐτοῦ	his	αὐτῆς	hers	αὐτοῦ	its
D. αὐτῷ	to or for him	αὐτῇ	to or for her	αὐτῷ	to or for it
A. αὐτόν	him	αὐτήν	her	αὐτό	it

Plural

N. αὐτοί	they	αὐταί	they	αὐτά	they
G. αὐτῶν	theirs	αὐτῶν	theirs	αὐτῶν	theirs
D. αὐτοῖς	to or for them	αὐταῖς	to or for them	αὐτοῖς	to or for them
A. αὐτούς	them	αὐτάς	them	αὐτά	them

8. Notice that the first person of the personal pronoun is found in the genitive, dative and accusative singular in two forms, the longer form being accented and the shorter unaccented. The second person of the personal pronoun also has two possible forms, the same words being accented or unaccented. The first form is the "emphatic"; the second, the "unemphatic." The emphatic form is, as a rule, used to put some stress on the pronoun, and also when it follows a preposition. (But see **§10**). Remember that the unemphatic forms are enclitic and may transfer the accent which all one syllable enclitics lose to the preceding word (**cf. 10, § 8**)

9. It is necessary to remind ourselves that the genitive usually expresses the idea of possession. This also applies to the personal pronoun. In the 1st person the unemphatic form is used for this purpose. Thus τὸ βιβλίον μου *(my book)*; ὁ διδάσκαλος ὑμῶν *(your teacher).*

10. Remember the elision which takes place in prepositions ending in a vowel when the word which follows begins with a vowel, with the exception of the prepositions περί and πρό (**9 § 5**). This also applies to the personal pronoun when it begins with a vowel; i.e. in all persons except the 2nd person singular. It must be added that after a preposition, whether this ends in a vowel or in a consonant, the emphatic form of the pronoun in the 1st person singular is used. Thus, παρ᾽ ἐμοῦ, σὺν ἐμοί, σὺν σοί, δι᾽ ἐμέ, διὰ σέ. (Not παρά μου, σύν μοι, σύν σοι διά με, διά σε). The only exception is the preposition πρός (with the accusative) which can be followed by the personal pronoun either in the emphatic or the unemphatic form. It is equally correct to write πρὸς ἐμὲ (John 6:37) and πρός με (Luke 18:16).

11. As already stated, the personal pronoun is used in the place of a noun. However, sometimes the personal pronoun in the 3rd person is used *together with the noun,* and can have one of two different meanings depending on its position in connection with the article:

(i) If the pronoun follows immediately the article (the attributive position), it means "the same." The interposition of the words μέν, δέ, γάρ between the pronoun and the article does not affect the application of this rule. Thus, τὸ δὲ αὐτὸ πνεῦμα *(but the same Spirit;* 1 Cor. 12:4).

(ii) If the pronoun does not immediately follow the article (the predicative position), it is used for purposes of emphasis. Thus, αὐτὸς δὲὁ θεὸς τῆς εἰρήνης *(The God of peace himself;* 1 Thess. 5:23).

12. For purposes of emphasis this pronoun can also be used together with another pronoun, expressed or implied. Thus, ἐγὼ αὐτὸς γράφω *(I myself write)*; αὐτοὶ οἴδατε *(you yourselves know;* 1 Thess. 2:1–here ὑμεῖς is the implied pronoun).

VOCABULARY

ἀποκαλύπτω:	I uncover, I reveal
διαθήκη, ἡ:	covenant
διδασκαλία, ἡ:	teaching, instruction
διδαχή, ἡ:	teaching, instruction
δικαιοσύνη, ἡ:	righteousness
εὐλογία, ἡ:	blessing
θρόνος, ὁ:	throne
θυσία, ἡ:	sacrifice
κενός, ή, όν:	empty; figuratively: without effect
κεφαλή, ἡ:	head
κοινωνία, ἡ:	fellowship, communion
κριτής, ὁ:	judge
μέσος, η, ον:	middle
ἐν μέσῳ:	in the midst
ἐκ μέσου:	from among
μισθός, ὁ:	wages
μυστήριον, τό:	mystery
μωρός, ά, όν:	foolish
νόμος, ὁ:	law
παλαιός, ά, όν:	old (never used of persons)
πρόβατον, τό:	sheep

σοφός, ή, όν:	wise
τέλειος, α, ον:	perfect, complete, mature
φρόνιμος, ος, ον:	prudent
φυλάσσω:	I guard, I keep

EXERCISES

I.

Translate into English:

1. αὐτὸς ὁ κύριος ἀποκαλύπτει σοι τὰ μυστήρια αὐτοῦ. 2. τέλειός ἐστιν ὁ νόμος μου καὶ μακάριαί εἰσιν αἱ ἐντολαί μου. 3. ὁ μὲν μισθὸς τῆς ἁμαρτίας θάνατός ἐστι, τὸ δὲ δῶρον τοῦ θεοῦ ζωὴ αἰώνιος. 4. ὁ Χριστὸς ἡ κεφαλή ἐστι τῆς ἐκκλησίας, ἡμεῖς δέ ἐσμεν τὰ πρόβατα αὐτοῦ. 5. αὐτοὶ βλέπομέν σε, ὦ θεέ, καὶ τὸν ἅγιον θρόνον σου. 6. ὑμεῖς μὲν τῆς παλαιᾶς διαθήκης ἐστὲ μαθηταί, ἡμεῖς δὲ τῆς καινῆς. 7. καὶ αὐτὸς πονηρὸς εἶ καὶ τὰ ἔργα σου πονηρά ἐστιν. 8. ἐν τῇ αὐτῇ ἐκκλησίᾳ αὐτοὶ οἱ πρεσβύτεροι προσέφερον τὸν ἄρτον καὶ τὸν οἶνον τῆς κοινωνίας πρὸς τοὺς ἀδελφοὺς αὐτῶν. 9. τὰ δῶρά σου τέλειά ἐστιν. 10. τὰς αὐτὰς ἐντολὰς αὐτοὶ φυλάσσετε. 11. κατὰ τὴν ἐντολὴν τοῦ νόμου ἀνεβαίνομεν σὺν τοῖς ἀδελφοῖς ἡμῶν εἰς τὸ ἱερόν. 12. μακάριοί ἐστε ὅτι κατεκρίνετε τοὺς πονηροὺς καὶ ἐξεβάλλετε τοὺς ἀπίστους ἐκ μέσου ὑμῶν. 13. οὐκ εἰσι μαθηταὶ τοῦ Χριστοῦ οἱ ἄλλοι διδάσκαλοι, οὐ γὰρ παραλαμβάνουσι τὰς ἐπαγγελίας τοῦ σταυροῦ. 14. τὰς αὐτὰς ἐντολὰς τοῦ νόμου αὐτοὶ οἱ προφῆται γράφουσί σοι καὶ τοῖς τέκνοις σου. 15. φρόνιμοί εἰσιν οἱ ἀδελφοί σου ὅτι προσέφερον θυσίας πρὸς τὸν θεὸν ἐν τῷ ἱερῷ κατὰ τὴν διδαχὴν τῶν διδασκάλων αὐτῶν. 16. αὐτὸς ὁ Ἰησοῦς ἐν μέσῳ τῶν μαθητῶν αὐτοῦ ἐστι καὶ λέγει αὐτοῖς, Εἰρήνη ὑμῖν. 17. ἀπ᾽ ἐμοῦ ἤκουες τὴν διδαχὴν περὶ τῆς βασιλείας καὶ ἔμενες παρ᾽ ἐμοὶ μετὰ τῶν φίλων σου. 18. κρύπτει τὸ πρόσωπον αὐτοῦ ὁ θεὸς ἀπὸ τοῦ υἱοῦ αὐτοῦ ἐπὶ τοῦ σταυροῦ, ὅτι φέρει τὴν ἁμαρτίαν τοῦ κόσμου ὅλου. 19. κοινωνίαν ἔχομεν ἡμεῖς μεθ᾽ ὑμῶν, ἀδελφοὶ ἡμῶν γάρ ἐστε ἐν τῷ κυρίῳ. 20. ὑμεῖς μὲν σοφοί ἐστε κατὰ κόσμον, ἡμεῖς δὲ ἐπιγινώσκομεν τὴν σοφίαν τὴν

ἀληθινήν, ἀπεκάλυπτε γὰρ ἡμῖν ὁ θεὸς τὰ μυστήρια τῆς βασιλείας αὐτοῦ. 21. αὐτὸς διδάσκει αὐτοὺς αὐτὴν τὴν ἐπαγγελίαν τῆς αὐτῆς διαθήκης. 22. οὐδὲ αὐτοὶ οἱ σοφοὶ διδάσκαλοί σου καθαροί εἰσιν ἀπὸ τῆς ἁμαρτίας. 23. οἱ τελῶναι οὔκ εἰσι καθ' ἡμῶν, μεθ' ὑμῶν γὰρ μένουσιν. 24. αὐτοὶ γινώσκετε ὅτι ὑπὲρ ὑμῶν προσέφερε τὴν αἰώνιον θυσίαν ὁ Χριστός. 25. οὐ δι' ἐμοῦ αλλὰ διὰ τῶν διδασκάλων σου αὐτὸς ὁ θεὸς ἀποκαλύπτει σοι τὴν ἀγάπην τῆς διαθήκης αὐτοῦ.

II.

Translate into Greek:

In our exercises, to let you know whether to use the first or second person personal pronouns in the nominative for emphasis or the third person intensive pronoun (see **§ 12**), we will use parentheses for the former and no parentheses for the later. Thus: *we (ourselves) write* (ἡμεῖς γράφομεν) *we ourselves write* (αὐτοὶ γράφομεν).

1. There isn't fear in the perfect love. 2. Christ himself is our life and we have fellowship with him. 3. Neither do I (myself) condemn thee. 4. Thou art revealing to me, O God, the mysteries of thy covenant, for life eternal is in my heart. 5. Thy tongue is unclean and without effect are thy sacrifices. 6. Blessed are thy children for they see the face itself of the Lord and receive from him the same eternal blessings. 7. Foolish are thy slaves for they do not keep the commandments of their church. 8. Your promises are not true for you are not disciples of Christ. 9. We both hear thee, O faithful prophet of our God, and we believe thee, for we ourselves are faithful. 10. In the fellowship of our brethren Christ is guarding us from the devil and from his works. 11. Blessed are the clean in the heart because they see the face of God. 12. The Lord himself knows his sheep and they know him. 13. The enemies of the cross are against you, but you (yourselves) have peace in your hearts, for the Lord of glory is with you. 14. Both wise and prudent you are in the midst of your friends, but the other disciples in the same church do not obey the voice of their Lord. 15. We are not perfect, but you are baptizing us and the Lord himself is sanctifying both us and you. 16. Thou thyself eatest the same bread and drinkest the same wine with thy

brothers in the hour of the communion. 17. The foolish ones (fem.) are saying unjust words against me, but the prudent ones (fem.) are in favor of me. 18. Are you teachers in the old synagogue, thou and thy friends? 19. The judge in his house is judging us, but God himself in the heavens is judging him. (be sure to bring out the contrast). 20. The prophet himself was casting out of you the demons and was teaching both you and your children. 21. In the same hour instead of you we (ourselves) were preaching to your brothers the gospel of peace. 22. Your slaves were bringing to me your letters of love. 23. The angels of God are around his throne. 24. Because of the work of the cross your sins no longer are upon you. 25. The teacher himself reveals the same truths both to you and to us.

Lesson Thirteen

The Pronoun: The Demonstrative Pronouns
The Adjective: Comparison of Adjectives

1. The Demonstrative Pronouns. The demonstrative pronouns are used to point out and designate certain objects in distinction from others.

2. There are two principal demonstrative pronouns in NT Greek: οὗτος (m.), αὕτη (f.), τοῦτο (n.) and ἐκεῖνος, ἐκείνη, ἐκεῖνο, used in the case of a near or remote antecedent respectively *(this, that)*.

3. There is a third demonstrative pronoun, ὅδε, ἥδε, τόδε which, however, is very rarely used in the NT. It consists of the article regularly declined plus δέ. Several times it is used in the neuter plural with the meaning of *"these things"* (see Rev. 2:1).

4. These demonstrative pronouns:

(i) Can be accompanied by a noun. In this case they are placed in the predicative position; i.e., they never follow the article immediately, and must agree with the noun they qualify in case, gender, and number. Contrary to English usage, the article is never omitted. Thus, οὗτος ὁ ἀπόστολος or ὁ ἀπόστολος οὗτος; ἐκεῖνος ὁ δοῦλος or ὁ δοῦλος ἐκεῖνος.

(ii) Can stand alone. Thus, οὗτος πιστεύει *(this [man] believes)*.

5. The demonstrative pronouns are declined as follows:

Singular

Masculine	**Feminine**	**Neuter**
N. οὗτος	αὕτη	τοῦτο
G. τούτου	ταύτης	τούτου
D. τούτῳ	ταύτῃ	τούτῳ
A. τοῦτον	ταύτην	τοῦτο

Plural

Masculine	**Feminine**	**Neuter**
N. οὗτοι	αὗται	ταῦτα
G. τούτων	τούτων	τούτων
D. τούτοις	ταύταις	τούτοις
A. τούτους	ταύτας	ταῦτα

Singular

Masculine	**Feminine**	**Neuter**
N. ἐκεῖνος	ἐκείνη	ἐκεῖνο
G. ἐκείνου	ἐκείνης	ἐκείνου
D. ἐκείνῳ	ἐκείνῃ	ἐκείνῳ
A. ἐκεῖνον	ἐκείνην	ἐκεῖνο

Plural

Masculine	**Feminine**	**Neuter**
N. ἐκεῖνοι	ἐκεῖναι	ἐκεῖνα
G. ἐκείνων	ἐκείνων	ἐκείνων
D. ἐκείνοις	ἐκείναις	ἐκείνοις
A. ἐκείνους	ἐκείνας	ἐκεῖνα

6. Specific features of the demonstrative pronouns.

(i) Both demonstrative pronouns have the regular endings of the first-second declension adjectives in all three genders, the only deviation from the rule being that the neuter drops the final **ν** in the nominative and the accusative singular, just as it does in the article.

(ii) The interchange of **αυ** and **ου** in the stem of οὗτος, αὕτη and τοῦτο is subject to the rule that there is **ου** in the stem when there is an **ο** or **ω** in the ending; otherwise the stem has **αυ**. The initial letter is a vowel with a rough breathing in the same places where the article begins with a vowel and rough breathing.

(iii) The demonstrative pronouns have no vocative case.

(iv) A clear distinction should be made between αὕτη, αὗται (demonstrative) and αὐτή, αὐταί (personal). The distinction hangs on the place of the accent and the different breathing.

7. Comparison of Adjectives. An adjective can be used in an absolute sense (a good man) or to indicate a comparison of the noun it qualifies (i) with certain other nouns (a better man), or (ii) with all others (the best man). There are, therefore, three degrees in the adjective: *positive, comparative,* and *superlative.*

8. The adjectives of the first and second declensions, with which we are familiar, form the comparative and superlative degrees by adding to the stem the endings – ότερος, – οτέρα, – ότερον and – ότατος, – οτάτη, – ότατον respectively, and are declined exactly as the basic adjective is.

9. The **ο** at the beginning of these endings is turned into **ω** if the last vowel in the stem of the adjective is short. Thus μωρός, μωρότερος but σοφός, σοφώτερος. A difficulty arises when the last vowel in the stem is one of the three "dichrons" **α**, **ι**, **υ** which can be either long or short. The difficulty is substantially lessened through the application of the following rules:

(i) The **ι** is short in adjectives ending in – ιος, – ικος, – ιμος and – ινος.

(ii) All three "dichrons" are long if they are immediately followed by two or more consonants in a row.

10. A small number of adjectives of common use form the comparative or superlative degree, or both, in an irregular way. We shall reserve the examination of these for the stage of our study in which we shall deal with the adjectives of the third declension.

11. μικρός forms its superlative: ἐλάχιστος. However, besides its regular comparative, μικρός also has an alternative one declined according to the third declension.

12. The superlative form (degree) is rather rarely found in the

NT, the comparative being used in the sense of the superlative. Thus, context indicates that. ὁ δὲ μικρότερος ἐν τῇ βασιλείᾳ τῶν οὐρανῶν: should be translated: *"but the least in the kingdom of heaven"* (Matt. 11:11).

13. Comparison is made either by putting the object of comparison (the noun or pronoun with which the first one is compared) in the genitive, or by having the particle **ἢ**, *than*, follow the adjective and putting the second noun or pronoun in the same case as the first. Thus, σοφώτερος τοῦ ἀδελφοῦ αὐτοῦ or σοφώτερος ἢ ὁ ἀδελφὸς αὐτοῦ *(wiser than his brother).*

VOCABULARY

ἄξιος, α, ον:	worthy
διάκονος, ὁ:	servant, deacon
ἐκλεκτός, ή, όν:	chosen, elect
ἐργάτης, ὁ:	worker
ἤ:	either, or, than
θεραπεύω:	I heal
κρυπτός, ή, όν:	hidden, concealed, secret
λευκός, ή, όν:	white
λοιπός, ή, όν:	remaining,
τὸ λοιπὸν	the rest (of group)
or τοῦ λοιποῦ:	henceforth, from now on
μαρτυρία, ἡ:	testimony (of what one has witnessed)
μετάνοια, ἡ:	repentance
ὅτε:	when (adverb)
πλούσιος, α, ον:	rich
πτωχός, ή, όν:	poor
ὑποκριτής, ὁ:	hypocrite
φανερός, ά, όν:	manifest, in public
Φαρισαῖος, ὁ:	Pharisee
χαρά, ἡ:	joy
χωλός, ή, όν:	lame, crippled

EXERCISES

I.

Translate into English:

1. οὗτός ἐστιν ὁ υἱός μου ὁ ἀγαπητός. 2. τὸ μωρὸν τοῦ θεοῦ σοφώτερον τῶν ἀνθρώπων ἐστίν. 3. ἐκεῖνοι οἱ προφῆται μακαριώτεροί εἰσιν ἢ οὗτοι οἱ διδάσκαλοι ἡμῶν, ἀλλ᾽ οὐχ ἁγιώτεροι αὐτῶν. 4. ὁ θεὸς ἤκουε τὰς προσευχὰς τῶν πιστῶν τούτων ἐν τῷ κρυπτῷ καὶ ἔπεμπε τὰς εὐλογίας τοῖς τέκνοις αὐτῶν ἐν τῷ φανερῷ. 5. ἐν ἐκείναις ταῖς ἡμέραις ἔλεγον οἱ Ἰουδαῖοι πρὸς αὐτούς, ὑμεῖς μὲν ἐκείνου ἐστὲ μαθηταί, ἡμεῖς δὲ τῶν ἁγιωτάτων προφητῶν μαθηταί ἐσμεν. 6. μετὰ ταῦτα αὐτοὶ ἠσθίετε οὐ σὺν τοῖς λοιποῖς μαθηταῖς ἀλλὰ σὺν ἐκείνοις τοῖς ἀδίκοις τελώναις. 7. ὁ μικρότερος ἐν τῇ βασιλείᾳ τῶν οὐρανῶν μακαριώτερός ἐστι τῶν λευκοτάτων ἀγγέλων. 8. ἐγὼ γάρ εἰμι ὁ ἐλάχιστος τῶν ἀποστόλων. 9. τελειότερά ἐστι τὰ ἔργα τούτων τῶν ἀποστόλων ἢ τὰ ἔργα ἐκείνων τῶν διακόνων τῆς ἐκκλησίας. 10. αὐτοὶ οἱ πρεσβύτεροι ταύτης τῆς ἐκκλησίας ἐβάπτιζον καὶ φρονίμους καὶ μωρούς, οὗτοι γὰρ οἱ ἐκλεκτοὶ τοῦ θεοῦ εἰσιν. 11. οὗτοι πτωχοὶ μὲν ἐν τῷ κόσμῳ εἰσίν, πλούσιοι δὲ ἐν τῇ κοινωνίᾳ τῶν πιστῶν. 12. φανερὰ ἐστιν ἐν ὅλῃ τῇ ἐκκλησίᾳ τούτων τῶν διακόνων ἡ μαρτυρία. 13. τὸ λοιπὸν οἱ τελῶναι ἐκεῖνοι φέρουσι καρπὸν ἄξιον τῆς μετανοίας αὐτῶν. 14. ὀλίγοι εἰσὶν οἱ ἐκλεκτοί. 15. σοφώτεροί εἰσιν οὗτοι οἱ μαθηταὶ ἢ οἱ διδάσκαλοι αὐτῶν; 16. αὗται μὲν χαρὰν ἔχουσιν ἐν τῇ καρδίᾳ αὐτῶν, ἐκεῖναι δὲ φόβον διὰ τὴν ἁμαρτίαν αὐτῶν. 17. ἐν ἐκείναις ταῖς ἡμέραις οὐχ οὗτοι οἱ προφῆται ἀλλ᾽ οἱ διάκονοι ταύτης τῆς μικρᾶς ἐκκλησίας ἐθεράπευον καὶ χωλοὺς καὶ τυφλούς. 18. αὕτη ἔχει αὐτὴν τὴν ἀλήθειαν ἐν τῇ ψυχῇ αὐτῆς. 19. ταπεινότεροι τῶν ἐσχάτων δούλων εἰσὶν οὗτοι οἱ υἱοὶ τῆς βασιλείας. 20. ταῦτα τὰ αὐτὰ μυστήρια τῆς αἰωνίου διαθήκης αὐτοῦ ἀποκαλύπτει τούτοις τοῖς ταπεινοῖς αὐτὸς ὁ κύριος διὰ τῶν προφητῶν αὐτοῦ. 21. δικαιότεροι ἐκείνων τῶν τελωνῶν οὔκ εἰσιν οὗτοι οἱ Φαρισαῖοι. 22. πρὸς ἐκείνας τὰς ἐκκλησίας ἐπέμπομεν ἐπιστολὰς εἰρήνης, ἀγαπητότεροι γὰρ εἰσι τῶν λοιπῶν. 23. αὐτοὺς τοὺς υἱοὺς ἐκείνων τῶν ὑποκριτῶν

κατεκρίνομεν, ὅτι οὐκ ἐφύλασσον τὴν ψυχὴν αὐτῶν ἀπὸ τῆς ἁμαρτίας. 24. οὗτος ἐξ αὐτῶν ἐστιν. 25. γινώσκεις τοῦτο, ὅτι τὰ κρυπτὰ τῆς καρδίας σου φανερά ἐστι τῷ θεῷ.

II.

Translate into Greek:

1. This is my joy. 2. This is the son himself of God. 3. These (women) are more blessed than those (women) for more manifest are their good works. 4. I (myself) am that prophet. 5. More prudent are the sons of this world than the children of the kingdom of glory. 6. The deacons themselves of this smallest church were showing thee the most perfect way of life. 7. After these things; (neuter) we were offering with our brethren those remaining sacrifices in the same temple. 8. These unrighteous workers were knowing thoroughly those Holy Scriptures. 9. More prudent art thou than thy teachers and are thy works more perfect than the works of those? 10. The hypocrites are more unclean than even the unbelievers themselves. 11. These few (fem.) know the commandments themselves. 12. These wise teachers judge those hypocrites and lead them into the same way of peace. 13. Thou (thyself) knowest us thoroughly and we know thee and from thee we receive these promises of the holiest covenant. 14. There is love in this fellowship of the believers. 15. Worthy of their wages (sing.) are the sons of the other workers. 16. Both these rich ones and those poor ones we were rebuking on account of their evil works. 17. Without effect is the repentance of these Pharisees. 18. From among those hypocrites the Messiah gathers together these his sheep. 19. Those children of the covenant go up into this temple and read in that holiest book the words of the true promises themselves. 20. Not on account of our righteousness but on account of the work of the cross God saves us and we receive from him that most blessed wisdom. 21. Those teachers are reading the same books. 22. These are the parables of the kingdom. 23. These used to baptize our children, but now (they) no longer baptize them. 24. We are the sons of the kingdom, but both you and those are disciples of the evil one. 25. Those (fem.) see that prophet in the same place.

Lesson Fourteen

The Verb: Middle and Passive Voice:
Present and Imperfect Indicative
Deponent Verbs
Imperfect Indicative of the Verb εἰμί

1. The Middle and Passive Voices. In all languages a statement can be made in two forms: active and passive. An active sentence can be turned into a passive one and vice-versa without the content of the statement being affected; e.g., "the apostle teaches the disciple"; "the disciple is being taught by the apostle." We have, therefore, in the verb the active and the passive voices.

2. In Greek we also have, as has already been stated in a previous lesson (**3 § 6, ii**), the middle voice–not as common as the others – in which the subject acts upon himself, as in Mark 14:67, "warming himself," or with reference to himself, as in Acts 25:11, "I appeal (call upon in my own behalf) to Caesar."

3. In turning an active sentence into a passive one, the object in the active sentence becomes the subject ("the disciple," in the above example), while the subject in the active sentence becomes the "agent" by which the action is performed ("by the apostle"). The word "by" is expressed in Greek by the preposition ὑπό followed by the noun or adjective, etc. in the genitive case: ὁ διδάσκαλος γράφει τὴν ἐπιστολὴν—ἡ ἐπιστολὴ γράφεται ὑπὸ τοῦ διδασκάλου *(the letter is being written by the teacher)*. This sentence might also be translated: *(the letter is written by the teacher)*, but this rendering might give the impression of a completed action, which is the role assigned to another tense, while the present tense represents a process of continuous action. In order to avoid the possibility of confusion the first of the renderings is to be preferred.

4. Sometimes a sentence contains a noun which expresses the instrument or the means that was used in bringing about the action described: "the prophet teaches the disciple *by means of his word.*" In Greek this is expressed by putting this noun in the dative case: "τῷ λόγῳ αὐτοῦ." This is called the "Dative of Instrument."

The dative of instrument is best translated: "by means of." Remember that the indirect object is also put in the dative; herein lies a danger of possible confusion. In translating, therefore, a Greek sentence one should be careful to ascertain, with the aid of the context, whether a dative in it represents an indirect object or a dative of instrument.

5. Present and Imperfect Indicative. The endings which we attach to the stem, already known to us from the active voice, in order to form the present and imperfect indicative are identical in both the middle and passive voices. The context as well as the nature of the verb will usually decide whether the verb in a given text is in the middle or the passive voice. These endings are as follows:

Present	**Imperfect**
–ομαι	–ομην
–ῃ	–ου
–εται	–ετο
–ομεθα	–ομεθα
–εσθε	–εσθε
–ονται	–οντο

The verb λύω in the present and imperfect indicative, middle and passive voices is conjugated as follows:

Present

	Middle	**Passive**
λύομαι	—I loose for myself	I am being loosed
λύῃ	—Thou loosest for thyself	Thou art being loosed
λύεται	—He looses for himself	He is being loosed
λυόμεθα	—We loose for ourselves	We are being loosed
λύεσθε	—You loose for yourselves	You are being loosed
λύονται	—They loose for themselves	They are being loosed

Imperfect

	Middle	Passive
ἐλυόμην	—I was loosing for myself	I was being loosed
ἐλύου	—Thou wast loosing for thyself	Thou wast being loosed
ἐλύετο	—He was loosing for himself	He was being loosed
ἐλυόμεθα	—We were loosing for ourselves	We were being loosed
ἐλύεσθε	—You were loosing for yourselves	You were being loosed
ἐλύοντο	—They were loosing for themselves	They were being loosed

6. Notice that as in the active voice, the imperfect requires the "augment" to be prefixed to the stem. All the rules which govern the augment in the active voice apply also to the two other voices.

7. Deponent Verbs. Certain verbs are of the middle voice in form, although they are active in meaning; e.g., πορεύομαι *(I go).*

8. Some other verbs are in the active voice in certain tenses and in the middle voice in others; this happens more often in the future tense. Thus, λαμβάνω—λήμψομαι.

9. A few deponent verbs form the future and aorist in the passive voice; e.g., ἀποκρίνομαι, aorist: ἀπεκρίθην. However, the middle form ἀπεκρινάμην is also found in the NT. Such verbs will be marked in the vocabularies as "passive deponent."

10. A few verbs in the middle voice have a meaning entirely different from that which they have in the active voice; e.g., ἄρχω *(I rule)*; ἄρχομαι *(I begin).*

11. Imperfect of the Verb εἰμί. The verb εἰμί is conjugated in the imperfect indicative as follows:

ἤμην	—I was	ἦμεν or ἤμεθα	—we were
ἦς	—thou wast (rarely: ἦσθα–Matt. 26:69)	ἦτε	—you were
ἦν	—he, she, it was	ἦσαν	—they were

VOCABULARY

ἀποκρίνομαι:	I answer (pass. dep.; with dat.)
ἅπτομαι:	I touch (with gen.)
ἀρχή, ἡ:	beginning

ἄρχομαι:	I begin
ἄρχω:	I rule (with gen.)
γεύομαι:	I taste (with gen.; only exceptions: John 2:9; Heb. 6:5)
γίνομαι:	I become (with a predicate nominative), to come to pass
δέχομαι:	I receive
ἐντέλλομαι:	I command
ἐργάζομαι:	I work
ἔρχομαι:	I come

The following compound words are formed by prefixing a preposition to ἔρχομαι:

ἀν (α):	ἀνέρχομαι	I come or go up
ἀπ (ο):	ἀπέρχομαι	I go away
δι (α):	διέρχομαι	I go through
εἰσ:	εἰσέρχομαι	I enter in (I enter)
ἐξ:	ἐξέρχομαι	I go out
κατ(α):	κατέρχομαι	I go down
προσ:	προσέρχομαι	I go to (towards) (with dat.)
συν:	συνέρχομαι	I gather together; I go with

Some of the compounds of ἔρχομαι are good examples of the application of the rule in **11 § 3** which says that quite often the preposition which has been used in the formation of the compound verb has to be repeated after the verb. This is done especially when there is the need to specify the place or person *from* which one goes *away* (ἀπό); *through* (διά); *into* (εἰς); *out of* (ἐκ). The verb διέρχομαι is used in the NT text sometimes by applying the above rule (Luke 4:30: "διελθὼν διὰ μέσου αὐτῶν" – "passing through the midst of them") and on other occasions by simply having the accusative follow the verb (Luke 19:1: "διήρχετο τὴν Ἰεριχὼ . . . *he was passing through Jericho*").

εὐαγγελίζομαι:	I bring good news, I evangelize (The εὐ is treated as if it were a preposition.)
οὔπω:	not yet (adverb)

πορεύομαι:	I go (mid. dep. in future; pass. dep. in aorist)
προσεύχομαι:	I pray

EXERCISES

I.

Put the following sentences in Greek in both the active and the passive voices:

1. This good teacher is teaching that faithful disciple. 2. The prophets themselves were baptizing those tax-collectors. 3. We were sending you. 4. The sinners are persecuting the righteous ones. 5. The same elders were offering gifts to God.

II.

Translate into English:

1. ἐν ἀρχῇ ἦν ὁ λόγος, καὶ ὁ λόγος ἦν πρὸς τὸν θεόν, καὶ θεὸς ἦν ὁ λόγος. 2. ἐν αὐτῇ τῇ ἐκκλησίᾳ ἀναγινώσκονται αἱ ἐπαγγελίαι τοῦ θεοῦ ὑπὸ τοῦ αὐτοῦ μαθητοῦ. 3. οὗτοι προσηύχοντο, ἀλλ᾽ οὐκ ἀπεκρίνετο αὐτοῖς ὁ θεὸς διὰ τὴν ἁμαρτίαν ἐν ταῖς καρδίαις αὐτῶν. 4. διερχόμεθα διὰ τῆς ἐρήμου τοῦ κόσμου τούτου καὶ πορευόμεθα πρὸς τὴν μακαρίαν βασιλείαν. 5. ταῦτα ἐνετέλλετο ὑμῖν ὁ κύριος. 6. προσεύχου ὑπὲρ αὐτῶν τῶν ἐχθρῶν σου; 7. καὶ τοῖς Φαρισαίοις εὐηγγελίζεσθε τὴν βασιλείαν τοῦ θεοῦ καὶ αὐτοὶ ἐδέχοντο τὸν λόγον ὑμῶν καὶ ἐγεύοντο ζωῆς αἰωνίου. 8. οἱ ὑποκριταὶ ἐξεβάλλοντο ἐκ τοῦ οἴκου τῆς προσευχῆς ὑπὸ τῶν διακόνων. 9. ἦσαν δὲ οἱ μαθηταὶ ἐν τῇ ὁδῷ καὶ ἀνήρχοντο εἰς τὸ ἱερόν. 10. καὶ φρονίμους καὶ μωροὺς ἐδέχετο ὁ Ἰησοῦς καὶ ἐγίνοντο αὐτοὶ μαθηταὶ αὐτοῦ. 11. τὴν ἁμαρτίαν ἐργάζῃ καὶ ἠλέγχου ὑπὸ τοῦ πιστοῦ προφήτου. 12. κατὰ τὴν ἐντολὴν τοῦ κυρίου ἐξήρχεσθε ἐκ τοῦ κόσμου τῆς ἁμαρτίας καὶ εἰσήρχεσθε εἰς τὴν κοινωνίαν τῶν πιστῶν. 13. οὐ τοῖς ἔργοις σου τοῖς ἀγαθοῖς ἀλλὰ τῇ αἰωνίῳ θυσίᾳ τοῦ Χριστοῦ σῴζῃ καὶ γίνῃ μαθητὴς αὐτοῦ. 14. διὰ τὸν φόβον τοῦ ἀδίκου κριτοῦ ἐξεβάλλεσθε ἐξ ἐκείνης τῆς

συναγωγῆς καὶ ἤγεσθε εἰς ἄλλον τόπον. 15. ὑπ᾽ ὀλίγων πτωχῶν πλούσιαι θυσίαι προσεφέροντο ἐν τῷ ἱερῷ. 16. ἐν ἐκείναις ταῖς ἡμέραις ἐδιδασκόμεθα ὑπὸ τῶν προφητῶν, νῦν δὲ αὐτοὶ διδάσκομεν ἐν ταῖς αὐταῖς ἐκκλησίαις. 17. ἐκρύπτετο τὰ μυστήρια τῆς βασιλείας ἀπὸ τῶν σοφῶν καὶ ἀπεκαλύπτετο τοῖς ταπεινοῖς. 18. ὁ κύριος ἄρχει τῆς ἐκκλησίας αὐτοῦ. 19. ἐν τῷ ἀγρῷ ἦν ὁ θησαυρός, ἀλλ᾽ οὐχ εὑρίσκετο ὑπὸ τῶν ἐργατῶν. 20. τῇ ἀγαθῇ γλώσσῃ τοῦ υἱοῦ σου ἐλέγοντο τούτοις τοῖς ἁμαρτωλοῖς λόγοι ἀληθείας καὶ ἀγάπης. 21. ταῦτα τὰ δαιμόνια ἐξεβάλλοντο ἀπὸ τῶν ἀπίστων τελωνῶν ὑφ᾽ ὑμῶν ταῖς προσευχαῖς τῶν ἀδελφῶν. 22. συνήρχοντο οἱ λοιποὶ φίλοι περὶ τὸν σοφὸν διδάσκαλον καὶ προσηύχοντο σύν αὐτῷ πρὸς τὸν θεόν. 23. δι᾽ ὅλης τῆς ἡμέρας κατὰ τὴν ἐντολὴν αὐτοῦ τοῦ κυρίου ἦμεν μετὰ τῶν ἀδελφῶν ἡμῶν, ἐδιώκοντο γὰρ αὐτοὶ ὑπὸ τῶν ἀπίστων τοῖς δούλοις αὐτῶν. 24. τότε μὲν οὐκ ἦτε ἐν τῇ κοινωνίᾳ τῶν πιστῶν, νῦν δὲ καὶ διδάσκαλοί ἐστε ἐν αὐτῇ. 25. οὐχ ὑφ᾽ ἡμῶν ἀλλ᾽ ὑπ᾽ αὐτῶν τῶν προφητῶν ἠγείροντο οἱ νεκροὶ τῷ λόγῳ τοῦ σταυροῦ.

III.

Translate into Greek:

1. After these (things) you were no longer coming together in the synagogue. 2. Not on account of the bread of this world are we working. 3. You were going into the whole world and were evangelizing the sinners. 4. Both the faithful (fem.) and the unfaithful (fem.) were being cast out from the church by the deacons. 5. Through (by means of) the word of the Lord both dead ones were being raised up and lepers were being cleansed. 6. Thou art going away, for thou art being reproved by the words of the commandment. 7. Those humble disciples were coming out of their houses and were going to Christ. 8. The Pharisees were being offended because Jesus was receiving sinners and humble tax-collectors. 9. In those days neither your bread nor your wine were we touching. 10. The same disciples were being sent by the elders themselves and were evangelizing the unbelievers. 11. These books concerning the kingdom of the heavens were being written by that prophet. 12. The Lord was being glorified by you for you were the beloved disciples of the blessed apostles. 13. Thou wast not yet a true

slave of the Lord and your testimony was not manifest in the midst of the sinners. 14. Christ was the friend of the humble ones and they were themselves coming out of their houses and were going to him. 15. In those days neither our bread was being eaten nor our wine was being drunk by you, for you were not yet our friends. 16. The promises of the new covenant were being preached by you and the voices of angels were being heard in the place of prayer. 17. There were faithful deacons in that small church and good words were being said by them concerning this brother. 18. After these things the truth concerning the glory of the cross was being revealed to me by you. 19. By means of the testimony of those faithful apostles we were becoming true disciples. 20. The Lord himself was in the midst of us and our prayers were being heard by him. 21. Not a few unrighteous ones but the believers themselves were being offended by thee by means of thy foolish works. 22. Thou art tasting the new wine of the covenant and thou receivest the true promises of the gospel. 23. Thou wast answering that friend of thine that by means of the sacrifice of Christ thou art no longer being condemned by the just God. 24. We were being taught the eternal promises by our friends by means of the holy Scriptures. 25. The Lord was touching the leper and he himself was being healed by means of God's blessing.

Lesson Fifteen

The Verb:
Future Active Indicative

1. Distinctive Features of the Future Active Indicative. In conjugating the future in the indicative the basic fact to remember is that **σ** is the distinctive consonant of this tense. This consonant is inserted between the stem of the verb and the ending of the present active, as follows:

λύ –σ – ω	I shall loose	λύ –σ – ομεν	We shall loose
λύ –σ – εις	Thou shall loose	λύ –σ – ετε	You shall loose
λύ –σ – ει	He shall loose	λύ –σ – ουσι (ν)	They shall loose

2. If the stem ends:

(i) In a labial (**π**, **β**, **φ**) this, combined with **σ**, produces **ψ**: πέμπω—πέμψω.

(ii) In a guttural (**κ**, **γ**, **χ**) this, combined with **σ**, produces **ξ**: ἄγω—ἄξω.

(iii) In a dental (**τ**, **δ**, **θ**) this is dropped before the **σ** πείθω–πείσω.

3. Present and Verbal Stems. Quite a large number of verbs have two stems: the *present stem,* used for the formation of the present and imperfect, and the *verbal stem,* used for the formation of the other tenses.

(The verbal stem is the original and basic stem of the verb. The present stem was formed through the lengthening of the verbal stem).

The following are the three main groups of such verbs:

(i) Verbs whose present stem ends in **σσ** have a verbal stem ending in **κ**. Thus, φυλάσσω; verbal stem: φυλάκ; future: φυλάκ + **σ** + **ω**, results in φυλάξω.

(ii) Verbs whose present stem ends in **ζ** have a verbal stem ending in **δ**. Thus, βαπτίζω; verbal stem: βαπτιδ (future) + **σ** + **ω,** (the dental **δ** according to rule 2 iii is dropped): βαπτίσω. Exception in this group: κράζω (actual stem, κραγ)–κράξω.

(iii) Verbs whose present stem ends in **πτ** have a verbal stem ending in **π**. Thus, κρύπτω; verbal stem: κρυπ; future: κρύψω.

4. Non-Regular Formation of Future. Several verbs or groups of verbs form the future according to patterns other than the one indicated in **§1**. We shall deal with these in the proper places.

5. Verbs whose stem ends in a nasal (**μ**, **ν**) or liquid (**λ**, **ρ**) consonant form the future and aorist active, middle and passive in a special way and will be dealt with separately in Lesson 22. The verbs ἁμαρτάνω, βαίνω, βλαστάνω, λαμβάνω, πίνω, φέρω, χαίρω, although their stem ends in a nasal or liquid consonant, are not included in the nasal/liquid group of verbs so far as the formation of the future and the aorist is concerned, because they do not follow the rules which govern this group of verbs.

6. There are also a few verbs which form the future in an irregular way. Of the verbs we have so far found the following should be noticed:

Present	**Future**
ἁμαρτάνω	ἁμαρτήσω
δεικνύω	δείξω
διδάσκω	διδάξω
εὑρίσκω	εὑρήσω
κλαίω	κλαύσω
κράζω	κράξω
φέρω	οἴσω

7. The verb ἔχω forms the future in a regular way, but in this tense it has the rough breathing: ἔχω–ἕξω.

The verb βλέπω forms its active future regularly: βλέψω. But this is rarely used except in the compound forms of the verb, e.g.

ἀναβλέπω. Much more commonly used is the deponent future of ὁράω (a contract verb): ὄψομαι.

The verb λέγω forms its active future from another stem: ἐρ– (ἐρῶ) and is conjugated on the pattern of the nasal/liquid verbs. We will discuss this more it in Lesson 22.

8. The future in Greek does not present the distinction between continuous and non-continuous action which other Greek tenses present. λύσω is basically *(I shall loose)* but, may at times have the idea of *(I shall be loosing).*

VOCABULARY

ἁμαρτάνω:	I sin
βαστάζω:	I carry, I bear
ἕκαστος, η, ον:	each, every
ἐλπίζω:	I hope, I trust in
ἐξουσία, ἡ:	authority
θαυμάζω:	I wonder at, I marvel
ἱκανός, ή, όν:	sufficient, able, large or many enough, or simply; large, many
καθίζω:	I sit: (trans.), I cause to sit; (intrans.)
κράζω:	I cry out
ὅμοιος, α, ον:	resembling, like (with dat.)
ὀφθαλμός, ὁ:	eye
ὄχλος, ὁ:	crowd, multitude
πειράζω:	I test, I tempt
πράσσω:	I do, I accomplish, I practice
σημεῖον, τὸ:	sign, miracle

EXERCISES

I.

Translate into English:

1. ἀκούσει τὴν προσευχήν σου ὁ κύριος, καὶ δείξει σοι τὴν ὁδὸν τῆς ζωῆς καὶ σώσει σε. 2. οὐδὲ κηρύξετε τὸ εὐαγγέλιον τοῖς πονηροῖς οὐδὲ ἐλέγξετε αὐτούς, αὐτοὶ γὰρ οὔκ ἐστε πιστοί. 3. τὸ

λοιπὸν κρύψει ὁ κύριος τὰ μυστήρια τῆς βασιλείας ἀπὸ τῶν σοφῶν καὶ ἀποκαλύψει αὐτὰ τοῖς ταπεινοῖς. 4. τότε κλαύσουσιν οἱ ὄχλοι, οὐ γὰρ εὑρήσουσι τὴν θύραν τῆς ζωῆς. 5. τὰ ἔργα τοῦ πονηροῦ πράξετε, ὅμοιοι γάρ ἐστε αὐτῷ. 6. οὐ τὸν διδάσκαλον μόνον ἀλλ᾽ ὅλην τὴν ἐκκλησίαν ἑκάστην ἡμέραν πειράσει ὁ διάβολος. 7. καὶ ὑμᾶς καὶ τὰ τέκνα ὑμῶν συνάξει ὁ κύριος ἐκ μέσου τῶν ἁμαρτωλῶν καὶ ἁγιάσει ὑμᾶς τῷ λόγῳ αὐτοῦ. 8. ἐν ἐκείνῃ τῇ ἡμέρᾳ ἐπιστρέψουσιν οἱ υἱοί σου ἀπὸ τῶν πονηρῶν ὁδῶν αὐτῶν καὶ καθαρίσει αὐτοὺς τὸ εὐαγγέλιον. 9. οὐχ ἁμαρτήσεις, φυλάξει γὰρ τὴν καρδίαν σου ὁ κύριος. 10. ὑμεῖς μὲν διδάξετε τοὺς ὄχλους, ἡμεῖς δὲ βαπτίσομεν τὰ τέκνα αὐτῶν. 11. πέμψει ὁ κύριος τῇ ἐκκλησίᾳ αὐτοῦ προφήτας καὶ διδασκάλους. 12. καὶ τοὺς ὀφθαλμοὺς τῶν τυφλῶν ἀνοίξεις καὶ τοὺς λεπροὺς βαπτίσεις τῇ ἐξουσίᾳ τοῦ λόγου τοῦ σταυροῦ. 13. ἐν τῇ βασιλείᾳ τῶν οὐρανῶν καθίσει ὁ Χριστὸς ἕκαστον τῶν πιστῶν ἐπὶ θρόνου δόξης. 14. ἕξουσιν οἱ πτωχοὶ ἀδελφοί σου χαρὰν ἐν τῷ κόσμῳ τούτῳ τῷ πονηρῷ, πιστεύσουσι γὰρ οὐκ ἀνθρώποις ἀλλ᾽ εἰς αὐτὸν τὸν κύριον. 15. ἕκαστος ὑμῶν δοξάσει τὸν θεὸν τοῖς ἔργοις αὐτοῦ καὶ ἀκούσουσι καὶ οἱ πιστοὶ καὶ οἱ ἄπιστοι περὶ τῆς ὑπομονῆς ὑμῶν. 16. πειράσει σε ὁ πονηρὸς ἐν τῇ ὥρᾳ τοῦ θανάτου, ἀλλ᾽ ἱκαναί εἰσί σοι αἱ ἐπαγγελίαι τῆς διαθήκης. 17. οὐχ οἱ ὑποκριταὶ ἀλλ᾽ ὑμεῖς βαστάσετε τὸν χωλὸν καὶ ἄξετε αὐτὸν εἰς τὸν αὐτὸν τόπον. 18. ἔλεγον οἱ Φαρισαῖοι, οὐκ οὗτός ἐστιν ὁ τυφλός, ἀλλ᾽ ὅμοιος αὐτῷ ἐστιν. 19. κράξεις μετὰ ταῦτα καὶ κλαύσεις ἐν μέσῳ ἱκανοῦ ὄχλου ἀλλ᾽ οὐχ ἕξει χαρὰν ἡ καρδία τῶν μωρῶν. 20. οἴσουσι πρός σε τὰς γραφὰς οἱ ταπεινοὶ ἐργάται καὶ διδάξουσί σε περὶ δικαιοσύνης καὶ σὺ εὑρήσεις εὐλογίας ἱκανάς. 21. τὸ λοιπὸν κηρύξετε τοῖς ἁμαρτωλοῖς περὶ τῆς αἰωνίου θυσίας τοῦ Χριστοῦ καὶ αὐτοὶ ἄξια τῆς μετανοίας ἔργα πράξουσιν. 22. τοῖς λόγοις αὐτῶν πειράσουσιν ὑμᾶς οἱ ἄδικοι, ἀλλ᾽ αὐτὸς ὁ θεὸς δείξει αὐτοῖς σημεῖα ἀπ᾽ οὐρανοῦ. 23. ἀνοίξεις τὴν καρδίαν σου τῇ φωνῇ τοῦ κυρίου καὶ πιστεύσεις εἰς αὐτόν. 24. γράψομεν τὰς αὐτὰς ἐπιστολάς, καὶ πέμψομεν αὐτὰς αὐτοῖς τοῖς πιστοῖς διδασκάλοις τῶν αὐτῶν ἐκκλησιῶν. 25. ἁμαρτήσουσιν οἱ ἄνθρωποι, ἀλλ᾽ ὁ κύριος οὐ κλείσει αὐτοῖς τὴν θύραν τῆς μετανοίας καὶ σώσει αὐτούς.

II.

Translate into Greek:

1. The evil ones will persecute thee, but in the kingdom of the heavens thou wilt have joy in thy soul. 2. The blind will recover their sight and will glorify God because of His love. 3. In the hour of prayer God will hear thee in secret and will send to thee His rich blessings in public. 4. Even these stones will proclaim the perfect works of God. 5. You will cry out to the Lord and he will open to you the door of life. 6. Will not the prophet show to thee good signs and will heal both thee and thy friends? 7. You will no longer practice works worthy of death, because the Lord will gather you together from among the crowd. 8. The foolish ones will weep because their sin will hide from their eyes the real treasures. 9. The evil one will tempt us but we (ourselves) shall not sin. 10. You will both have authority and you will teach in the midst of the church. 11. Both good ones and bad ones will hear thy voice and will return to the same place. 12. These works you will do and the faithful ones in the whole church will wonder on account of them. 13. Not yet perfect are our friends, but the Son of Man will reveal to them the mysteries of his kingdom and they will obey him. 14. The sons of the kingdom will find their enemies, and will cry out to them and will show to them the everlasting way. 15. The prophets will write these holy words in a book and thou (thyself) wilt teach them to thy children and they will glorify God. 16. In those days we were not yet in the fellowship of the believers, but now we shall no longer weep for the Lord himself will open to us the door of the life. 17. God will lead his sons into that small church and they themselves will show to the disciples many enough signs. 18. The Lord himself will rule his church and from now on his disciples will preach to the crowds the whole truth of his commandments. 19. Wilt thou bring gifts into the temple and wilt thou sanctify the day of the Lord? 20. The Pharisees will fast on the day of the Sabbath but will not find peace in their hearts. 21. Thou wilt hear the words of the eternal truth and the Lord will open to thee his house. 22. In those days thou wast being taught by others, but now thou (thyself) will teach the faithful disciples. 23. The humble ones will obey the voice of Jesus and they

will find treasures of (the) wisdom. 24. Not to the righteous ones (fem.) but to the unrighteous (fem.) you will preach the gospel of the glory of the kingdom, and they will weep and the Lord will cleanse them. 25. Henceforth you will have authority upon evil spirits, and you will accomplish sufficient miracles in the midst of the crowd.

Lesson Sixteen

The Verb: Future Indicative Middle and Passive
Future of the Verb εἰμί • *The Adjective:* μέγας, πολύς

1. Distinctive Features of the Future Indicative Middle and Passive. As indicated in the previous lesson, **σ** is the characteristic consonant of the future. The middle voice of the future is formed by having this characteristic consonant inserted between the stem of the verb and the ending of the present middle: λύσομαι.

2. The passive voice of the future has **θη** inserted between the stem and the endings of the future middle voice: λυθήσομαι.

3. A small number of verbs whose stem ends in a vowel insert a **σ** between the stem and **θη**. Thus ἀκού – ω: ἀκουσθήσομαι.

4. The conjugation of λύω in the future middle and passive is as follows:

Middle	**Passive**
λύσομαι, I shall loose for myself	λυθήσομαι, I shall be loosed
λύσῃ	λυθήσῃ
λύσεται	λυθήσεται
λυσόμεθα	λυθησόμεθα
λύσεσθε	λυθήσεσθε
λύσονται	λυθήσονται

5. The rules governing the changes which certain consonants suffer when followed by **σ** (**15 § 2**) apply to the future in the middle voice also: ἄγω—ἄξομαι, etc.

6. The rules concerning the verbal stem, outlined in **15 § 3**, have an application in the future middle and passive, with the following adjustments in regard to the **θη** of the passive:

(i) In verbs whose verbal stem ends in a labial (**π**, **β**, **φ**), the labial before the **θ** is turned into the softest of the labials **φ**: καλύπτω; verbal stem: καλυπ; future: καλυφθήσομαι.

(ii) In verbs whose verbal stem ends in a guttural (**κ**, **γ**, **χ**), the guttural before the **θ** is turned into the softest of the gutturals **χ**: κηρύσσω; verbal stem: κηρυκ; future: κηρυχθήσομαι.

(iii) In verbs whose verbal stem ends in a dental (**τ**, **δ**, **θ**), the dental before the **θ** is turned into **σ**: βαπτίζω; verbal stem: βαπτιδ; future: βαπτισθήσομαι, πείθω, πεισθήσομαι. But σῴζω: σωθήσομαι, ἐμπαίζω: ἐμπαιχθήσομαι.

As already indicated (**15 § 4**), verbs whose stem ends in a liquid or nasal will be dealt with separately in Lesson 22.

7. The following verbs form the future passive in an irregular way:

βάλλω	—βληθήσομαι	εὑρίσκω	—εὑρεθήσομαι
βλέπω	—ὀφθήσομαι*	λαμβάνω	—λημφθήσομαι
διδάσκω	—διδαχθήσομαι	σῴζω	—σωθήσομαι
ἐγείρω	—ἐγερθήσομαι		

*(It uses the future passive of ὁράω)

8. As already noted, there are certain verbs which are deponent only in the future tense, forming it on the pattern of the middle or passive voice. Following are the verbs we have so far learned that do so, most of them forming the future in an irregular way. (Only those verbs are listed here which occur in the NT text in the future tense). All are middle except for χαίρω, whose future is an irregular passive.

βαίνω	—βήσομαι	πίνω	—πίομαι
βλέπω (ὁράω)	—ὄψομαι	τίκτω	—τέξομαι
γινώσκω	—γνώσομαι	φεύγω	—φεύξομαι
ἐσθίω	—φάγομαι	χαίρω	—χαρήσομαι
λαμβάνω	—λήμψομαι		

9. The future of the verb ἀκούω, besides its regular form ἀκούσω, is also occasionally found as a deponent in the middle voice ἀκούσομαι.

The verbs ἀποθνῄσκω, ἐλπίζω, καθαρίζω and πίπτω also form the future on the pattern of the middle voice, but these will be dealt with in more detail after the study of the contract verbs.

10. Of the regular deponent verbs we have dealt with so far, the verb ἀποκρίνομαι forms its future in the passive voice: ἀποκριθήσομαι, and the verbs ἔρχομαι and γίνομαι form it from different stems: ἐλεύσομαι, γενήσομαι.

11. Future of the Verb εἰμί. The verb εἰμί forms the future as a deponent, as follows:

ἔσομαι	ἐσόμεθα
ἔσῃ	ἔσεσθε
ἔσται	ἔσονται

12. The Adjectives μέγας, πολύς. These two adjectives, very common in the NT, are declined partly in an irregular way. Features which they have in common are:

(i) The feminine is declined regularly on the pattern of the–**η** group of the first declension.

(ii) The masculine and neuter are declined on the pattern of the second declension in the genitive and dative of the singular and in all cases of the plural.

(iii) The other four forms are declined in the third declension on shortened root forms, with the λ being dropped in the first, and the second λ being dropped in the second.

Singular

	Masculine	Feminine	Neuter
N.	μέγας	μεγάλη	μέγα
G.	μεγάλου	μεγάλης	μεγάλου
D.	μεγάλῳ	μεγάλῃ	μεγάλῳ
A.	μέγαν	μεγάλην	μέγα
V.	μέγα	μεγάλη	μέγα

Plural

	Masculine	**Feminine**	**Neuter**
N.	μεγάλοι	μεγάλαι	μεγάλα
G.	μεγάλων	μεγάλων	μεγάλων
D.	μεγάλοις	μεγάλαις	μεγάλοις
A.	μεγάλους	μεγάλας	μεγάλα
V.	μεγάλοι	μεγάλαι	μεγάλα

Singular

	Masculine	**Feminine**	**Neuter**
N.	πολύς	πολλή	πολύ
G.	πολλοῦ	πολλῆς	πολλοῦ
D.	πολλῷ	πολλῇ	πολλῷ
A.	πολύν	πολλήν	πολύ
V.	πολύ	πολλή	πολύ

Plural

	Masculine	**Feminine**	**Neuter**
N.	πολλοί	πολλαί	πολλά
G.	πολλῶν	πολλῶν	πολλῶν
D.	πολλοῖς	πολλαῖς	πολλοῖς
A.	πολλούς	πολλάς	πολλά
V.	πολλοί	πολλαί	πολλά

VOCABULARY

ἐκπορεύομαι:	I go out
ἐμπαίζω:	I scorn, I mock
ἴδιος, α, ον:	one's own
κατ' ἰδίαν:	privately, apart
καλύπτω:	I cover
μέγας, μεγάλη, μέγα:	great, large
παρουσία, ἡ:	presence, coming, the Second Coming of Christ.
πείθω:	I persuade, (I obey, passive voice)
πολύς, πολλή, πολύ:	much; (pl.), many

ποτήριον, τό:	cup
στέφανος, ὁ:	crown
ταράσσω:	I disturb, I trouble
τίκτω:	I give birth, I bear
τράπεζα, ἡ:	table

EXERCISES

I.

Translate into English:

1. ἀπὸ τῶν καρπῶν αὐτοῦ γνώσεσθε τὸ δένδρον. 2. ἐν τῇ παρουσίᾳ τοῦ Χριστοῦ λήμψονται στέφανον οἱ πιστοὶ καὶ δοξασθήσονται. 3. οὐ φεύξομαι ἀφ᾽ ὑμῶν, ἀλλ᾽ ἀναβήσομαι εἰς τὸν ἴδιον οἶκον. 4. πολλοὶ προσελεύσονται εἰς τὴν τράπεζαν τοῦ κυρίου καὶ φάγονται τὸν ἄρτον καὶ πίονται τὸν οἶνον τῆς κοινωνίας καὶ ἕξουσι χαρὰν μεγάλην ἐν ταῖς ἰδίαις ψυχαῖς. 5. καὶ τὰ τέκνα ἡμῶν ἁγιασθήσονται τῷ λόγῳ τῆς ἀληθείας καὶ γενήσονται μαθηταὶ τοῦ κυρίου. 6. ἐν ἐκείνῃ τῇ ἡμέρᾳ οὐ ταραχθήσῃ αὐτὸς γὰρ ὁ κύριος ἔσται μετὰ σοῦ. 7. συναχθήσονται κατ᾽ ἰδίαν αἱ ταπειναὶ καὶ διδαχθήσονται ὑφ᾽ ὑμῶν. 8. οὐ καταλειφθήσῃ μόνος ἐν μέσῳ τῶν πονηρῶν, τῇ μετανοίᾳ σου γὰρ γεύσῃ τῆς ἀγάπης τοῦ θεοῦ καὶ ἀναβήσῃ εἰς τὸν οἶκον αὐτοῦ. 9. οὔπω ἀποκαλυφθήσεται τοῖς τέκνοις ὑμῶν τὰ μυστήρια τῆς βασιλείας τοῦ Μεσσίου. 10. ἐν τῇ παρουσίᾳ τοῦ Χριστοῦ οἱ νεκροὶ ἐγερθήσονται τῷ λόγῳ τοῦ κυρίου. 11. πολλοὶ ἄδικοι καὶ ἀκάθαρτοι ἀπελεύσονται ἐκ μέσου ὑμῶν καὶ καθαρισθήσεται ἡ ἐκκλησία ἀπὸ τῆς ἁμαρτίας. 12. τὸ μυστήριον τοῦτο μέγα ἐστίν, ἐγὼ δὲ λέγω περὶ τοῦ Χριστοῦ καὶ περὶ τῆς ἐκκλησίας. 13. τὸ λοιπὸν θύρα μεγάλη ἀνοιχθήσεται ὑμῖν καὶ κηρυχθήσεται ὑφ᾽ ὑμῶν τὸ εὐαγγέλιον ἐν ὅλῳ τῷ κόσμῳ 14. φωνὴ ἀπὸ τοῦ οὐρανοῦ ἀκουσθήσεται καὶ ἐλεύσεται ὁ υἱὸς τοῦ ἀνθρώπου μετὰ δόξης πολλῆς, καὶ ὄψονται αὐτὸν οἱ πιστοί, καὶ δοξασθήσεται ἡ ἐκκλησία αὐτοῦ σὺν αὐτῷ. 15. καὶ αὐτῶν τῶν ἀγγέλων μακαριώτεροι ἔσεσθε, γνώσεσθε γὰρ τὴν ὁδον τῆς εἰρήνης καὶ αὐτὸς ὁ κύριος δέξεται ὑμᾶς κατὰ τὴν ἐπαγγελίαν αὐτοῦ. 16. ἐν

ἐκείνῃ τῇ ὥρᾳ οἱ μὲν πονηροὶ ἐλεγχθήσονται οἱ δὲ πιστοὶ ἀναβήσονται εἰς τὸν οὐρανόν. 17. τὰ δῶρα ὑμῶν λημφθήσεται ὑπὸ τῶν αὐτῶν προφητῶν. 18. πειρασθήσῃ ὑπὸ τοῦ πονηροῦ καὶ διωχθήσῃ ὑπὸ τῶν ὑποκριτῶν, ἀλλὰ προσεύξῃ τῷ θεῷ καὶ σωθήσῃ. 19. ἀναγνωσθήσονται αἱ ἐπαγγελίαι τῆς καινῆς διαθήκης ἐν ἐκείνῃ τῇ μεγάλῃ ἐκκλησίᾳ καὶ πολλοὶ πεισθήσονται περὶ τῆς ἀληθείας αὐτῶν καὶ πορεύσονται εἰς τοὺς ἰδίους οἴκους ἐν εἰρήνῃ. 20. ἀπελεύσεται ὁ προφήτης ἐκ μέσου τῶν μαθητῶν καὶ αὐτοὶ ταραχθήσονται ἀλλ᾽ ἐλεύσεται αὐτὸς ὁ κύριος καὶ χαρήσονται αἱ ψυχαὶ αὐτῶν. 21. ἑτοιμασθήσεταί σοι τόπος ἐν τῷ οὐρανῷ ἀποκαλυφθήσεταί σοι γὰρ τὰ μυστήρια τῆς βασιλείας καὶ γενήσῃ υἱὸς τοῦ θεοῦ. 22. μετὰ ταῦτα δέξονται αὐτοὶ οἱ ἀδελφοὶ ὑμῶν μετὰ τῶν ἰδίων τέκνων τὰς ἐπαγγελίας τοῦ λόγου τοῦ θεοῦ καὶ ἐπιστρέψουσιν ἀπὸ τῶν πονηρῶν ὁδῶν αὐτῶν. 23. ἐν ταῖς ἡμέραις ταῖς πρώταις προσηύχου τῷ κυρίῳ, ἀλλὰ νῦν οὐκέτι προσεύξῃ αὐτῷ. 24. ἀχθήσονται οἱ τυφλοὶ πρὸς τὸν κύριον καὶ αὐτὸς θεραπεύσει αὐτοὺς καὶ ἀναβλέψουσιν. 25. ἐκπορεύσῃ ἐκ τοῦ οἴκου τοῦ ἀδελφοῦ σου καὶ οὐδὲ ἄρτον φάγῃ οὐδὲ οἶνον πίῃ, ὅτι διώξουσί σε οἱ υἱοὶ τοῦ κόσμου τούτου. 26. πολλοί, καὶ μεγάλοι καὶ μικροί, συναχθήσονται ἐν τῇ ἐκκλησίᾳ καὶ βαπτισθήσονται καὶ ἔσται χαρὰ μεγάλη ἐν τῷ οὐρανῷ. 27. τότε προσεύξῃ κατ᾽ ἰδίαν τῷ κυρίῳ καὶ ὁ πονηρὸς φεύξεται ἀπὸ σοῦ καὶ σὺ ἔσῃ μακάριος.

II.

Translate into Greek:

1. We shall be taught the truth by the wise teacher, and the door of the true promises will be opened to us. 2. Both you and your children will be cleansed from your sins and will enter into the fellowship of the believers. 3. Thou wilt pray to the Lord and wilt be saved and wilt become a disciple of him. 4. You will not yet go up into heaven, but with patience you will be sanctified. 5. The sins of the hypocrites will no longer be covered from the eyes of the Lord. 6. The disciples will be led privately by their own elders. 7. Your sons will take authority from the church and will go away and will evangelize the whole world. 8. In the great day of the second coming of the Messiah both thou and the

other believers will take the crown of glory. 9. You will cry out to the Lord and your prayer will be heard by him. 10. Many believers will be tempted in the midst of the great hypocrites. 11. There will be revealed in the presence of God the hidden (things) of the heart of each (man). 12. Many sinners will be saved by means of your word and will enter into the life of joy and peace. 13. Many of our beloved teachers will be persecuted by the workers of the sin on account of the truth of the gospel, but the church will pray on their behalf. 14. Thou wilt be persuaded concerning the truth of the promises of the covenant, and thou wilt be baptized, and thou wilt be a deacon in that large church. 15. Many and great signs will be in the sky and the hearts of the sinners will be troubled. 16. Even the enemies of the perfect wisdom will be saved, and will eat the bread and drink the wine of the communion and will be true disciples of Christ. 17. The holy Scriptures will be read in the midst of the crowd, and many (fem.) will be led to the elders of that church and will rejoice. 18. Thy works will not be done according to the commandment and thou wilt be reproved and wilt be condemned by thine own brothers. 19. These lepers will be sent by the righteous judge into other places and will not be offended. 20. We shall go up into the house of God, for his table by means of his word will be prepared both for you and for us. 21. Those many enemies of the eternal truth will believe in (to) the Lord because they will be taught by thee. 22. The evil ones will be many and the saints will be persecuted by them, but these will have peace in their hearts. 23. Thou wilt not flee from among thy enemies, but the Lord himself will touch thee. 24. You will know thoroughly the truth and many will come to the church by means of your testimony. 25. There will be many (fem.) in that place and thou wilt evangelize them.

Lesson Seventeen

The Verb: First Aorist Active Indicative
The Pronoun: The Relative Pronoun

1. Distinctive Features in the Meaning of the First Aorist Active Indicative . As already indicated (**8 § 1**), there are other tenses besides the imperfect which denote an action in the past. Such is the aorist. However, strictly speaking, the aorist denotes past time only in the indicative; in the other moods the aorist is not confined exclusively to action in the past. Unlike the imperfect, the aorist is used to express an action that is not continuous or habitual. ἔγραφον means *"I was writing"* or *"I used to write"*; ἔγραψα (aorist) means *"I wrote."* This can equally be rendered *"I have written"*; however, for reasons to be explained in the proper place we shall reserve the expression *"I have . . ."* for the rendering of the perfect tense. For the sake of a clear distinction between the imperfect and the aorist in the exercises, it is advisable that the aorist should be translated simply as *"I wrote."*

2. The term "first" in our tense title implies the existence of a "second aorist." We shall deal with it in the next lesson. The difference between the two does not lie in the meaning they convey, but in the way each of them is constructed. Some verbs form the aorist one way, some the other, and a few both ways. Of the verbs which have both a first and a second aorist, there are a few in which the first aorist has a meaning different to that of the second.

3. In conjugating the first aorist active indicative we should notice three basic points.

(i) Like the future, the first aorist has **σ** as its distinctive consonant which is inserted between the stem of the verb and the remainder of the ending. The rules which govern both the combination of certain consonants and **σ** and the verbal stem in the future (**15 § 2, 3**) apply to the first aorist also. Thus γράφω—ἔγραψα, κηρύσσω—ἐκήρυξα, πείθω—ἔπεισα, βαπτίζω—ἐβάπτισα, κρύπτω—ἔκρυψα, διώκω—ἐδίωξα.

(ii) The endings of the first aorist present a striking similarity to those of the imperfect, the main difference consisting in the preponderance of the **α** sound in the aorist. The similarity is made clear in the following table:

Imperfect	**Aorist**
–ον	–σ –α
–ες	–σ –ας
–ε (ν)	–σ –ε (ν)
–ομεν	–σ –αμεν
–ετε	–σ –ατε
–ον	–σ –αν

(iii) Like the imperfect, the first aorist takes the augment.

4. The verb λύω in the first aorist active indicative is conjugated as follows:

ἔλυσα	I loosed	ἐλύσαμεν	we loosed
ἔλυσας	loosedst, didst loose	ἐλύσατε	you loosed
ἔλυσε (ν)	he, she, or it loosed	ἔλυσαν	they loosed

5. Of the verbs we have learned so far the following form the first aorist in an irregular way:

ἁμαρτάνω	ἡμάρτησα
βλαστάνω	ἐβλάστησα
δεικνύω	ἔδειξα
διδάσκω	ἐδίδαξα
κλαίω	ἔκλαυσα
κράζω	ἔκραξα
φέρω	ἤνεγκα

6. The Relative Pronoun. A relative pronoun usually has two uses: it serves in some function in an adjectival relative clause (as its subject, direct object, object of a preposition, etc.) and it connects that relative clause with the rest of the sentence by pointing to the clause's antecedent (the word it modifies or refers to). For example in the sentence "The man who lives in this house is a disciple of Christ," we have two clauses: one main clause and one dependent clause. The main clause is "the man is a disciple of Christ," but in order to make clear which man we are speaking about, the dependent clause "who lives in this house" is added, with the relative pronoun "who" linking the two together. The noun, pronoun, participle, etc. which the relative pronoun refers to is its *antecedent.* Sometimes; however, the antecedent is not expressed, but implied. In that case the mere relative pronoun **ὅς** has the meaning "he who" or "that one who," e.g,. "ὅς οὐ λαμβάνει τὸν σταυρὸν αὐτοῦ . . . οὐκ ἔστιν μου ἄξιος" or, *(He) who does not take his cross . . . is not worthy of me"* (Matt. 10:38).

7. The main relative pronoun is **ὅς**, **ἥ**, **ὅ**, and is declined in a way identical to that of the first-second declension adjectives, the only deviation being that the neuter drops the **ν** in the nominative and the accusative singular. There is no vocative case.

Singular

	Masc.	**Fem.**	**Neu.**
N.	ὅς	ἥ	ὅ
G.	οὗ	ἧς	οὗ
D.	ᾧ	ᾗ	ᾧ
A.	ὅν	ἥν	ὅ

Plural

	Masc.	**Fem.**	**Neu.**
N.	οἵ	αἵ	ἅ
G.	ὧν	ὧν	ὧν
D.	οἷς	αἷς	οἷς
A.	οὕς	ἅς	ἅ

8. The relative pronoun must agree with its antecedent in gender and number–not necessarily in case; this depends on the function which is assigned to the pronoun in the dependent clause: if it is the subject of the verb in its clause, it will be put in the nominative; if the direct object, generally in the accusative; if the indirect object, in the dative. Thus, ὁ ἄνθρωπος, ὃν εἶδες, προφήτης ἐστίν *(The man whom thou didst see is a prophet)*; ὁ κύριος ὑφ' οὗ σωζόμεθα, ἁγιάσει ἡμᾶς *(The Lord, by whom we are being saved, will sanctify us)*.

9. In spite of the above rule, not infrequently in the NT text, the relative pronoun is put not in the case which its function in the dependent clause would require, but in the same case as its antecedent; e.g. ἔπεισα αὐτοὺς τοῖς λόγοις οἷς (instead of οὓς) ἔλεγον *(I persuaded them by means of the words which I was speaking)*. This irregularity is called "attraction" because the pronoun, so far as the case is concerned, is attracted by the case of its antecedent. However, in the English to Greek exercises the rule outlined in **§ 8** should be applied.

10. The relative pronoun is also used in the NT as a demonstrative pronoun in a distributive sense; i.e., ὃς μὲν . . . ὃς δὲ (this one . . . that one)."

VOCABULARY

αἴρω:	I take up, I take away, I remove
ἀπαγγέλλω:	I announce, I proclaim
βαπτιστής, ὁ:	Baptist (used in the NT only as a title for John)
βλαστάνω:	I sprout (spring up, bring forth)
ἤδη:	already (adverb)
ἱμάτιον, τὸ:	garment
Ἰωάννης, ὁ:	John
καιρός, ὁ	time, due time, appointed time, opportunity (See also χρόνος)
λαός, ὁ:	people
οὖν:	therefore, accordingly (postpositive).
Παῦλος, ὁ:	Paul
Πέτρος, ὁ:	Peter
ὑποτάσσω:	I subject, I submit
φονεύω:	I kill

χρεία, ἡ:	necessity, need
χρόνος, ὁ	time (See also καιρός)

EXERCISES

I.

Translate into English:

1. ἤκουσεν οὖν ὁ Ἰωάννης περὶ τῶν ἔργων, ἃ ἔπραξεν ὁ Ἰησοῦς, καὶ ἔπεμψε τοὺς μαθητὰς αὐτοῦ πρὸς αὐτόν. 2. οὐχ οὗτός ἐστιν ὃν ἡγίασεν ὁ θεὸς καὶ ἔπεμψεν εἰς τὸν κόσμον; 3. οὐδὲ ὁ Παῦλος οὐδὲ ὁ Πέτρος οὐδὲ οἱ λοιποὶ ἀπόστολοι ἔσωσαν ἡμᾶς, ἀλλ' αὐτὸς ὁ κύριος ἐν ᾧ ἠλπίσαμεν. 4. ἤκουσεν ὑμῶν ὁ κύριος καὶ ἡτοίμασεν ὑμῖν εὐλογίας κατὰ τὴν χρείαν ὑμῶν. 5. ὃς ἦν μετὰ τοῦ Ἰωάννου τοῦ βαπτιστοῦ οὗτος ἐβάπτισε πολλούς. 6. ἐκηρύξαμεν οὖν λόγους μετανοίας καὶ αὐτοῖς τοῖς Φαρισαίοις, οἳ ἐφόνευσαν τοὺς πιστοὺς προφήτας. 7. ὁ ἄνθρωπος ὃν ἐθεράπευσεν ὁ Χριστὸς ἐπέστρεψεν εἰς τὸ ἱερὸν καὶ ἐδόξασε τὸν θεόν. 8. οὐ γὰρ ἀγγέλοις ἀλλὰ τῷ υἱῷ αὐτοῦ ὑπέταξεν ὁ θεὸς τὸν κόσμον ὃν βλέπετε. 9. οἱ διδάσκαλοι οὓς ἠκούσατε ἔπεισαν ὑμᾶς περὶ τῆς ἀληθείας τῆς διδαχῆς αὐτῶν. 10. ἐντολὰς ἀγάπης ἔγραψαν ἐν ἐκείνῳ τῷ καιρῷ οἱ ἀπόστολοι καὶ ἤδη ἔπεμψαν αὐτὰς πρὸς τὰς ἐκκλησίας, καὶ τὰς μεγάλας καὶ τὰς μικράς. 11. ὁ κύριος ἐκαθάρισέ με ἀπὸ τῆς ἁμαρτίας μου, ἐγὼ οὖν ἐδόξασα αὐτὸν καὶ ἐκήρυξα τὰς ἐπαγγελίας αὐτοῦ τῷ λαῷ. 12. ὁ Χριστὸς προσήνεγκε τὴν αἰώνιον θυσίαν διὰ τὰς ἁμαρτίας ὅλου τοῦ κόσμου, πολλοὶ οὖν οἳ ἦσαν ταπεινοὶ ἐπίστευσαν εἰς αὐτόν. 13. ἐθαύμασεν ὁ λαὸς ἐπὶ τοῖς ἔργοις τοῦ κυρίου καὶ πολλοὶ ἔκλαυσαν. 14. ὁ υἱός τοῦ ἀνθρώπου ἡτοίμασε τόπον ἐν τῷ οὐρανῷ τοῖς ἰδίοις μαθηταῖς καὶ αὐτοὶ χαρήσονται. 15. ἐδίδαξέ σε κατ' ἰδίαν ὁ προφήτης ᾧ ἤγγισας ἐν τῷ ναῷ καὶ ἔδειξέ σοι τὴν θύραν τῆς ζωῆς καὶ σὺ προσήνεγκας αὐτῷ δῶρα. 16. ὁ πονηρὸς ἐπείρασε τοὺς υἱοὺς ὑμῶν, ἀλλ' αὐτοὶ ἤνοιξαν τὰς καρδίας αὐτῶν τῷ κυρίῳ. 17. οἱ διδάσκαλοι, οἳ ἦσαν ἐν τῷ ἀγρῷ ἔδειξαν ὑμῖν ταῦτα τὰ μεγάλα μυστήρια, ἃ ἀπεκάλυψεν αὐτοῖς αὐτὸς ὁ θεός. 18. οἱ ἄνθρωποι οὓς ἐδίωξαν οἱ Φαρισαῖοι

ἔπεμψαν ὑμῖν τὰ βιβλία ἃ ἔγραψαν οἱ ἀπόστολοι. 19. ἕκαστος τῶν προφητῶν ἡτοίμασε τὸν ἴδιον οἶκον, ἐν ᾧ ἤλεγξε τοὺς ἐχθροὺς τῆς ἀληθείας. 20. οὗτος ὁ σοφὸς διδάσκαλος ἔπεισέ με περὶ τῶν ἐπαγγελιῶν τοῦ θεοῦ, ἐγὼ οὖν ὑπήκουσα τῇ φωνῇ τοῦ εὐαγγελίου. 21. ἤγγισεν ὁ καιρὸς τῶν καρπῶν, οἱ δοῦλοι οὖν ἡτοίμασαν τὴν τράπεζαν τοῖς κυρίοις αὐτῶν. 22. μετὰ πολὺν χρόνον ἐπέστρεψεν ὁ κύριος τῶν δούλων ἐκείνων καὶ ἔκραξεν αὐτοῖς φωνῇ μεγάλῃ. 23. ἀπεκαλύψαμεν ὑμῖν τὰς ἐντολὰς τοῦ νόμου καὶ ὀλίγοι ἐξ ὑμῶν ἡγιάσατε τὴν ἡμέραν τοῦ κυρίου καὶ ἐδοξάσατε τὸν θεὸν τοῖς ἔργοις ἃ ἐπράξατε. 24. ὃς μὲν ἔκλαυσε διὰ τὰς ἁμαρτίας αὐτοῦ καὶ ὁ θεὸς ἡγίασεν αὐτόν, ὃς δὲ ἔκλεισε τὴν καρδίαν αὐτοῦ. 25. ἐφύλαξεν ὁ κύριος τοὺς πιστοὺς κατὰ τὴν χρείαν ἑκάστου.

II.

Translate into Greek:

NOTE: In translating relative clauses into Greek, use commas in your Greek translation whenever the English has commas. Then accent enclitics accordingly.

1. Life and truth is the teaching which you heard. 2. The teachers whom the Lord sent preached to the people the great mysteries of the kingdom. 3. I cried out to Thee, O Lord, and Thou didst hear me and didst save me. 4. We reproved, therefore, the brethren, for the works which they performed were not worthy of the new covenant. 5. The wise ones did not offend the remaining beloved disciples. 6. Both lepers Christ cleansed and humble ones he taught. 7. The devil tempted thee but the Lord guarded thee. 8. The prophet in whom you hoped did not save you from your sins. 9. Those workers, whom thou didst send to the righteous judge, did not return to thee. 10. These are the Scriptures, which the elders in that large synagogue taught to thee. 11. Many tax-collectors, whom thou didst reprove, wept and showed much love to others. 12. By means of his work on the cross Christ saved thee, thou therefore by means of thy testimony persuaded many of thy friends concerning the truth of his promises. 13. In that (due) time you taught us concerning the kingdom of the heavens, but not yet shall we

receive the crown of glory. 14. We revealed the commandments of the new covenant to many and we baptized those who believed. 15. A few are in the whole church, both rich and poor, whom thou didst heal and they themselves glorified God. 16. The unrighteous ones (fem.), whom you reproved with patience, did works which were worthy of their repentance. 17. Did the Lord reveal to thee the times and seasons of his blessed and eternal kingdom? 18. The elders of these large churches showed even to the men of this world the great mysteries of both death and life, those therefore believed. 19. Those other friends of ours returned from their sinful ways to Christ and he himself saved them. 20. On the authority of the word of the Lord, blind ones recovered their sight, the multitudes therefore marveled on account of it. 21. Not you but the Lord himself, in (into) whom we believed, cleansed us from our sins. 22. The sin of man closed the door of heaven, but the sacrifice of Christ upon the cross opened it. 23. Those few sons of the prophets, whom thou didst hide in thy large house, fasted on account of the sins of the whole synagogue. 24. Both you and we are now children of God, we sat therefore with our brothers around the table of the communion. 25. Those evil ones who troubled each of you will not be worthy of Christ in his second coming.

Lesson Eighteen

The Verb: The Second Aorist Active Indicative
Indirect Speech

1. Distinctive Features of the Second Aorist Active Indicative. The second aorist, or "strong," aorist does not use the **σ** as a distinctive consonant or the endings of the first aorist at all. Instead, the endings of the imperfect active are used and it is distinguished from that tense by virtue of a change which takes place within the stem or of the use of an entirely different stem. This process is not unknown in the English language. The past tense in language is normally formed through the addition of the ending –"ed" to the present: "I walk–I walked." However, in a number of verbs this tense is formed by means of a change within the stem: "I write–I wrote," and in others through the use of a different stem: "I go–I went."

2. A very small number of verbs have both a first and second aorist: ἁμαρτάνω—ἡμάρτησα, ἥμαρτον.

3. Like the imperfect and the first aorist, the second aorist takes the augment; this is governed by the same rules which apply to the two other tenses.

4. The second aorist of βάλλω is formed as follows:

ἔβαλον	ἐβάλομεν
ἔβαλες	ἐβάλετε
ἔβαλε	ἔβαλον

(Notice the endings, identical with those of the imperfect, and the difference in the stem βαλλ—, βαλ—).

5. Following is a list of verbs we have seen so far which have a second aorist:

ἄγω—	ἤγαγον
ἁμαρτάνω—	ἥμαρτον
ἀποθνῄσκω—	ἀπέθανον
βάλλω—	ἔβαλον
βλέπω—	εἶδον (It uses the second aorist of the verb ὁράω.)
ἔρχομαι—	ἦλθον
ἐσθίω—	ἔφαγον
εὑρίσκω—	εὗρον
ἔχω—	ἔσχον
λαμβάνω—	ἔλαβον
λέγω—	εἶπον
λείπω—	ἔλιπον
μανθάνω—	ἔμαθον
πάσχω—	ἔπαθον
πίνω—	ἔπιον
πίπτω—	ἔπεσον (Only in moods other than the indicative. In the indicative: ἔπεσα.)
τίκτω—	ἔτεκον
φεύγω—	ἔφυγον

All the above are conjugated with the regular endings of the imperfect attached to the verbal stem.

6. Exceptions to the rule that the second aorist has endings identical to those of the imperfect are the verbs γινώσκω, ἀναβαίνω (βαίνω), which form the second aorist as follows:

ἔγνων	ἀνέβην
ἔγνως	ἀνέβης
ἔγνω	ἀνέβη
ἔγνωμεν	ἀνέβημεν
ἔγνωτε	ἀνέβητε
ἔγνωσαν	ἀνέβησαν

The verb φέρω, as we have seen (**17 § 5**), has a first aorist formed on a different stem: ἐνεγκ–. It also has a second aorist formed on the same stem to which the imperfect active endings are added: ἤνεγκον. However, this form of the aorist is much less frequently used.

7. The second aorist of the verbs βλέπω, ἔρχομαι and λέγω is often found in the NT text with first aorist endings:

ἃ εἴδαμεν* καὶ ἠκούσαμεν (Acts 4:20).
παρεκάλεσαν τοὺς ἀδελφοὺς καὶ ἐξῆλθαν (Acts 16:40).
Ἐγὼ εἶπα, θεοί ἐστε; (John 10:34).

* Some manuscripts have the regular 2nd aorist: εἴδομεν.

8. Indirect Speech. Consider These Sentences: "The man said, 'I believe'"; "The man said that he believed." Both of them make the same statement, but in different ways. The first, in which the actual words of the speaker, thinker, etc., are reproduced within single quotation marks, is called "direct speech"; the second, in which a report is given of that which was spoken, thought of, etc., is called "indirect speech."

9. In NT Greek there are two ways to construct indirect speech: (i) by putting the dependent clause in the infinitive (see Lesson **31 § 13**), or (ii) by using ὅτι to introduce the dependent clause.

10. An important difference from the English usage is that in Greek the verb in the dependent clause is usually preserved in the same tense which would have been used in the direct speech: "ἡ οὖν Μάρθα ὡς ἤκουσεν ὅτι Ἰησοῦς ἔρχεται" (lit.*) "therefore when Martha heard that Jesus is coming"* (John 11:20). In English the correct form of the dependent clause is "that Jesus *was coming."* Be sure to give the correct form for indirect speech in your translations. This may involve shifting a Greek present tense into an English past tense or a Greek aorist into an English past perfect in your translation. For example in the Greek "ἔλεγεν ὅτι εἶδε τὸν Χριστόν," the original statement was probably "εἶδον τὸν Χριστόν *(I saw Christ)*. But with the proper tense sequence shift, the best English translation would be, "*He was saying that he had seen Christ.*"

VOCABULARY

ἥλιος, ὁ:	sun
θάλασσα, ἡ:	sea
κακός, ή, όν:	bad, evil
κώμη, ἡ:	village
ὀργή, ἡ:	anger, wrath
παραλυτικός, ή, όν:	paralytic
παρθένος, ἡ:	virgin
πειρασμός, ὁ:	temptation
ποταμός, ὁ:	river
σωτηρία, ἡ:	salvation
τέ:	and, both . . . and (when followed by . . . καί or another . . . τέ; enclitic.)

EXERCISES

I.

Translate into English:

1. εἶπεν ὁ μαθητὴς ἐκεῖνος πρὸς τὸν ἀδελφὸν αὐτοῦ ὅτι εὗρε τὸν Μεσσίαν, καὶ ἤγαγεν αὐτὸν πρὸς τὸν Ἰησοῦν. 2. εἰσῆλθεν οὖν ὁ Ἰησοῦς εἰς τὴν συναγωγὴν καὶ ἀνέγνω ἐν τῷ βιβλίῳ τοῦ νόμου. 3. μικρά ἐστιν ἡ κώμη ἐν ᾗ ἔτεκεν ἡ παρθένος τὸν υἱὸν αὐτῆς. 4. καὶ τὸν ἄρτον τῆς κοινωνίας ἐφάγομεν καὶ τὸν οἶνον ἐπίομεν, ὅτι αὕτη ἐστὶν ἡ ἡμέρα τοῦ κυρίου. 5. μετὰ ταῦτα ἔπεσας εἰς πειρασμὸν καὶ ἐγκατέλιπες τὰς ἐπαγγελίας τῆς διαθήκης. 6. ἐμάθομεν ὅτι οἱ τελῶναι ἐκεῖνοι ἀνέβησαν εἰς τὸ ἱερὸν καὶ προσήνεγκαν πλουσίας θυσίας τῷ κυρίῳ. 7. ἐξῆλθες καὶ εὗρες τὸν ἄνθρωπον, ἀφ᾽ οὗ ἐξέβαλεν ὁ Ἰησους τὰ δαιμόνια. 8. ἥμαρτον οἱ υἱοί σου, ἀλλ᾽ οὐκ ἀπέθανον ἐν τῇ ἁμαρτίᾳ αὐτῶν ὅτι ἔλαβον ἀπὸ τοῦ κυρίου τὸ δῶρον τῆς σωτηρίας. 9. νῦν μὲν ἔπαθες κακὰ διὰ τὴν μαρτυρίαν τοῦ εὐαγγελίου, τότε δὲ δοξασθήσῃ ὑπὸ τοῦ κυρίου. 10. ἐν ἐκείνῃ τῇ ἡμέρᾳ ἔσχετε καὶ τὰς ἐντολὰς καὶ τὰς ἐπαγγελίας τῆς διαθήκης. 11. ἀγαθοῖς τε καὶ

πονηροῖς εἴπομεν τὴν ἀλήθειαν καὶ αὐτοὶ εὗρον τὴν σωτηρίαν ἐν Χριστῷ Ἰησοῦ. 12. εἶδεν ὁ Ἰωάννης ὁ βαπτιστὴς τὸν Ἰησοῦν παρὰ τὸν ποταμὸν καὶ ἐβάπτισεν αὐτόν. 13. καὶ τὰς ἐπαγγελίας τῆς διαθήκης ἔγνωτε καὶ ἐξουσίαν ἐπὶ τῶν δαιμονίων παρελάβετε ἀπὸ τοῦ κυρίου. 14. ταῦτα εἴπετε ἡμῖν ἐν τῇ συναγωγῇ, ἐκεῖνα δὲ καὶ αὐτοὶ οἱ δοῦλοι εἶπον καὶ ἀπήλθομεν. 15. μετὰ ταῦτα κατέβη ὁ τελώνης ἀπὸ τοῦ δένδρου καὶ ἦλθε πρὸς τὸν Χριστὸν καὶ ἔλαβε τὴν χαρὰν τῆς σωτηρίας. 16. πολλὰ ἔπαθεν ὁ κύριος ὑπὲρ τῶν ἁμαρτωλῶν, ὅτι ἔσχε μεγάλην ἀγάπην ἐν τῇ καρδίᾳ αὐτοῦ. 17. οὐ κατέλιπεν ἡμᾶς μόνους ὁ κύριος ἐν τῇ ὥρᾳ τοῦ πειρασμοῦ, ἀλλ᾽ ἕκαστος ἡμῶν ἔλαβεν εὐλογίας κατὰ τὴν χρείαν αὐτοῦ. 18. ὁ ἀπόστολος εἶπε τοῖς ὄχλοις ὅτι ἔπεσαν οἱ πονηροὶ ἄγγελοι ἐκ τοῦ οὐρανοῦ ὅτι οὐκ ἔσχον τὴν σοφίαν τοῦ θεοῦ. 19. οὔπω τοῖς ἰδίοις ὀφθαλμοῖς εἴδομεν τὴν δόξαν τοῦ οὐρανοῦ, ἀλλ᾽ εἰσήλθομεν εἰς τὴν αἰώνιον βασιλείαν καὶ ἐλάβομεν ἀγαθὰς ἐπαγγελίας. 20. ὁ παραλυτικός, ὃν εἴδετε, οὐκ ἔπεσεν, ἤγαγον γὰρ αὐτὸν οἱ φίλοι αὐτοῦ πρὸς τὸν Χριστὸν ἐν τῇ συναγωγῇ. 21. μετὰ ταῦτα ἀπέθανεν ὁ διδάσκαλος ἀφ᾽ οὗ ὑμεῖς τε καὶ οἱ φίλοι ὑμῶν ἐμάθετε τὴν ἀλήθειαν. 22. καὶ οἱ τελῶναι εἶπόν σοι ὅτι ἤγαγον τὰ ἴδια τέκνα εἰς τὴν αὐτὴν συναγωγὴν καὶ προσήνεγκαν αὐτὰ τῷ κυρίῳ. 23. πλούσιοί τε καὶ πτωχοὶ εἰσῆλθον νῦν εἰς τὴν ἐκκλησίαν, ἐν δὲ τῷ καιρῷ αὐτῶν εἰσελεύσονται εἰς αὐτὸν τὸν οὐρανόν. 24. ἔχαιρον οἱ μαθηταὶ ὅτε εἶδον τὸν κύριον. 25. οὐ θυσίας ἀλλὰ τὴν ἰδίαν ζωὴν προσηνέγκαμεν ἐκείνῳ ὃς ἔπαθεν ὑπὲρ ἡμῶν.

II.

Translate into Greek:

1. To the humble ones who went up into our synagogue in that village we did read the letter of the blessed apostle. 2. We learned that that beloved deacon had died. 3. You are more blessed than the remaining churches for you did cast the hypocrites out of your midst. 4. That prudent prophet gathered together the poor ones and they themselves ate bread and drank wine in his house. 5. Did you offer gifts of love to your teachers on account of their faithful teaching? 6. The disciples said that they had seen that one who suffered upon the cross on their

behalf and were rejoicing in their hearts. 7. We found treasures of blessings because we forsook the ways of sin. 8. Both from the synagogue and from the temple, you went away because of that one whom the virgin bore. 9. A few of the lame ones fell by the road. 10. Your children sinned against the holy law of the covenant and went down into the way which led them into death. 11. You said to those paralytics that the teacher had come into their village. 12. Both you sinned and your children sinned, therefore you fled from the face of the judge. 13. The paralytic, whom those others led to Jesus, did not die but found salvation for he had (aorist) repentance in his own heart. 14. Neither to the righteous (fem.) nor to the unrighteous ones (fem.) but to the deacons themselves you said privately that you had seen the men who had learned the appointed times of the kingdom. 15. Didst thou read in the book of the law that those who have sinned have already fallen under the wrath of God? 16. The elders went out of their houses but did not find the man who said to you the mysteries which troubled your souls. 17. There died those faithful ones who suffered many (things), because they saw by means of their own eyes the glory of heaven. 18. Now the disciples said that they had already found blessings according to the need of each of them. 19. The sons of the prophets said that the people of the Messiah had seen (sing.) signs both in the sun and in the whole world. 20. To many beloved disciples, who went up into their own synagogue, we did read the great letters of that most wise apostle. 21. More blessed are you than the remaining churches, for you rebuked a few unbelievers. 22. You neither ate our bread nor drank our wine. 23. We gathered together privately the workers who forsook their sinful ways. 24. By means of the eyes of your soul you saw Christ, who suffered upon the cross, and you found salvation. 25. Those evil men went away into the sea.

Lesson Nineteen

The Verb: Aorist Indicative, Middle and Passive

1. Distinctive Features of the Aorist Indicative Middle. We have already seen the similarity between the endings of the first aorist active and those of the imperfect active, the difference consisting mainly in the preponderance of the **α** sound in the aorist (**17 § 3, ii**). This similarity is just as striking in the middle voice. As in the active voice, the aorist in the middle voice has **σ** as its distinctive consonant, inserted between the stem and the remainder of the ending. Thus the aorist indicative middle is formed as follows:

ἐ λυ σ άμην*	ἐ λυ σ άμεθα
ἐ λύ σ ω	ἐ λύ σ ασθε
ἐ λύ σ ατο	ἐ λύ σ αντο

*"I loosed for myself."

The rules which govern the combination of certain consonants with **σ**, and the verbal stem (**15 § 2, 3**) apply here also. Thus, ἄρχομαι—ἠρξάμην, ἅπτομαι—ἡψάμην.

2. The largest number of verbs which have an aorist in the middle voice are deponent verbs.

3. Some verbs have a second, or strong, aorist in the middle voice formed without the **σ**, developing certain changes within the stem and adopting the endings of the imperfect middle/passive. Most important of these are the verbs γίνομαι and λείπομαι which form the aorist as follows:

ἐγενόμην	ἐγενόμεθα	ἐλιπόμην	ἐλιπόμεθα
ἐγένου	ἐγένεσθε	ἐλίπου	ἐλίπεσθε
ἐγένετο	ἐγένοντο	ἐλίπετο	ἐλίποντο

The deponent verb ἔρχομαι forms the second aorist by attaching the endings of the imperfect active to the stem ἐλθ—ἦλθον.

4. Distinctive Features of the Aorist Passive Indicative. The aorist passive indicative is formed as follows:

ἐλύθην	ἐλύθημεν
ἐλύθης	ἐλύθητε
ἐλύθη	ἐλύθησαν

Here again we notice the resemblance to the endings of the imperfect active, in all but the 3rd person plural, with all vowels in those endings being replaced by **η** preceded by the characteristic consonant **θ** of the future and aorist passive. The augment is prefixed to the stem. One of the distinctive marks of the aorist passive is its use of the active endings throughout the system.

5. The deponent verb γίνομαι, besides its second aorist middle, has a passive aorist form that is commonly used in the NT text: ἐγενήθην. The deponent verb ἀποκρίνομαι also forms the aorist in both the middle and the passive voice: ἀπεκρινάμην, ἀπεκρίθην, the latter being more frequently used in the NT text. The deponent verb πορεύομαι forms the aorist in the passive voice: ἐπορεύθην.

6. The changes caused by certain consonants before the **θ** of the future passive outlined in **(16 § 6)** occur in the aorist passive as well. Thus ἄγω—ἤχθην, βαπτίζω—ἐβαπτίσθην, πράσσω—ἐπράχθην, ἀποκαλύπτω—ἀπεκαλύφθην, πείθω—ἐπείσθην.

7. Certain verbs form the aorist passive:

(i) As a second aorist by dropping the **θ**. γράφω—ἐγράφην, χαίρω—ἐχάρην. ἐχάρην is a deponent form: "*I rejoiced.*"

(ii) By inserting a **σ** between the stem and the regular ending, if their stem ends in a long vowel: ἀκούω—ἠκούσθην, κλείω—ἐκλείσθην, (cf. **16 § 3**). However, this does not apply, to all verbs whose stem ends in a long vowel; e.g. λύω—ἐλύθην.

(iii) By making changes within the stem or by using a different stem. Of the verbs we have so far learned such are the following:

ἀνοίγω—	ἠνεῴχθην (also ἀνεῴχθην, ἠνοίγην, and the regular ἠνοίχθην).
βλέπω—	ὤφθην
γινώσκω—	ἐγνώσθην
δεικνύω—	ἐδείχθην
διδάσκω—	ἐδιδάχθην
εὑρίσκω—	εὑρέθην
κρύπτω—	ἐκρύβην
λαμβάνω—	ἐλήμφθην
λέγω—	ἐρρέθην
στρέφω—	ἐστράφην
σῴζω—	ἐσώθην
τίκτω—	ἐτέχθην
φέρω—	ἠνέχθην

NOTE: This list does not include verbs of the liquid/nasal group.

VOCABULARY

ἀσπάζομαι:	I greet
γάμος, ὁ:	marriage, wedding (Sometimes in the plural, of the wedding festivities)
γενεά, ἡ:	generation, race
ἐλεύθερος, α, ον:	free, free person
ἔξω:	outside (an adverb [With gen. when preceding a noun.])
μνημεῖον, τό:	grave, tomb
νεφέλη, ἡ:	cloud.
νύμφη, ἡ:	bride.
νυμφίος, ὁ:	bridegroom.
παιδίον, τό:	little child, infant
στρέφω:	I turn.
τάλαντον, τό:	talent (sum of money)

τιμή, ἡ:	price, honor
φυλακή, ἡ:	prison, a watch period (as in the third watch)

EXERCISES

I.

Translate into English:

1. ἐρρέθη ὑπὸ τοῦ Ἰησοῦ ὅτι τὸ σάββατον διὰ τὸν ἄνθρωπον ἐγένετο καὶ οὐχ ὁ ἄνθρωπος διὰ τὸ σάββατον. 2. τὰ μυστήρια τῆς βασιλείας ἐκρύβη ἀπὸ τῶν ὀφθαλμῶν τῶν σοφῶν καὶ ἀπεκαλύφθη τοῖς ταπεινοῖς. 3. τὰ τέκνα τῆς γενεᾶς ταύτης ἠλέγχθησαν ἀλλ᾽ ἐσώθησαν διὰ τὴν μετάνοιαν αὐτῶν. 4. εἰς τὰ ἴδια ἦλθε καὶ οἱ ἴδιοι οὐκ ἐδέξαντο αὐτόν. 5. οὐ θυσίαι ἀλλὰ μετάνοια ταπεινῆς καρδίας προσηνέχθη τῷ θεῷ ὑπὸ τῶν πιστῶν μαθητῶν. 6. αὐτοὶ ἐπειράσθητε ὑπὸ τοῦ πονηροῦ, ἀλλ᾽ ἐφυλάχθητε ἀπὸ τῆς ἁμαρτίας ὑπὸ τοῦ φίλου τῶν ἁμαρτωλῶν. 7. νῦν ἐδιώχθη ἡ ἐκκλησία, ὅτι ἀπῆλθον ἀπ᾽ αὐτῆς οἱ ἄνθρωποι ὑφ᾽ ὧν ἐπράχθησαν τὰ πονηρὰ ἔργα ἐκεῖνα. 8. προσηύξω τῷ κυρίῳ καὶ αὐτὸς ἐδέξατό σε καὶ ἐγένου μαθητὴς αὐτοῦ καὶ ἠσπάσαντό σε οἱ ἀδελφοί. 9. σὺ εὗρες τὸν Χριστὸν ἢ αὐτὸς εὑρέθης ὑπ᾽ αὐτοῦ; 10. εἰς ὅλον τὸν κόσμον ἐπέμφθητε καὶ ἐκηρύχθη τὸ εὐαγγέλιον τῆς εἰρήνης ὑφ᾽ ὑμῶν καὶ πολλοὶ ἐχάρησαν. 11. ὀλίγων τελωνῶν οἱ υἱοί, οὓς εἴδετε ἐν τῇ ἐκκλησίᾳ, προσηύξαντο τῷ θεῷ καὶ ὑπετάχθησαν τῷ νόμῳ αὐτοῦ. 12. οὔπω ἦλθεν ὁ νυμφίος, ἀλλ᾽ ἐλεύσεται ἐπὶ τῶν νεφελῶν τοῦ οὐρανοῦ ἐν τῷ ἰδίῳ καιρῷ καὶ παραλήμψεται τὴν ἐκκλησίαν, ἥ ἐστιν ἡ νύμφη αὐτοῦ. 13. τοῖς λόγοις οἳ ἐρρέθησάν σοι ἐγνώσθη σοι ἡ ἀλήθεια καὶ ἐγένου αὐτῶν τῶν διδασκάλων σου σοφώτερος. 14. οἱ διάκονοι τῆς ἐκκλησίας ὑμῶν, οἳ ἀνέβησαν εἰς τὸ ἱερόν, εἶπον ὑμῖν ὅτι λόγοι αἰωνίου εὐλογίας ἠκούσθησαν καὶ πολλοὶ ἐσώθησαν. 15. πολλὰ τάλαντα παρελήμφθησαν ὑπὸ ἐκείνου τοῦ πιστοῦ δούλου, ὃς ἠργάσατο πολλὰ αὐτοῖς, ἠσπάσατο οὖν αὐτὸν ὁ κύριος αὐτοῦ. 16. ὁ προφήτης ἤχθη πρὸς τὸν κριτήν, ὅτι ἠλέγχθη ὑπ᾽ αὐτοῦ ἐκεῖνος ὁ πονηρὸς ἄνθρωπος. 17. τὰ ἔργα ἃ

ἐπράχθη ὑφ᾽ ὑμῶν τε καὶ τῶν τέκνων ὑμῶν ἐν τῷ κρυπτῷ ἀποκαλυφθήσεται ἐν τῷ φανερῷ ἐν τῇ παρουσίᾳ τοῦ κυρίου. 18. οὐδὲ ὑπὸ τῶν φίλων οὐδὲ ὑπὸ τῶν ἐχθρῶν εὑρέθη ἐκεῖνος ὁ θησαυρὸς ὃς ἐκρύβη ὑπὸ σοῦ ἐν ἄλλῳ τόπῳ. 19. ἔγνωτε τὸν κύριον ὅτι ὑμεῖς ἐπεγνώσθητε ὑπ᾽ αὐτοῦ. 20. οὐκ ἐδέξαντο τοὺς ἀποστόλους οἱ πρεσβύτεροι ταύτης τῆς συναγωγῆς, ἐπορεύθησαν οὖν αὐτοὶ εἰς ἑτέραν κώμην. 21. ἐκηρύχθη τὸ εὐαγγέλιον ὑπὸ τῶν υἱῶν ἡμῶν, οἳ ἐπέμφθησαν ὑπὸ τῆς ἐκκλησίας, καὶ ἠκούσθη ἡ φωνὴ αὐτῶν ἐν ὅλῳ τῷ κόσμῳ. 22. ὑπ᾽ αὐτῶν τῶν ἀποστόλων ἐν τῷ αὐτῷ βιβλίῳ ἐγράφησαν αὗται αἱ ἐντολαί. 23. ἡ ταπεινὴ ἐκείνη ἥψατο τῶν ἱματίων τοῦ Ἰησοῦ καὶ ἐθεραπεύθη. 24. κατέλιπες τὴν ὁδὸν τῆς ἀληθείας, ἀλλὰ σὺ οὐ κατελείφθης ὑπὸ τοῦ θεοῦ. 25. ὤφθη καὶ ὑπ᾽ ἐμοῦ, τοῦ ἐσχάτου τῶν ἁμαρτωλῶν, ὁ κύριος, ὃς ἦλθεν εἰς τὸν κόσμον.

II.

Translate into Greek:

1. A rich treasure was brought by the slaves of the tax-collectors outside the house of the unjust judge. 2. We ate the bread and drank the wine, which was offered to us, and we went away from the table of the communion. 3. The words of God's covenant were read into the hearts of the humble, and these were loosed from the law of sin and became free. 4. Your sons turned from their evil ways in repentance, and were saved and were sanctified. 5. Not to the righteous but to the sinners was the gospel of God's salvation preached, and these were convicted, and were cleansed, and were baptized. 6. The bride of the Lord was not glorified but was disturbed by the hypocrites. 7. Many words of love were heard by the crowds which were turned from the kingdom of sin into life eternal. 8. Both you and your children were persecuted on account of the truth and you suffered many (things), but you prayed to the Lord and He, himself answered your prayers. 9. The words of thy repentance were heard and thou didst become wiser than thy beloved brothers. 10. Didst thou rejoice because of the child which was borne (given birth) by the virgin? 11. (It) was said to us that many letters had been written by you to both great and small churches and sacrifices had been offered by the believers. 12. In those days we were slaves of (the)

sin, but now we became disciples of Christ and are free. 13. Our sins were covered from the eyes of God by means of the eternal sacrifice which was offered upon the cross. 14. Some (on the one hand) were disturbed, others (on the other hand) rejoiced when (it) was heard that the evil judge had died. 15. When Christ went up into the heaven, the disciples were not left behind alone. 16. Not on account of the good but on account of the evil works which were done by thee thou wast reproved by the whole church. 17. We were not persuaded concerning the truth of the words which were said by you, both in the church and outside the synagogue. 18. Thy soul was prepared, and it received the word which led thee into the fellowship of love. 19. To this generation many signs were shown, and many mysteries were revealed, but it did not find salvation. 20. Many (people) were found in the roads, both poor and lame, and were led into the festivities of the wedding and rejoiced. 21. Thou wast persecuted by those evil ones, and thou didst depart into other places, but thou wast not disturbed, for thou didst pray to God, and he himself answered thee. 22. The man who was reproved by the whole church, on account of the evil works which were done by him obeyed the voice of God and the brothers greeted him. 23. These friends of mine became disciples when they were persuaded concerning the love of that one who was (borne) given birth by the virgin. 24. Thou didst work (the) sin, and thou wast hidden from the face of the Lord. 25. We were turned from the ways of death, and the Lord of life received us.

Lesson Twenty

The Contract Verbs: Present and Imperfect
Active, Middle and Passive.

1. The Contract Verbs: General Rules. If a verb has a stem ending in one of the short vowels **α, ε, ο,** a contraction takes place with the last vowel of the stem combining with the first vowel of the ending to produce one long vowel or diphthong. See **§ 6**, below, for a discussion of accenting in contract verbs. We have three groups of such verbs: the **–αω**, **–εω** and **–οω** verbs.

2. The rules which govern the contraction of the vowels are very important. These rules, which should be well memorized, are as follows:

(i) **–αω** verbs

α + ο, ω, or ου = ω	τιμά – ομεν—τιμῶμεν
	τιμά – ουσι—τιμῶσι
α + ε or η = α	τιμά – ετε, τιμά – ητε—τιμᾶτε.

In the case of the contraction of **α** with the diphthong **ει** or with **η** the **ι** appears as a subscript: τιμά – ει, τιμάῃ—τιμᾷ.

(ii) **–εω** verbs

ε + ε = ει	φιλέ + ετε—φιλεῖτε
ε + ο = ου	φιλέ + ομεν—φιλοῦμεν

ε + long vowel or diphthong = the **ε** is absorbed without changing the long vowel or diphthong:

φιλέ + ω—φιλῶ, φιλέ + ουσι—φιλοῦσι.

(iii) -**οω** verbs
ο + short vowel (even when this is the **ο** in the diphthong ου) = ου, δηλό + ετε–δηλοῦτε, δηλό + ουσι–δηλοῦσι
ο + long vowel = ω, δηλό + ω—δηλῶ
ο + diphthong **ει** or **ῃ**= οι;
δηλό - ει, δηλό + ῃ—δηλοῖ.

3. The contract verbs of the three groups are conjugated in the present and imperfect indicative active and middle/passive as follows:

Present Active

τιμά+ω=τιμῶ	φιλέ+ω=φιλῶ	δηλό+ω=δηλῶ
τιμά+εις=τιμᾷς	φιλέ+εις=φιλεῖς	δηλό+εις=δηλοῖς
τιμά+ει=τιμᾷ	φιλέ+ει=φιλεῖ	δηλό+ει=δηλοῖ
τιμά+ομεν=τιμῶμεν	φιλέ+ομεν=φιλοῦμεν	δηλό+ομεν=δηλοῦμεν
τιμά+ετε=τιμᾶτε	φιλέ+ετε=φιλεῖτε	δηλό+ετε=δηλοῦτε
τιμά+ουσι(ν)=τιμῶσι(ν)	φιλέ+ουσι(ν)=φιλοῦσι(ν)	δηλό+ουσι(ν)=δηλοῦσι(ν)

Imperfect Active

ἐτίμα+ον=ἐτίμων	ἐφίλε+ον=ἐφίλουν	ἐδήλο+ον=ἐδήλουν
ἐτίμα+ες=ἐτίμας	ἐφίλε+ες=ἐφίλεις	ἐδήλο+ες=ἐδήλους
ἐτίμα+ε=ἐτίμα	ἐφίλε+ε=ἐφίλει	ἐδήλο+ε=ἐδήλου
ἐτιμά+ομεν=ἐτιμῶμεν	ἐφιλέ+ομεν=ἐφιλοῦμεν	ἐδηλό+ομεν=ἐδηλοῦμεν
ἐτιμά+ετε=ἐτιμᾶτε	ἐφιλέ+ετε=ἐφιλεῖτε	ἐδηλό+ετε=ἐδηλοῦτε
ἐτίμα+ον=ἐτίμων	ἐφίλε+ον=ἐφίλουν	ἐδήλο+ον=ἐδήλουν

Present Middle/Passive

τιμά+ομαι=τιμῶμαι	φιλέ+ομαι=φιλοῦμαι	δηλό+ομαι=δηλοῦμαι
τιμά+ῃ=τιμᾷ	φιλέ+ῃ=φιλῇ	δηλό+ῃ=δηλοῖ
τιμά+εται=τιμᾶται	φιλέ+εται=φιλεῖται	δηλό+εται=δηλοῦται
τιμα+όμεθα=τιμώμεθα	φιλε+όμεθα=φιλούμεθα	δηλο+όμεθα=δηλούμεθα
τιμά+εσθε=τιμᾶσθε	φιλέ+εσθε=φιλεῖσθε	δηλό+εσθε=δηλοῦσθε
τιμά+ονται=τιμῶνται	φιλέ+ονται=φιλοῦνται	δηλό+ονται=δηλοῦνται

Imperfect Middle/Passive

ἐτιμα+όμην=ἐτιμώμην	ἐφιλε+όμην=ἐφιλούμην	ἐδηλο+όμην=ἐδηλούμην
ἐτιμά+ου=ἐτιμῶ	ἐφιλέ+ου=ἐφιλοῦ	ἐδηλό+ου=ἐδηλοῦ
ἐτιμά+ετο=ἐτιμᾶτο	ἐφιλέ+ετο=ἐφιλεῖτο	ἐδηλό+ετο=ἐδηλοῦτο
ἐτιμα+όμεθα=ἐτιμώμεθα	ἐφιλε+όμεθα=ἐφιλούμεθα	ἐδηλο+όμεθα=ἐδηλούμεθα
ἐτιμά+εσθε=ἐτιμᾶσθε	ἐφιλέ+εσθε=ἐφιλεῖσθε	ἐδηλό+εσθε=ἐδηλοῦσθε
ἐτιμά+οντο=ἐτιμῶντο	ἐφιλέ+οντο=ἐφιλοῦντο	ἐδηλό+οντο=ἐδηλοῦντο

Remember the present and imperfect are conjugated in the middle and passive voices in an identical way.

4. Contraction can take place only when the ending begins with a vowel; i.e. only in the present and the imperfect.

5. Apart from the application of the contraction rules, the conjugation of the contract verb is normal, the regular endings of the verb being used. However, the fact that the contraction of the **α** of the stem, in the **–αω** verbs, with either **ει** or **η** of the regular ending of the verb results in **ᾳ** is a source of possible confusion in that the 3rd person singular present active indicative and the 2nd person singular present middle/passive of the same mood are identical in their contracted form: τιμά + ει = τιμᾷ, τιμά + η = τιμᾷ. In the subjunctive mood (Lesson 32) the possibility of a confusion of an even greater nature is created by identical contracted endings in the **–αω** verbs group. On a somewhat smaller scale the same problems are created by the contraction in the **–οω** group.

6. If either of the component syllables in the uncontracted form of the verb would receive the accent in accordance with the special rule of the accent applying to the verb (**2 § 4, iii**), the resulting new syllable also receives the accent, and this is always the circumflex, provided the basic rules of the accent (**2 § 5, i–iii**) will allow. Thus, τιμά + ομεν = τιμῶμεν, but τιμα + όμεθα = τιμώμεθα; ἐφιλε + όμην = ἐφιλούμην. In the present active, middle, and passive, the accent is always placed on the contracted syllable.

7. Although the contracted form of the verb is generally used in the NT, the uncontracted forms will be given in the vocabularies, so that the student will know to which of the three groups a verb belongs.

VOCABULARY

ἀγαπάω:	I love
αἰτέω:	I ask, I make a request
ἀκολουθέω:	I follow (with dat.)
ἀρνέομαι:	I deny
δηλόω:	I declare, I signify
διψάω:	I thirst
ἐρωτάω:	I ask a question, I inquire, I beseech
εὐλογέω:	I bless
ζητέω:	I seek
θανατόω:	I put to death, I kill
καλέω:	I call
λαλέω:	I speak
μαρτυρέω:	I bear witness, I testify (with dat.)
μετανοέω:	I repent
ὁμολογέω:	I confess, I declare publicly
ὁράω:	I see (In the imperfect it is a double augment: ἑώρων)
πεινάω:	I hunger
ποιέω:	I make, I do
σταυρόω:	I crucify
τηρέω:	I keep, I observe
τιμάω:	I honor
φανερόω:	I make manifest, I show, I make clear
φιλέω:	I love
φοβέομαι:	I fear, I am afraid (pass. depon.)

EXERCISES

I.

Translate into English:

1. ὑπ᾽ ἐκείνων τιμᾶται ὁ θεός, οἳ τὰς ἀγαθὰς ἐντολὰς αὐτοῦ τηροῦσιν. 2. μακάριοι οἳ πεινῶσι καὶ διψῶσι τὴν δικαιοσύνην, ὅτι αὐτοὶ ἀγαπῶνται. 3. οἱ ὑποκριταὶ ἐκεῖνοι οὐ μετενόουν, ἀλλ᾽ ἠρνοῦντο τὴν ἀλήθειαν καὶ οὐκ ἠκολούθουν τῷ κυρίῳ. 4. ἠρωτῶμεν

τὸν προφήτην περὶ τῆς βασιλείας καὶ αὐτὸς ἐφανέρου ἡμῖν τὰ μεγάλα μυστήρια αὐτῆς. 5. ἀγαπᾷ σε ὁ ἀδελφός σου καὶ σὺ ἀγαπᾷς αὐτόν. 6. καλεῖ σε ἐκεῖνος ὁ πιστὸς διδάσκαλος καὶ σὺ ὁμολογεῖς τὴν ἀλήθειαν. 7. καὶ φίλοι καὶ ἐχθροὶ ἐμαρτύρουν περὶ σοῦ ὅτι φοβῇ τὸν θεόν. 8. φιλοῦμεν ὑμᾶς ὅτι οὐ ζητεῖτε τὴν ἰδίαν δόξαν. 9. ἐθανατοῦντο οἱ πιστοὶ ὑπὸ τῶν πονηρῶν, ὅτι ἐλάλουν τὴν ἀλήθειαν καὶ ὡμολόγουν τὸν Χριστόν. 10. ᾔτεις τὰ δῶρα τοῦ θεοῦ καὶ ηὐλογοῦ. 11. ἠκολούθει αὐτῷ ὄχλος πολύς, ὅτι ἑώρων τὰ σημεῖα ἃ ἐποίει. 12. ἐκάλει ὑμᾶς τε καὶ τὰ τέκνα ὑμῶν ἡ νύμφη τοῦ Χριστοῦ καὶ ὑμεῖς ἠκολουθεῖτε αὐτῷ καὶ ηὐλογεῖσθε. 13. ὁ κύριος ηὐλόγει ἐκείνους τοὺς πονηροὺς ἀνθρώπους οἳ ἐσταύρουν αὐτόν. 14. τὰ τέκνα ἃ αἰτοῦσιν ἄρτον οὐ λήμψονται λίθον. 15. σὺ ἀγαπᾷς τὸν κύριον καὶ σὺ ἀγαπᾷ ὑπ᾽ αὐτοῦ. 16. ἐκαλοῦ εἰς τὴν βασιλείαν τῶν οὐρανῶν ὑπὸ τοῦ υἱοῦ τοῦ θεοῦ, ὃς ἐσταυροῦτο διὰ τὰς ἁμαρτίας σου. 17. ἐγὼ ἐτίμων ἐκείνους τοὺς σοφοὺς διδασκάλους, αὐτοὶ γὰρ ἐτίμων τὸν νόμον τῆς διαθήκης. 18. ἐν ταῖς συναγωγαῖς καὶ ταῖς ὁδοῖς ἐλάλουν οἱ ἀπόστολοι περὶ τῆς σωτηρίας καὶ πολλοὶ ἤκουον καὶ μετενόουν. 19. οὐκ ὀλίγοι ἐκ τοῦ ὄχλου ἐπίστευσαν εἰς τὸν Χριστόν, ἀλλὰ διὰ τοὺς Φαρισαίους οὐχ ὡμολόγουν, ἠγάπων γὰρ τὴν δόξαν τῶν ἀνθρώπων. 20. οὔπω ὁρῶμεν νῦν τὴν δόξαν τοῦ οὐρανοῦ, ὀψόμεθα δὲ αὐτὴν ἐν τῇ παρουσίᾳ τοῦ κυρίου. 21. ἐν ἐκείναις ταῖς ἡμέραις οὐκ ἐφοβοῦντο οἱ πιστοί, ἀλλ᾽ ἐμαρτύρουν τῷ κυρίῳ αὐτῶν. 22. ὡμολόγουν αὐτοὶ οἱ υἱοὶ ὑμῶν καὶ οὐκ ἠρνοῦντο ὅτι ἐγένοντο μαθηταὶ τοῦ Μεσσίου καὶ ἠκολούθουν αὐτῷ. 23. ταῦτα ἐποίουν πολλοὶ ὑποκριταί, ὅτι οὐδὲ τὸν κύριον οὐδὲ τὴν ἐκκλησίαν αὐτοῦ ἐφίλουν. 24. ἐκεῖνος ὁ μαθητὴς ἠρνεῖτο ὅτι γινώσκει τὸν Ἰησοῦν, ἀλλ᾽ ὁ ἄλλος ὡμολόγει αὐτόν. 25. αὐτὸς ὁ κύριος ὤφθη ὑπὸ τῶν ἀνθρώπων οἳ ἑώρων τὰ ἔργα ἃ ἐποίουν οἱ μαθηταὶ αὐτοῦ. 26. ἐκάλει σε ὁ πονηρὸς κριτής, ἀλλὰ σὺ οὐκ ἐπορεύου πρὸς αὐτόν, ἐφοβοῦ γὰρ αὐτόν. 27. φιλεῖς τοὺς φίλους σου καὶ φιλῇ ὑπ᾽ αὐτῶν.

II.

Translate into Greek:

1. Thou art being loved by thy friends and art fearing thine enemies. 2. We were confessing that one who was being crucified on our behalf. 3. Thou wast not being blessed, for thou wast not doing the works of (the)

truth. 4. Both thee and thy children the Lord is calling and is speaking to you words of love. 5. Thou art being honored and loved by us for thou makest manifest to us the way of (the) salvation. 6. We declare to you that the righteous one was being crucified on behalf of the unrighteous. 7. They themselves are denying the truth and are not repenting, for they do not see the great and perfect works which God does. 8. Wast thou requesting loaves for (to) thy children? 9. In those days you were hungry and thirsty (for) the righteousness and you were witnessing (concerning) him whom you were following. 10. The unrighteous judges were inquiring concerning the eternal life and I (myself) was witnessing to them. 11. You were not being blessed because you were not keeping the commandments of the new covenant. 12. Not with (by means of) the tongues of the angels, but with the tongues of men each of you is speaking, and by means of them you witness to your Lord. 13. Wast thou being blessed by the prophet, who was calling thee into his house? 14. A few small children of this generation were following that beloved prophet who was speaking to the multitudes, but they themselves were not repenting. 15. When you were hungering and thirsting, you were asking (for) bread and wine. 16. You (yourselves) declare publicly that our sons with their own friends were honoring the fellowship of the believers and were keeping the commandments of the law, for they were loving the coming of the Lord. 17. The deacons of the church in that village told us that they were seeking God's kingdom and his righteousness. 18. By means of thine own eyes thou used to see the Lord himself in the hour of the temptation, but now thou no longer seest him for thou no longer followest him. 19. The man whom we were inquiring of concerning both (postpositive) the love and the wrath of God told us that the Lord was calling us into his church. 20. The apostle in that ship was not afraid for he was seeing an angel who was speaking to him words of peace. 21. Art thou confessing and honoring that (one) who was being put to death on thy behalf? 22. Thou wast speaking privately to thine own brothers, and that (one) who was borne by the virgin was seeing thee and was hearing thee. 23. Salvation and life eternal Christ offered to both rich and poor (ones) who were repenting. 24. John the Baptist was confessing and was not denying that, "I myself am not the Christ." 25. God is blessing those who are hungering and thirsting (for) the truth and are following it out of their whole heart.

Lesson Twenty-One

The Contract Verbs: Future and Aorist Indicative
The Verb ζάω • *The Adjective: Contract Adjectives*

1. Contract Verbs: Future and Aorist Indicative. As has already been stated, in the contract verbs, contraction takes place only in the present and the imperfect. The remaining tenses are formed by having the regular endings of each tense added to the stem and by lengthening the **α** and **ε** of the **–αω** and **–εω** verbs into **η**, and the **ο** of the **–οω** verbs into **ω**. Thus:

Future Active:	τιμήσω	φιλήσω	δηλώσω
Aorist Active:	ἐτίμησα	ἐφίλησα	ἐδήλωσα
Future Passive:	τιμηθήσομαι	φιληθήσομαι	δηλωθήσομαι
Aorist Passive:	ἐτιμήθην	ἐφιλήθην	ἐδηλώθην

2. There are several exceptions to the above rule:

(i) In the –**αω** group the **α** is retained when it is preceded by **ε, ι,** or **ρ**; also in the verbs πεινάω and κλάω. Thus, ἰάομαι—ἰάθην, θεάομαι—ἐθεασάμην, καταράομαι—κατηράσθην, πεινάω—ἐπείνασα, κλάω—ἔκλασα.

(ii) In the –**εω** group the verb καλέω retains the **ε** before the **σ** of the future and aorist active (καλέσω, ἐκάλεσα), but turns it into **η** before the **θ** of these tenses in the passive (κληθήσομαι, ἐκλήθην). The future and aorist passive, are formed on the stem **κλ**–. The verb τελέω retains the **ε** in all tenses; and in the future, and aorist passive inserts a **σ** between the stem and the ending. Thus: τελέσω, ἐτέλεσα, τελεσθήσομαι, ἐτελέσθην. The **ε** contract vowel of the verb δοκέω does not show up at all in the future and aorist tenses. δόξω and ἔδοξα.

3. The Verb ζάω. A slightly irregular contract verb is ζάω, which is conjugated as follows:

Present Indicative		Imperfect	
ζῶ	ζῶμεν	ἔζων	ἐζῶμεν
ζῇς	ζῆτε	ἔζης	ἐζῆτε
ζῇ	ζῶσι(ν)	ἔζη	ἔζων

The other tenses are formed by applying the rules in **§ 1**. The future is deponent: ζήσομαι (rarely: ζήσω).

4. Contract Adjectives. There is a small number of adjectives of the first-second declension with a stem ending in **ε**- to which the rules of contraction are applied. Such are: χρυσοῦς *(golden)*, ἀργυροῦς *(silver)*, ἁπλοῦς *(single, sincere)*, διπλοῦς *(double)*, τετραπλοῦς *(fourfold)*. These are conjugated as follows:

Single

	Masc.	Fem.	Neut.
N.V.	ἁπλοῦς	ἁπλῆ	ἁπλοῦν
G.	ἁπλοῦ	ἁπλῆς	ἁπλοῦ
D.	ἁπλῷ	ἁπλῇ	ἁπλῷ
A.	ἁπλοῦν	ἁπλῆν	ἁπλοῦν

Plural

	Masc.	Fem.	Neut.
N.V.	ἁπλοῖ	ἁπλαῖ	ἁπλᾶ
G.	ἁπλῶν	ἁπλῶν	ἁπλῶν
D.	ἁπλοῖς	ἁπλαῖς	ἁπλοῖς
A.	ἁπλοῦς	ἁπλᾶς	ἁπλᾶ

It will be noticed that the feminine follows the first declension pattern unaltered, the only indication of its contract nature being the circumflex in all cases.

VOCABULARY

ἀγνοέω:	I am ignorant
ἀδικέω:	I act unjustly, I wrong someone
ἀθετέω:	I reject, I nullify
ἁπλοῦς, ῆ, οῦν	single, clear, good, sincere
ἀσθενέω:	I am weak, sick
βλασφημέω:	I speak reproachfully, I blaspheme
διακονέω:	I serve, I minister (with dat.)
δικαιόω:	I justify
δοκέω:	I suppose, I seem (It is also used as an impersonal verb; cf. **31 § 12**.)
ἐλεέω:	I have mercy on, I pity
ἐλευθερόω:	I set free
ἐπιτιμάω:	I rebuke (with dat.)
εὐχαριστέω:	I give thanks (with dat.)
ζάω:	I live
θεάομαι:	I behold
ἰάομαι:	I heal
κατηγορέω:	I accuse (with gen.)
κλάω:	I break (always with ἄπτον, bread)
λυπέω:	I cause grief
μεριμνάω:	I am anxious
μισέω:	I hate
οἰκοδομέω:	I build, I build up, I edify
παρακαλέω:	I exhort, I beseech, I comfort
περιπατέω:	I walk
πλανάω:	I lead astray
ἀποπλανάω:	I lead astray
πληρόω:	I fill, I fulfill
προσκυνέω:	I worship (usually with dat.)
σιωπάω:	I am silent
συντελέω:	I accomplish
τελέω:	I finish

EXERCISES

I.

Translate into English:

1. οὐ μισήσεις τὸν ἀδελφόν σου, ἀλλ' ἀγαπήσεις αὐτὸν καὶ ἐλεήσεις αὐτόν. 2. ἐδικαιώθη ἡ σοφία ἐκ τῶν ἔργων αὐτῆς. 3. ἐλύπησα ὑμᾶς καὶ χαίρω ὅτι ἐλυπήθητε κατὰ θεόν. 4. συντελέσω ἐφ' ὑμᾶς διαθήκην καινήν. 5. οὐ μεριμνήσομεν περὶ ἄρτου, ἐκλήθημεν γὰρ ὑπὸ τοῦ θεοῦ καὶ ἠλεήθημεν ὑπ' αὐτοῦ. 6. σὺ μὲν ἠδίκησάς με, ἐγὼ δὲ εὐλογήσω σε καὶ διακονήσω σοι. 7. οἳ μὲν ἠθέτησαν τὰς ἐντολὰς τοῦ θεοῦ καὶ ἐβλασφήμησαν αὐτόν, οἳ δὲ προσεκύνησαν αὐτῷ καὶ ηὐλογήθησαν ὑπ' αὐτοῦ. 8. ὁ λεπρὸς ὃς ἰάθη ὑπὸ τοῦ Χριστοῦ ἐπέστρεψε καὶ ηὐχαρίστησεν αὐτῷ. 9. ἐπὶ τοῦ σταυροῦ τοῦ Χριστοῦ ἐπληρώθη ὁ νόμος, ἡμεῖς οὖν μετενοήσαμεν καὶ ηὐλογήθημεν. 10. ἐν μέσῳ τῶν μαθητῶν αὐτοῦ ὁ κύριος ἔκλασε τὸν ἄρτον. 11. ἠλευθέρωσέ σε ὁ υἱὸς τοῦ θεοῦ ἀπὸ τῶν ἁμαρτιῶν σου, καὶ ἐκάλεσέ σε εἰς τὴν βασιλείαν αὐτοῦ, ζήσῃ οὖν εἰς ζωὴν αἰώνιον. 12. ἐν τῷ προσώπῳ τοῦ Χριστοῦ ἐθεασάμεθα τὴν δόξαν τοῦ θεοῦ. 13. κατηγόρησαν τοῦ Χριστοῦ οἱ Φαρισαῖοι ὅτι μετὰ τελωνῶν ἐσθίει. 14. ἐπείνασας καὶ ἐδίψησας τὴν δικαιοσύνην καὶ οὐκ ἐφοβήθης. 15. οὐ φοβηθησόμεθα, ἐκλήθημεν γὰρ ὑπὸ τοῦ θεοῦ καὶ ἠλεήθημεν ὑπ' αὐτοῦ. 16. οὐκ ἠρνήσασθε τὸν κύριον ὑμῶν, ἀλλ' ἐμαρτυρήσατε αὐτῷ καὶ παρεκλήθητε ὑπ' αὐτοῦ. 17. ἔργα ἀγαθὰ ἤδη ἐποίησας κατὰ τοὺς λόγους οὓς ἐλάλησάν σοι οἱ διδάσκαλοί σου. 18. ἐδόξατε ὅτι ἐκεῖνοι οἱ μαθηταὶ ἐφοβήθησαν τοὺς ὑποκριτὰς καὶ οὐκ ηὐχαρίστησαν τῷ κυρίῳ ὃς ἠλέησεν αὐτούς. 19. οὐκ ἐθεάσαντο οἱ ἀδελφοὶ ἡμῶν τὸ πρόσωπον τοῦ κυρίου, ἀλλ' ἠγαπήθησαν ὑπ' αὐτοῦ καὶ προσεκύνησαν αὐτῷ ἐν τῇ ἐκκλησίᾳ. 20. τὰ τέκνα τῶν προφητῶν ἃ συνήχθησαν ἐν τῷ ἱερῷ ηὐχαρίστησαν τοῖς διδασκάλοις διὰ τοὺς λόγους οἷς παρεκλήθησαν. 21. πιστὸς ὁ θεός, ὑφ' οὗ ἐκλήθητε εἰς τὴν κοινωνίαν τοῦ υἱοῦ αὐτοῦ Ἰησοῦ Χριστοῦ τοῦ κυρίου ἡμῶν. 22. ὤφθη ὁ θεὸς τῆς δόξης καὶ ὑπὸ τῶν πτωχῶν ἀδελφῶν ἡμῶν, ὅτε αὐτοὶ ἦσαν ἐν τῷ ἱερῷ. 23. κατηγόρησαν τοῦ Ἰησοῦ οἱ ἐχθροὶ αὐτοῦ ὅτι ἐν τῇ ἡμέρᾳ τοῦ σαββάτου ἰάσατο πολλοὺς οἳ ἠσθένησαν. 24. ηὐχαρίστησας τῷ

κυρίῳ ὅτι ἠλευθέρωσέ σε ἀπὸ τοῦ νόμου τῆς ἁμαρτίας καὶ τοῦ θανάτου; 25. πολλοὶ ἐλεύσονται καὶ κράξουσιν, Ἐγώ εἰμι ὁ Χριστός, καὶ πολλοὺς ἁπλοῦς μαθητὰς πλανήσουσιν. 26. οὐ σιωπήσομεν, ἀλλὰ φανερώσομεν τὰς ἐντολὰς τῆς διαθήκης τοῦ θεοῦ τοῖς ἀνθρώποις οἳ ἠρώτησαν ἡμᾶς περὶ αὐτῶν.

II.

Translate into Greek:

1. We shall speak to thee words of truth and shall not be silent. 2. God will have mercy (on) thee and thou (thyself) wilt give thanks to him. 3. You both beheld the Messiah and you worshiped him. 4. We shall not be anxious about our life for the Lord did set us free. 5. Thou didst keep the commandments and thou was blessed for God did not nullify his promises. 6. I am not worthy but I was pitied by God. 7. Thou wilt bless those who hated thee and wronged thee. 8. The sinners confessed thy truth and worshiped thee because they repented from their sins. 9. We shall not be led astray but we shall live, for we were called by him who was crucified on our behalf. 10. We did not deny him who loved us. 11. In those days we spoke to thee privately words of eternal joy, but we shall no longer speak, for thou thyself didst not repent. 12. You asked good gifts from that (one) who was crucified in behalf of you; and he will have mercy (on) you, therefore you will give thanks to him. 13. You were not afraid (of) the sons of this generation, but you beheld the Messiah who made manifest to you his glory and you worshiped him. 14. Those who led astray many disciples from the truth neither repented nor did they seek the way of life according to the simple words which were spoken to them. 15. The enemies of our fellowship who walked with the disciples beheld the works which Jesus did and they rebuked them. 16. I thanked the Son of God because he had mercy (on) me and set me free from (the) sin. 17. These were the men who loved Jesus and followed him, for they were loved and blessed by him. 18. Our friend said that he was justified not by means of his own works but by means of the work which Jesus accomplished when he was crucified. 19. You were silent in the synagogue because you were afraid (of) those who wronged you. 20. We both spoke and shall speak concerning (the things) which were accomplished in the

midst of us. 21. Many were healed by Christ, but few returned and gave thanks to him. 22. The men who built our house were sick, but the Lord pitied them and healed them. 23. Not righteous (ones) but sinners Christ called and they themselves repented. 24. Were you (yourselves) also called into life eternal and did you confess that (one) who was crucified in your behalf? 25. Both thee and the other disciples were accused by the unrighteous (ones) that you had nullified the law concerning the Sabbath.

Lesson Twenty-Two

Liquid and Nasal Verbs: Future and Aorist Indicative;
The Pronoun: The Possessive Pronoun.

1. Liquid and Nasal Verbs. Liquid and nasal verbs are those whose stem ends in one of the liquid consonants **λ**, **ϱ** or in one of the nasal consonants **μ**, **ν** respectively. These verbs present a peculiarity in the formation of the future and aorist tenses in all three voices.

2. Future Active and Middle. The future in these two voices is formed as follows:

(i) The characteristic consonant of this tense (**σ**) is dropped.

(ii) The verb is conjugated as if it were a contract verb of the **-εω** group, with the accent on the contracted syllable. The accent is the circumflex provided it does not violate the basic rule of the accent (**2 § 5, i**). In the case of certain nasal verbs, the accent is the only way the future active can be distinguished from the present active in the three persons of the singular and the third person of the plural: μένω—μενῶ.

(iii) The verbal stem is used if it differs from the present stem. Thus, αἴϱω—ἀϱῶ, ἀϱοῦμαι, ἀποστέλλω—ἀποστελῶ, ἀποστελοῦμαι.

3. The verb λέγω forms its future active from the stem **ἐϱ–**. Since this ends in a liquid consonant the future of this verb follows the rules of the liquid/nasal verbs: ἐϱῶ, ἐϱεῖς, ἐϱεῖ, ἐϱοῦμεν, ἐϱεῖτε, ἐϱοῦσιν.

4. The verbs ἀποθνήσκω and πίπτω, deponent only in the future, form this tense by adding to the verbal stems–θαν and πεσ, respectively–the endings of the present middle of the contract verb of the **-εω** group. Thus (in the persons met in the NT) ἀποθανεῖται, ἀποθανεῖσθε; πεσοῦμαι, πεσεῖται, πεσοῦνται.

The verbs ἐλπίζω and καθαρίζω form the future active on the same pattern of the contract verb. Thus (in the persons met in the NT): ἐλπιοῦσιν, καθαριεῖ.

5. Aorist Active and Middle. This tense is formed as follows:

(i) The consonant **σ** is dropped and the normal endings of the first aorist are used.

(ii) The augment is prefixed.

(iii) A change is sometimes effected within the stem, usually by lengthening the verbal stem. Thus, ἀναγγέλλω—ἀνήγγειλα, αἴρω—ἦρα. In the verb βάλλω the second aorist ending is used: ἔβαλον.

6. Future and Aorist Passive. The normal endings of these tenses are added to the verbal stem, and some of the nasal verbs drop the **ν**. Thus, κρίνω—κριθήσομαι, ἐκρίθην. But the **λ** or **ρ** of the liquid verbs is retained. Thus, ἐγείρω—ἠγέρθην.

7. Following is a table of the liquid/nasal verbs most frequently found in the NT text, in the future and the aorist.

Present Active	**Future Active**	**Future Middle**	**Future Passive**	**Aorist Active**	**Aorist Passive**
ἀγγέλλω	ἀγγελῶ			ἤγγειλα	ἠγγέλην
αἴρω	ἀρῶ		ἀρθήσομαι	ἦρα	ἤρθην
ἀνατέλλω				ἀνέτειλα	
ἀποκρίνομαι					ἀπεκρίθην
ἀποκτείνω	ἀποκτενῶ			ἀπέκτεινα	ἀπεκτάνθην
βάλλω	βαλῶ		βληθήσομαι	ἔβαλον	ἐβλήθην
ἐγείρω	ἐγερῶ		ἐγερθήσομαι	ἤγειρα	ἠγέρθην
κρίνω	κρινῶ		κριθήσομαι	ἔκρινα	ἐκρίθην
μένω	μενῶ			ἔμεινα	
ξηραίνω				ἐξήρανα	ἐξηράνθην
ποιμαίνω	ποιμανῶ			ἐποίμανα	
σπείρω				ἔσπειρα	ἐσπάρην
στέλλω	στελῶ			ἔστειλα	ἐστάλην
φαίνω		φανοῦμαι or φανήσομαι			ἐφάνην
χαίρω			χαρήσομαι		ἐχάρην

Notice that the verbs (ἀν–, ἀπ–) ἀγγέλλω, σπείρω, (ἀπο) στέλλω, φαίνω and χαίρω form the passive aorist as 2nd aorist by dropping the **θ**.

8. The Possessive Pronoun. We have already seen that the sense of possession is obtained by using the genitive of the personal pronoun: τὸ βιβλίον μου. The same meaning, with an even more emphatic force, can be obtained by using the possessive pronoun: τὸ ἐμὸν βιβλίον. We remind you that several pronouns are used (**12 § 1**). Such is the case of the so-called possessive pronoun, which does not take the place of a noun, but qualifies it as an adjective.

9. The possessive pronoun is found only in the first and second persons in all three genders. It is declined on the pattern of the first-second declension adjectives and must agree in case, gender, number, and with the noun it qualifies.

10. The possessive pronouns are:

1st person singular: ἐμός, ἐμή, ἐμόν
1st person plural: ἡμέτερος, α, ον

2nd person singular: σός, σή, σόν
2nd person plural: ὑμέτερος, α, ον

11. The possessive pronoun can be used either in the attributive or in the predicative sense: ὁ ἐμὸς δοῦλος, ἐμός ἐστιν ὁ δοῦλος.

VOCABULARY

ἄκανθα, ης, ἡ:	thorn, a thornbush
ἀναγγέλλω:	I announce, I make known
ἀνατέλλω:	(trans.) I cause to rise (intrans.) I rise. (usually, but not exclusively of the sun.)
βλαστάνω:	I sprout
δεῖπνον, τὸ:	supper
ἐμβαίνω:	I go into, I embark
ἐπαίρω:	I lift up; (pass.), I exalt myself
ἐπιβάλλω:	I lay upon, I beat upon
ἐπιμένω:	I continue, I persevere
κατοικέω:	I dwell

ξηραίνω:	I dry; (pass.), I become dry, I wither
ὅτε:	when (adverb)
ποιμαίνω:	I tend sheep
ῥίζα, ἡ:	root
σκάνδαλον, τό:	stumbling block
ὑπομένω:	I endure
φαίνω:	I shine; (pass.), I appear

EXERCISES

I.

Translate into English:

Note: In these exercises use the true possessive pronoun (ἐμός, etc.) whenever you can.

1. ἡ βασιλεία ἡ ἐμὴ οὔκ ἐστιν ἐκ τοῦ κόσμου τούτου. 2. οἱ δὲ εἶπον, οἱ μαθηταὶ Ἰωάννου νηστεύουσιν, οἱ δὲ σοὶ ἐσθίουσι καὶ πίνουσιν. 3. ἄλλα δὲ ἐσπάρη ἐπὶ τὰς ἀκάνθας καὶ ἐβλάστησεν, ἀλλ᾽ ὅτε ἀνέτειλεν ὁ ἥλιος ἐξηράνθη. 4. ποιμανῶ τὰ ἐμὰ πρόβατα καὶ ἀποκτενῶ τοὺς ἐχθροὺς αὐτῶν. 5. ἐρεῖ ὁ κύριος τοῖς ἀγγέλοις αὐτοῦ καὶ ἀροῦσι τὰ σκάνδαλα ἐκ μέσου τῆς ἡμετέρας ἐκκλησίας, αὐτὸς δὲ ἐγερεῖ τοὺς νεκρούς. 6. ἐκ τοῦ ἐμοῦ λήμψεται ἐκεῖνος καὶ ἀναγγελεῖ αὐτὸ πρὸς ὑμᾶς. 7. καὶ τότε φανήσεται τὸ σημεῖον τοῦ υἱοῦ τοῦ ἀνθρώπου ἐν τῷ οὐρανῷ καὶ οἱ ἐμοὶ ἀδελφοὶ χαρήσονται. 8. ἐπίομεν τὸν οἶνον τῆς κοινωνίας ἐν τῇ ὥρᾳ τοῦ δείπνου τοῦ κυρίου. 9. ὅτε οἱ ἡμέτεροι υἱοὶ προσήνεγκαν τὴν θυσίαν ἐν τῷ ἱερῷ ἐφάνη αὐτοῖς ἄγγελος. 10. ἐπαροῦσιν οἱ προφῆται τὴν φωνὴν αὐτῶν καὶ ἐροῦσι τοῖς ὑμετέροις τέκνοις ὅτι κατακριθήσονται διὰ τὰ ἔργα τὰ πονηρὰ αὐτῶν. 11. οὗτοι ἐνέβησαν εἰς τὸ σὸν πλοῖον ὅτι ἀπεστάλησαν ὑπὸ τοῦ κυρίου. 12. οὐ μενεῖτε ἐν τοῖς ὑμετέροις οἴκοις, ἀπηγγείλαμεν γὰρ ὑμῖν ὅτι ὁ κύριος ἀπέστειλεν ὑμᾶς εἰς τὸν πονηρὸν κόσμον. 13. οὐ κρινοῦμεν τοὺς ἀνθρώπους οἳ ἀπέκτειναν τὸν κύριον τῆς δόξης, αὐτοὶ γὰρ ἤδη κατεκρίθησαν καὶ οὐ ζήσονται τὴν αἰώνιον ζωὴν ἀλλ᾽ ἀποθανοῦνται ἐν ταῖς ἁμαρτίαις αὐτῶν. 14. ὅτε οἱ πιστοὶ ᾠκοδόμησαν τὸ ἱερόν, ὑμεῖς ἐσπείρατε ἐν ταῖς καρδίαις αὐτῶν

τὰς ἐπαγγελίας τῆς εἰρήνης. 15. οὔπω ἤγειρεν ὁ κύριος τοὺς νεκρούς, ἀλλ᾽ ἐγερεῖ ἐκείνους οἳ οὐκ ἠδίκησαν τοὺς ταπεινοὺς ἀλλὰ κατῴκησαν σὺν τοῖς υἱοῖς τοῦ ἡμετέρου λαοῦ. 16. ὁρᾶτε νῦν τὰς παρθένους τῆς ὑμετέρας κώμης, αἳ ἐπλανήθησαν ἀπὸ τῆς ὁδοῦ τῆς ἁπλῆς σοφίας ὅτι οὐκ ἐπέμειναν ἐν τῇ ἀληθινῇ διδαχῇ. 17. ἡμεῖς ἐξεβάλομεν ἐκ τῆς ἡμετέρας συναγωγῆς τοὺς ὑποκριτάς, ὅτε ὑμεῖς ἐξεβάλλετε ἐκ τῆς ὑμετέρας πολλοὺς φρονίμους μαθητάς. 18. καὶ μικροὺς καὶ μεγάλους ἀποστελεῖ ὁ κύριος καὶ ἀπαγγελλοῦσι τοῖς ὑμετέροις υἱοῖς λόγους οἷς εὐλογηθήσονται. 19. παρακαλῶ σε περὶ τοῦ ἐμοῦ τέκνου. 20. ὁ λόγος ὁ σὸς ἀλήθειά ἐστιν. 21. μακάριοι οἱ πτωχοί, ὅτι ὑμετέρα ἐστιν ἡ βασιλεία τῶν οὐρανῶν. 22. ἀποστελεῖ ὁ κύριος ἀξίους διδασκάλους καὶ αὐτοὶ ποιμανοῦσι τὸν ἐκλεκτὸν λαὸν αὐτοῦ. 23. ἐν ἐκείναις ταῖς ἡμέραις σὺ ἐγκατέλειπες τὴν ὥραν τῆς προσευχῆς, ἀλλ᾽ ὁ κύριος οὐκ ἐγκατέλιπέ σε. 24. σὺν ἐμοὶ ἦσαν οἱ ἐμοὶ δοῦλοι ὅτε ἀπηγγέλη ἡμῖν ὅτι οἱ ἐργάται τῆς ἁμαρτίας ἀπέκτειναν τὸν προφήτην ἐν τῷ σῷ οἴκῳ. 25. ἤρθησαν ἐκ μέσου ὑμῶν ἐκεῖνοι οἳ ἐποίουν τὰ σκάνδαλα, κατεκρίθησαν γὰρ ὑφ᾽ ὅλης τῆς ἐκκλησίας.

II.

Translate into Greek:

In this exercise whenever there is more than one Greek verb which conveys the meaning of an English verb, use the one which belongs to the liquid/nasal group. Whenever the need of expressing possession arises, use the possessive pronoun.

1. Both our own sons and yours will persevere in the true teaching and will not be condemned in the last day. 2. In the hour of prayer angels appeared to thy slaves. 3. The wise teacher will lift up his voice and will say to me and to my brethren words of salvation. 4. Those evil men will be condemned, for they killed the righteous prophet. 5. We sowed the promise of life in the hearts of the men for we were sent by that one who tended (as a shepherd) his people and took away their sins. 6. It was announced to the deacons of your church that those beloved disciples had been condemned and killed, but the Lord will raise them up. 7. Shall we drink both out of the cup of the holy com-

munion and out of the cup of the demons? 8. You are blessed because you cast out of your midst those men who were the root of the sin. 9. We rejoiced because our sons no longer sinned. 10. We neither ate nor drank but went down to the houses of the poor and remained in them. 11. Your disciples cast out demons and announced the promises of the gospel. 12. Those (things) which you sowed in your fields did not wither but sprouted and brought good fruit. 13. Neither us nor our children will the wise teacher lead astray, but will say both to us and to them words of salvation and we shall live. 14. Not by those deacons, but by the apostles themselves there were sown in your souls words of great joy, because these persevered in the love of that one by whom they will not be condemned. 15. Those hypocrites neither ate bread nor drank wine according to the commandment, but remained in the house of the men who wronged both me and thee. 16. You will not judge the enemies of the eternal covenant, for they were already judged by God himself. 17. Those who forsook houses and fields on account of me will receive a crown of glory in my kingdom. 18. You were sent into the world of the sinners by that (one) who was raised from the dead (ones). 19. Shall we say to our brothers that we shall persevere in the sin? 20. A few friends of yours used to forsake the prophet, but he himself did not forsake them. 21. Thou wilt speak and wilt tell to the whole church that when thou didst remain in the temple many angels appeared to thee. 22. The new life withered in the hearts of our disciples because there was not a root in their hearts and they themselves exalted themselves. 23. Thou didst sow sin in thy life and thou wilt receive death. 24. In thy village remained those unjust (ones; fem.) by whom the remaining prophets were killed, but the Lord will raise them from the dead (ones) in the last day. 25. In the midst of you there was sown the word of the eternal salvation, but you persevered in your foolish ways and you will be cast out of the fellowship of the believers.

Lesson Twenty-Three

The Noun:
The Third Declension:
1. Masculine and Feminine Nouns
With Stem Ending in a Consonant

1. Distinctive Features of the Third Declension Nouns. The third declension nouns present a greater difficulty than those of the other two, primarily because the stem may undergo a variety of changes. Many of these changes can be grouped together within the framework of concrete rules; some others are, or at least seem to be, arbitrary. As a consequence, the student will have to apply memorization to a greater degree than he did in the study of the previous two declensions.

2. We shall start by making two basic distinctions:

(i) Between masculine and feminine nouns on the one hand, and neuter nouns on the other.

(ii) Between masculine and feminine nouns whose stem ends in a consonant and those whose stem ends in a vowel. Most of the nouns of the third declension have their stem end in a consonant.

3. The natural procedure in declining a noun is to add the proper ending to the stem. However, in the third declension the stem cannot be singled out by dropping the ending of the nominative singular, as is done in the other declensions, because the nominative case has usually already been altered by the change. The genitive singular will have to be used; after eliminating the ending of this case, what is left is usually the stem. For this reason a third declension noun is given in vocabularies and dictionaries in the nominative followed by the genitive or its ending. Because masculine and feminine nouns take the same endings in the third declension, the student should take care to ascertain from the dictionary or vocabulary the gender of the noun he is dealing with.

4. Nouns of this declension present a further peculiarity in that the genitive, dative and accusative singular and all cases of the plural usually have one syllable more than the nominative singular does.

5. Endings. The endings of masculine and feminine nouns of the third declension, of both groups, are as follows:

Singular	**Plural**
N. ς /-	–ες
G. –ος	–ων
D. –ι	–σι (ν)
A. –α/ν	–ας
V. (usually same as in nominative)	–ες

6. Most of the masculine and feminine nouns in the third declension which end in a consonant take the **α** ending for the accusative singular, but a few take the **ν** (see below, **§ 9 ii**). The **α** and **ι** in the endings of this declension are short.

7. Masculine and Feminine Nouns with a Stem ending in a Consonant. Nouns with a stem which ends in a labial (β, π, φ), guttural (γ, κ, χ and –κτ), or dental (δ, θ, τ) form the nominative singular by having **ς** added to the stem. This undergoes the same changes we are familiar with from the formation of the future and the first aorist of the verb (**15 § 2, 3**). Thus, λαιλαπ+ς—λαῖλαψ, φυλακ+ς—φύλαξ, νυκτ+ ς—νύξ, ἐλπιδ+ς—ἐλπίς, ποδ+ς—πους.

In nouns ending in a nasal or liquid the mere stem, with its last vowel lengthened if it is short usually, forms the nominative singular. Thus ποιμέν—ποιμήν, ἀστέρ—ἀστήρ.

8. The same changes take place before the **σ** of the ending of the dative plural. In nouns with stem ending:

(i) In **ϱ**, the **ϱ** is retained before the **σ**. Thus, σωτήϱ—σωτῆϱσι.

(ii) In a nasal, the **ν** is dropped. Thus, ἡγεμών—ἡγεμόσι.

(iii) In **ντ**, the **ντ** is dropped and the preceding vowel is lengthened as follows:

αντ+σι—ασι
εντ+σι—εισι
οντ+σι—ουσι

Thus, ἄρχων, ἄρχοντος, ἄρχουσι (ν).

9. Nouns whose stem end in a dental preceded by **ι**:

(i) If they are accented on the ultima in the nominative, they form the accusative singular by adding the normal **α** ending to the normal stem. Thus, ἐλπὶς—ἐλπίδα.

(ii) If they are accented on the penult in the nominative, they form the accusative singular by adding the alternative **ν** ending to a shortened stem. Thus, χάρις—χάριν (In the NT the form χάριτα is also found twice: Acts 24:27, Jude 4.).

10. Nouns of one syllable in the nominative singular deviate from the rule which governs the accent of the noun in that they drop the accent to the ultima in the genitive and dative of both numbers instead of retaining the accent on the stem (as represented by the nominative singular). Thus, χείρ—χειρός, χειρί, χειρῶν, χερσί (ν) but χεῖρα, χεῖρες, χεῖρας. See also νύξ, and θρήξ below.

11. Examples of nouns of this group which are regularly declined:

Singular

N.	ὁ φύλαξ	ἡ νύξ	ὁ ἄρχων
G.	φύλακος	νυκτός	ἄρχοντος
D.	φύλακι	νυκτί	ἄρχοντι
A.	φύλακα	νύκτα	ἄρχοντα
V.	φύλαξ	νύξ	ἄρχων

Plural

N.	φύλακες	νύκτες	ἄρχοντες
G.	φυλάκων	νυκτῶν	ἀρχόντων
D.	φύλαξι (ν)	νυξί (ν)	ἄρχουσι (ν)
A.	φύλακας	νύκτας	ἄρχοντας
V.	φύλακες	νύκτες	ἄρχοντες

Singular

N.	ὁ ποιμήν	ὁ σωτήρ
G.	ποιμένος	σωτῆρος
D.	ποιμένι	σωτῆρι
A.	ποιμένα	σωτῆρα
V.	ποιμήν	σῶτερ

Plural

N.	ποιμένες	σωτῆρες
G.	ποιμένων	σωτήρων
D.	ποιμέσι (ν)	σωτῆρσι (ν)
A.	ποιμένας	σωτῆρας
V.	ποιμένες	σωτῆρες

12. Examples of nouns of this group irregularly declined:

Singular

N.	ὁ πατήρ	ὁ ἀνήρ	ἡ γυνή	ἡ θριξ
G.	πατρός	ἀνδρός	γυναικός	τριχός
D.	πατρί	ἀνδρί	γυναικὶ	τριχί
A.	πατέρα	ἄνδρα	γυναῖκα	τρίχα
V.	πάτερ	ἄνερ	γύναι	θρίξ

Plural

N.	πατέρες	ἄνδρες	γυναῖκες	τρίχες
G.	πατέρων	ἀνδρῶν	γυναικῶν	τριχῶν
D.	πατράσι (ν)	ἀνδράσι (ν)	γυναιξί (ν)	θριξί (ν)
A.	πατέρας	ἄνδρας	γυναῖκας	τρίχας
V.	πατέρες	ἄνδρες	γυναῖκες	τρίχες

The nouns θυγάτηρ and μήτηρ are declined on the pattern of πατήρ; the accent on the vocative singular of θυγάτηρ is on the antepenult: θύγατερ. Notice the interchange of **θ** and **τ** in θριξ; when the harsher **χ** sound at the end of the stem is softened by adding the **σ** sound, the initial **τ** is softened to **θ**.

VOCABULARY

αἰών, αἰῶνος, ὁ:	age
(εἰς τὸν αἰῶνα:	forever
εἰς τοὺς αἰῶνας τῶν αἰώνων:	forever and ever
ἀνήρ, ἀνδρός, ὁ:	man (as distinct from woman, compare ἄνθρωπος) husband, male
ἄρχων, ἄρχοντος, ὁ:	ruler
ἀστήρ, ἀστέρος, ὁ:	star
γυνή, γυναικός, ἡ:	woman, wife
διαφέρω:	I differ
Ἕλλην, Ἕλληνος, ὁ:	Greek
ἐλπίς, ἐλπίδος, ἡ:	hope
ἡγεμών, ἡγεμόνος, ὁ:	governor, king
θρίξ, τριχός, ἡ:	hair
θυγάτηρ, θυγατρός, ἡ:	daughter
μάρτυς, μάρτυρος, ὁ:	witness
μήτηρ, μητρός, ἡ:	mother
νύξ, νυκτός, ἡ:	night
παῖς, παιδός, ὁ, ἡ:	child (boy or girl), servant
πατήρ, πατρός, ὁ:	father
ποιμήν, ποιμένος, ὁ:	shepherd
πούς, ποδός, ὁ:	foot
σάρξ, σαρκός, ἡ:	flesh
σωτήρ, σωτῆρος, ὁ:	savior
χάρις, χάριτος, ἡ:	grace
χείρ, χειρός, ἡ:	hand
ὡς:	as, how, about, like (adverb)

EXERCISES

I.

Translate into English:

1. βλέπετε, γὰρ ἀδελφοί, ὅτι οὐ πολλοὶ σοφοὶ κατὰ σάρκα ἐκλήθησαν. 2. ἔλαβεν ὁ κύριος ἐν ταῖς χερσὶν ἄρτον καὶ ἔκλασεν

αὐτόν. 3. ἔσομαι ὑμῖν εἰς πατέρα καὶ ὑμεῖς ἔσεσθέ μοι εἰς υἱοὺς καὶ θυγατέρας. 4. εὕρομεν ἐν Χριστῷ ἐλπίδα ἀγαθὴν ἐν χάριτι. 5. οἱ νεκροὶ ἐγερθήσονται ἐν τῇ ἐσχάτῃ ἡμέρᾳ καὶ ζήσονται εἰς τοὺς αἰῶνας τῶν αἰώνων. 6. ἄλλη δόξα ἀστέρων, ἀστὴρ γὰρ ἀστέρος διαφέρει ἐν δόξῃ. 7. ὀργὴ γὰρ ἀνδρὸς δικαιοσύνην θεοῦ οὐκ ἐργάζεται. 8. καὶ ἐκ τῶν ἀρχόντων πολλοὶ ἐπίστευσαν εἰς αὐτόν, ἀλλὰ διὰ τοὺς Φαρισαίους οὐχ ὡμολόγουν. 9. ἔσεσθέ μου μάρτυρες ἐν ὅλῳ τῷ κόσμῳ. 10. προσηύξω τῷ σῷ πατρὶ ὑπὲρ τῶν ἀρχόντων κατὰ τὴν ἐντολὴν τοῦ νόμου; 11. εἶπεν Ἡρώδης τοῖς παισὶν αὐτοῦ, Οὗτός ἐστιν Ἰωάννης ὁ Βαπτιστής· αὐτὸς ἠγέρθη ἀπὸ τῶν νεκρῶν. 12. τούτου τοῦ αἰῶνος τὰ τέκνα οὐδὲ τὴν χάριν τοῦ σωτῆρος ἔγνωσαν οὐδὲ τὴν ἐλπίδα τῆς αἰωνίου ζωῆς ἔσχον ἐν ταῖς καρδίαις αὐτῶν. 13. καὶ τοῖς πατράσιν ὑμῶν καὶ ταῖς μητράσιν ὑμῶν ἀπαγγελοῦμεν τὰς ἐπαγγελίας ἐκείνου ὃν ἀπέκτειναν οἱ ἁμαρτωλοί, καὶ αὐτοὶ ἔσονται μάρτυρες τοῦ Χριστοῦ. 14. ἐχθροῖς τε καὶ φίλοις ἐροῦμεν ὅτι ὑπὸ τὴν χεῖρα τοῦ ἡμετέρου πατρὸς ἀδελφοὶ αὐτῶν ἐσόμεθα καὶ μενοῦμεν μετ᾽ αὐτῶν τὸ λοιπὸν. 15. οὐκ ἐν τῇ σαρκὶ ἕξετε τὴν ἐλπίδα ὑμῶν, ἀλλ᾽ ἐν τῇ χάριτι τοῦ σωτῆρος, ὃς ἦρε τὰς ἁμαρτίας τοῦ κόσμου. 16. τῷ λόγῳ τῆς χάριτος, ὃς ἐσπάρη κατ᾽ ἰδίαν ἐν ταῖς καρδίαις τῶν σῶν θυγατέρων, αὗται οὐ κριθήσονται, ἀλλ᾽ ὁ κύριος ἐγερεῖ αὐτὰς ἐν τῇ ἐσχάτῃ ἡμέρᾳ καὶ ζήσονται εἰς τοὺς αἰῶνας τῶν αἰώνων. 17. οὗτοι οἱ ἄνδρες σὺν ταῖς γυναιξὶν αὐτῶν ἐδέξαντο ἀπὸ τῶν χειρῶν αὐτοῦ τοῦ σωτῆρος τὴν ἐπαγγελίαν τῆς αἰωνίου ζωῆς, καὶ ἀπεστάλησαν ὑπ᾽ αὐτοῦ πρὸς τοὺς παῖδας τῶν ἀρχόντων. 18. ἐν τῇ νυκτὶ τούτου τοῦ ἁμαρτωλοῦ αἰῶνος ἐκβαλοῦμεν ἐκ τῆς ἐκκλησίας τοὺς ὑποκριτάς, οἳ ζῶσι καὶ περιπατοῦσι κατὰ τὴν σάρκα. 19. ἔδειξεν αὐτοῖς τὰς χεῖρας καὶ τοὺς πόδας. 20. ποιμανεῖ ὁ σωτὴρ τοὺς πιστοὺς ὡς ὁ ποιμὴν ποιμαίνει τὰ πρόβατα αὐτοῦ. 21. ἐροῦσιν οἱ σοφοὶ προφῆται τοῖς ἄρχουσι ταύτης τῆς κώμης ὅτι οὐκ ἄρχουσι τῶν ἀδελφῶν αὐτῶν κατὰ τὸν νόμον τοῦ θεοῦ. 22. ἀπεκρίθη τῷ ἡγεμόνι ὁ Ἰησοῦς, Ἡ βασιλεία ἡ ἐμὴ οὐκ ἔστιν ἐκ τοῦ κόσμου τούτου. 23. ἐκεῖναι αἱ ἐπιστολαὶ ἃς ἀνέγνωτε τῇ ἐμῇ χειρὶ ἐγράφησαν. 24. ὅτε ἠγέρθη ἀπὸ τῶν νεκρῶν ὁ Χριστός, ὤφθη ὑπ᾽ ἀνδρῶν τε καὶ γυναικῶν, οἳ νῦν μάρτυρες αὐτῷ εἰσιν. 25. ζῶμεν νῦν καὶ ὁμολογοῦμεν τὸν κύριον ἐπὶ τῇ ἐλπίδι τῆς ἐπαγγελίας ἣ ἐγένετο τοῖς πατράσιν ἡμῶν.

II.

Translate into Greek:

1. Because of the night the rulers sent their boy-servants to the governor. 2. Not in the flesh of men have we our hope. 3. The Savior himself will have mercy (on) your sons and daughters forever and ever. 4. Doesn't your Father know even the hairs of your head? 5. By means of the grace of God, I am (that) which I am. 6. The witnesses beheld his hands and his feet. 7. Daughter, not I but the grace of God healed thee. 8. The good shepherds lead the governor into repentance. 9. To your fathers and your mothers you will say the words of the Savior. 10. These rulers exalted themselves, for they did not have the grace of the Savior in their hearts. 11. Thy feet led thee into the ways of the Savior himself. 12. Neither to men nor to women but to the boy-servants of the rulers of this age our beloved fathers will announce the promises of the true hope. 13. Not by means of the works of the flesh but through the grace of the Savior thou wast saved, and thou wilt be raised by means of his hand. 14. In the hands of the Savior we have both his grace and our hope. 15. No longer do I know the Lord according to the flesh. 16. Thy throne, O Lord, will remain forever and ever. 17. That woman touched by means of the (her) hands the garments of Jesus and was healed. 18. The word became flesh. 19. Even the servants of that evil governor will be raised from the dead ones by means of the grace of the Father, who is in the heavens. 20. When those wise men saw the star they rejoiced. 21. The multitudes wondered at the many great miracles which were being done by means of the hands of the Lord. 22. When the rulers persecuted thee, thou wast not afraid, but thou didst persevere in the grace by means of which thou wast saved. 23. The unbelievers who live according to the flesh will die the eternal death. 24. We did not speak to you the wisdom of this age. 25. Through the whole night those women were praying and the Lord answered them and blessed them.

Lesson Twenty-Four

The Third Declension Nouns:

2. Masculine and Feminine Nouns with Stem Ending in a Vowel

The Dative of Respect

1. The second group of third declension nouns, composed of masculine and feminine nouns with a stem which ends in a vowel, is made up of three smaller groups.

2. The First Group: Stems Ending in a Variable Vowel. The nouns in this group have a variable stem which becomes **ι** in the nominative, accusative and vocative singular, and becomes an **ε** in all other cases. All nouns of this group are feminine and are mainly abstract nouns.

3. In this group there are certain departures from the regular third declension endings:

(i) The ending –**ος** of the genitive singular is lengthened to –**ως**. For accent purposes the **εω** in the genitive singular and plural is considered a single syllable, allowing accent to remain on the antepenult.

(ii) In the accusative singular the alternative ending –**ν**, instead of –**α**.

(iii) When the **ε** of the stem is followed by the **ες** of the nominative plural ending or the **ας** of the accusative plural ending a contraction takes place resulting in **ει**.

4. The nouns of this group must be carefully distinguished from nouns whose stem ends in a consonant and have their ending in –**ις** in the nominative singular. The genitive singular will supply the means for the distinction: χάρις, χάριτος; πίστις, πίστεως.

5. The nouns of this group are declined as follows:

		Singular	**Plural**
N.	ἡ	πόλις	πόλεις
G.		πόλεως	πόλεων
D.		πόλει	πόλεσι (ν)
A.		πόλιν	πόλεις
V.		πόλι	πόλεις

6. The Second Group: Stems Ending in - ευ. All nouns in this group are masculine, mainly describing those in particular occupations.

7. In this group, also, there are certain departures from the regular third declension endings, similar to those of the previous group:

(i) The ending –**ος** of the genitive singular is lengthened to –**ως**. However, the **εω** in the genitives of this group is not considered as a single syllable as it is in the first group (thus the accent on the **ε** as the penult).

(ii) The **υ** of the stem is dropped whenever followed by a vowel ending; and whenever this vowel is **ε** as in the nominative plural, a contraction takes place between this and the **ε** of the stem resulting in **ει**. A contraction also takes place in the accusative plural between the **ε** of the stem and the **α** of the regular ending –**ας** resulting in **ει**. The nominative singular is formed by adding a **ς** to the stem.

8. Notice that nouns of both this group and the previous one have similar endings in the plural. The nominative, accusative and vocative plural in both groups have the same endings.

9. The nouns of this group are declined as follows:

		Singular	**Plural**
N.	ὁ	ἱερεύς	ἱερεῖς
G.		ἱερέως	ἱερέων
D.		ἱερεῖ	ἱερεῦσι (ν)
A.		ἱερέα	ἱερεῖς
V.		ἱερεῦ	ἱερεῖς

10. The Third Group: Stems Ending in υ. This group includes a small number of nouns, both masculine and feminine, which are declined in a way similarly to that of the first group, in the singular. The most distinctive feature of this small group is the diaresis (**1 § 4**) which marks the **ι** of the dative singular ending as a separate syllable rather than part of a diphthong. Notice that the **υ** sometimes drops out of the **ου** dipththong in the genitive singular form of the word νοῦς.

11. The nouns of this group are declined as follows:

	Singular	**Plural**
N. ὁ	ἰχθύς	ἰχθύες
G.	ἰχθύος	ἰχθύων
D.	ἰχθύϊ	ἰχθύσι (ν)
A.	ἰχθύν	ἰχθύας
V.	ἰχθύ	ἰχθύες

	Singular	**Plural**
N. ἡ	ἰσχύς	No plurals found in the NT.
G.	ἰσχύος	Quite similar is the declension of ὀσφύς
D.	ἰσχύϊ	(waist, loins), and στάχυς (ear of grain).
A.	ἰσχύν	
V.	ἰσχύ	

	Singular	**Plural**	
N. ὁ	νοῦς	νόες	Quite similar is the declension of
G.	νοός	νοῶν	βοῦς (ox), πλοῦς (voyage), and
D.	νοΐ	νουσί (ν)	χοῦς (dust).
A.	νοῦν	νόας	
V.	νοῦ	νόες	

12. The Dative of Respect. Besides the other services the dative case of the noun renders in the sentence it is also employed to indicate a specific relationship which may exist between various parts of a sentence and define its limits. This is the "dative of respect." For example: τὸν δὲ ἀσθενοῦντα τῇ πίστει προσλαμβάνεσθε: "and welcome him who is weak (not in all respects–actually he may be a strong man, but) *so far as the faith is concerned*" (Rom. 14:1).

VOCABULARY

ἀδύνατος, ον:	weak
ἁλιεύς, ἁλιέως, ὁ:	fisherman
ἀνάστασις, ἀναστάσεως, ἡ:	resurrection
ἀποκάλυψις, ἀποκαλύψεως, ἡ:	revelation
ἀρχιερεύς, ἀρχιερέως, ὁ:	high priest
ἄφεσις, ἀφέσεως, ἡ:	release, forgiveness
βασιλεύς, βασιλέως, ὁ:	king
γνῶσις, γνώσεως, ἡ:	knowledge
γονεύς, γονέως, ὁ:	parent (only in the plural in the NT)
γραμματεύς, γραμματέως, ὁ:	scribe
δέησις, δεήσεως, ἡ:	supplication, prayer
δύναμις, δυνάμεως, ἡ:	power, miracle
θλῖψις, θλίψεως, ἡ:	affliction, tribulation
ἱερεύς, ἱερέως, ὁ:	priest
ἰχθύς, ἰχθύος, ὁ:	fish
κρίσις, κρίσεως, ἡ:	judgment
κτίσις, κτίσεως, ἡ:	creation, creature
νοῦς, νοός, ὁ:	mind, discernment
παράδοσις, παραδόσεως, ἡ:	tradition
παράκλησις, παρακλήσεως, ἡ:	exhortation, consolation
πίστις, πίστεως, ἡ:	faith, belief
πόλις, πόλεως, ἡ:	city
συνείδησις, συνειδήσεως, ἡ:	conscience
φύσις, φύσεως, ἡ:	nature

EXERCISES

I.

Translate into English:

1. ὁ κύριος ἡμῶν τῇ χάριτι αὐτοῦ ἐποίησεν ἡμᾶς βασιλεῖς καὶ ἱερεῖς τῷ θεῷ καὶ πατρὶ αὐτοῦ. 2. δι᾽ ἀποκαλύψεως τοῦ Ἰησοῦ Χριστοῦ ἐδεξάμην τὸ εὐαγγέλιον καὶ δοξασθήσεται ὁ κύριος ἐν

τῇ σαρκί μου. 3. ἄνδρες ἀδελφοί, περὶ ἐλπίδος καὶ ἀναστάσεως νεκρῶν κρίνομαι. 4. ἐκ δὲ τῆς πόλεως ἐκείνης πολλοὶ ἐπίστευσαν εἰς αὐτὸν διὰ τὸν λόγον τῆς γυναικός. 5. ἐν τῷ κόσμῳ θλῖψιν ἕξετε, ἀλλὰ προσεύξεσθε τῷ πατρὶ καὶ λήμψεσθε δύναμιν ἐν τῇ χάριτι καὶ τῇ γνώσει τοῦ κυρίου καὶ σωτῆρος ἡμῶν Ἰησοῦ Χριστοῦ. 6. ὑμεῖς δὲ ἐχάρητε ἐπὶ τῇ παρακλήσει. 7. τῇ γὰρ χάριτι ἐσώθητε διὰ πίστεως. 8. καὶ ἐν τῷ νοῒ καὶ ἐν τῇ καρδίᾳ προσκυνοῦμεν τῷ σωτῆρι ἡμῶν. 9. οἱ ἱερεῖς ἠγνόουν τὴν δύναμιν τοῦ λόγου τοῦ θεοῦ. 10. ποιήσω ὑμᾶς ἁλιεῖς ἀνθρώπων. 11. οὐκ ἐσθίομεν ἄρτον διὰ τὴν συνείδησιν τοῦ ἀδυνάτου ἀδελφοῦ. 12. οὐκ ἀποθανούμεθα ἀλλὰ ζησόμεθα, ἔχομεν γὰρ τὴν ἐλπίδα τῆς ἀναστάσεως ἐν ταῖς καρδίαις ἡμῶν. 13. ἐκ πίστεως ἐδικαιώθητε καὶ ἐβαπτίσθητε ὑπὸ τῶν πρεσβυτέρων τῆς ἐκκλησίας. 14. εἰς κρίσιν οὐκ ἐλευσόμεθα, ἀλλ᾽ ἐγερθησόμεθα ἐν δόξῃ ἐν τῇ μεγάλῃ ὥρᾳ τῆς ἀναστάσεως. 15. ἐν ἐκείναις ταῖς μεγάλαις πόλεσι κηρυχθήσεται τὸ εὐαγγέλιον τῆς ἀποκαλύψεως τοῦ θεοῦ ἐν δυνάμει καὶ τοῖς ἀνδράσι καὶ ταῖς γυναιξίν. 16. οὐδὲ τοῖς βασιλεῦσιν οὐδὲ τοῖς ἄρχουσιν άλλὰ τοῖς γραμματεῦσιν ἀπεστάλησαν αἱ γραφαὶ τῆς αἰωνίου ἐλπίδος. 17. ἡμεῖς μὲν ἀνέβημεν εἰς τὸν οἶκον τοῦ ἀρχιερέως, ὑμεῖς δὲ μενεῖτε ἐν ταύτῃ τῇ ταπεινῇ πόλει. 18. πτωχοὶ μὲν τῷ κόσμῳ, πλούσιοι δὲ τῷ θεῷ εἰσιν οἱ υἱοὶ τῆς ἀναστάσεως. 19. οὗτοι οἱ ἱερεῖς ἐλάλησαν τοῖς γονεῦσι κατὰ τὴν παράδοσιν τῶν γραμματέων. 20. ἔλαβε γνῶσιν σωτηρίας ὁ λαὸς τοῦ θεοῦ ἐν ἀφέσει τῶν ἁμαρτιῶν αὐτῶν. 21. τότε μὲν ἤμεθα φύσει τέκνα ὀργῆς ὡς καὶ οἱ λοιποί, ἀλλὰ τῇ χάριτι τοῦ Χριστοῦ καὶ διὰ τῆς πίστεως ἐγενόμεθα υἱοὶ καὶ θυγατέρες τοῦ θεοῦ. 22. οἱ ἄνδρες οἳ μετενόησαν καὶ ἐπίστευσαν τῷ σωτῆρι ἔλαβον ἄφεσιν ἁμαρτιῶν καὶ ζήσονται εἰς τοὺς αἰῶνας τῶν αἰώνων. 23. προσηυξάμεθα τῷ βασιλεῖ τῶν οὐρανῶν καὶ αὐτὸς ἀπεκρίθη ταῖς δεήσεσιν ἡμῶν. 24. οἱ ἄνδρες καὶ αἱ γυναῖκες ἔφαγον τοὺς ἄρτους καὶ τοὺς ἰχθύας, οὓς ἔλαβον ἀπὸ τῶν χειρῶν τῶν ἀποστόλων. 25. δυνάμει μεγάλῃ ἐκήρυξαν οἱ ἡμέτεροι φίλοι ἐν ἐκείναις ταῖς πόλεσι καὶ ἐγένοντο μάρτυρες τῆς ἀναστάσεως τοῦ κυρίου.

II.

Translate into Greek:

1. Not by means of the works of the flesh, but by means of the power of the resurrection of the Savior we were saved. 2. In your afflictions you have the knowledge of the promises of your Father. 3. More righteous are the kings of these cities than (disjunctive particle) the priests themselves. 4. In the last hour the voice of the angel will be heard, and after these (things) judgment. 5. You are walking according to the traditions of your fathers. 6. The fishermen brought the fishes into the other city. 7. The disciples persevered in prayers and supplications. 8. Through (the) faith and by means of the grace of God you will receive the forgiveness of your sins. 9. You offered to your parents love in the power of your hearts. 10. The kings in those great cities killed a few priests and scribes. 11. The servants of the rulers in the other cities sowed the word of the faith in the hearts of the men and the women of this sinful age. 12. In the hour of their affliction the sons and the daughters of the evil kings will pray to their Savior and will receive from his hands revelations of his power. 13. The priests will remain in the house which the servants of our fathers built, for they have faith and hope in their hearts. 14. The witnesses of the truth will announce to the scribes both the judgment and the hope of the resurrection. 15. Both the priests and the scribes nullified the revelation of God because of their traditions. 16. Didst thou know in thine own life the power of the supplications to God? 17. By means of the grace of the Savior the sun of righteousness rose in our hearts and we learned the knowledge of God in the face of Christ. 18. You know that because of a sickness of the flesh I brought the good news to you, and you yourselves received me as an angel of God. 19. The humble ones will persevere in their supplications and will take both in their mind and in their conscience the consolation of God. 20. Not the high priest but our king himself we shall worship. 21. Blessed are the clean so far as the heart is concerned. 22. Many have the knowledge concerning the resurrection of the Savior but not concerning its power also. 23. In the whole creation there appeared the glory of God. 24. In those days by means of the sign of the fish the disciples used to find their brethren. 25. In our afflictions we shall lift up our hearts to our Father who is in the heavens.

Lesson Twenty-Five

The Third Declension Nouns:
3. Neuter Nouns

1. There are two groups of neuter nouns of the third declension. Nouns of both groups have stems ending in a consonant, though this is not immediately apparent in the second group. The endings in both groups are basically the regular endings of the third declension; however, as in all neuter nouns, the nominative, accusative and vocative in both numbers have identical endings.

2. First Group: Stems Ending in -ματ. A large number of neuter nouns have endings in –**ματ**, and are declined in the third declension. The final –**τ** drops out when no ending is added in the nominative, accusative, and vocative singular, and before the **σι** of the dative plural.

Singular	**Plural**	**Singular**	**Plural**
N.–	–ατ - α	ὄνομα	ὀνόματα
G.–ατ - ος	–ατ - ων	ὀνόματος	ὀνομάτων
D.–ατ - ι	–α - σι (ν)	ὀνόματι	ὀνόμασι (ν)
A.–	–ατ - α	ὄνομα	ὀνόματα
V.–	–ατ - α	ὄνομα	ὀνόματα

3. There are a number of nouns with slight variations from the –**ματ**, pattern. The most common of these are given here with the nominative singulars and any other forms found in the NT. Some have an –**ατ** ending add a –**σ** as the ending for the nominative, accusative, and vocative singular with the –**τ** dropping out: ἅλας, ἅλατος, ἅλατι (*salt*); κρέας, κρέα (pl.) (*meat*). Others form similarly on an –**οτ** or –**ωτ** stem with a –**σ** in the nominative, accusative, and vocative singular: οὖς, ὦτα, ὠσί (*ear*); φῶς, φωτός, φωτί, φῶτα (*light*). Additional variations are: γόνυ, γόνατα, γόνασι (*knee*); ὕδωρ, ὕδατος, ὕδατι, ὕδατα, ὑδάτων (*water*); φρέαρ, φρέατος (*well, a pit*, not a condition of health).

4. The monosyllable (in the nominative) nouns of this group are accented on the ultima in all cases in the singular and in the dative in the plural (see οὖς and φῶς, in **§ 3**).

5. Second Group: Stems Ending in – εσ. Another fairly large number of neuter nouns in the third declension have stems ending in **– εσ**. Whenever the ending begins with a vowel, i.e. in all cases except the dative plural, the **σ** is dropped and a contraction takes place between the remaining **ε** of the stem and the vowel of the ending. In the nominative, accusative and vocative singular the **ε** is turned into **ο** and the **σ** is retained.

6. Most of the nouns of this group are declined as follows:

Singular	**Plural**	**Singular**	**Plural**
N.– :ος	–ε (σ): η	γένος	γένη
G.– :ε (σ)ος: ους	–ε (σ) ων: ων	γένους	γενῶν
D.– :ε (σ)ι: ει	–εσι (ν)	γένει	γένεσι (ν)
A.– :ος	–ε (σ): η	γένος	γένη
V.– :ος	–ε (σ): η	γένος	γένη

Learn the nouns in this group very well and be careful in translating them, because three of the forms are so easily misidentified: γένος, γένους, γένη. This is one place where the article, if present, becomes even more important in identification.

7. Two nouns in this group have slight irregularities in one form. πῦρ is irregular in the dative singular: πῦρί: and ὄρος is irregular in the genitive plural: ὀρέων.

VOCABULARY

αἷμα, αἵματος, τό:	blood
βάπτισμα, βαπτίσματος, τό:	baptism
γεννάω:	I beget, (pass.) I am born
γένος, γένους, τό:	offspring, race

δουλεύω:	I serve (with dative)
ἔθνος, ἔθνους, τό:	nation; in the plural (usually Gentiles)
ἔλεος, ἐλέους, τό:	mercy
θέλημα, θελήματος, τό:	will
μέλος, μέλους, τό:	member
μέρος, μέρους, τό:	part
ὄνομα, ὀνόματος, τό:	name
ὄρος, ὄρους, τό:	mountain
οὖς, ὠτός, τό:	ear
πλῆθος, πλήθους, τό:	multitude, crowd
πνεῦμα, πνεύματος, τό:	spirit
πῦρ, πυρός, τό:	fire
ῥῆμα, ῥήματος, τό:	word
σκεῦος, σκεύους, τό:	vessel
σκότος, σκότους, τό (also σκοτία, ἡ):	darkness
σπέρμα, σπέρματος, τό:	seed
στόμα, στόματος, τό:	mouth
σῶμα, σώματος, τό:	body
τέλος, τέλους, τό:	end
ὕδωρ, ὕδατος, τό:	water
φῶς, φωτός, τό:	light
χάρισμα, χαρίσματος, τό:	spiritual gift

EXERCISES

I.

Translate into English:

1. ἐγὼ ἐβάπτισα ὑμᾶς ὕδατι, ἐκεῖνος δὲ ὃς ἐλεύσεται βαπτίσει ὑμᾶς πνεύματι ἁγίῳ καὶ πυρί. 2. τῇ χάριτι τοῦ σωτῆρος μέλη ἐγενόμεθα τοῦ σώματος αὐτοῦ, ὅ ἐστιν ἡ ἐκκλησία. 3. οἱ πατέρες ἡμῶν ἐν τῷ ὄρει τούτῳ προσεκύνησαν. 4. οὗτοι οὐκ ἐξ αἱμάτων οὐδὲ ἐκ θελήματος σαρκὸς οὐδὲ ἐκ θελήματος ἀνδρός, ἀλλ' ἐκ θεοῦ ἐγεννήθησαν. 5. πολλοὶ ἐροῦσι μοι ἐν ἐκείνῃ τῇ ἡμέρᾳ, κύριε, οὐ τῷ σῷ ὀνόματι δαιμόνια ἐξεβάλομεν καὶ δυνάμεις πολλὰς

ἐποιήσαμεν; 6. οἳ μὲν σκεύη ὀργῆς, οἳ δὲ σκεύη ἐλέους. 7. υἱοὶ φωτός ἐστε· οὐκ ἐσμεν νυκτὸς οὐδὲ σκότους. 8. ἐκ τοῦ στόματός σου κρινῶ σε, δοῦλε πονηρέ. 9. ἠκολούθει δὲ αὐτῷ πολὺ πλῆθος τοῦ λαοῦ ἀνδρῶν τε καὶ γυναικῶν. 10. ἐκ μέρους γὰρ γινώσκομεν καὶ ἐκ μέρους προφητεύομεν. 11. ὃν γὰρ ἀπέστειλεν ὁ θεὸς τὰ ῥήματα τοῦ θεοῦ λαλεῖ. 12. ἐγερθήσεται γὰρ ἔθνος ἐπὶ ἔθνος καὶ βασιλεία ἐπὶ βασιλείαν. 13. τῷ ῥήματι τοῦ γραμματέως τὰ ἔθνη γνώσεται καὶ τὸ ὄνομα καὶ τὸ θέλημα τοῦ κυρίου. 14. διὰ τοῦ αἵματος τοῦ Ἰησοῦ Χριστοῦ καὶ οἱ βασιλεῖς καὶ οἱ ἄρχοντες ἐκαθαρίσθησαν ἀπὸ τῶν ἁμαρτιῶν αὐτῶν. 15. κατακριθήσεσθε ὅτι τοῖς ἰδίοις ὠσὶν ἠκούσατε περὶ τῆς δυνάμεως τῆς ἀναστάσεως τοῦ Χριστοῦ, ἀλλ᾽ οὐ μετενοήσατε. 16. οἱ πατέρες ἡμῶν ἐν ταύτῃ τῇ πόλει ἐβαπτίσθησαν εἰς τὸ ὄνομα τοῦ πατρὸς καὶ τοῦ υἱοῦ καὶ τοῦ ἁγίου πνεύματος κατὰ τὴν παράδοσιν τῆς ἐκκλησίας. 17. ἐκήρυσσεν ὁ Ἰωάννης βάπτισμα μετανοίας εἰς ἄφεσιν ἁμαρτιῶν. 18. ἐν ἐκείνῳ τῷ καιρῷ ἐποιεῖτε τὸ θέλημα τῶν ἐθνῶν. 19. ὅτε εἶδε τὰ πλήθη τῶν ἀνδρῶν ὁ Ἰησοῦς ἀνέβη εἰς τὸ ὄρος. 20. κύριε, οὐχὶ σπέρμα καλὸν ἔσπειρας ἐν τῷ σῷ ἀγρῷ; 21. καὶ τῆς βασιλείας αὐτοῦ οὐκ ἔσται τέλος. 22. οἱ υἱοὶ τοῦ αἰῶνος τούτου φρονιμώτεροί εἰσιν ὑπὲρ τοὺς υἱοὺς τοῦ φωτός. 23. οὗτοι οἱ ἡγεμόνες οὐ μετενόησαν ὅτι οὔπω ἔγνωσαν ἐν τῇ ἰδίᾳ ζωῇ τὴν δύναμιν τοῦ πυρὸς τοῦ ἁγίου πνεύματος. 24. αὕτη ἐστὶν ὑμῶν ἡ ὥρα καὶ ἡ ἐξουσία τοῦ σκότους. 25. ἐν τῷ φωτὶ περιπατοῦμεν καὶ τὸ αἷμα τοῦ Ἰησοῦ καθαρίζει ἡμᾶς ἀπὸ τῆς ἁμαρτίας.

II.

Translate into Greek:

1. The Lord took bread and said, This is my body, and took a cup of wine and said, This is my blood. 2. You did (have) not yet come out of this world of darkness, but you remain in the light of the truth. 3. According to the will of God and by means of his power we shall serve the members of his body. 4. By means of your ears you heard words of mercy. 5. These men with their wives were more prudent than the others, for they did not receive the unclean words from the mouth of the evil teacher. 6. Not by means of the blood of sheep, but by means of the grace of God through faith we were saved. 7. Because of the evil

teaching of your fathers the name of the Savior was being blasphemed in the nations. 8. The daughters of this shepherd are walking not according to the flesh but according to the Spirit. 9. The Savior of the nations is rich in mercy both to rulers and to priests. 10. God called you vessels of mercy. 11. You (yourselves) were baptized in water, but we in the baptism of the Holy Spirit. 12. Not only the hands and the feet, but the ears also are members of our body. 13. The rulers in your great city will not remain in the darkness, but will live in the light of the faith. 14. On the authority of the name of the evil king the scribes will cast the scriptures into the fire. 15. Many priests in our cities were sent (liquid verb) to the Gentiles and spoke (contract verb) to them concerning the grace and the mercy of the Savior. 16. The seeds of the truth, which were sown in the heart of thy father, led him into the knowledge of the eternal grace. 17. The members of the body of Christ drank the water of life and will persevere in the light. 18. The bodies of those who were saved by means of the grace of Christ will be raised in the hour of the resurrection according to the words of God's revelation. 19. You (yourselves) are disciples of the darkness, but we (ourselves) are witnesses of the light of the church. 20. Wast thou baptized both in water and in fire? 21. According to the will of our Father and through his grace our names were written in the book of life. 22. In the flesh we shall die, but through the spirit we shall be raised into life eternal. 23. You will say to the rulers of this multitude, Do you see that city on the mountain? 24. Our ears were opened and we heard the words of the Holy Spirit. 25. We were saved by means of the mercy of the son of man and through his blood.

Lesson Twenty-Six

The Verb: Perfect and Pluperfect Indicative

1. Perfect and Pluperfect: Their Meaning.

(i) The *perfect* tense denotes an action which took place in the past and is perfected in the sense that its effects still remain at the time of speaking. The distinction between the aorist and the perfect is that in the latter the emphasis is placed on the abiding results of the action. For example, "πεπίστευκα εἰς τὸν Χριστόν: *I have believed in Christ,*" would indicate that I have placed my faith in Christ and I am still believing (cf. Mark 5:34). In this sense it is quite correct to speak of the perfect as both a past and a present tense.

(ii) The *pluperfect* tense resembles the perfect in the sense of the continuity of its effects, but differs from it in that the effects are viewed as existing at a certain time in the past or prior to another event expressed or implied in the text. Thus, "ἐπεπιστεύκει ὁ Παῦλος εἰς τὸν Χριστόν*: Paul had believed in Christ,*" would indicate that, at some time in the past which I am describing, Paul had placed his faith in Christ, and that he was still believing at that time.

2. Formation of the Perfect. The distinctive feature of this tense in all three voices is the "reduplication." This consists in its initial consonant being followed by **ε** as a prefix to the stem; e.g., λύω—λέλυκα.

In contrast to the augment in the imperfect and the aorist, the reduplication is retained in all moods. In compound verbs the reduplication is placed immediately before the stem.

3. Certain groups of verbs depart from the above pattern of the reduplication. Reduplication is formed:

(i) In verbs beginning with a vowel or diphthong by lengthening these. Thus, ἐλπίζω—ἤλπικα, οἰκοδομέω—ᾠκοδόμηκα.

(ii) In verbs beginning with the consonants **θ**, **φ**, **χ** by substituting for these the hardest consonants of their respective groups **τ**, **π**, **κ** as the reduplication consonant. Thus, θεραπεύω—τεθεράπευκα, φανερόω—πεφανέρωμαι, χαρίζομαι—κεχάρισμαι.

(iii) In verbs beginning with the consonants **ζ** and **ξ**, by prefixing **ἐ**. Thus, ζητέω—ἐζήτηκα, ξηραίνω—ἐξήραμμαι.

(iv) In verbs beginning with two consonants:

(a) Generally, by prefixing **ἐ**; σταυρόω—ἐσταύρωμεμαι.

(b) If the second of these consonants is a liquid or nasal (λ, ν or ρ), the reduplication is built on the first consonant as if it were the only one: γράφω—γέγραφα; θνήσκω—τέθνηκα; πληρόω—πεπλήρωκα; χρηματίζω—κεχρημάτισμαι.

4. Perfect Active. The endings of this tense follow the pattern of the first aorist active, with the perfect tense suffix **κ** being substituted for the aorist tense suffix **σ.** The only form that will not be exactly the same is the 3rd person plural: –κασι (ν), although this is sometimes in the expected form: καν.

Thus,	λέ – λυ – κα	λε – λύ – καμεν
	λέ – λυ – κας	λε – λύ – κατε
	λέ – λυ – κε (ν)	λε – λύ – κασι (ν) or λέ – λυ – καν.

5. If the stem ends in a dental or a **ν**, these are dropped. Thus, ἐλπίζω (ἐλπιδ—)—ἤλπικα, κρίνω—κέκρικα.

6. Some verbs have a second perfect, known also as a strong perfect. This is formed by omitting the **κ**: γράφω—γέγραφα.

7. Perfect Middle and Passive. The endings are identical with those of the present passive, with the connecting vowel between the stem and ending being omitted, and the second person singular ending in –σαι. Thus,

λέ – λυ – μαι	λε – λύ – μεθα
λέ – λυ – σαι	λέ – λυ – σθε
λέ – λυ – ται	λέ – λυ – νται

8. The short vowel in the contract verb stem endings will lengthen before the **κ** of the perfect active and the consonantal endings of the middle and passive, just as they did before the **σ** of the future and the aorist. Thus:

Perfect Active:	τετίμηκα	πεφίληκα	δεδήλωκα
Perfect Passive:	τετίμημαι	πεφίλημαι	δεδήλωμαι.

9. If the stem ends in certain consonants, these undergo the following changes in the aorist or perfect passive:

(i) For the gutturals, **γ**, **κ**, **χ**:
Any guttural before **μ** becomes **γ**; δέχομαι—δέδεγμαι.
Any guttural before **τ** becomes **κ**; ἄγω—ἧκται.
Any guttural before **θ** becomes **χ**; ἄγω—ἤχθη.

(ii) For the labials, **β**, **π**, **φ**:
Any labial before **μ** becomes **μ**; γράφω—γέγραμμαι.
Any labial before **τ** becomes **π**; γράφω—γέγραπται.

(iii) For the dentals, **δ**, **θ**, **τ**:
Any dental before **μ** or **τ** becomes **σ**; ἑτοιμάζω—ἡτοίμασμαι, ἡτοίμασται.
Any dental before **κ** is dropped: βαπτίζω—βεβάπτικα.

(iv) The nasal **ν** before **κ**, **μ**, **τ** is usually dropped: κρίνω—κέκριμαι; but ξηραίνω—ἐξήραμμαι. Sometimes the **ν** is retained and **η** is inserted between this and the ending: μένω—μεμένηκα.

In applying these changes, the rules governing verbs with a verbal stem which is different from the present stem (**15 § 3**) should be borne in mind (σσ—κ, ζ—δ, πτ—π).

10. No verb with a stem ending in a consonant occurs in the NT in the perfect middle or passive indicative with a second person singular or plural or a third person plural ending. Therefore, we do not have to be concerned with what happened with a consonantal stem with a **σ** or **ντ** ending.

11. Of the verbs we have so far learned the following form the perfect, in one or all voices and one or more moods, in an irregular way:

Pres. Act	Per. Act.	Per. Mid	Pres. Act.	Per. Act	Per. Mid
ἀγγέλω:	ἤγγελκα,	—μαι	κράζω:	κέκραγα	
αἴρω:	ἦρκα,	—μαι	λαμβάνω:	εἴληφα,	—μαι
ἀκούω:	ἀκήκοα		λέγω:	εἴρηκα,	—μαι
ἁμαρτάνω:	ἡμάρτηκα		μανθάνω:	μεμάθηκα	
ἀνοίγω:	ἀνέῳγα,	—μαι	μένω:	μεμένηκα	
βαίνω:	βέβηκα		ξηραίνω:	ἐξήραμμαι	
βάλλω:	βέβληκα,	—μαι	ὁράω:	ἑώρακα	
γίνομαι:	γέγονα,	—γεγένημαι		or ἑόρακα	
γινώσκω:	ἔγνωκα,	—σμαι	πάσχω:	πέπονθα	
δεικνύω:	δέδειγμαι		πείθω:	πέποιθα (act.)	
ἐγείρω:	ἐγήγερμαι			πέπεισμαι (pass.).	
ἐλπίζω:	ἤλπικα		πίπτω:	πέπτωκα	
ἔρχομαι:	ἐλήλυθα		πράσσω:	πέπραχα,	—γμαι
εὑρίσκω:	εὕρηκα		σπείρω:	ἔσπαρμαι	
ἔχω:	ἔσχηκα		στέλλω:	ἔσταλκα,	—μαι
θνήσκω:	τέθνηκα		στρέφω:	ἔστραμμαι	
καλέω:	κέκληκα,	—μαι	τελέω:	τετέλεκα,	—σμαι
κλείω:	κέκλεισμαι		φέρω:	ἐνήνοχα	
κοπιάω	κεκοπίακα		φεύγω:	πέφευγα	

12. Formation of the Pluperfect Active and Passive. This tense takes the reduplication preceded by the augment (which occasionally is omitted in the NT text). Whereas the perfect active is characterized by **-κα** endings, the pluperfect active is characterized by **-κει** endings. And, just as the perfect middle and passive added the present endings without connecting vowel, the pluperfect middle and passive adds the imperfect endings without connecting vowels. The pluperfect is rather rare in the New Testament.

Active	Middle and Passive
ἐ – λε – λύ – κειν	ἐ – λε – λύ – μην
ἐ – λε – λύ – κεις	ἐ – λέ – λυ – σο
ἐ – λε – λύ – κει	ἐ – λέ – λυ – το
ἐ – λε – λύ – κειμεν	ἐ – λε – λύ – μεθα
ἐ – λε – λύ – κειτε	ἐ – λέ – λυ – σθε
ἐ – λε – λύ – κεισαν	ἐ – λέ – λυ – ντο

13. Principal Parts. A brief overview of an English verb could be given with just six verb phrases:

Present	I see
Past	I saw
Future	I will see
Present Perfect	I have seen
Past Perfect	I had seen
Future Perfect	I will have seen

And since the auxilliary verbs ("will . . . have . . . had . . . will have . . .") never change form, we really need only these words, which are called *Principal Parts*: the simple present, *see*; the simple past, *saw*; and whatever word is used in the perfect tenses, *seen*. With just these three principle parts I can sum up all of the variations in the verb paradigm for any English verb. For example:

see	saw	seen
drive	drove	driven
hit	hit	hit
run	ran	run
swim	swam	swum
think	thought	thought
turn	turned	turned

In a similar way, an overview of the paradigm for any Greek verb can be given with just six forms, four actives and two passives, traditionally given in this order:

Pres. Act.	**Fut. Act.**	**Aor. Act.**	**Perf. Act.**	**Perf. Pass.**	**Aor. Pass.**
λύω	λύσω	ἔλυσα	λέλυκα	λέλυμαι	ἐλύθην

Any irregularities in the verb system will be indicated in these six principal parts. All of the presents and all of the imperfects are formed on the first; the future active and middle are formed on the second, the aorist active and middle are formed on the third; the perfect active and pluperfect active are formed on the fourth; the perfect and pluperfect middle and passive are formed on the fifth; and the future passive and aorist passive are formed on the sixth. A few minor variations will have to be learned separately; e.g., all aorist forms outside the indicative drop their augment, and the unaugmented forms are not always predictable (εἶπον – εἰπ; εἶδον, – ἰδ). But the vast majority of the Greek verb system can be developed from these six principal parts. If one tense system is not used, that form is usually left blank (as with the perf. act. of ἄγω, below). Middle deponent forms are listed in the place of the active in those tenses in which a particular verb is deponent (notice ἔρχομαι, below). A list of principal parts is given in the Summary of Morphology in the back of this book for most of the verbs in this book that show any irregularities. Examine the partial list of principal parts given below to get acquainted with the concept.

Pres. Act.	Fut. Act.	Aor. Act.	Perf. Act.	Perf. Pass.	Aor. Pass.
ἄγω	ἄξω	ἤγαγον		ἦγμαι	ἤχθην
γράφω	γράψω	ἔγραψα	γέγραφα	γέγραμμαι	ἐγράφην
ἔρχομαι	ἐλεύσομαι	ἦλθον	ἐλήλυθα		
κρίνω	κρινῶ	ἔκρινα	κέκρικα	κέκριμαι	ἐκρίθην

VOCABULARY

δέω:	I bind
εἰ:	if
Ἰερουσαλήμ, ἡ:	Jerusalem (indecl.)
Ἱεροσόλυμα, τά:	Jerusalem (regular neuter plural)
κοπιάω:	I toil, I work hard, I get tired
κόπος, ὁ:	work, labor
κρατέω:	I take hold of, I hold
κωφός, ή, όν:	dumb, deaf
Μωϋσῆς (—έως—εῖ or—ῇ—ῆν) ὁ:	Moses
πῶς:	how? (adverb)

EXERCISES

I.

Translate into English:

1. ἄλλοι κεκοπιάκασιν, καὶ ὑμεῖς εἰς τὸν κόπον αὐτῶν εἰσεληλύθατε. 2. πεπλήρωται ὁ καιρὸς καὶ ἤγγικεν ἡ βασιλεία τοῦ θεοῦ. 3. ἐγὼ ἑώρακα καὶ μεμαρτύρηκα ὅτι οὗτός ἐστιν ὁ υἱὸς τοῦ θεοῦ. 4. εἰ δὲ ἀνάστασις νεκρῶν οὐκ ἔστιν, οὐδὲ Χριστὸς ἐγήγερται. 5. καὶ ὑπὸ τῶν ἐθνῶν δέδεκται τὸ εὐαγγέλιον τῆς βασιλείας. 6. ἤχθης εἰς τὴν ὥραν τοῦ πειρασμοῦ, ἀλλ᾽ ὁ σωτὴρ κεκράτηκέ σε ἐν τῇ χειρὶ καὶ ηὐλόγηκέ σε. 7. ὃν ἔγραψε Μωϋσῆς ἐν τῷ νόμῳ εὑρήκαμεν. 8. πειρασμὸς ὑμᾶς οὐκ εἴληφεν. 9. ὑμεῖς ἀπεστάλκατε πρὸς Ἰωάννην καὶ μεμαρτύρηκε τῇ ἀληθείᾳ. 10. ἡ πίστις σου σέσωκέ σε. 11. κέκλεισται ἡ θύρα τῆς ζωῆς τούτοις τοῖς ἀνδράσιν, οὐ γὰρ μετενόησαν. 12. οὐ γέγραπται, Ὁ οἶκός μου οἶκος προσευχῆς; 13. ἡ πίστις τῶν ταπεινῶν ἀνδρῶν τούτων, οἳ εἰσεληλύθασιν εἰς τὸ ἱερόν, σέσωκεν αὐτοὺς καὶ αὐτοὶ τετιμήκασι τοὺς πατέρας τῆς ἐκκλησίας. 14. ὅτε προσηύξω τῷ θεῷ, αὐτὸς ἀκήκοέ σε καὶ πεφανέρωκέ σοι τὸ θέλημα αὐτοῦ, σὺ οὖν ἔγνωκας τὴν δύναμιν τῆς προσευχῆς. 15. εἰρήκαμεν ἤδη ὑμῖν ὅτι ἑωράκαμεν τὸν Μεσσίαν καὶ μεμαρτυρήκαμεν τοῖς ἀνδράσι ταύτης τῆς πόλεως ὅτι οὗτός ἐστιν ὁ υἱὸς τοῦ θεοῦ καὶ ἐν αὐτῷ εὑρήκαμεν τὴν εἰρήνην τῆς ψυχῆς ἡμῶν. 16. ἡ καινὴ ἀποκάλυψις, ἣ γέγραπται ῥήμασιν οὐ σαρκὸς καὶ σκότους ἀλλὰ πνεύματος καὶ φωτός, ἀπέσταλται καὶ τοῖς ἔθνεσιν. 17. οὐ τοῖς ἱερεῦσι καὶ γραμματεῦσιν ἀλλὰ τῷ ἡμετέρῳ βασιλεῖ ἐληλύθαμεν καὶ λελαλήκαμεν αὐτῷ περὶ τῆς χάριτος τοῦ σωτῆρος καὶ τῆς ἐλπίδος τῆς ἀναστάσεως, αὐτὸς οὖν πεπίστευκε καὶ βεβάπτισται ἐν ὕδατι καὶ πνεύματι. 18. ἀπεκρίθη ὁ ἡγεμὼν καὶ εἶπε τοῖς ἀρχιερεῦσιν, Ὃ γέγραφα γέγραφα· αὐτοὶ οὖν ἀπεληλύθασιν, ὅτι ἡ σωτηρία διὰ τῆς πίστεως οὐκ ἔγνωσται ὑπ᾽ αὐτῶν. 19. τέθνηκεν ὁ προφήτης ὃς λελάληκε τοῖς σοῖς ὠσὶ ῥήματα ἐλέους, ἀλλὰ σὺ μεμίσηκας τὴν ἀποκάλυψιν τῆς κρίσεως τοῦ θεοῦ. 20. οἱ ἄνδρες οὓς ἐκβεβλήκατε ἐκ τῆς ὑμετέρας συναγωγῆς οὐκ εὑρήκασι χάριν καὶ ἐλπίδα ἐν τῷ ὀνόματι τοῦ σωτῆρος, οὐ γὰρ ἐγνώκασι τὴν δύναμιν τῆς πίστεως.

21. εἶπον τοῖς ἀποστόλοις οἱ ἀρχιερεῖς, Πεπληρώκατε τὴν Ἰερουσαλὴμ τῆς διδαχῆς ὑμῶν. 22. μακάριός ἐστιν ἐκεῖνος ὁ ταπεινός, ὅτι δεδίωκται διὰ τὸ ὄνομα τοῦ σωτῆρος. 23. οἱ πονηροὶ ἄνδρες οὗτοι εἰλήφασι λίθους καὶ βεβλήκασιν αὐτοὺς ἐπὶ τοὺς προφήτας. 24. ᾔτηκας ἀπὸ τοῦ θεοῦ εὐλογίας καὶ ἤλπικας εἰς αὐτὸν καὶ ἡτοίμασταί σοι τόπος ἐν τῷ οὐρανῷ. 25. οὐ κατακεκρίκασί σε οἱ πρεσβύτεροι τῆς ἐκκλησίας, ἐπιμεμένηκας γὰρ τῇ πίστει καὶ ἀνέῳκταί σοι θύρα μεγάλη γνώσεως.

II.

Translate into Greek:

1. The Lord has taken the bread and the wine in his own hands. 2. We are persuaded (lit. have been persuaded) that our Savior has been risen from the dead. 3. Your teachers have announced to you that the Son of God has come into the world. 4. Even the deaf ones by means of the grace of God have heard and the blind ones have seen. 5. We have believed and have known that thou thyself art the holy one of God. 6. We (ourselves) have come out of the house of sin, but you (yourselves) have remained in it. 7. Hast thou believed because thou hast seen me? 8. The good prophet has blessed your sons and daughters, but even he himself has been blessed by his Savior. 9. You have not believed in the testimony which your fathers have testified concerning the resurrection of the dead. 10. That one who has been crucified has said, "(It) is finished." 11. Our daughters have entered into the house of the king of that city and have seen the grace of the Savior and have heard the words of (the) hope and have been blessed by the elders. 12. We have hoped that the witnesses of the power of the resurrection have spoken to the servants of thy rulers and the multitude has been prepared not according to the flesh but according to the will of the Father. 13. By means of my own hand I have written to the elders of thy synagogue and have called them to (lit.: into) the promises of God's mercy. 14. Not through our hands but by means of the grace of God himself we have been saved and have come out of this age of darkness and we have found the Savior and have kept his commandments. 15. The Lord himself hast sent thee to the Gentiles and thou hast become to them the witness to the revelation of God. 16. Jesus has opened the

eyes of that blind one, and he himself has remained beside him. 17. Thou hast been kept from the evil one by means of the power of thy Savior. 18. He has been persecuted by the sons of the darkness, but he has not fled into another city. 19. The promises of the Holy Spirit have been fulfilled in the life of each man of this multitude and they have confessed to their Savior. 20. Each of us in this whole city has been saved from our sins and we have become members of the body of Christ. 21. The Father, who is in the heavens, has heard our supplications, for we have put our trust (lit. been persuaded) in him. 22. Thou hast suffered many (things–neuter) on account of the name of that one who has loved thee and has been crucified in behalf of thee and has saved thee. 23. The hands of the enemies of the truth have been raised against those who have followed the voice of their own conscience. 24. You have loved the Savior and you have been loved by him. 25. God has not nullified his covenant and you (yourselves) have been called into it.

Lesson Twenty-Seven

The Participle:

1. General Rules. Active Voice

The Verb οἶδα

1. General Rules Governing the Participle. The participle is used in the nature of two parts of speech: the verb and the adjective. As a verb, it has tense and voice and may have an object. As an adjective it is declined and must agree in case, gender, and number with the noun or pronoun, expressed or implied, which it qualifies. Depending on the role which it plays in a sentence, a participle is *adjectival* or *adverbial.*

2. In the *adjectival participle* the element of the adjective is the predominant one. The adjectival participle is generally preceded (not always immediately) by the article. It is also called the *attributive participle* because it performs in the sentence the same functions as those of the attributive adjective; e.g., ὁ καλὸς μαθητής, *the good disciple*; ὁ μαθητὴς ὁ βλέπων τὸν κύριον, *the disciple who sees the Lord*—both the adjective καλός and the participle βλέπων indicate which disciple we are speaking about; both are attributive. The participle can be used in the same sense as the indicative preceded by the relative pronoun: ὁ βλέπων τὸν κύριον, ὃς βλέπει τὸν κύριον, *he who sees the Lord.*

Like the attributive adjective, the participle can also be used with the article as a noun; οἱ βλέποντες τὸν κύριον: *(the people) who see the Lord.*

It is not always easy or possible to render a Greek participle literally into English. The best way to treat an attributive participle is by using the relative pronoun, as in the above example.

3. In the *adverbial participle* the element of the verb is the most prominent, and the participle is never preceded by the article. An adverbial participle may convey a variety of meanings, and, as a rule, is meant to supply the answer to one of the questions: "when," "why," or "how" did the action indicated by the main verb take place? To these must be added the "concessive participle" which serves to explain that the action of the main verb was done in spite of a certain state of things: "οἵτινες τὸ δικαίωμα τοῦ θεοῦ ἐπιγνόντες . . . αὐτὰ ποιοῦσιν, *Who* ***though they know well*** *the righteous decree of God . . . do them*" (Rom. 1:32). Also the "intensive participle" (a "hebraism"): "εὐλογῶν εὐλογήσω σε" (Heb. 6:14), "*I will bless thee* ***abundantly*** (lit. blessing, *I will bless thee*)." By removing the article preceding the participle in the first example, ὁ μαθητὴς βλέπων τὸν κύριον, we may have the meaning: "*while the disciple was seeing the Lord*," "*because . . .*"; "*by seeing the Lord, the disciple . . .*"; or something else. The context will usually indicate which service is rendered by the adverbial participle in a given text.

The presence or absence of the article in the following sentences will make clear the difference between the adverbial and the adjectival participle: ὁ διδάσκαλος μένων ἐν ταύτῃ τῇ οἰκίᾳ ἐκήρυσσεν: "*the teacher*, ***while he was remaining*** in this house, *was preaching*"; ὁ διδάσκαλος ὁ μένων ἐν ταύτῃ τῇ οἰκίᾳ ἐκήρυσσεν: "*the teacher* ***who is remaining*** *in this house had preached.*"

4. The Time Element of Adjectival Participles. Although the future and perfect participles maintain the same time element as their indicative counterparts in all constructions, there is no time element at all in present and aorist participles when they are used as adjectives or substantives. Just as there is no difference in time between the imperfect and aorist indicatives (see **17 § 1**), the only difference between present and aorist participles is the aspect of linear, progressive action versus a simple undefined or punctiliar action. Thus ὁ βλέπων, *the one who is seeing* as opposed to ὁ βλέψας, *the one who* ***sees.***

5. The Time Element of Adverbial Participles. There is, however, a secondary time element with adverbial participles, showing the time relationship of the action of the participle to the action of the principal verb with which the participle is used. Thus, the participle is put:

(i) In the *present*, if the action denoted by it is contemporaneous with that of the principal verb in the sentence "*. . . they will see* *the Son of Man while he is coming in the clouds. . ."* (Matt. 24:30). Since the participle has no imperfect, the present is used in its place with past tense verbs.

(ii) In the *future,* if the action denoted by it is subsequent to that of the principal verb: *"who had come as one who will worship"* (technically, *in order to worship*; Acts 8:27b).

(iii) In the *aorist,* if the action denoted by it is represented as having taken place before that of the principal verb: *"Therefore having been justified* (lit., *being justified*) *by faith, we are having peace. . ."* (Rom. 5:1). If the main verb is a future, it may well be that this aorist denotes an action which still lies in the future to the speaker: *"And when he was come* (lit., *coming*), *he will reprove. . ."* (John 16:8).

In all three of the above cases it makes no difference whether the action denoted by the principal verb takes place in the present, the future, or the past.

6. The Participle in the Active Voice. The stem for the present active participle is λυοντ–. The masculine and neuter genders are declined on the pattern of the third declension nouns (like ἄρχων). The feminine gender adds a **–σ** to the stem (with the **–ντ** dropping out before the **σ**, and the **ο** lengthening to **ου** as in the masculine dative plural, λύουσι), and then adds the first declension endings of the **α** group with stems ending in **σ**.

Singular

	Masculine	**Feminine**	**Neuter**
N. V.	λύων	λύουσα	λῦον
G.	λύοντος	λυούσης	λύοντος
D.	λύοντι	λυούσῃ	λύοντι
A.	λύοντα	λύουσαν	λῦον

Plural

	Masculine	**Feminine**	**Neuter**
N. V.	λύοντες	λύουσαι	λύοντα
G.	λυόντων	λυουσῶν	λυόντων
D.	λύουσι (ν)	λυούσαις	λύουσι (ν)
A.	λύοντας	λυούσας	λύοντα

As can be noticed in the above table, the feminine participle does not follow the adjective in the matter of the accentuation of the genitive plural, but, like the noun of the first declension, places the genitive plural accent on the ultima.

7. The participle of contract verbs in all voices follows the rules of contraction which we have already seen (**20 § 2, 5**). For example, τιμά + ων = τιμῶν, and τιμά + ουσα = τιμῶσα: φιλῶν, φιλοῦσα, φιλοῦν; δηλῶν, δηλοῦσα, δηλοῦν.

8. The *future* is formed by inserting **σ** between the stem and the endings of the present, as follows:

	Singular		
	Masculine	**Feminine**	**Neuter**
N. V.	λύσων	λύσουσα	λῦσον
G.	λύσοντος	λυσούσης	λύσοντος
D.	λύσοντι	λυσούσῃ	λύσοντι
A.	λύσοντα	λύσουσαν	λῦσον

	Plural		
	Masculine	**Feminine**	**Neuter**
N. V.	λύσοντες	λύσουσαι	λύσοντα
G.	λυσόντων	λυσουσῶν	λυσόντων
D.	λύσουσι (ν)	λυσούσαις	λύσουσι (ν)
A.	λύσοντας	λυσούσας	λύσοντα

Verbs whose stems end in a liquid or nasal consonant (**λ, μ, ν, ρ**) follow the same rule for the future participle that they do for the future indicative (**22 § 2**). The sign of the future is **εσ**, with the sigma dropping out and the **ε** combining with the vowel endings according to the **ε** contract verb rules. Thus, ἀποστελῶν, ἀποστελοῦσα, ἀποστελοῦν; κρινῶν, κρινοῦσα, κρινοῦν. Notice that in some forms of verbs like μένω or κρίνω, which do not have a vowel change in the stem, the only difference between the active participle and the present active participle may be the circumflex accent on the future participle which reflects the contraction of the ε in the ending.

9. The *first aorist* is formed by inserting **σ** between the stem and the endings of the present and substituting **α** for **ο** or **ου** sounds at the head of the ending in all three genders and in all cases. In the nominative and vocative singular of the masculine the final **ν** is turned into **ς**. Thus,

Singular

	Masculine	**Feminine**	**Neuter**
N. V.	λύσας	λύσασα	λῦσαν
G.	λύσαντος	λυσάσης	λύσαντος
D.	λύσαντι	λυσάσῃ	λύσαντι
A.	λύσαντα	λύσασαν	λῦσαν

Plural

	Masculine	**Feminine**	**Neuter**
N. V.	λύσαντες	λύσασαι	λύσαντα
G.	λυσάντων	λυσασῶν	λυσάντων
D.	λύσασι (ν)	λυσάσαις	λύσασι (ν)
A.	λύσαντας	λυσάσας	λύσαντα

Verbs whose stem ends in a liquid or nasal consonant (**λ, μ, ν, ϱ**) follow the same rule in the aorist participle that they do for the aorist indicative (**22 § 5, i, iii**). Thus, ἀποστείλας, κϱίνας.

The *second aorist* is formed by adding to the stem of this tense the endings of the present participle and moving the accent one syllable to the right. Thus, ἀγαγών, ἀγαγοῦσα, ἀγαγόν; ἰδών, ἰδοῦσα, ἰδόν; ἐλθών, ἐλθοῦσα, ἐλθόν. But ἀνα (κατα) βάς, (ἀναβάντος); –βᾶσα, βάν. (See list of verbs and their second aorist in **18 § 4**.) The verb πίπτω forms the participle on the pattern of the second aorist from the stem πεσ-; πεσών, πεσοῦσα, πεσόν.

Notice that the aorist participle takes no augment, this being the exclusive characteristic of the indicative mood.

10. The *perfect* is formed in the masculine and neuter on the general pattern of the third declension noun (resembling somewhat the declension of the neuter noun with stems ending in **-ατ**), and in the feminine on the pattern of the first declension noun of the **-α** group with stems ending in a vowel or **ϱ**. The reduplication is retained in all moods. The perfect active is declined as follows:

Singular

	Masculine	Feminine	Neuter
N. V.	λελυκώς	λελυκυῖα	λελυκός
G.	λελυκότος	λελυκυίας	λελυκότος
D.	λελυκότι	λελυκυίᾳ	λελυκότι
A.	λελυκότα	λελυκυῖαν	λελυκός

Plural

	Masculine	Feminine	Neuter
N. V.	λελυκότες	λελυκυῖαι	λελυκότα
G.	λελυκότων	λελυκυιῶν	λελυκότων
D.	λελυκόσι (ν)	λελυκυίαις	λελυκόσι (ν)
A.	λελυκότας	λελυκυίας	λελυκότα

The circumflex in the nominative and accusative singular feminine is due to the application of the rule governing the adjectives of the third declension (See **29 § 4, iii**).

Verbs which have a second perfect retain it in the participle. Thus, γέγραφα—γεγραφώς; ἀκήκοα—ἀκηκοώς.

11. The present participle of the verb εἰμὶ consists of the simple endings of the present: ὤν, οὖσα, ὄν .

12. The participle is negated by use of μή.

13. Indirect Discourse. Many times an accusative participle without an article is joined with an accusative direct object to form the equivalent of an ὅτι indirect discourse clause (**18 § 10**). For example: John 6:19 says "θεωροῦσιν τὸν Ἰησοῦν περιπατοῦντα ἐπὶ τῆς θαλάσσης, *they see Jesus walking upon the sea.*" The emphasis is not simply on who they see (Jesus), with the added time element, while he was walking upon the sea; rather it is upon the whole participial phrase, what they see Jesus doing, equivalent to θεωροῦσιν ὅτι ὁ Ἰησοῦς περιπατεῖ ἐπὶ τῆς θαλάσσης, "*They see that Jesus is walking upon the sea.*" Indirect discourse participial phrases may be used with any verb expressing the idea of saying, seeing, thinking, finding. etc.

14. Periphrastic Tenses. The participle is occasionally used in the NT text (chiefly in the gospels of Mark and Luke) in combination with the verb εἰμὶ to produce a distinct form of certain tenses, especially the imperfect and the future. This is the "periphrastic" (roundabout) structure of these tenses. The periphrastic imperfect is formed by the present participle of the verb preceded by the imperfect of εἰμί: "καὶ ἦσαν οἱ μαθηταὶ Ἰωάννου καὶ οἱ Φαρισαῖοι νηστεύοντες: *and the disciples of John and the Pharisees were fasting*" (Mark 2:18). The periphrastic future is formed by the present participle of the verb and the future of εἰμί: "καὶ ἰδοὺ ἔσῃ σιωπῶν: *and behold, thou wilt be silent*" (Luke 1:20).

15. The Verb οἶδα. The verb οἶδα is found only in the perfect and pluperfect which are used with the meaning of the non-existent present and imperfect respectively. "The pluperfect of οἶδα probably has the same impact as the aorist of other verbs." It is conjugated as follows:

Indicative

Singular

Perfect	Pluperfect
οἶδα	ᾔδειν
οἶδας	ᾔδεις
οἶδε (ν)	ᾔδει

Plural

οἴδαμεν	ᾔδειμεν
οἴδατε	ᾔδειτε
οἴδασι (ν)	ᾔδεισαν

Participle: εἰδώς (-ότος), εἰδυῖα, εἰδός

16. Like the verb οἶδα, the verb πείθω is also used in the perfect tense with a present meaning, with both the active and passive having the thought of "I put trust in; have confidence in."

VOCABULARY

Γαλιλαία, ἡ:	Galilee
ἐπερωτάω:	I ask, I question
θεωρέω:	I look at, I observe
κρούω:	I knock
οἶδα:	I know (in the perfect tense)

παραγγέλλω: I command, I charge (with dat. of the person)
πενθέω: I mourn
πέποιθα: I put trust in, have confidence in (perfect of πείθω)
περισσεύω: I exceed a certain number, I abound
πρᾶγμα, πράγματος, τό: thing, matter, deed, event
χορτάζω: I feed, I satisfy myself with food

EXERCISES

I.

Translate into English:

1. ὁ αἰτῶν λαμβάνει, καὶ ὁ ζητῶν εὑρίσκει, καὶ τῷ κρούοντι ἀνοιγήσεται. 2. ὁ τὸν λόγον μου ἀκούων καὶ πιστεύων τῷ πέμψαντί με ἔχει ζωὴν αἰώνιον. 3. μακάριοι οἱ πενθοῦντες, ὅτι αὐτοὶ παρακληθήσονται. 4. τότε μὴ εἰδότες θεὸν προσεκυνεῖτε τοῖς φύσει μὴ οὖσιν θεοῖς. 5. οἱ μὴ ὁμολογοῦντες τὸν Χριστὸν ἐν σαρκὶ ἐληλυθότα ἐκ τοῦ θεοῦ οὐκ εἰσιν. 6. μακάριοί εἰσιν οἱ μὴ ἰδόντες καὶ πιστεύσαντες. 7. ἐκείνη πορευθεῖσα ἀπήγγειλε τοῖς μαθηταῖς πενθοῦσι καὶ κλαίουσιν. 8. Καταβὰς ἀπὸ τοῦ ὄρους καὶ περιπατῶν παρὰ τὴν θάλασσαν εἶδε τὸν ὄχλον κοπιῶντα. 9. πεφανέρωκεν ὁ θεὸς τὸ θέλημα αὐτοῦ τοῖς ἀγαπῶσι τὴν ἀλήθειαν καὶ ζητοῦσιν αὐτήν. 10. προσκυνοῦμεν τῷ σεσωκότι ἡμᾶς καὶ ἠλευθερωκότι ἀπὸ τῶν ἁμαρτιῶν ἡμῶν. 11. ἐξεληλυθότες ἐκ τῆς πόλεως ἀπηγγέλκαμεν ταῦτα ταῖς γυναιξὶ ταῖς διακονησάσαις τοῖς προφήταις. 12. ὄψεσθε τὸν οὐρανὸν ἀνεῳγότα καὶ τοὺς ἀγγέλους τοῦ θεοῦ ἀναβαίνοντας καὶ καταβαίνοντας ἐπὶ τὸν υἱὸν τοῦ ἀνθρώπου. 13. εἶπεν ὁ ἄρχων τῷ Ἰησοῦ, Οἴδαμεν ὅτι ἀπὸ θεοῦ ἐλήλυθας διδάσκαλος. 14. ἐλάλησεν αὐτοῖς ὁ Παῦλος πείθων αὐτοὺς περὶ τοῦ Ἰησοῦ ἀπό τε τοῦ νόμου Μωϋσέως καὶ ἀπὸ τῶν προφητῶν. 15. ἐγὼ δὲ οὐ ζητῶ καὶ κρίνω· ἔστιν ὁ ζητῶν καὶ κρίνων. 16. λαβὼν ὁ κύριος ἄρτον καὶ εὐλογήσας ἔκλασεν. 17. λαλήσας δὲ ὁ Πέτρος εἶπε, Σὺ εἶ ὁ Χριστὸς ὁ υἱὸς τοῦ θεοῦ τοῦ ζῶντος. 18. ἔτι ὢν ἐν τῇ

συναγωγῇ ὁ κύριος ἐθεράπευσε τὸν ἀσθενοῦντα ἄνδρα. 19. ἠκούσαμεν τὸν προφήτην λαλοῦντα ῥήματα ἀληθείας. 20. ἠκούσαμεν τὸν λαλοῦντα ῥήματα ἀληθείας. 21. ὁ ἀθετῶν ἐμὲ καὶ μὴ λαμβάνων τὰ ῥήματά μου ἔχει τὸν κρίνοντα αὐτόν· ὁ λόγος ὃν ἐλάλησα ἐκεῖνος κρινεῖ αὐτὸν ἐν τῇ ἐσχάτῃ ἡμέρᾳ. 22. εἶδες τὸν ἱερέα προσενέγκαντα τὴν θυσίαν ἐν τῷ ἱερῷ; 23. εἶδες τὸν ἱερέα τὸν προσενεγκόντα τὴν θυσίαν ἐν τῷ ἱερῷ; 24. λαβόντες τὰς γραφὰς αἳ ἐγράφησαν ὑπὸ τῶν ἀνθρώπων τοῦ θεοῦ ἀνέγνωμεν καὶ ἐσώθημεν. 25. ἀγαγόντες τοὺς υἱοὺς ἡμῶν τοῖς ἀναβάσιν εἰς τὸν οἶκον τοῦ βασιλέως εἴδομεν αὐτοὺς λαλοῦντας μετ᾽ αὐτοῦ. 26. αὐτοὶ ἠκούσαμεν τὸν κύριον λέγοντα τοῖς ὄχλοις τὴν παραβολὴν τοῦ σπείροντος. 27. ἡ δὲ γυνή, εἰδυῖα ὃ γέγονεν αὐτῇ, ἦλθε καὶ προσεκύνησεν αὐτῷ. 28. ἰδόντες τοὺς ἱερεῖς εἰσελθόντας εἰς τὴν συναγωγὴν εἴδομεν καὶ τοὺς ἐλθόντας ἐξ αὐτῆς. 29. εὑρόντες τοὺς ὄντας μετ᾽ αὐτοῦ καὶ ἰδόντες αὐτοὺς ἁμαρτάνοντας ἠλέγξαμεν αὐτούς, ὅτι οὐκ ᾔδεισαν τὴν ἀλήθειαν. 30. ὁ ἁμαρτήσας ἀποθανὼν κρινεῖται.

II.

Translate into Greek:

In this exercise and in the exercise of the next lesson certain parts of some sentences are in parenthesis. Give the translation for both alternatives. Be careful to use the right kind of participle: adjectival or adverbial–and in the right tense. In translating "who looses," "while he looses," "is loosing" or "was loosing," use the present; for "who loosed," "when he loosed," "after he loosed," use the aorist; for "having loosed" or "after he had loosed" use the perfect. In a similar way treat verbs in the passive voice. Use participial phrases whenever you can.

1. Believing in (lit.: into) the Lord Jesus we have life eternal. 2. Although we have not seen the Lord in the flesh nor have heard him, we believed in (lit., into) him. 3. Having received the Holy Spirit the apostles came to (those) who were living in sin. 4. Because he prepared a place for thee, the Lord will come and will receive thee. 5. Having repented from your sins, you came to (those) who were not repenting. 6. When we came out of the synagogue we saw those who were coming into it. 7. Because we follow (him) who loved us and died on our

account we love even (those) who persecute us. 8. (He) who endured in the temptations will enter into the kingdom of the heavens. 9. The Lord prayed on behalf of (those) who crucified him. 10. When thou art seeking God thou approachest (him) who hears thee. 11. We heard the apostles (teaching) (who were teaching) in the temple. 12. Having this hope in our hearts we shall receive glory in heaven. 13. (Because they believe) (those who believe) in the promises of their Father, will receive a crown of glory. 14. After the rulers of the nations learned the tongue of love, they taught it even to them who have not yet known it. 15. We saw the prophet (who was opening) (opening) the door of the synagogue in that city. 16. (While they were writing) (After they had written) these words in the book, those priests saw God's mercy in the light of the resurrection. 17. After they repented from their sins the kings of these cities have come to (those) who were not yet repenting. 18. The priests, because they follow (him) who loved them and suffered in their behalf love even (those) who wronged them. 19. Although thou hast known the consolation of God and hast seen many miracles, thou hast not believed in (lit., into) the Savior. 20. (Those) who believed and persevered in the faith dwell with their brothers. 21. (Those who feed) (Because they feed) (those who are hungry) will also themselves be fed. 22. (Those) who have not seen (him), who came down from heaven, have not known peace so far as God is concerned. 23. After (they) received the power of the Holy Spirit the believers preached the gospel to (those) who were dwelling in other places. 24. We saw the women who died, but we did not see their husbands mourning. 25. (Those) who preached the promises of the covenant to the Gentiles will return to (him) who sent (liquid verb) them.

Lesson Twenty-Eight

The Participle:

2. Middle and Passive Voice

Genitive Absolute

The Article: Unusual Usage of the Article

1. The Participle in the Middle and Passive Voices. In all tenses in the middle and passive voices, with the exception of the aorist passive, the participle is declined like the adjective, ἀγαθός, η, ον, in the masculine and the neuter on the pattern of the second declension noun, and in the feminine on that of the first declension noun of the **η** group. Thus:

	Masculine	**Feminine**	**Neuter**
Present Middle/Passive:	λυόμενος	λυομένη	λυόμενον.
Future Middle:	λυσόμενος	λυσομένη	λυσόμενον.
Future Passive:	λυθησόμενος	λυθησομένη	λυθησόμενον.
Aorist Middle:	λυσάμενος	λυσαμένη	λυσάμενον.
Perfect Middle/Passive:	λελυμένος	λελυμένη	λελυμένον.

2. The aorist passive participle is formed on the stem λυθεντ–. The masculine and neuter are formed on the pattern of the third declension nouns; A **σ** is added and to the feminine stem, which is then formed like a first declension noun of the **α** group with stems ending in a **σ**. The **ντ** drops out before a **σ**, as they did in the present active participle, and the **ε** lengthens to **ει**. Notice the shift of accent to the first syllable of the ending.

Singular

	Masculine	Feminine	Neuter
N.V.	λυθεὶς	λυθεῖσα	λυθὲν
G.	λυθέντος	λυθείσης	λυθέντος
D.	λυθέντι	λυθείσῃ	λυθέντι
A.	λυθέντα	λυθεῖσαν	λυθὲν

Plural

	Masculine	Feminine	Neuter
N.V.	λυθέντες	λυθεῖσαι	λυθέντα
G.	λυθέντων	λυθεισῶν	λυθέντων
D.	λυθεῖσι (ν)	λυθείσαις	λυθεῖσι (ν)
A.	λυθέντας	λυθείσας	λυθέντα

3. The second aorist middle is formed by adding the endings of the present middle participle to the verbal stem: γινόμενος—γενόμενος.

The second aorist passive is formed by omitting the **θ** in the ending: ἀποστέλλω—ἀποσταλείς.

Remember that not all verbs which have a second aorist in the active voice necessarily have one in the passive.

4. Of the verbs we have dealt with so far, the following form the aorist and perfect (active, middle or passive) in an irregular way or as a second aorist/perfect. All the liquid/nasal verbs we have learned are included. Only verbs found in some form in these tenses in the NT are included in this list.

Present Indicative	Aorist Active	Aorist Middle or Passive	Perfect Active	Perfect Passive
ἀγγέλλω	ἀγγείλας	ἀγγειλάμενος		ἠγγελμένος
ἄγω	ἀγαγών	ἀχθείς (P)		
αἴρω	ἄρας			ἠρμένος
ἀκούω			ἀκηκοώς	
ἁμαρτάνω	ἁμαρτήσας			
ἀνατέλλω	ἀνατείλας			

Present Indicative	**Aorist Active**	**Aorist Middle or Passive**	**Perfect Active**	**Perfect Passive**
			ἀνεῳγώς	ἀνεῳγμένος or ἠνεῳγμένος
ἀποκτείνω	ἀποκτείνας	ἀποκτανθείς		
βαίνω	βάς		βεβηκώς	
βάλλω	βαλών	βαλόμενος	βεβληκώς	
		βληθείς (P)		βεβλημένος
βλαστάνω	βλαστήσας			
βλέπω (see ὁράω)				
γίνομαι		γενόμενος	γεγονώς	
γινώσκω	γνούς	γνωσθείς	ἐγνωκώς	ἐγνωσμένος
δεικνύω or δείκνυμι		δειχθείς		
δέω	δήσας			
ἐγείρω	ἐγείρας	ἐγερθείς		ἐγηγερμένος
ἔρχομαι	ἐλθών		ἐληλυθώς	
ἐσθίω	φαγών			
εὑρίσκω	εὑρών	εὑράμενος		
		εὑρεθείς (P)		
ἔχω	σχών		ἐσχηκώς	
θέλω	θελήσας			
θνῄσκω	θανών		τεθνηκώς	
καλέω	καλέσας	καλεσάμενος	κεκληκώς	κεκλημένος
		κληθείς (P)		
κλείω				κεκλεισμένος
κράζω	κράξας			
κρίνω	κρίνας			κεκριμένος
λαμβάνω	λαβών	λαβόμενος	εἰληφώς	εἰλημμένος
		λημφθείς (P)		
λέγω		ῥηθείς (P)		εἰρημένος
λείπω	λείψας or λιπών			λελειμμένος
μανθάνω	μαθών		μεμαθηκώς	
ξηραίνω				ἐξηραμμένος
οἶδα			εἰδώς	

Present Indicative	Aorist Active	Aorist Middle or Passive	Perfect Active	Perfect Passive
	ἰδών	ὀφθείς (P)	ἑωρακώς	
πάσχω	παθών			
πείθω			πεποιθώς	
πίνω	πιών			
πίπτω	πεσών		πεπτωκώς	
σπείρω	σπείρας	σπαρείς		ἐσπαρμένος
στέλλω	στείλας			ἐσταλμένος
στρέφω		στραφείς		ἐστραμμένος
τελέω	τελέσας	τελεσθείς (P)		
τίκτω		τεχθείς (P)		
φέρω	ἐνέγκας	ἐνεχθείς (P)		
φεύγω	φυγών			

5. Genitive Absolute. A noun or pronoun in the genitive case which is qualified by a participle may function independently, being neither the subject nor the object–direct or indirect–of the principal verb in the sentence. They are detached from the main part of the sentence; hence this construction is known as "genitive absolute" (from the Latin "absolvo": "to loose from").

Notice the use of this construction in the second sentence of the following comparison: ὁ ἀπόστολος θεραπεύσας τὸν τυφλὸν ἀπῆλθεν: *The apostle, after healing the blind man, went away.*" In this first sentence the noun ἀπόστολος, which is qualified by the participle, is the subject of the main verb; therefore, both this and the participle occur in the nominative. But: τοῦ ἀποστόλου θεραπεύσαντος τὸν τυφλόν ὁ μαθητής ἀπῆλθεν*: The apostle having healed the blind man, the disciple went away.*" In this second sentence μαθητής rather than the noun ἀπόστολος, is the subject of the principal verb of the sentence ἀπῆλθεν; in this case, both the participle and the noun qualified by it are independent of the principal verb and its subject and occur in the genitive. Genitive absolutes usually occur at the beginning of the sentence as a time element, and are very frequent in the gospels.

6. Special Usages of the Article. When a prepositional phrase is preceded by an article, it functions adjectivally. For example, "οἱ ἐν τῇ ἐκκλησίᾳ διδάσκαλοι: (Lit., "*The in the church teachers); that, is, the teachers who are (*or *were) in the church.*" And just as with the adjective, the prepositional phrase with the article can be used as a substantive. Thus: "οἱ ἐν τῇ ἐκκλησίᾳ: *those who are in the church.*"

7. Similar to the second usage above is the use of an article with:

(i) An adverb as a substantive which is being treated as if it were a noun: "τοὺς ἔξω: *those who are outside*" (1 Cor. 5:13).

(ii) A noun in the genitive: "τὰ τοῦ κόσμου: *the things of the world*" (1 Cor. 7:34).

VOCABULARY

βηθλεέμ, ἡ:	Bethlehem (indeclinable)
Δαυίδ, ὁ:	David (indeclinable)
ἐπιπίπτω:	I fall upon
ἔτι:	still (adverb)
εὐθέως, εὐθύς:	immediately (as an adverb)
ἰδού:	behold
Ἰουδαία, ἡ:	Judaea
κάθημαι:	I sit, I am seated
κλίνη, ἡ:	bed
οἰκία, ἡ:	house
ὁμοιόω:	I liken, I compare
παραγίνομαι:	I arrive, I come
προάγω:	(transitive) I lead forward; (intransitive) I go before, I precede
ὑπάγω:	(intransitive) I depart, I go. (found in the NT only in the present in all moods, and the imperfect in the indicative).

EXERCISES

I.

Translate into English:

1. καὶ οἱ προάγοντες καὶ οἱ ἀκολουθοῦντες ἔκραζον, Εὐλογημένος ὁ ἐρχόμενος ἐν ὀνόματι κυρίου. 2. τοῦ δὲ Ἰησοῦ γεννηθέντος ἰδοὺ ποιμένες παρεγένοντο εἰς Βηθλεὲμ τῆς Ἰουδαίας. 3. εὐθὺς ἔρχεται ὁ πονηρὸς καὶ αἴρει τὸν λόγον τὸν ἐσπαρμένον ἐν αὐτοῖς. 4. καὶ ἀπελθοῦσα εἰς τὸν οἶκον αὐτῆς εὗρε τὸ παιδίον βεβλημένον ἐπὶ τὴν κλίνην καὶ τὸ δαιμόνιον ἐξεληλυθός. 5. ἔτι λαλοῦντος τοῦ Πέτρου τὰ ῥήματα ταῦτα ἐπέπεσε τὸ πνεῦμα τὸ ἅγιον ἐπὶ τοὺς ἀκούοντας τὸν λόγον. 6. ὁμοία ἐστὶν ἡ βασιλεία τῶν οὐρανῶν θησαυρῷ κεκρυμμένῳ ἐν τῷ ἀγρῷ, ὃν εὑρὼν ἄνθρωπος ἔκρυψεν. 7. καὶ ἐσθιόντων αὐτῶν λαβὼν ἄρτον εὐλογήσας ἔκλασεν. 8. δικαιωθέντες οὖν ἐκ πίστεως εἰρήνην ἔχομεν πρὸς τὸν θεόν. 9. τότε ὄψονται τὸν υἱὸν τοῦ ἀνθρώπου ἐρχόμενον μετὰ δυνάμεως πολλῆς καὶ δόξης. 10. καὶ ἰδοὺ ἀνήρ, ὃς ἐξεληλύθει προσκυνήσων εἰς Ἰερουσαλήμ. 11. καὶ πορευομένων αὐτῶν εἶπέ τις ἄνθρωπος πρὸς αὐτόν. 12. ὁ σπείρων τὸν λόγον σπείρει, οὗτοι δέ εἰσιν οἱ παρὰ τὴν ὁδόν, ὅπου σπείρεται ὁ λόγος. 13. παραγενομένου τοῦ κληθέντος ὑπὸ τοῦ ἄρχοντος εἰς τὸν ἀγρὸν εὐθὺς τὰ σπέρματα ἐσπάρησαν ὑπὸ τῶν ἐργατῶν. 14. καὶ ἐκβληθέντος τοῦ δαιμονίου λαλήσει οὗτος ὁ ἄνθρωπος. 15. τοῦ βασιλέως τῆς πόλεως προσαγαγόντος τὴν θυγατέρα αὐτοῦ τοῖς ἱερεῦσι καὶ ἡμῶν προσευχομένων ὁ Ἰησοῦς ἰάσατο αὐτήν. 16. προσενέγκαντος τὴν θυσίαν ἐν τῷ ἱερῷ τοῦ θεραπευθέντος ὑπὸ τοῦ κυρίου οἱ καθήμενοι ἐχάρησαν. 17. οἱ χορτασθέντες τοῖς ἄρτοις τοῖς προσενεχθεῖσιν αὐτοῖς μένοντες ἔτι παρὰ τῷ Ἰησοῦ ἐθεώρουν τὰ ἔργα τὰ ποιούμενα ὑπ᾽ αὐτοῦ. 18. εἰσελθόντος δὲ αὐτοῦ εἰς τὴν πόλιν προσῆλθεν αὐτῷ ὁ ἄρχων παρακαλῶν αὐτὸν καὶ λέγων κύριε, ὁ παῖς μου βέβληται εἰς τὴν οἰκίαν παραλυτικός. 19. καὶ οἱ ὄχλοι θεωρήσαντες τὰ γενόμενα ὑπέστρεφον. 20. ἰδὼν ὁ προφήτης τοὺς παρὰ τὴν ὁδὸν ἐλάλησεν αὐτοῖς καὶ εἶπε τὰ ὑπὸ τοῦ Ἰησοῦ πραχθέντα. 21. πιστεύομεν καὶ λαλοῦμεν εἰδότες ὅτι ὁ ἐγείρας τὸν κύριον Ἰησοῦν καὶ ἡμᾶς σὺν αὐτῷ ἐγερεῖ. 22. γραφεισῶν τῶν

ἐπιστολῶν ὑπὸ τῶν ἐν τῇ συναγωγῇ γραμματέων ἐπῆραν τὴν φωνὴν αὐτῶν οἱ ἐν τῇ οἰκίᾳ. 23. αἱ ὑπὸ τῶν ἀποστόλων γραφεῖσαι ἐπιστολαὶ ἀπεστάλησαν τοῖς ἐξ ἐθνῶν ἀδελφοῖς. 24. ὁ λαὸς ὁ καθήμενος ἐν σκότει φῶς εἶδε μέγα. 25. σιωπησάντων τῶν μαθητῶν αὐτοὶ οἱ λίθοι κράξουσιν. 26. ἔτι ἁμαρτωλῶν ὄντων ἡμῶν Χριστὸς ὑπὲρ ἡμῶν ἀπέθανεν. 27. οἱ ἀκηκοότες ταῦτα καὶ ἑωρακότες τὰς δυνάμεις τὰς ὑπὸ τοῦ Ἰησοῦ ποιηθείσας ἐμαρτύρουν περὶ αὐτοῦ καὶ τοῖς μήπω πεπεισμένοις. 28. εἰληφότες τὴν δύναμιν τοῦ ἁγίου πνεύματος ἐμείναμεν παρὰ τοῖς ἐγνωκόσι τὰ περὶ τοῦ Χριστοῦ. 29. ἰαθέντος τοῦ λεπροῦ οἱ ὄχλοι ἐθαύμαζον.

II.

Translate into Greek:

1. The blind man after he received the prophet into his house was baptized by him. 2. After the apostles arrived into the temple the Lord went away into other cities. 3. While the prophet was preaching in the synagogue I saw the women (who were praying) (who prayed) (while they were praying). 4. After they received the power of the Holy Spirit the believers came out and preached the gospel to (those) who were repenting. 5. After the Lord comes in his glory, the church will be saved from the power of sin. 6. We saw the child which had been cast out of the house, but we did not see his father and his mother seeking it. 7. While the Lord was still in the flesh (those) who were believing in him were not yet being comforted by (those) who had the words of the covenant. 8. The kingdom of heaven was likened to a seed which was sown in a field. 9. After the disciples went away on account of the fear of the Jews, the Lord appeared to (those) who were worshiping him. 10. (He) who believed and was baptized will be saved. 11. (While men and women are praying) (Those who are praying) see the face of the Lord. 12. God knows (use the new verb) the names of (those) who have been saved. 13. Those who were in the church (prepositional phrase) were comforting (those) who were persecuted on account of the name of the Savior. 14. Having heard the promises of God and having believed in (lit., into) the Lord and having been baptized in his name we preached the gospel to (those) who have not yet believed. 15. Because these (things) have been written in the Holy Scriptures the

priests have told to the multitudes words of mercy. 16. When the Lord was raised from the dead he came to (those) who were praying and blessed them. 17. When the sun rose, the (things) which were in the field (prepositional phrase) withered. 18. We did not see the Savior while he was still in the flesh, but (those) who believe in him see him in the spirit while they are praying. 19. (Those) who dwelt in this great city having observed signs in the heaven did not enter into their houses. 20. Because the sons of this age did not repent on account of their sins the prophets did not bless them. 21. (Those) who called us into the church, having themselves been called by (him) who was crucified both in their and our own behalf, glorified him. 22. After the disciples had said these (things) to (those) who brought the blind one to Jesus, we saw the rulers. 23. (Those) who have put their trust in the Savior will have hope in their hearts. 24. Having put our trust in the Savior we shall have hope in our hearts. 25. Because the rulers had not come into Jerusalem the priests were afraid. 26. When the workers built a house to the Lord we came and worshiped him. 27. Our Father who art in the heavens (prepositional phrase).

Lesson Twenty-Nine

The Adjective:
Adjectives of the Third Declension
Comparison of These Adjectives

1. Adjectives of the Third Declension. The adjectives of the third declension can be classified into three groups. To the first two groups belong adjectives which are declined in all three genders on the pattern of the third declension noun and in accordance with concrete rules. The third group is composed of adjectives which defy a well-defined and all-embracing classification, and each of them or small groups of them have to be dealt with separately.

Since the third declension uses the same endings for masculine and feminine nouns, the masculine and feminine adjectives will be the same for any third-declension adjective, just as with the adjective αἰώνιος. These will be indicated in the vocabulary with just two endings: ἀληθής, ές. When you see a word in the vocabulary with only one other ending indicated and no article to indicate gender (as for nouns), assume that it is an adjective with the first ending for masculine and feminine and the second ending for neuter.

2. First Group. The adjectives of this group have their stem end in –**εσ**. As in the corresponding neuter nouns (**25 § 5, 6**), the **σ** is dropped and a contraction takes place between the **ε** of the stem and the initial vowel of the regular endings of the third declension. The nominative singular of the masculine and feminine ends in –**ης**, while the vocative singular of these two genders, as well as the nominative, accusative and vocative singular of the neuter, consists of the bare stem. In the dative plural the **σ** of the stem is dropped before the **σ** of the ending. The adjectives of this group are declined as follows:

	Singular		Plural	
	Masc. and Fem.	**Neuter**	**Masc. and Fem.**	**Neuter**
N.	ἀληθής	ἀληθές	ἀληθεῖς	ἀληθῆ
G.	ἀληθοῦς	ἀληθοῦς	ἀληθῶν	ἀληθῶν
D.	ἀληθεῖ	ἀληθεῖ	ἀληθέσι (ν)	ἀληθέσι (ν)
A.	ἀληθῆ	ἀληθές	ἀληθεῖς	ἀληθῆ
V.	ἀληθές	ἀληθές	ἀληθεῖς	ἀληθῆ

3. Second Group. The adjectives of this extremely small group have their stems end in **-ον**, to which the regular endings of the third declension are added. In the masculine and feminine the **ο** is turned into **ω** in the nominative and vocative singular. In the dative plural the **ν** of the stem is dropped before the **σ** of the ending. The adjectives of this group are declined as follows:

	Singular		Plural	
	Masc. and Fem.	**Neuter**	**Masc. and Fem.**	**Neuter**
N. V.	ἄφρων	ἄφρον	ἄφρονες	ἄφρονα
G.	ἄφρονος	ἄφρονος	ἀφρόνων	ἀφρόνων
D.	ἄφρονι	ἄφρονι	ἄφροσι (ν)	ἄφροσι (ν)
A.	ἄφρονα	ἄφρον	ἄφρονας	ἄφρονα

4. Third Group. Of the miscellaneous adjectives which make up this group the most important–some of the commonest in the NT text–are the following:

(i) πᾶς, πᾶσα, πᾶν. The masculine and the neuter follow the third declension, while the feminine follows the first declension noun of the **-α** group with stem which ends in a consonant other than **ρ**. The declension of this adjective presents no difficulty because in all three genders it follows exactly the pattern of the first aorist participle active **(27 § 9)**, the only difference being that in the masculine and the neuter the adjective follows the accent rule which governs the monosyllable noun of the third declension and drops the accent to the ultima in the genitive and dative–but only in the singular. Thus: παντός, παντί

The adjective πᾶς can be used in the following ways:

(a) Without the article it means *every* in the singular and *all* in the plural–πᾶς ἄνθρωπος: *every man,* πᾶσιν ἀνθρώποις: *to all men.* Sometimes the noun qualified by this adjective is implied: πάντες ἥμαρτον, "all (have) sinned."

(b) With the article usually following it, it means as a rule *the whole* in the singular and *all* in the plural–πᾶσα ἡ πόλις: *the whole city,* πᾶσαι αἱ πόλεις: *all the cities.*

(ii) ἅπας, ἅπασα, ἅπαν is an emphatic form of πᾶς and is declined on the same pattern, but does not drop the accent to the ultima.

(iii) εὐθύς, εὐθεῖα, εὐθύ The masculine is declined irregularly according to the 3rd declension. In the NT text it is found only in the feminine: nominative and accusative singular and accusative plural: εὐθεῖα, εὐθεῖαν, εὐθείας. Like εὐθύς: πραΰς, πραεῖα, πραΰ. In the NT text it is found only in the masculine nominative, the genitive singular and nominative plural πραΰς, πραέως, πραεῖς; and in the neuter genitive singular: πραέως.

Feminine adjectives which are declined according to the first declension, while the masculine follows the third, have the **α** of the ending in the nominative and accusative singular short; hence the circumflex on εὐθεῖα.

(iv) μέγας and πολύς. We have already become acquainted with these (**16 § 12**).

5. Comparison of the Adjectives. The adjectives of the first group form the comparative and superlative degrees by adding to the stem –τερος, α, ον and –τατος, η, ον respectively: ἀληθέστερος, α, ον; ἀληθέστατος, η, ον; the adjectives of the second group, by adding to the stem –εστερος, α, ον and –εστατος, η, ον respectively: ἀφρονέστερος, α, ον; ἀφρονέστατος, η, ον. The adjectives of the third group, as well as some of the first-second declension ones, form these degrees <u>irregularly</u> as follows:

ἀγαθός—	κρείσσ (ττ) ων, ον; κράτιστος, η, ον
κακός—	χείρων, ον
μέγας—	μείζων, ον; μέγιστος, η, ον

μικρός—	ἐλάσσ (ττ) ων, ον and μικρότερος, α, ον; ἐλάχιστος, η, ον
πολύς—	πλείων, ον or πλέον; πλεῖστος, η, ον

All of the above ending in **ων** are declined regularly according to the third declension, like ἄφρων. But also: μείζω instead of μείζονα; (acc. fem. sing. and nom. and acc. neuter plural); ἐλάσσω instead of ἐλάσσονα (acc. masc. sing.); πλείω instead of πλείονα (acc. neuter sing.); πλείους instead of πλείονες, πλείονας.

VOCABULARY

ἀληθής, ές:	true, truthful
ἀπαιτέω:	I demand
ἅπας, ἅπασα, ἅπαν	whole, all (pl.)
ἀσθενής, ές:	weak, sick
ἄφρων, ον:	foolish
γῆ, γῆς, ἡ:	earth, land, ground, (circumflex accent on all forms)
δουλεύω:	I serve
ἐκκόπτω:	I cut down
εὐθύς, εῖα, ύ:	straight, right (as adjective)
ἰσχυρός, ά, όν:	strong, powerful
κληρονομέω:	I inherit
μονογενής, ές:	only begotten
ὅσος, η, ον:	as much as; as many as (pl.)
πᾶς, πᾶσα, πᾶν:	every, all (pl.)
πλήρης, ες:	full (with genitive)
πραῢς, εῖα, πραῢς:	meek
προσδοκάω:	I expect, I look for
ὑγιής, ές:	sound, healthy
χήρα, ας, ἡ:	widow

EXERCISES

I.

Translate into English:

1. ἐθεασάμεθα τὴν δόξαν αὐτοῦ, δόξαν ὡς μονογενοῦς παρὰ πατρός. 2. ὁ μείζων δουλεύσει τῷ ἐλάσσονι. 3. ἄνδρας ἐξ ὑμῶν μαρτυρουμένους πλήρεις πνεύματος καὶ σοφίας. 4. ὅλον ἄνθρωπον ὑγιῆ ἐποίησα ἐν σαββάτῳ. 5. ὁ πιστὸς ἐν ἐλαχίστῳ καὶ ἐν πολλῷ πιστός ἐστιν. 6. μακάριοι οἱ πραεῖς, ὅτι αὐτοὶ κληρονομήσουσι τὴν γῆν. 7. εὐθείας ποιεῖτε τὰς ὁδοὺς τοῦ κυρίου. 8. τὸ ἀσθενὲς τοῦ θεοῦ ἰσχυρότερον τῶν ἀνθρώπων. 9. ὃς ὤφθη ἐπὶ ἡμέρας πλείους τοῖς συναναβᾶσιν αὐτῷ ἀπὸ τῆς Γαλιλαίας. 10. πάντα ὅσα εἶπεν Ἰωάννης περὶ τούτου ἀληθῆ ἦν. 11. ἡ χήρα αὕτη ἡ πτωχὴ πλεῖον πάντων ἔβαλεν. 12. γίνεται τὰ ἔσχατα τοῦ ἀνθρώπου χείρονα τῶν πρώτων. 13. δαιμόνια πολλὰ ἐξέβαλεν. 14. λαβόντες κρείσσονα διαθήκην γενομένην ἐν τῷ αἵματι τοῦ μονογενοῦς υἱοῦ τοῦ θεοῦ ἀπαγγελοῦμεν αὐτὴν τοῖς μήπω εὐλογηθεῖσιν. 15. λαλήσαντος τοῦ προφήτου ταῦτα τὰ ῥήματα ἐν πάσαις ταῖς πόλεσι πολλοὶ ἀσθενεῖς ὑγιεῖς γεγόνασιν. 16. ὁ Ἰησοῦς Χριστὸς ἀποθανὼν διὰ τὰς ἁμαρτίας πάντων ἡμῶν ἐγήγερται ἀπὸ τῶν νεκρῶν δεξάμενος ἅπασαν τὴν δόξαν τοῦ οὐρανοῦ. 17. πολλοὶ ἄνδρες πλήρεις πνεύματος ἁγίου καὶ ἔχοντες τὴν ἀληθῆ πίστιν ἐκήρυξαν τὰς ἐπαγγελίας τοῦ θεοῦ πᾶσι τοῖς ἔθνεσιν. 18. καὶ αὐτῶν τῶν ὑποκριτῶν χείρονές ἐστε, γνόντες γὰρ τὰ ἀληθῆ μυστήρια τῆς βασιλείας οὐχ ὡμολογήσατε τὸν σωτῆρα. 19. γεγραφότος τοῦ προφήτου πάσαις ταῖς ἐκκλησίαις ἅπασαν τὴν ἀλήθειαν περὶ τῆς ἐλπίδος τῆς ἀναστάσεως πολλοὶ ἀδελφοὶ ἀποσταλέντες ὑπὸ τοῦ κυρίου ἐλάλουν καὶ τοῖς μὴ πιστεύσασιν. 20. πᾶς ὁ ἀρνούμενος τὸν υἱὸν οὐδὲ τὸν πατέρα ἔχει. 21. ἄλλος ἐστὶν ὁ μαρτυρῶν περὶ ἐμοῦ, καὶ οἶδα ὅτι ἀληθής ἐστιν ἡ μαρτυρία ἣν μαρτυρεῖ περὶ ἐμοῦ. 22. πλήρη ὕδατος ἦσαν τὰ σκεύη. 23. πάντες ὅσοι εἶχον ἀσθενοῦντας ἤγαγον αὐτοὺς πρὸς αὐτόν. 24. πραΰς εἰμι καὶ ταπεινὸς τῇ καρδίᾳ. 25. εὐθεῖαί εἰσιν αἱ ὁδοὶ τοῦ κυρίου καὶ πλήρεις δώρων ἀγαθῶν τοῖς πιστοῖς.

II.

Translate into Greek:

(In translating each English sentence into Greek use the participle whenever this is possible.)

1. And he taught them many (things) in parables. 2. (They) who seek the glory of (him) who sent them are true. 3. He who believes in me will do the works which I do; and greater (works) than these he will do. 4. These disciples were full of (the) Holy Spirit and of faith. 5. He who destroys the least of these commandments shall be called least in the kingdom of the heavens. 6. Having come into the city they announced to the high priests all (the things) which they had done. 7. He sent other slaves, more than the first. 8. Every tree which does not make good fruit is cut down and is cast into the fire. 9. Woman, great is thy faith. 10. The disciples preached the gospel into the whole world. 11. (The things) which were said by these foolish men and women are not true. 12. Great are our enemies, but greater than them is the power of our faith. 13. The hypocrites are worse than the unrighteous (ones). 14. After the daughters of this woman heard concerning the great miracles which were done by Jesus, the scribes brought many sick (ones) to the Savior. 15. All (the things), as many as have been written in the book of God's revelation are true and full of power. 16. Having believed by means of the grace of the only begotten Son of God, these men (in distinction to women) announced the knowledge of the true will of God to all (those) who were in the darkness. 17. As many as received Jesus as their own Savior became true children of God. 18. The life of the evil (ones) is not by nature straight. 19. Not all (those) who live on the earth will inherit the kingdom. 20. But I have a testimony (that which testifies to me) greater than (that) of John. 21. The brethren who are with me greet every saint in Christ Jesus. 22. All the words which thou hast spoken to us are true. 23. After he gathered together the high priests and the scribes of the people, the disciples made manifest to all every commandment of the law of God. 24. To all the members of the church the whole judgment of the Lord was made manifest. 25. After the only-begotten son of that widow died, Jesus with his disciples entered into the city.

Lesson Thirty

The Interrogative Pronoun • *The Indefinite Pronoun*
The Indefinite-Relative Pronoun
The Noun: The Cases Indicating Time and Space

1. The Interrogative Pronoun. The interrogative pronoun, corresponding to the English *"who?"* or *"which?"* is τίς, τί. It preserves the acute on the one syllable forms, never turning it into a grave and is declined on the pattern of the third declension, as follows:

	Singular		Plural	
	Masc. and Fem.	**Neuter**	**Masc. and Fem.**	**Neuter**
N.	τίς	τί	τίνες	τίνα
G.	τίνος	τίνος	τίνων	τίνων
D.	τίνι	τίνι	τίσι (ν)	τίσι (ν)
A.	τίνα	τί	τίνας	τίνα

The interrogative pronoun is also used to introduce an indirect question: "Γινωσκετε τί πεποίηκα ὑμῖν" (John 13:12).

2. The interrogative pronoun in the neuter accusative singular, either by itself or preceded by the preposition διά, is also used in the sense of *why?* For example: "τί δὲ Βλέπεις . . ." (Matt. 7:3).

3. The Indefinite Pronoun. The indefinite pronoun corresponds to the English *a certain, some* or other similar expressions. The indefinite pronoun is in form identical to the interrogative, but its accent, if it has one, will be on the ultima. The indefinite pronoun usually follows the noun which it qualifies, the noun taking no article.

4. The indefinite pronoun is an enclitic (See rules **10 § 9**). διδάσκαλοί τινες: *"certain teachers."*

5. The indefinite pronoun is frequently used without qualifying a noun. In this case it is a pronoun in the proper sense of the term. Example: "Εἰσ τί ἡ ἀπώλεια" (Mark 14:4).

6. The Indefinite Relative Pronoun. The indefinite relative pronoun differs from the ordinary relative pronoun in that it may mean, but not always, *whoever, whichever.* In form it is the combination of the relative and the indefinite pronouns in one word: ὅστις, ἥτις, ὅ τι. In the neuter the two pronouns are separated by a space in order that it may be distinguished from ὅτι: *that, because.* Both components of the pronoun are declined regularly according to the rules of their respective declensions: ὅστις, οὗτινος, etc. However, in the NT text this pronoun is found only in the nominative of both numbers in the masculine and feminine and the accusative singular in the neuter, thus: ὅστις, ἥτις, οἵτινες, αἵτινες, ὅ τι. It also occurs 5 times as an old form of the genitive singular ὅτου in the combination ἕως ὅτου: *until* (Luke 13:8).

7. Use of the Cases to Indicate Time or Space. Sometimes nouns are used in the objective cases adverbially to show certain relationships in time or space, as follows:

(i) Time.

(a) The accusative is used to express the *length* of time.
e.g., "Mary remained with her ὡς μῆνας τρεῖς: *about three months.*" (Luke 1:56).

(b) The genitive is used to indicate the time *within* which an event takes place: the kind of time.
e.g., "This one came to him νυκτὸς: *at night,* (by night) . . ." (John 3:2).

(c) The dative is used to indicate a particular point of time *at* which an event takes place.
e.g., "ταύτῃ τῇ νυκτί: *in this night* . . . you will deny me three times" (Mark 14:30).

However, the above distinctions are not applied consistently in the NT text.

(ii) Space. The accusative is used to indicate the *extent* of space or distance.

e.g., "... into a village which was σταδίους ἑξήκοντα: *sixty stadia* (*seven miles*) from Jerusalem" (Luke 24:13).

VOCABULARY

εἰκών, εἰκόνος, ἡ:	image
καθεύδω:	I sleep, (fig.) I am dead
κλέπτω:	I steal
κοιμάομαι:	I sleep, (fig.), I die
κραυγή, ῆς, ἡ:	shout
μεταξύ:	between (prep. with gen.); meanwhile, in the meantime (an adverb)
μισθός, οῦ, ὁ:	wages, reward
πέτρα, ας, ἡ:	rock
πότε:	when? (an adverb)
ποτέ:	at some time in the past, formerly, ever (enclitic) (an adverb).
ῥύομαι:	I deliver, I rescue (dep.)
σήμερον:	today
στρατιώτης, ου, ὁ:	soldier
ταλαίπωρος, ος, ον:	miserable
ταπεινόω:	I humble, I humiliate

EXERCISES

I.

Translate into English:

1. στραφεὶς ὁ Ἰησοῦς ἠρώτησε τοὺς ἐν τῷ πλήθει ἄνδρας, τίς μου ἥψατο τῶν ἱματίων; 2. ἐπηρώτησαν δὲ αὐτὸν λέγοντες, Διδάσκαλε, πότε ταῦτα ἔσται, καὶ τί τὸ σημεῖον τῆς σῆς παρουσίας; 3. πῶς λέγουσιν ἐν ὑμῖν τινες ὅτι ἀνάστασις νεκρῶν οὐκ ἔστιν; 4. οἱ μαθηταὶ αὐτοῦ νυκτὸς ἐλθόντες ἔκλεψαν αὐτὸν ἡμῶν κοιμωμένων. 5. τίνι ὁμοία ἐστὶν ἡ βασιλεία τοῦ θεοῦ; 6. διὰ τί ἡμεῖς καὶ οἱ Φαρισαῖοι νηστεύομεν, οἱ δὲ μαθηταί σου οὐ

νηστεύουσιν; 7. ἄφρων, ταύτῃ τῇ νυκτὶ τὴν ψυχήν σου ἀπαιτοῦσιν ἀπὸ σοῦ. 8. ἦν δὲ τὰς ἡμέρας ἐν τῷ ἱερῷ διδάσκων. 9. ὁ δὲ ἐγερθεὶς παρέλαβε τὸ παιδίον καὶ τὴν μητέρα αὐτοῦ νυκτός. 10. τίς μὲ ῥύσεται ἐκ τοῦ σώματος τοῦ θανάτου τούτου; 11. ὅστις δὲ οὐκ ἔχει, καὶ ὃ ἔχει ἀρθήσεται ἀπ᾽ αὐτοῦ. 12. οἱ γὰρ καθεύδοντες νυκτὸς καθεύδουσιν. 13. τίνι γὰρ εἶπέν ποτε τῶν ἀγγέλων, Υἱός μου εἶ σύ, ἐγὼ σήμερον γεγέννηκά σε; 14. εἴδομέν τινα ἐν τῷ ὀνόματί σου ἐκβάλλοντα δαιμόνια. 15. ἐξελθόντι δὲ αὐτῷ ἐπὶ τὴν γῆν προσῆλθε αὐτῷ ἀνήρ τις ἐκ τῆς πόλεως. 16. ἄνθρωπός τις ἐποίει δεῖπνον μέγα καὶ ἐκάλεσε πολλούς, καὶ ἀπέστειλε τὸν δοῦλον αὐτοῦ τῇ ὥρᾳ τοῦ δείπνου τοῖς κεκλημένοις καὶ ἀνήγγειλεν αὐτοῖς ὅτι πάντα ἡτοίμασται. 17. εἰδὼς ὁ Ἰησοῦς τί ἦν ἐν τῇ καρδίᾳ αὐτῶν εἶπεν αὐτοῖς, τί οὐ μετανοεῖτε; 18. καὶ ἰδόντες οἱ ἐν τῇ οἰκίᾳ Φαρισαῖοι ἔλεγον τοῖς μαθηταῖς αὐτοῦ, διὰ τί μετὰ τελωνῶν καὶ ἁμαρτωλῶν ἐσθίει ὁ ὑμέτερος διδάσκαλος; 19. τινὲς δὲ τῶν γραμματέων ἀκούσαντες ταῦτα εἶπον, οὗτος βλασφημεῖ. 20. τί δέ με καλεῖτε, κύριε, κύριε; 21. ἦσαν δὲ καὶ γυναῖκές τινες, αἳ ἦσαν τεθεραπευμέναι ἀπὸ πνευμάτων πονηρῶν, αἵτινες διηκόνουν αὐτοῖς. 22. πᾶς οὖν ὅστις ἀκούει μου τοὺς λόγους τούτους καὶ ποιεῖ αὐτοὺς ὁμοιωθήσεται ἀνδρὶ φρονίμῳ, ὅστις ᾠκοδόμησεν αὐτοῦ τὴν οἰκίαν ἐπὶ τὴν πέτραν. 23. καὶ ἐπηρώτησέ τις ἄρχων αὐτὸν λέγων, Διδάσκαλε ἀγαθέ, τί ποιήσας ζωὴν αἰώνιον κληρονομήσω; 24. ἄνθρωπός τις ἐν πνεύματι ἀκαθάρτῳ ἔκραξε λέγων, Οἶδά σε τίς εἶ. 25. ἐλπίζω ὅτι μενῶ μεθ᾽ ὑμῶν ἡμέρας τινάς.

II.

Translate into Greek:

1. Whose is this image? 2. Why do you speak to them in parables? 3. A certain ruler of the Jews came to Jesus at night. 4. Whoever believes in (lit., into) the Savior becomes a child of God. 5. And certain miserable soldiers took at some time in the past their wages (singular). 6. Who are sleeping at night? 7. Did you ever speak to certain women about the hope of the second coming of Christ? 8. When did we see thee being hungry or being thirsty? 9. You did not follow certain hypocrites but (him) who delivered you from your sins. 10. Who is (he)

who was born king of the Jews? 11. Whoever will be humbled will be called greater than all the others. 12. This day certain evil men with their wives came to a certain great synagogue. 13. After a certain man sowed in his field certain seeds, these brought much and good fruit. 14. Certain priests said to the king, "To whom (plural) in this city shall we announce today thy judgment?" 15. Who of (lit., out of) you knowing (that) his brother is sinning (participle) will not rebuke him by means of words full of mercy? 16. The women who were in the city (prepositional phrase) did not know that, while they were sleeping, certain sick (people) were brought into their house. 17. What art thou demanding from me? 18. By whom (plural) were the mysteries of the kingdom known? 19. A certain foolish (man) asked, "Who is greater and better than me?" 20. Certain soldiers rescued us at night from the hands of certain evil men. 21. Why did you not prepare something for the priests? 22. As many as were led astray from the straight way returned (on) a certain day into the fellowship of the believers. 23. In the whole creation there are certain (people) who are not anxious (participle) on account of the needs of the flesh. 24. Who was the (one) who called thee (participle) by means of his grace into his eternal kingdom? 25. What is this which I hear about thee?

Lesson Thirty-One

Infinitives in All Voices • *Articular Infinitive*
Impersonal Verbs • *Indirect Speech*
The Verbs δύναμαι *and* γίνομαι

1. The Infinitive. We have already seen that the participle is a "verbal adjective," describing someone doing an action. The infinitive is a "verbal noun," describing the action itself. This mood derives its name from the fact that it serves to express the general (infinite) concept of the action or state denoted by the verb without necessarily linking this concept with a certain person, as is done in other moods; e.g., *"to err* is human."

2. As a *verb* the infinitive has tense and voice, and may have a subject or an object.

The following sentence in two forms, one with the infinitive in the active voice and the other with the infinitive in the passive, makes clear the fact that the infinitive may have a subject or an object: ἐκέλευσεν αὐτοὺς ἄγειν τὸν τυφλὸν πρὸς αὐτόν*: "he commanded that (they) should lead the blind man to him."* Here αὐτοὺς is the subject and τυφλὸν is the object of the infinitive ἄγειν.

"ἐκέλευσε τὸν τυφλὸν ἄγεσθαι πρὸς αὐτόν*:" "he commanded that the blind man should be led to him." Here* τυφλὸν is the subject of the infinitive ἄγεσθαι.

Notice that whereas the finite verb always has a nominative case subject, the infinitive always takes an accusative subject.

3. As a *noun* the infinitive can itself be the subject or object of another verb. The following two verses will make this clear: " Ἔξεστιν τῷ σαββάτῳ θεραπεῦσαι*; Is it lawful to heal on the Sabbath?*" (Luke 14:3). In this sentence the infinitive θεραπεῦσαι is the *subject* of the verb ἔξεστιν.

"βασιλεῖς ἠθέλησαν ἰδεῖν ἃ ὑμεῖς βλέπετε . . . *Kings have desired to see . . . that which you see . . .* " (Luke 10:24). In this sentence the infinitive ἰδεῖν is the *object* of the verb ἠθέλησαν, and the relative clause ἃ ὑμεῖς βλέπετε is the object of the infinitive ἰδεῖν .

4. The infinitive is formed by adding to the stem of the verb the following endings:

(i) Present Active: ειν—λύειν.

(ii) Present Middle & Passive: εσθαι—λύεσθαι.

The rule which governs the contract verbs applies here also except that the **ι** in the present active ending does not show up in the **α** contract or **ο** contract verbs. Notice that the contracted syllable is accented and the accent is the circumflex. Thus, ἀγαπᾶν, ἀγαπᾶσθαι; φιλεῖν— φιλεῖσθαι; φανεροῦν–φανεροῦσθαι. ζάω forms the present active infinitive in an irregular way: ζῆν.

(iii) Future Active: σειν—λύσειν.

(iv) Future Middle: σεσθαι—λύσεσθαι.

(v) Future Passive: θήσεσθαι—λυθήσεσθαι.

(vi) First Aorist Active: σαι—λῦσαι.

(vii) First Aorist Middle: σασθαι—λύσασθαι.

(viii) First Aorist Passive: θῆναι—λυθῆναι.

(In verbs whose stem ends in a nasal or liquid consonant the same rule applies which governs this tense in the indicative [**22 § 5, i, iii**]). Thus, κρίνω–κρῖναι, ἀποστέλλω–ἀποστεῖλαι.

(ix) Perfect Active: κέναι—λελυκέναι.

(x) Perfect Middle & Passive: σθαι—λελύσθαι.

The *second aorist* is formed by adding to the verbal stem εῖν in the active voice (but γνῶναι), έσθαι in the middle, and ῆναι in the passive: βαλεῖν; βαλέσθαι; βληθῆναι.

The *second perfect active* is formed by adding to the reduplicated stem έναι: γεγραφέναι. The same process is followed in the verbs which form the perfect in an irregular way (**26 § 11**); e.g., λέγω—εἰρηκέναι, γίνομαι— γεγονέναι, ἔρχομαι—ἐληλυθέναι.

In the aorist and perfect, both first and second, active and passive there is a deviation from the rule of the accent which governs the verb in that the accent is not pushed up to the antepenult although the ultima is short: διῶξαι, διωχθῆναι, λελμκέναι, λελύσθαι.

5. The infinitive of the verb εἰμί in the present is εἶναι, future: ἔσεσθαι.

6. The infinitive is negated by means of μή, μηδέ, μηκέτι, μήπω.

7. Of the verbs we have so far learned the following form the infinitive for the aorist and perfect (active, middle or passive) in an irregular way or as a second aorist/perfect. All the liquid/nasal verbs we have learned are also included. Only verbs found in the NT in some form of these tenses are included in this list.

Present Indicative	**Aorist Active**	**Aorist Passive (or Middle)**	**Perfect Active**
ἀγγέλλω	ἀγγεῖλαι		
ἄγω	ἀγαγεῖν		
αἴρω	ἆραι		
ἀνατέλλω	ἀνατεῖλαι		
ἀνοίγω		ἀνεῳχθῆναι	
ἀποκτείνω	ἀποκτεῖναι	ἀποκτανθῆναι	
–βαίνω–	βῆναι		
βάλλω	βαλεῖν	βληθῆναι	
βλέπω (see ὁράω)			
γίνομαι		γενέσθαι	γεγονέναι
γινώσκω	γνῶναι	γνωσθῆναι	ἐγνωκέναι
δεικνύω	δεῖξαι		
δείκνυμι	δεῖξαι		
δέω	δῆσαι		
διδάσκω	διδάξαι		
ἐγείρω	ἐγεῖραι	ἐγερθῆναι	
ἔρχομαι	ἐλθεῖν		
ἐσθίω	φαγεῖν		
εὑρίσκω	εὑρεῖν	εὑρεθῆναι	εὑρηκέναι
θνήσκω	θανεῖν		
καλέω	καλέσαι	καλέσασθαι or κληθῆναι	
κρίνω	κρῖναι	κριθῆναι	

Present Indicative	Aorist Active	Aorist Passive (or Middle)	Perfect Active
κρύπτω		κρυβῆναι	
λαμβάνω	λαβεῖν	λαβέσθαι	εἰληφέναι
λέγω	εἰπεῖν		
λείπω		λειφθῆναι	
μανθάνω	μαθεῖν		
μένω	μεῖναι		
οἶδα			εἰδέναι
ὁράω	ἰδεῖν		ἑωρακέναι
πάσχω	παθεῖν		
πίνω	πιεῖν or πεῖν		
πίπτω	πεσεῖν		
σπείρω	σπεῖραι		
–στέλλω	–στεῖλαι		
σῴζω	σωθῆναι		
τελέω	τελέσαι		
τίκτω	τεκεῖν		
φέρω	ἐνεγκεῖν or ἐνέγκαι		
φεύγω	φυγεῖν		πεφευγέναι
χαίρω		χαρῆναι	

8. There is no real element of time with the infinitive as there is with the finite verb in the indicative. The present does not necessarily refer to an action taking place now, or the aorist to one which took place in the past. The present in the infinitive denotes an action which is continued or repeated (Mark 4:1). When there is no such definite suggestion, the infinitive is placed in the aorist (Luke 14:6), which is more frequently used than the present in the NT text.

9. The Noun Uses of the Infinitive. At the beginning of the chapter we saw examples of the infinitive as both the subject and the object of a verb (§ 3). As a noun, the infinitive may take a neuter article (called an articular infinitive), and may be used in any way any other noun is used:

(i) As a subject, particularly with the impersonal verbs ἔξεστι, *it is lawful* and δεῖ, *it is necessary*, (See **§ 12**). Thus: "Ἡμῖν οὐκ ἔξεστιν ἀποκτεῖναι οὐδένα: *It is not lawful for us to kill anyone* (lit., *to kill anyone is not lawful for us*"; John 18:31). "δεῖ με καὶ Ῥώμην ἰδεῖν: *I must see Rome also* (lit., *me to see Rome is also necessary*"; Acts 19:21).

(ii) As a direct object, particularly with the verb ἄρχομαι, *I begin*, and with verbs of wishing, like βούλομαι (1 Tim. 6:9) and θέλω (Matt. 19:21), or of commanding, like κελεύω (Acts 22:30) and παραγγέλλω (1 Tim. 6:17). Thus: "ἤρξατο ὁ Ἰησοῦς κηρύσσειν καὶ λέγειν, . . . *Jesus began to preach and to say* . . ." (Matt. 4:17).

(iii) As the object of a preposition, as discussed later in (**§ 11**) under the adverbial uses. This use is one that is very much unlike the English infinitives. Note that although the infinitive is not declined, any article used with it will be declined in the neuter gender according to the case used.

10. The Adjective and Complementary Uses of the Infinitive. One use of the infinitive in both English and Greek is to modify certain verb, noun or adjective ideas by explaining them, such as in what way is one able or worthy. δύναμαι, *I am able*, for example, is usually followed by an infinitive which explains what one is able to do. Thus, "Οὐδεὶς δύναται δυσὶ κυρίοις δουλεύειν: *No one is able to serve two masters* . . ." (Matt. 6:24). Infinitives are also frequently used to explain nouns like ἐξουσία, *authority* or *power* (John 1:12), and adjectives like δυνατός, *able* (2 Tim. 1:12), and ἄξιος, *worthy* (Luke 15:19). In a similar way, an infinitive usually follows the verb μέλλω, *I am about to*, to complete the idea of what one is about to do. Thus: "αὐτὸς γὰρ ᾔδει τί ἔμελλεν ποιεῖν: *for he knew what he was going to do*" (John 6:6).

11. The Adverbial Uses of the Infinitive. The infinitive is frequently used in Greek, either by itself, or as the object of a preposition with the corresponding neuter article, to show a variety of adverbial uses. Three of the most important adverbial uses are to show time, purpose or cause, as follows.

(i) To show the relationship between the infinitive and the main verb in terms of *time*. Thus:

(a) Antecedent time: before the time of the main verb, with πρὸ τοῦ: "Πρὸ τοῦ σε Φίλιππον φωνῆσαι . . . εἶδόν σε: *before Philip called thee* (lit., *before Philip to call thee . . . I saw thee*" [John 1:48]). Notice the two accusatives in the sentence, the first being the object and the second the subject of the infinitive.

(b) Contemporaneous time: *during* the time of the main verb, *while*, with ἐν τῷ: "καὶ ἐν τῷ κατηγορεῖσθαι αὐτὸν ὑπὸ τῶν ἀρχιερέων . . . *and while he was accused* (lit., *in the him to be accused by the chief priests . . .*"; Matt. 27:12).

(c) Subsequent time: *after* the time of the main verb with μετὰ τὸ: "μετὰ τὸ παθεῖν αὐτὸν . . . *after he had suffered*" (lit., *after the him to suffer;* Acts 1:3).

(ii) To show the purpose or aim of the action denoted by the main verb. There are three primary constructions with the infinitive to show purpose.

(a) The simple infinitive by itself: "μὴ νομίσητε ὅτι ἦλθον καταλῦσαι . . . *Do not suppose that I came to destroy . . .*" (Matt. 5:17).

(b) The infinitive with the neuter article τοῦ: "τοῦ ἀπολέσαι αὐτό: *in order to destroy him.*" (Matt. 2:13).

(c) The infinitive with the prepositions (and neuter article) εἰς τὸ or πρὸς τὸ: "εἰς τὸ θανατῶσαι αὐτὸν . . . *in order to put him to death . . .*" (Mark 14:55); "πρὸς τὸ ἐπιθυμῆσαι αὐτὴν . . . *in order to desire her . . .*" (Matt. 5:28).

(iii) To show the cause for the action of the main verb, used with διὰ τὸ: "διὰ τὸ πληθυνθῆναι τὴν ἀνομίαν . . . *Because lawlessness will have increased*" (lit., *because lawlessness to have increased;* Matt. 24:12).

12. Impersonal Verbs. There is a group of verbs called impersonal because in the construction of the sentence they do not, or do not seem to have a subject and are employed only in the third person singular. Of these the most common are δεῖ (imperfect ἔδει): *it is necessary*; ἔξεστι (ν): *it is lawful;* μέλει: *it is a care, it concerns;* and δοκεῖ: *it seems.*

13. Indirect Speech. We have already seen **(18 § 9)** that in indirect speech ὅτι is used to introduce the dependent clause. Indirect speech can also be done by putting the dependent clause in the infinitive: "πῶς λέγουσι τὸν Χριστὸν **εἶναι** Δαυίδ υἱόν; *How do they say that Christ is David's son?"* (lit., *Christ to be David's son;* Luke 20:41).

14. The Verbs δύναμαι, γίνομαι. The verb δύναμαι (deponent) is conjugated as follows:

Present Indicative		Imperfect	
Singular	**Plural**	**Singular**	**Plural**
δύναμαι	δυνάμεθα	ἐδυνάμην	ἐδυνάμεθα
δύνασαι or δύνῃ	δύνασθε	ἐδύνω	ἐδύνασθε
δύναται	δύνανται	ἐδύνατο	ἐδύναντο

Future		Aorist Passive	
Singular	**Plural**	**Singular**	**Plural**
δυνήσομαι	δυνησόμεθα	ἠδυνήθην	ἠδυνήθημεν
δυνήσῃ	δυνήσεσθε	ἠδυνήθης	ἠδυνήθητε
δυνήσεται	δυνήσονται	ἠδυνήθη	ἠδυνήθησαν

The verb γίνομαι (deponent) is conjugated as follows:

Present Indicative		Future	
Singular	**Plural**	**Singular**	**Plural**
γίνομαι	γινόμεθα	γενήσομαι	γενησόμεθα
γίνῃ	γίνεσθε	γενήσῃ	γενήσεσθε
γίνεται	γίνονται	γενήσεται	γενήσονται

Second Aorist		Aorist Passive	
Singular	**Plural**	**Singular**	**Plural**
ἐγενόμην	ἐγενόμεθα	ἐγενήθην	ἐγενήθημεν
ἐγένου	ἐγένεσθε	ἐγενήθης	ἐγενήθητε
ἐγένετο	ἐγένοντο	ἐγενήθη	ἐγενήθησαν

Perfect		Perfect Passive	
Singular	**Plural**	**Singular**	**Plural**
γέγονα	γεγόναμεν	γεγένημαι	γεγενήμεθα
γέγονας	γεγόνατε		γεγένησθε
γέγονεν	γέγοναν or γεγόνασι(ν)		

As we have already learned (Lesson 14, Vocabulary) the verb γίνομαι means basically: *I become, to come to pass.* It also has, however, a variety of other meanings, such as *to happen, to appear, to be made,* etc., some of which defy a literal translation into English. One use of this verb, common in the first three gospels and the Acts, is the use of the second aorist middle in the third person singular preceded by καί (probably a Hebraism introduced into the *Koine* through the *Septuagint)* to mean: *and it happened that,* regularly translated in the KJV *and it came to pass.* The most common forms of this idiomatic expression are καὶ ἐγένετο.

(i) Followed by an infinitive and its subject (Mark 2:23).

(ii) Followed (not necessarily immediately) by a finite verb preceded by καὶ (Luke 24:15).

(iii) Followed by a finite verb not preceded by καὶ (Mark 1:9). Many modern versions leave καὶ ἐγένετο untranslated.

VOCABULARY

Ἀβραάμ, ὁ:	Abraham (indeclinable)
ἀδελφή, ῆς, ἡ:	sister
βούλομαι:	I am willing, I wish
δεῖ:	must, ought, it is necessary
δοκεῖ:	it is thought, it seems, it is supposed (with dative)
δύναμαι:	I can, I am able
ἐμπίπτω:	I fall in
ἔξεστι (ν):	It is lawful (with dative indicating person, something is lawful for)
ἐπάγω:	I bring upon
Ἡρῴδης, ου, ὁ	Herod
θέλω:	I am willing, I wish
Ἰάκωβος, ου, ὁ:	James
καθώς:	just as (adverb)
κελεύω:	I command
κέρδος, ους, τό:	gain

μέλει:	it is a care, it concerns, it matters (with dative)
μέλλω	I am about to (+ infinitive), I am going to (+ infinitive)
πάλιν:	again (adverb)
πλουτέω:	I become rich
Σαδδουκαῖος, ου, ὁ:	Sadducee
συνεσθίω:	I eat together (with someone)
φωνέω:	I call
ὡσεί:	as, like (adverb)
ὥστε:	so that, therefore

EXERCISES

I.

Translate into English:

1. ὁ υἱὸς τοῦ ἀνθρώπου οὐκ ἦλθε διακονηθῆναι, ἀλλὰ διακονῆσαι. 2. δύναται ὁ θεὸς ἐκ τῶν λίθων τούτων ἐγεῖραι τέκνα τῷ Ἀβραάμ. 3. ἤρξατο διδάσκειν αὐτοὺς ὅτι δεῖ τὸν υἱὸν τοῦ ἀνθρώπου πολλὰ παθεῖν. 4. ἐν δὲ τῷ ἄρξασθαί με λαλεῖν ἐπέπεσε τὸ πνεῦμα τὸ ἅγιον ἐπ᾽ αὐτούς. 5. πάντα μοι ἔξεστιν, ἀλλ᾽ οὐ πάντα οἰκοδομεῖ. 6. πρὸ τοῦ γὰρ ἐλθεῖν τινας ἀπὸ Ἰακώβου μετὰ τῶν ἐθνῶν συνήσθιεν. 7. κύριε, οὐ μέλει σοι ὅτι ἡ ἀδελφή μου μόνην με κατέλιπε διακονεῖν; 8. οὐκ ἔχετε διὰ τὸ μὴ αἰτεῖσθαι ὑμᾶς. 9. εἶπεν αὐτὸν φωνηθῆναι, καὶ φωνοῦσι τὸν τυφλόν. 10. ἔρχεται γὰρ ἡμέρα ἐν ᾗ μέλλει ὁ θεὸς κρίνειν τὸν κόσμον ἐν δικαιοσύνῃ. 11. καὶ ἐν τῷ σπείρειν αὐτὸν ἃ μὲν ἔπεσε παρὰ τὴν ὁδόν. 12. μετὰ τὸ λαλῆσαι αὐτοῖς ὁ κύριος Ἰησοῦς ἀνελήμφθη εἰς τὸν οὐρανόν. 13. καὶ συνέρχεται πάλιν ὁ ὄχλος, ὥστε μὴ δύνασθαι αὐτοὺς μηδὲ ἄρτον φαγεῖν. 14. ἔδει δὲ αὐτὸν διέρχεσθαι διὰ τῆς πόλεως ἐκείνης. 15. παρηγγείλαμεν ὑμῖν μὴ διδάσκειν ἐπὶ τῷ ὀνόματι τούτῳ, καὶ ἰδοὺ βούλεσθε ἐπαγαγεῖν ἐφ᾽ ἡμᾶς τὸ αἷμα τοῦ ἀνθρώπου τούτου. 16. καὶ ἐγένετο ὡσεὶ νεκρός, ὥστε τοὺς πολλοὺς λέγειν ὅτι ἀπέθανεν. 17. οὐ γὰρ ἔκρινά τι εἰδέναι ἐν ὑμῖν εἰ μὴ Ἰησοῦν Χριστόν. 18. ἐμοὶ γὰρ τὸ

ζῆν Χριστὸς καὶ τὸ ἀποθανεῖν κέρδος. 19. ἐν τῷ λαλεῖν τὸν Ἰησοῦν ταῦτα οἱ μαθηταὶ ἤκουον εἰς τὸ μαθεῖν αὐτοὺς τὰ μυστήρια τῆς βασιλείας. 20. ἔδει τοὺς ἁμαρτωλοὺς μετανοῆσαι τοῦ σωθῆναι αὐτοὺς πρὸ τοῦ ἐλθεῖν τὴν ἐσχάτην ἡμέραν. 21. ὁ Ἰωάννης οὖν γράψει ἃ εἶδε καὶ ἅ εἰσὶν καὶ ἃ μέλλει γενέσθαι μετὰ ταῦτα. 22. ἔγραψα ὑμῖν πρὸς τὸ ἐπιγνῶναι ὑμᾶς τὰς ἀληθεῖς ἐντολὰς τῆς καινῆς διαθήκης. 23. ἐκέλευσεν ὁ ἄρχων τοὺς πιστοὺς φεύγειν ἐκ τῆς πόλεως διὰ τὸ μισεῖσθαι αὐτοὺς ὑπὸ τῶν Φαρισαίων. 24. ὁ δὲ Ἡρῴδης ἰδὼν τὸν Ἰησοῦν ἐχάρη, ἦν γὰρ ἐξ ἱκανῶν χρὸνων θέλων ἰδεῖν αὐτόν, διὰ τὸ ἀκούειν περὶ αὐτοῦ. 25. μακάριος ὁ θεὸς πάσης παρακλήσεως, ὁ παρακαλῶν ἡμᾶς ἐπὶ πάσῃ τῇ θλίψει ἡμῶν εἰς τὸ δύνασθαι ἡμᾶς παρακαλεῖν τοὺς ἐν πάσῃ θλίψει.

II.

Translate into Greek:

Use the articular infinitive whenever possible. In translating the parts of the last four sentences in italics use (a) the genitive absolute, (b) the articular infinitive.

1. You cannot drink both the cup of the Lord and the cup of the demons. 2. Dost thou wish to become healthy? 3. It is not lawful to thee to have the wife of thy brother. 4. It is necessary that I should go (depart) to other cities and preach the gospel to them. 5. O teacher, thou canst cleanse me by means of thy power. 6. I go to prepare a place for you. 7. For there is not another name through which it is necessary that we should be saved. 8. Is it lawful to be healing on the Sabbath or not? 9. After I am raised up I will go before you to Galilee. 10. Are you able to drink the cup which I drink or to be baptized (by means of) the baptism (by means of) which I am baptized? 11. We were exhorting both Jews and Greeks to be obeying the commandments of the (one) who was born in Bethlehem. 12. Many therefore of his disciples said, Who is able to be hearing him? 13. The king was wishing to send (liquid) his slaves to call the poor and the blind ones. 14. (Those) who were eating together with us were wishing to see and read the books which thou didst write in order that they should

become members of the body of Christ. 15. Christ was wishing to cleanse those sinful men (in distinction to women) so that they should be saved, but they themselves could not believe in him. 16. Those meek brethren who were in thy city (prepositional phrase) began to command both rich and poor ones to be baptized in water and in (the) spirit. 17. The Son of Man came to find and save (those) who were wishing to be set free from the power of sin. 18. It is not lawful to thee to be persecuting us because we are loving the Lord. 19. It is necessary for me to go (depart) to the Gentiles in order to bring the light of the resurrection to (those) who wish to hear. 20. We repented because we knew that we were sinners and we were wishing to become children of God. 21. We have heard that thou hast written again to those who are in great affliction (prepositional phrase) words of consolation. 22. *While Jesus was remaining* in another place certain foolish (people) came to the disciples. 23. *After the elders baptized* the little children, we began to command the disciples not to be worshiping other gods. 24. *Because you have received* the hope of the resurrection your children have become better than the other ones. 25. *After Christ was raised* from the dead the believers began to be bearing witness to him because they were no longer fearing the hypocrites.

Lesson Thirty-Two

The Verb: The Subjunctive
Conditional Statements
The Particle ἄν

1. The Subjunctive: Its Formation. The sign of the subjunctive is a lengthened initial vowel for the ending: with **ε** lengthening to **η** and **ο** and **ου** lengthening to **ω**. The **ι** in the diphthongs **ει** and **ῃ** show up as a subscript under the **η**: **ῃ**. Thus:

Present Active		**Present Middle & Passive**	
λύω	λύωμεν	λύωμαι	λυώμεθα
λύῃς	λύητε	λύῃ	λύησθε
λύῃ	λύωσι (ν)	λύηται	λύωνται

Be careful with the forms that could be parsed more than one way. E.g.: λύω could be either , present active indicative, first singular, "*I am loosing,*" or present active subjunctive, first singular, *"I may be loosing.*" And λύῃ now could be present active subjunctive, third singular, "*He may be loosing;*" or second singular, middle or passive indicative, and middle or passive subjunctive.

2. The first aorist in the active and middle voices are formed by having **σ** inserted between the stem and the endings of the present subjunctive:

First Aorist Active		**First Aorist Middle**	
λύσω	λύσωμεν	λύσωμαι	λυσώμεθα
λύσῃς	λύσητε	λύσῃ	λύσησθε
λύσῃ	λύσωσι (ν)	λύσηται	λύσωνται

3. The second aorist active and middle is formed by adding the present endings to the 2d aorist stem:

Second Aorist Active		**Second Aorist Middle**	
βάλω	βάλωμεν	βάλωμαι	βαλώμεθα
βάλῃς	βάλητε	βάλῃ	βάλησθε
βάλῃ	βάλωσι (ν)	βάληται	βάλωνται

4. The aorist passive is formed by having **θε** inserted between the stem and the endings of the present active. Notice that the **ε** then combines with the ending and produces a circumflex accent on all forms:

Aorist Passive		**Second Aorist Passive**	
λυθῶ	λυθῶμεν	γραφῶ	γραφῶμεν
λυθῇς	λυθῆτε	γραφῇς	γραφῆτε
λυθῇ	λυθῶσι (ν)	γραφῇ	γραφῶσι (ν)

5. The second aorist subjunctive of the verb –βαίνω is:

–βῶ,	–βῶμεν
–βῇς,	–βῆτε
–βῇ	–βῶσι (ν),

of γινώσκω:

γνῶ	γνῶμεν
γνῷς	γνῶτε
γνῷ or γνοῖ	γνῶσι (ν).

Other second aorist subjunctives are built regularly upon the unaugmented aorist stem. Thus:

ἀποθνήσκω:	ἀποθάνω
ἔρχομαι:	ἔλθω
ἔχω:	σχῶ
λέγω:	εἴπω
ὁράω and βλέπω:	ἴδω

6. The present of the verb εἰμί is formed by the mere endings of the present active, as given above: ὦ, ᾖς, ᾖ, ὦμεν, ἦτε, ὦσι(ν). The subjunctive of the verb οἶδα is εἰδῶ.

7. The rules of contraction governing the contract verbs apply in this mood also: τιμῶ, τιμᾷς, etc. It has already been indicated **(20 § 5)** that the contract verbs of the **–αω** group present a possibility of confusion because of the fact that the contraction of **α** with either **ει** or **η** of the regular ending results in identical contracted endings. The possibility of confusion is intensified in the subjunctive by the fact that the contraction of **α** with either **ε** or **η** results in **α** and the contraction of **α** with **ο**, **ου** or **ω** results in **ω**. As a consequence it is impossible to distinguish the subjunctive from the indicative in the present tense. The danger of confusion is particularly strong in the "hortatory subjunctive" **(§ 14)** where the context may be less likely to offer the necessary aid.

8. We confine ourselves to the above tenses because in the NT text the subjunctive is only found, with very few exceptions, in the present and the aorist.

9. With regard to the element of time, the same rule applies in the subjunctive which governs the infinitive; i.e., the present is used to indicate a continuous or repeated action: "αὕτη δέ ἐστιν ἡ αἰώνιος ζωή, ἵνα γινώσκωσιν σὲ τὸν μόνον ἀληθινὸν θεόν: *and this is the eternal life, that they should know* (and go on knowing) *Thee, the only true God*" (John 17:3). Whenever such quality of the action is not suggested, the aorist is used: "ἵνα μὴ εἰσέλθητε εἰς πειρασμὸν: *that you may not enter into temptation*" (Matt. 26:41).

10. The Subjunctive: Its Role. While definite statements are made in the indicative, the subjunctive is used to make statements in which, in varying degrees, an element of vagueness is involved. As the Latin origin of the term *(subjungo)* indicates, the subjunctive is mainly used to introduce "subordinate" clauses, which, in one way or another, complete the statement made by the main verb of the sentence. There is, therefore, a variety of services which are rendered by this mood.

11. The Subjunctive of the "Final Clause." This is used to express purpose. In this role the verb is, as a rule, preceded by the particles ἵνα or, less frequently, ὅπως which are rendered: *in order that, so that:* " ̓ερωτῶ σε οὖν, πάτερ, ἵνα πέμψῃς αὐτὸν: *I beseech you,* *therefore, Father, that you should send him*" (Luke 16:27); "συμβούλιον ἐδίδουν κατ᾽ αὐτοῦ ὅπως αὐτὸν ἀπολέσωσιν: *They held counsel against him in order that they might destroy him*" (Mark 3:6). The negative is rendered by ἵνα . . . μή: *so that . . . not:* "ἵνα πᾶς ὁ πιστεύων εἰς αὐτὸν μὴ ἀπόληται: *so that everyone who believes in him should not perish*" (John 3:16).

12. The Subjunctive of the "Indefinite Clause." The element of indefiniteness is produced by the use of the particle ἄν (see below) or ἐάν. These particles may be rendered in English by the addition of *ever* to the proper word: *whoever, wherever,* etc. "εἰς ἣν δ᾽ ἂν εἰσέλθητε οἰκίαν: *and into whichever house you enter*" (Luke 10:5). The particle ἄν combined with ὅτε produces ὅταν: *whenever:* "καὶ ὅταν προσεύχησθε: *And whenever you are praying*" (Matt. 6:5).

13. The "Deliberative" Subjunctive. The subjunctive is also is used in questions which one may put to himself or to others either because the answer is not certain or with the intention of provoking a certain reaction on the part of the hearer: "τί οὖν ποίησωμεν: *What then should we do?*" (Luke 3:10). "τί οὖν; ἁμαρτήσωμεν ὅτι οὐκ ἐσμὲν ὑπὸ νόμον: *What then? Should we sin because we are not under law?*" (Rom. 6:15).

14. The "Hortatory" Subjunctive. The subjunctive may be used in the first person plural as an exhortation in which the speaker encourages the listener to join with him in a common effort. "ποιήσωμεν τρεῖς σκηνάς: *Let us make three booths*" (Mark 9:5).

15. The Subjunctive of the "Strong Denial." The subjunctive may be used to make a very strong denial if both negatives οὐ and μή are placed before the aorist subjunctive: "τὸν ἐρχόμενον πρός με οὐ μὴ ἐκβάλω ἔξω: *Him who comes to me I will by no means cast out*" (John 6:37). Ordinarily, the subjunctive is negated by the use of: μή.

There is also the "Subjunctive of Prohibition," but this will be dealt with in the lesson on the imperative mood.

16. Conditional Statements. A conditional statement is one in which the rise of a certain situation is made to depend on the realization of some other action or situation. Such a statement normally consists of two parts: (i) the "protasis" or "if clause," and (ii) the "apodosis," or "result clause": "if you believe, you will be saved." In the

Greek New Testament, the conditional statements can be divided into three groups:

(i) The "protasis" refers to a present or past event. The verb of the "protasis" is in the indicative preceded by εἰ: "εἰ δὲ πνεύματι ἄγεσθε, οὐκ ἐστὲ ὑπὸ νόμον: *But if you are being led according to the Spirit, you are not under (the) law*" (Gal. 5:18). Here, the clause is assumed to be true

(ii) The "protasis" refers to a future event. The verb of the "protasis" is in the subjunctive preceded by ἐάν (εἰ+ἄν): "ἐάν τις φάγῃ ἐκ τούτου τοῦ ἄρτου, ζήσει εἰς τὸν αἰῶνα: *If anyone eats of this bread, he will live forever*" (John 6:51). In groups (i) and (ii) only the "protasis" exhibits a variation in its construction; the "apodosis" is not affected. (In the NT text there is frequent deviation from the above rules.). Here the "if" clause may or may not be true.

(iii) The "protasis" refers to an event which did not materialize, and the "apodosis" states what the results might have been had the condition been fulfilled. The verbs in both sections of the statement are in a past tense of the indicative, the "protasis" preceded by εἰ and the "apodosis" preceded or followed by ἄν: "εἰ ὁ θεὸς πατὴρ ὑμῶν ἦν, ἠγαπᾶτε ἄν ἐμὲ: *If God were your father, you would be loving me*" (John 8:42).

17. The Particle ἄν. From what has been stated so far we can see that the particle ἄν (or ἐάν), used in a variety of ways, introduces into the sentence an element of generalization or uncertainty. Combined with καί it produces κἄν, normally found in a sentence with its verb in the subjunctive and meaning *if only, at least:* " ʼεὰν ἅψωμαι κἂν τῶν ἱματίων αὐτοῦ σωθήσομαι: *if only I touch his garments, I shall be saved*" (Mark 5:28).

VOCABULARY

ἀσθένεια, ας, ἡ:	weakness, illness
αὔριον:	tomorrow (adverb)
δεῦτε:	come (addressed to more that one person)
δωρεά, ᾶς, ἡ:	gift

ἐάν:	if
ἐκεῖ:	there (adverb)
ἐπαινέω:	I approve, I praise
Ἠλίας, ου, ὁ:	Elijah
κληρονομία, ας, ἡ:	inheritance
κληρονόμος, ου, ὁ:	heir
νικάω:	I overcome, I conquer
νίπτω:	I wash
ὅταν:	whenever, when, at the time that
οὔτε . . . οὔτε, μήτε . . . μήτε:	neither, nor
ὀφείλω:	I owe
πάσχα, τὸ:	Passover (indeclinable)

EXERCISES

I.

Translate into English:

1. ἐὰν πορευθῶ καὶ ἑτοιμάσω τόπον ὑμῖν, πάλιν ἔρχομαι καὶ παραλήμψομαι ὑμᾶς ἵνα ὅπου εἰμὶ ἐγὼ καὶ ὑμεῖς ἦτε. 2. ἴδωμεν εἰ ἔρχεται Ἠλίας σῶσαι αὐτόν. 3. εἰ γὰρ ἔγνωσαν, οὐκ ἂν τὸν κύριον τῆς δόξης ἐσταύρωσαν. 4. οὗτός ἐστιν ὁ κληρονόμος· δεῦτε ἀποκτείνωμεν αὐτὸν. 5. ἠρώτα αὐτὸν ἵνα τὸ δαιμόνιον ἐκβάλῃ ἐκ τῆς θυγατρὸς αὐτῆς. 6. ὅπου ἐὰν κηρυχθῇ τὸ εὐαγγέλιον τοῦτο ἐν ὅλῳ τῷ κόσμῳ, λαληθήσεται καὶ ὃ ἐποίησεν αὕτη. 7. ἐὰν μὴ στραφῆτε καὶ γένησθε ὡς τὰ παιδία, οὐ μὴ εἰσέλθητε εἰς τὴν βασιλείαν τῶν οὐρανῶν. 8. τί ποιῶμεν ἵνα ἐργαζώμεθα τὰ ἔργα τοῦ θεοῦ; 9. ποῦ θέλεις ἀπελθόντες ἑτοιμάσωμεν ἵνα φάγῃς τὸ πάσχα; 10. ἐπαινέσω ὑμᾶς ἐν τούτῳ; οὐκ ἐπαινῶ. 11. ἐὰν μὴ νίψω σε, οὐκ ἔχεις μέρος μετ᾽ ἐμοῦ. 12. ὃς ἂν ἐμὲ δέξηται, δέχεται τὸν ἀποστείλαντά με. 13. οὐκ εἶπόν σοι ὅτι ἐὰν πιστεύσῃς ὄψῃ τὴν δόξαν τοῦ θεοῦ; 14. ὁ Ἰωάννης ἦλθεν ἵνα μαρτυρήσῃ περὶ τοῦ φωτός. 15. πορευθῶμεν καὶ εἰς τὰς ἄλλας κώμας, ἵνα καὶ ἐκεῖ παρακαλέσω τοὺς πιστούς. 16. τί με δεῖ ποιεῖν ἵνα σωθῶ; 17. ὁ υἱὸς τοῦ θεοῦ ἐσταυρώθη καὶ ἀπέθανεν ἵνα πάντες ἡμεῖς ἔχωμεν ζωήν. 18. ἐν τῷ λαλεῖν τὸν

προφήτην τὰ ῥήματα ταῦτα ἦλθον οἱ ὄχλοι ὅπως ἀκούσωσι καὶ διδαχθῶσι περὶ τῆς κρίσεως τοῦ θεοῦ. 19. βούλομαι γράψαι ὑμῖν ἐπιστολὴν ἵνα γνῶτε τὰς ἐπαγγελίας τοῦ θεοῦ καὶ εἰσέλθητε ἐις τὴν κοινωνίαν τῶν πιστῶν. 20. φάγωμεν καὶ πίωμεν, αὔριον γὰρ ἀποθνήσκομεν. 21. εἰ δέ τις πνεῦμα Χριστοῦ οὐκ ἔχει, οὗτος οὐκ ἐστιν αὐτοῦ. 22. οὔτε ἐμὲ οἴδατε οὔτε τὸν πατέρα μου, εἰ γὰρ ἐμὲ ᾔδειτε, καὶ τὸν πατέρα μου ἂν ᾔδειτε. 23. εἰς μὴ ἴδωσιν οὗτοι σημεῖα, οὐ ταπεινωθήσονται ἵνα δέξωνται τὴν ἐπαγγελίαν τοῦ θεοῦ καὶ ζήσωσιν. 24. ἀγαπήσωμεν τοὺς ἀδελφοὺς ἡμῶν καθὼς ὁ Χριστὸς ἠγάπησεν ἡμᾶς. 25. ἐάν τις τὸν ἐμὸν λόγον τηρήσῃ, θάνατον οὐ μὴ θεωρήσῃ εἰς τὸν αἰῶνα.

II.

Translate into Greek:

Translate the parts of the last two sentences in italics by using (a) the articular infinitive, (b) the subjunctive.

1. If you know these (things), blessed are you if you do them. 2. Let us also go, so that we may die with him. 3. And they were bringing little children to him, in order that he might touch them. 4. God sent his only begotten Son, so that every one who believes (participle) in him might have life eternal. 5. If you were (out) of the world, the world would love you. 6. Let us come into a new life and let us be doing good works, so that the name of our Savior may be glorified in the nations. 7. And they led him in order that they might crucify him. 8. If you keep my commandments, you will abide in my life. 9. If you believed Moses, you would believe me. 10. I have spoken these (things), so that my joy may be in you. 11. I sent you that you may bear fruit and your fruit may remain. 12. Let us be loving even our enemies, so that they may be blessed. 13. If someone is not born (out) of water and spirit, he cannot enter the kingdom of God. 14. They were saying these (things) in order that they may be justified. 15. If he were a sinner, he would not be casting out demons. 16. If you will not confess your sins, you will die the eternal death. 17. If you honor Christ, you will persevere in his grace and he (himself) will raise you

up in the day of the resurrection. 18. If God sent his Son into the world that he might save sinners, let us receive from his hands the gift of life. 19. After the apostle saw (use [a] genitive absolute, [b] articular infinitive) the Lord in his glory, the wives of the rulers took gifts in order to offer them to the poor ones in his name. 20. The repenting sinners have come to the Savior in order that they should have the power of the Holy Spirit in their hearts. 21. You have both seen the Lord and have heard his words and you have come into our house in order that you should learn and know his revelation. 22. If our names have been written (periphrastic) in the book of life, the Lord will glorify us in his kingdom. 23. If the men who are in these cities (prepositional phrase) with their wives will repent and keep the commandments of the new covenant, God will have mercy (on) them. 24. When the Lord returned into the heaven, the apostles themselves and their friends went into all the cities *in order that they may preach* the promises of the hope. 25. Thou wilt not judge again thy brothers, but thou wilt proclaim the words of comfort to them, for the Lord sent thee *in order to announce* to them full salvation.

Lesson Thirty-Three

The Imperative Mood • *Prohibitions*
The Reflexive Pronoun • *The Reciprocal Pronoun*

1. The Imperative Mood. The imperative is used to give a command or to express a request. In the NT, the imperative occurs basically in the present and aorist tenses (with one occurrence of the perfect passive in Mark 4:39 πεδίμωτο). The most significant difference between the Greek and English imperative is that in Greek, the imperative can be used in the second and third persons in both numbers. Since English only has a second person imperative, we have a hard time understanding how an imperative can be in the third person–how can one give a command to someone he is not talking to?–and we don't have any way to render it accurately in our language. The closest we can come is a second person command for the hearer not to interfere with someone else. Thus: εἴ τις θέλει ὀπίσω μου ἐλθεῖν, ἀπαρνησάσθω ἑαυτὸν καὶ ἀράτω τὸν σταυρὸν αὐτοῦ καὶ ἀκολουθείτω μοι: *"If anyone wishes to come after me, let him deny himself and let him take up his cross and let him be following me"* (Matt. 16:24). Remember, this is a command for the one who wishes to come after Jesus to take up his cross and follow, not for some listener not to interfere.

2. As in the infinitive and the subjunctive, the only difference between the present and the aorist is in the kind of action pictured. The present tense is used when the order or request is pictured as a continuous or repeated action: μάνθανε: *be learning*, or *go on learning*; and the aorist tense is used if the action is thought of as simply to happen: μάθε: *learn.* Although it may not always be the smoothest English, in the exercises we will render present imperatives in the progressive form with the *-ing* participle, and aorist imperatives with the simple verb idea.

3. The imperative is conjugated as follows:

Present Active:	λῦε	λύετε
	λυέτω	λυέτωσαν
Present Middle and Passive:	λύου	λύεσθε
	λυέσθω	λυέσθωσαν
First Aorist Active:	λῦσον	λύσατε
	λυσάτω	λυσάτωσαν
First Aorist Middle:	λῦσαι	λύσασθε
	λυσάσθω	λυσάσθωσαν
First Aorist Passive:	λύθητι	λύθητε
	λυθήτω	λυθήτωσαν

4. The second aorist is formed on the aorist stem.

(i) In the active voice endings identical with those of the present active:

βάλε	βάλετε
βαλέτω	βαλέτωσαν

Always be alert to those imperative forms which look like another form. Notice in the present tense, the 2nd person plural indicative and imperative will look alike λύετε and λύεσθε. Consult a commentary for the possible interpretations of the two-fold use of πιστεύετε in John 14:1 (is it "*you believe,*" or "*believe ye*"?). Notice also that the 2nd singular of the aorist middle imperative and the aorist active infinitive, λύσαι look alike.

The following verbs (among the most common in the NT) have in the second person singular the accent on the ultima: ἐλθέ, εἰπέ). Unlike the compound verb in other moods and tenses (11, §, 6), the preposition is considered as part of the verb in the second aorist imperative, so that the accent may be placed in the preposition in the second singular: εἴσελθε.

(ii) In the middle voice endings identical with those of the present middle, the only difference consisting in that the accent drops to the ultima in the second person singular:

βαλοῦ	βάλεσθε
βαλέσθω	βαλέσθωσαν

(iii) In the passive voice endings similar to those of the first aorist passive, the difference consisting in that the **θ** (characteristic consonant of this tense) is dropped in all persons, and the **τ** in the second person singular is substituted by **θ**. Thus,

στέλλω—	στάληθι	στάλητε
	σταλήτω	σταλήτωσαν

5. The aorist active of –βαίνω is conjugated as follows:

	-βηθι or -βα	—βατε
	—βάτω	—βάτωσαν
of γινώσκω:		
	γνῶθι	γνῶτε
	γνώτω	γνώτωσαν

The aorist passive of γίνομαι (3rd person singular) is: γενηθήτω.

6. The imperative of the verb εἰμὶ is conjugated as follows:

ἴσθι	ἔστε
ἔστω	ἔστωσαν

7. The formation of the imperative of the contract verbs presents no difficulty, the rules which govern these verbs in the tenses of the indicative being applied here also. Thus,

Present Active:		**Aorist Active:**	
φίλει	φιλεῖτε	φίλησον	φιλήσατε
φιλείτω	φιλείτωσαν	φιλησάτω	φιλησάτωσαν

8. Prohibitions. A prohibition is expressed by **μή** followed by:

(i) The present imperative occurs, either (a) when the order is given to stop an action which is implied as already in the process of being done: "καὶ εἶπεν αὐτῇ, μὴ κλαῖε: *and he said to her, Do not weep* (actually: *Stop weeping*"; Luke 7:13), or (b) to forbid an action which is likely to be continuous or repeated: "μὴ οὖν βασιλευέτω ἡ ἁμαρτία ἐν τῷ θνητῷ ὑμῶν σώματι . . . *Let not sin therefore reign in your mortal body . . .*" (Rom. 6:12).

(ii) The aorist subjunctive, when there is no suggestion of an action already begun or likely to be protracted or repeated: "μὴ φονεύσῃς . . . *do not kill . . .*" (Mark 10:19).

9. The Reflexive Pronoun. The reflexive pronoun is one which refers back to the subject from an objective case position as oneself. It may be used.

(i) as *a direct object:* "ὅστις οὖν ταπεινώσει ἑαυτὸν: *therefore, whoever will humble himself*" (Matt. 18:4).

(ii) as an indirect object: " ἵνα . . . ἀγοράσωσιν ἑαυτοῖς βρώματα: in order that . . . they may buy food for themselves" (Matt. 14:15).

(iii) as an object of a preposition: "ἔλεγεν γὰρ ἐν ἑαυτῇ: for she was saying within herself." (Matt. 9:21), or

(iv) as *a possessive:* "ἄφες τοὺς νεκροὺς θάψαι τοὺς ἑαυτῶν νεκρούς: *let the dead bury their own dead*" (Matt. 8:22).

Do not confuse this use with that of the intensive pronoun, as in "God, himself, came down," or with the role of the middle voice of the verb.

10. Like the personal pronoun, the reflexive is found in three persons; in the masculine and feminine genders in all three persons and in the neuter only in the 3rd person. It is declined exactly like the personal pronoun in the 3rd person, the only differences consisting in that:

(i) In the 3rd person, **ἑ** is prefixed–ἑαυτοῦ, ἑαυτῆς: *of himself, of herself.* Sometimes in the third person singular the **ε** is omitted αὑτοῦ, etc. (Notice the difference from the personal pronoun in the rough breathing).

(ii) In the 1st person singular, **ἐμ** is prefixed–ἐμαυτοῦ, ἐμαυτῆς:–*of myself,* etc.

(iii) In the 2nd person singular, **σε** is prefixed–σεαυτοῦ, σεαυτῆς— *of thyself,* etc.

(iv) The plural in all three persons is identical, on the pattern of the 3rd person–ἑαυτῶν.

Because it is always used as an object, this pronoun has no nominative or vocative.

11. The Reciprocal Pronoun. The reciprocal pronoun conveys the meaning of two people reciprocating an action: "one another." It has no nominative or vocative and is found only in the plural; in the NT only in the masculine gender. It is as follows:

G. ἀλλήλων
D. ἀλλήλοις
A. ἀλλήλους

Sometimes the plural of the reflexive pronoun is used in the NT instead of the reciprocal. Thus: "ἀνεχόμενοι ἀλλήλων καὶ χαριζόμενοι ἑαυτοῖς: *bearing with one another; forgiving one another*" (rather than *'forgiving yourselves'*; Col. 3:13).

EXERCISES

I.

Translate into English:

Remember to use the progressive *-ing* translation for present imperatives and the simple verb form for aorist imperatives: λυέτω, *let him be loosing*; λυσάτω, *let him loose.*

1. πάτερ, ἐλήλυθεν ἡ ὥρα· δόξασόν σου τὸν υἱόν, ἵνα ὁ υἱὸς δοξάσῃ σέ. 2. ἁγιασθήτω τὸ ὄνομά σου, ἐλθέτω ἡ βασιλεία σου, γενηθήτω τὸ θέλημά σου, ὡς ἐν οὐρανῷ καὶ ἐπὶ γῆς. 3. ὁμολογεῖσθε οὖν ἀλλήλοις τὰς ἁμαρτίας καὶ προσεύχεσθε ὑπὲρ ἀλλήλων, ὅπως ἰαθῆτε. 4. μὴ κρίνετε, ἵνα μὴ κριθῆτε. 5. μὴ εἰσενέγκῃς ἡμᾶς εἰς πειρασμόν. 6. ἄλλους ἔσωσε, σωσάτω ἑαυτόν. 7. ὑπὲρ αὐτῶν ἐγὼ ἁγιάζω ἐμαυτόν, ἵνα ὦσι καὶ αὐτοὶ ἡγιασμένοι ἐν ἀληθείᾳ. 8. λάβετε φάγετε, τοῦτό ἐστι τὸ σῶμά μου. 9. σὺ περὶ σεαυτοῦ μαρτυρεῖς· ἡ μαρτυρία σου οὐκ ἔστιν ἀληθής. 10. εἰ υἱὸς εἶ τοῦ θεοῦ, εἰπὲ ἵνα οἱ λίθοι οὗτοι ἄρτοι γένωνται. 11. ὃς ἔχει ὦτα ἀκούειν ἀκουέτω. 12. κύριε, εἰ σὺ εἶ, κέλευσόν με ἐλθεῖν πρὸς

σὲ ἐπὶ τὰ ὕδατα. 13. μή μου ἅπτου, οὔπω γὰρ ἀναβέβηκα πρὸς τὸν πατέρα. 14. πίστευσον ἐπὶ τὸν κύριον Ἰησοῦν, καὶ σωθήσῃ. 15. ὁ καυχώμενος ἐν κυρίῳ καυχάσθω. 16. μαρτυρεῖτε ἑαυτοῖς ὅτι υἱοί ἐστε τῶν φονευσάντων τοὺς προφήτας. 17. μὴ θησαυρίζετε ὑμῖν θησαυροὺς ἐπὶ τῆς γῆς. 18. εἰ δὲ θέλεις εἰς τὴν ζωὴν εἰσελθεῖν, τήρει τὰς ἐντολάς. 19. ἀλλὰ ῥῦσαι ἡμᾶς ἀπὸ τοῦ πονηροῦ. 20. ποιήσατε οὖν καρπὸν ἄξιον τῆς μετανοίας. 21. μείνατε ἐν τῇ ἀγάπῃ τῇ ἐμῇ. 22. μὴ ταρασσέσθω ὑμῶν ἡ καρδία. 23. ὑμεῖς οὖν ἀκούσατε τὴν παραβολὴν τοῦ σπείραντος. 24. ὕπαγε, σεαυτὸν δεῖξον τῷ ἱερεῖ καὶ προσένεγκε τὸ δῶρόν σου κατὰ τὸν νόμον τοῦ Μωϋσέως. 25. πορεύεσθε οὖν καὶ ὅσους ἐὰν εὕρητε καλέσατε εἰς τοὺς γάμους.

II.

Translate into Greek:

Where there is no other clue in the sentence, "s." and "pl." in parenthesis are used to indicate "singular" or "plural" respectively.

1. We do not have our hope in ourselves but in the grace of the Savior. 2. Come, you who have been blessed (participle) by my Father, inherit the kingdom which has been prepared (participle) for you. 3. Do not be continually anxious about your life. 4. Close thy door and pray to thy Father. 5. Go up (pl.) into the synagogue. 6. Enter (s.) through my door. 7. Be loving your enemies, be blessing (those) who are cursing you, and be praying on behalf of (those) who are persecuting you. 8. Come unto me and thou wilt find peace. 9. Bless one another in the name of the Savior. 10. Keep thyself from the sin. 11. Preach (pl.) the gospel to the whole creation. 12. Be seeking and you will find, be knocking and (it) will be opened to you. 13. Repent and the promises of God will be fulfilled in you. 14. Have mercy (on) me, O God. 15. After you fast (art. inf.) go to the cities of the Gentiles. 16. Do not hide (s.) the rich inheritance of God's mercy from the multitudes, but reveal to them all his eternal promises. 17. Do not be sleeping, (pl.) but be working in the field of the will of God. 18. Heal thyself, as thou hast healed many others. 19. Do not be becoming rich (s.) so far as the world is concerned, but be feeding thyself by means of the grace of

thy Savior. 20. Pray to thy father who is in the heavens (prepositional phrase) and humble thyself before his face. 21. Release (pl.) the crowds and command them to go to their own houses. 22. Do not be fearing those miserable fishermen, but call thy friends to thyself. 23. Be doing as many (things) as are worthy of a believer and be dwelling in the city of the free men (in distinction to women). 24. Let all who live in this humble village be baptized in the name of Christ. 25. Be judging yourselves, not the others.

Lesson Thirty-Four

The Adverb: Comparison of the Adverb

1. The Adverb. The adverb is the part of speech which, as its name indicates, modifies a verb. Less frequently it is used to qualify an adjective or even another adverb. All adverbs are indeclinable.

2. Many adverbs which are derived from adjectives or other parts of speech are formed by adding the adverbial suffix **-ως** to the stem of the word. Thus, καλός: *good*, καλῶς: *well*, ἀληθής: *true*, ἀληθῶς: *truly*, μέγας (μεγαλ-): *great*, μεγάλως: *greatly*, οὗτος: *this*, οὕτως: *in this way*, κατά: *according to*, καθώς: *just as*. In a few cases the adjective in the neuter (accusative singular) is used as an adverb πολύ: *much, greatly*, μόνον: *only*, etc.

3. Adverbs can be classified into three main groups: those which indicate (i) *place*, (ii) *time*, and (iii) *manner*. Following is a list of the most common adverbs to be found in the NT. For convenience sake, even adverbs we have already studied are included in these lists. Browse through the list to get a good idea of the range of adverbs in the NT, and refer to this list for the exercises in this chapter. Then memorize the seven new more-frequently-used adverbs in the Vocabulary List.

Adverbs of Place: Most adverbs ending in "θεν" or "ου" are adverbs of place, others have endings in ι, σι. Nouns affected by an adverb of place are put in the genitive.

ἄνω: above.
ἄνωθεν: from above
(Also of time: from the beginning)
δεῦρο: hither (often used as an

ἔσωθεν: from within
κάτω: down, beneath, below
μακράν: far, at a distance
μακρόθεν: from afar

imperative, come hither, here)
δεῦτε: hither, come
ἐγγύς: near (Also of time, at hand)
ἐκεῖ: there
ἐκεῖθεν: thence
ἔμπροσθεν: before, in front of
ἐνθάδε: hither, in this place
ἐντεῦθεν: hence, on either side
ἔξω: outside
ἔξωθεν: without, outwardly, externally
ἐπάνω: over, on, above, upon
ἔσω: within
ὅθεν: whence, from the place of
ὄπισθεν: from behind
ὀπίσω: behind
ὅπου: where
οὗ: where, in what place
πανταχοῦ: everywhere
πέραν: on the other side, beyond
πλησίον: near
πόθεν: whence?
ποῦ: where?
ὧδε: here, hither, thus, in this place.

Adverbs of Time: Most adverbs ending in " **οτε** " are adverbs of time.

ἀεί: always, unceasingly
ἄρτι: now, just now
αὔριον: tomorrow
εἶτα: then, next
ἐπαύριον: on the next day
ἔπειτα: afterwards, thereupon
ἔτι: yet, still
εὐθέως, εὐθύς: immediately
ἕως: until
ἤδη: already
νῦν, νυνί: now
ὅτε: when
οὐδέποτε (μηδέποτε): never
οὐκέτι (μηκέτι): no longer
οὔπω (μήπω): not yet
πάλιν: again
πάντοτε: always
πολλάκις: often
πότε: when?
ποτέ: at some time (encl.)
πρωΐ: in the morning, early
πώποτε: ever, yet
σήμερον: today
τότε: then

Adverbs of Manner: Most adverbs ending in "**ως**" are adverbs of manner.

ἀληθῶς: truly
ἀμήν: amen, truly, verily
δικαίως: justly
δωρεάν: freely, in vain
εὖ: well
κακῶς: badly
ὁμοῦ: together
ὅμως: nevertheless, yet
ὄντως: really, truly
οὕτως; (οὕτω): so, thus, in this manner
παραχρῆμα: forthwith, immediately
πῶς: how, by what means

καλῶς: well

καθώς: as, even as, how, in what manner.

λάθρᾳ: secretly, privately

μᾶλλον: more, rather

ὁμοίως, likewise, similarly

σφόδρα: exceedingly

ταχέως: quickly, speedily, soon, shortly

χωρίς: separately, apart from, without

ὡς: as, like as, according as. (Also used correlatively with: οὕτως as . . . so.)

The Hebrew verbal adjective transliterated into Greek as **ἀμήν** is used in the NT mostly as an adverb, meaning "truly."

4. Comparison of the Adverb. As a rule, only the adverbs which are derived from adjectives can have comparative and superlative degrees. The comparative degree of the adjective in the neuter singular accusative serves as the comparative degree of the corresponding adverb, and the superlative degree of the adjective in the neuter singular nominative serves as the superlative of the adverb. Thus, μεγάλως—μεῖζον; πολύ—πλεῖον or πλέον.

A few adverbs not derived from adjectives; however, have a comparative and/or superlative degree. Thus, ἐγγὺς—ἐγγύτερον.

VOCABULARY

ἀμήν:	Amen
ἐγγύς:	near, (also of time, at hand)
ἑκατοντάρχης, ου, ὁ	centurion
ἔμπροσθεν:	before, in front of; (prep.) with gen.
νῦν:	now
ὅπου:	where
οὕτως:	so, thus, in this manner
ὧδε:	here, hither, in this place

EXERCISES

I.

Translate into English:

1. ἔξελθε εὐθὺς καὶ εἰσάγαγε τυφλοὺς καὶ χωλοὺς ὧδε. 2. σὺ τετήρηκας τὸν καλὸν οἶνον ἕως ἄρτι. 3. ἤδη δὲ αὐτοῦ οὐ μακρὰν ὄντος ἀπὸ τῆς οἰκίας, ἔπεμψε φίλους ὁ ἑκατοντάρχης. 4. οἴδαμεν ὅτι οὗτός ἐστιν ἀληθῶς ὁ σωτὴρ τοῦ κόσμου. 5. νῦν ἐγγύτερον ἡ σωτηρία ἢ ὅτε ἐπιστεύσαμεν. 6. ὁ ἄνωθεν ἐρχόμενος ἐπάνω πάντων ἐστίν. 7. μηκέτι ἐκ σοῦ καρπὸς γένηται εἰς τὸν αἰῶνα. 8. τίς οὖν αὐτὸν πλεῖον ἀγαπήσει; 9. πορεύου καὶ σὺ ποίει ὁμοίως. 10. δεῖ ὑμᾶς γεννηθῆναι ἄνωθεν. 11. οἱ δὲ μεῖζον ἔκραξαν λέγοντες, Κύριε, ἐλέησον ἡμᾶς. 12. ἐὰν οὖν ὁ Υἱὸς ὑμᾶς ἐλευθερώσῃ, ὄντως ἐλεύθεροι ἔσεσθε. 13. οὐ καλῶς λέγομεν ἡμεῖς ὅτι δαιμόνιον ἔχεις; 14. ἀμήν σοι λέγω, σήμερον μετ᾽ ἐμοῦ ἔσῃ ἐν τῷ παραδείσῳ. 15 ἡμεῖς μὲν δικαίως πάσχομεν, ἄξια ὧν ἐπράξαμεν, οὗτος δὲ ἀδίκως. 16. ὅταν ἔλθῃ ὁ υἱὸς τοῦ ἀνθρώπου καὶ πάντες οἱ ἄγγελοι μετ᾽ αὐτοῦ, τότε συναχθήσονται ἔμπροσθεν αὐτοῦ πάντα τὰ ἔθνη. 17. ἕως πότε μεθ᾽ ὑμῶν ἔσομαι; 18. καλῶς εἶπες ὅτι, Ἄνδρα οὐκ ἔχω. 19. οὕτως καὶ ὑμεῖς, ὅταν ἴδητε ταῦτα γινόμενα, γινώσκετε ὅτι ἐγγύς ἐστιν ἡ παρουσία τοῦ υἱοῦ τοῦ ἀνθρώπου. 20. ἐχάρην δὲ ἐν κυρίῳ μεγάλως. 21. ὁ θεὸς οὐκ ἔστιν θεὸς νεκρῶν ἀλλὰ ζώντων· πολὺ πλανᾶσθε. 22. ὁ δὲ ἐξελθὼν ἤρξατο κηρύσσειν πολλὰ, ὥστε μηκέτι τὸν Ἰησοῦν δύνασθαι φανερῶς εἰς πόλιν εἰσελθεῖν. 23. χωρὶς δὲ παραβολῆς οὐκ ἐλάλει αὐτοῖς. 24. εὖ, δοῦλε ἀγαθὲ καὶ πιστέ, εἴσελθε εἰς τὴν χαρὰν τοῦ κυρίου σου. 25. καὶ νῦν λάθρᾳ ἡμᾶς ἐκβάλλουσιν;

II.

Translate into Greek:

1. Truly thou (thyself) art the Son of God. 2. And having gone out they preached everywhere. 3. I trust in the Lord that I (myself) shall come again. 4. He is not here but has been raised. 5. Having come in the crowd from behind, she touched the garment of Jesus. 6. He

departed thence and his disciples immediately followed him. 7. Everyone who will confess me in front of (the) men, the Son of Man also will confess him in front of the angels of God. 8. Father, I am no longer worthy to be called thy son. 9. Lord, why cannot I follow thee now? 10. And Peter was following from afar. 11. All these evil (things) come out from within. 12. The Passover of the Jews was near. 13. If therefore you were raised with Christ, be seeking the (things which are) above. 14. Prepare (pl.) immediately the house for the king. 15. After the prophet healed (a: gen. absol.; b: art. inf.) a few sick (people) we came in front of him and thanked him. 16. In this manner (it) will be whenever the Son of Man comes. 17. These disciples remained near him, for they were loving him much. 18. The teachers who were in the synagogue (prepositional phrase) spoke openly to (the ones) who were there. 19. If thou wilt not follow him now, thou wilt not see him again. 20. The soldiers led Jesus into the house where the high priests and the scribes were sitting together. 21. Tomorrow the disciples will be found again inside, in the same place. 22. Because the sun has already risen, be sleeping no longer (pl.). 23. The Lord often said to his disciples that he will be with them always in order to comfort them. 24. You will return there where your Savior is. 25. Let us not yet eat the bread here.

Lesson Thirty-Five

The Numerals ● οὐδείς, μηδείς ● *Usages of* μή

1. The Numerals. A numeral can serve the following purposes:

(i) Indicate the number of persons or things: *cardinal* numerals; e.g., one, two, etc.

(ii) Indicate the respective order of such persons or things: *ordinal* numerals; e.g., first, second, etc.

(iii) Indicate frequency: *adverbial* numerals, e.g., once, twice, etc.

2. Below you will find a list of the numerals used in the NT. Browse through the list and use it for the exercises in this lesson. Then memorize the numerals in the vocabulary, which consist of all of those which occur 25 times or more.

Cardinals	**Ordinals**	**Adverbials**
1. εἷς, μία, ἕν	πρῶτος, η, ον	ἅπαξ
2. δύο	δεύτερος, α, ον	δίς
3. τρεῖς, τρία	τρίτος, η, ον	τρίς
4. τέσσαρες, τέσσαρα	τέταρτος, η, ον	τετραπλοῦς, ῆ, οῦν
5. πέντε	πέμπτος, η, ον	πεντάκις
6. ἕξ	ἕκτος, η, ον	
7. ἑπτά	ἕβδομος, η, ον	ἑπτάκις
8. ὀκτώ	ὄγδοος, η, ον	
9. ἐννέα	ἔνατος, η, ον	
10. δέκα	δέκατος, η, ον	

11. ἕνδεκα	ἑνδέκατος, η, ον	
12. δώδεκα	δωδέκατος, η, ον	
14. δεκατέσσαρες	τεσσαρεσκαιδέκατος, η, ον	
15. δεκαπέντε	πεντεκαιδέκατος, η, ον	
18. δέκα ὀκτὼ		
20. εἴκοσι		
30. τριάκοντα		
40. τεσσαράκοντα		
50. πεντήκοντα		
60. ἑξήκοντα		
70. ἑβδομήκοντα		ἑβδομηκοντάκις
80. ὀγδοήκοντα		
90. ἐνενήκοντα		
100. ἑκατὸν	ἑκατονταπλασίων, ον	
200. διακόσιοι, αι, α		
300. τριακόσιοι, αι, α		
400. τετρακόσιοι, αι, α		
500. πεντακόσιοι, αι, α		
1,000. χιλιάς, άδος, ἡ		
1,000. χίλιοι, αι, α		
2,000. δισχίλιοι, αι, α		
3,000. τρισχίλιοι, αι, α		
4,000. τετρακισχίλιοι, αι, α		
5,000. πεντακισχίλιοι, αι, α		
7,000. ἑπτακισχίλιοι, αι, α		
10,000. δέκα χιλιάδες,		

myriad, ten thousand: μύριοι, αι, α; μυριάς, άδος, ἡ
12,000. δώδεκα χιλιάδες,
double myriad, twenty thousand: δισμυριάς, άδος, ἡ

NOTE: The name for the Jewish feast being observed when the Holy Spirit empowered the disciples in Acts 2:1, πεντηκοστή, (ῆς, ἡ) means "*fiftieth*," since it is the "*fiftieth*" day after the Passover.

3. Of the cardinals, *one, three,* and *four* and from *two hundred* up are declinable and are found in all three genders. All the others are indeclinable. The cardinal *two* is indeclinable with the exception of the dative: δυσί (ν). The cardinals διακόσιοι, αι, α and upwards are declined on the pattern of the first-second declension adjectives. The cardinals χιλιάς—άδος, μυριάς—άδος are declined on the pattern of the third declension nouns.

4. The cardinals, *one*, *two, three*, and *four* are declined as follows (remember that, by the very nature of the numerals, there can be no plural for *one*, or singulars for *two*, *three*, or *four*):

	One			Two
	M.	**F.**	**N.**	**M., F. and N.**
N.	εἷς	μία	ἕν	δύο
G.	ἑνός	μιᾶς	ἑνός	δύο
D.	ἑνί	μιᾷ	ἑνί	δυσί (ν)
A.	ἕνα	μίαν	ἕν	δύο

	Three		Four	
	M. and F.	**N.**	**M. and F.**	**N.**
N.	τρεῖς	τρία	τέσσαρες	τέσσαρα
G.	τριῶν	τριῶν	τεσσάρων	τεσσάρων
D.	τρισί (ν)	τρισί (ν)	τέσσαρσι (ν)	τέσσαρσι (ν)
A.	τρεῖς	τρία	τέσσαρας	τέσσαρα

5. Both ordinals and (less frequently) cardinals may be preceded by the article: "καὶ προσελθὼν τῷ πρώτῳ εἶπεν: *and when he came to the first one he said*" (Matt. 21:28); ὁ εἷς παραλημφθήσεται . . . ἡ μία παραλημφθήσεται: *the one will be taken*" (Luke 17:34, 35).

6. ὁσάκις, ποσάκις. From the adjectives ὅσος and πόσος the corresponding adverbs ὁσάκις: *as often as,* ποσάκις: *how often* are derived.

7. οὐδείς, μηδείς and Double Negatives. The adjectives οὐδείς, οὐδεμία, οὐδέν (also: οὐθείς, οὐθέν) and μηδείς, μηδεμία, μηδέν: *no one, nothing* (used also as nouns) are declined regularly on the pattern of εἷς, etc. Οὐδείς is used with a verb in the indicative and μηδείς with a verb in all other moods. These adjectives may be found together with another negative in a sentence. For example, we find in Rom. 13:8, μηδενὶ μηδὲν ὀφείλετε . . . lit., *"owe no man nothing."* In Greek, a second negative strengthens the first negative. But in English, a second negative negates the first negative, making a positive; thus, if we translate both negatives into English, "*owe no man nothing,*" we are commanding our readers to owe every man something, the exact opposite of what Paul really said. Therefore, in translating a Greek double negative, we must make one of the negatives a positive. Either "*Owe no man anything,*" "*owe nothing to any man,*" or, perhaps, "*Do not owe any man anything.*"

8. Usages of μή. The particle μή (also μήτι, μήποτε) is used in the NT to introduce questions in which a certain degree of hesitation or doubt is implied: μήτι οὗτός ἐστιν ὁ Χριστός: *could this be the Christ?*" (John 4:29). One of these particles may also be used after verbs expressing fear or caution, in which it will usually be rendered in English by *lest:* "βλέπετε μή τις ὑμᾶς πλανήσῃ: *take care lest someone should lead you astray*" (Matt. 24:4).

9. The Negative in Direct Questions. Questions to which a negative answer is expected are also introduced by μή or μήτι: "μὴ σὺ μείζων εἶ τοῦ πατρὸς ἡμῶν Ἰακώβ: *Are you greater than our father Jacob?*" (John 4:12). We would phrase the question, "*You aren't greater than our father Jacob, are you?*" Questions to which a positive answer is expected are introduced by οὐ or οὐχί: "Οὐχ οὗτός ἐστιν ὃν ζητοῦσιν ἀποκτεῖναι: *Is not this the one whom they seek to kill?*" (John 7:25). Remember, the particular negative to be used–μή or οὐ–is determined by the expectation of the one asking the question, i.e., on the ground of the answer expected, not on the ground of that which might actually be given. The Samaritan woman in John 4:12 expected Jesus to answer "No, he was not greater than their father, Jacob."

10. εἰ μή and ἐὰν μή. μή preceded by εἰ or ἐάν means *except, unless:* ἐὰν μὴ πρῶτον τὸν ἰσχυρὸν δήσῃ: "*unless he first binds the strong man*" (Mark 3:27).

VOCABULARY

δέκα:	ten
δεύτερος, α, ον:	second
δύο:	two
δώδεκα:	twelve

εἷς, μία, ἕν:	one
ἑκατον:	one hundred
ἑπτά:	seven
ἔτος, ους, τό	year
κοιλία, ας, ἡ	womb, belly
μήν, μηνός, ὁ	month
ὅραμα, ατος, τό	vision
πέντε:	five
πρῶτος, η, ον:	first
τέσσαρες, τέσσαρα:	four
τεσσαράκοντα:	forty
τρεῖς, τρία:	three
τρίτος, η, ον:	third

EXERCISES

I.

Translate into English:

1. καὶ εἶδον, καὶ ἰδοὺ ὁ Χριστός, καὶ μετ' αὐτοῦ ἑκατὸν τεσσεράκοντα τέσσαρες χιλιάδες ἔχουσαι τὸ ὄνομα αὐτοῦ γεγραμμένον ἐπ' αὐτῶν. 2. ὃς ἐὰν οὖν λύσῃ μίαν τῶν ἐντολῶν τούτων τῶν ἐλαχίστων, ἐλάχιστος κληθήσεται ἐν τῇ βασιλείᾳ τῶν οὐρανῶν. 3. δεῖ αὐτὸν εἰς Ἱεροσόλυμα ἀπελθεῖν καὶ πολλὰ παθεῖν καὶ τῇ τρίτῃ ἡμέρᾳ ἐγερθῆναι. 4. ὁσάκις γὰρ ἐὰν ἐσθίητε τὸν ἄρτον τοῦτον καὶ τὸ ποτήριον πίνητε, τὸν θάνατον τοῦ κυρίου καταγγέλλετε. 5. μὴ Παῦλος ἐσταυρώθη ὑπὲρ ὑμῶν; 6. οὐ λέγω σοι ἕως ἑπτάκις, ἀλλὰ ἕως ἑβδομηκοντάκις ἑπτά. 7. οὐ διὰ τοῦτο πλανᾶσθε μὴ εἰδότες τὰς γραφάς; 8. τοῦτο ἤδη τρίτον ἐφανερώθη Ἰησοῦς τοῖς μαθηταῖς ἐγερθεὶς ἐκ νεκρῶν. 9. ὁρᾶτε μὴ σκανδαλίσητε ἑνὸς τῶν μικρῶν τούτων. 10. μὴ δύναται εἰς τὴν κοιλίαν τῆς μητρὸς αὐτοῦ δεύτερον εἰσελθεῖν καὶ γεννηθῆναι; 11. οὐδεὶς δύναται δυσὶ κυρίοις δουλεύειν. 12. ἀλλὰ ἐν ἐκκλησίᾳ θέλω πέντε λόγους τῷ νοΐ μου λαλῆσαι, ἵνα καὶ ἄλλους κατηχήσω, ἢ μυρίους λόγους ἐν γλώσσῃ. 13. ἐλθὼν ἐπ' αὐτὴν προσδοκῶν καρπόν, ούδένα εὗρεν. 14. οὐδεμίαν τῶν ἐντολῶν οἱ ὑπὸ τοῦ θεοῦ

εὐλογηθέντες ἠθετήκασιν. 15. χωρίς ἐμοῦ οὐ δύνασθε ποιεῖν οὐδέν. 16. οὐδένα εἶδον εἰ μὴ αὐτὸν Ἰησοῦν μόνον. 17. ὁ δὲ Πιλάτος πάλιν ἐπηρώτα αὐτὸν λέγων, Οὐκ ἀποκρίνῃ οὐδέν; ἴδου πόσα σου κατηγοροῦσιν. 18. ἐκλείσθη ὁ οὐρανὸς ἐπὶ ἔτη τρία καὶ μῆνας ἕξ. 19. ἐν οὐδενὶ αἰσχυνθήσομαι. 20. καὶ ἐγένετο ἐν μιᾷ τῶν ἡμερῶν καὶ αὐτὸς ἦν διδάσκων. 21. οὐχὶ καὶ οἱ τελῶναι τὸ αὐτὸ ποιοῦσιν; 22. μήτι δύναται τυφλὸς τυφλὸν ὁδηγεῖν; 23. μηδενὶ εἴπητε τὸ ὅραμα. 24. φοβοῦμαι μὴ ταπεινώσῃ με ὁ θεός μου. 25. καὶ οἱ δύο μάρτυρές μου κηρύξονται ἡμέρας χιλίας διακοσίας ἑξήκοντα.

II.

Translate into Greek:

1. Are not the hours of the day twelve? 2. And it was the third hour and they crucified him. 3. For none of us lives to himself, and none dies to himself. 4. And he sent the twelve in front of him. 5. This is the first and great commandment, and the second (is) like unto it. 6. Destroy this temple and in three days I shall raise it. 7. If I have all faith but have not love, I am nothing. 8. Peter was grieved because he said unto him the third time, art thou loving me? 9. Be seeking (pl.) first the kingdom of God and his righteousness. 10. No one can do these miracles which thou art doing, unless God is with him. 11. Truly I say to thee, this night thou shalt deny me three times. 12. When they came (participle) into the temple the priests saw no one there. 13. You are not more wise than our teachers, are you? 14. Be afraid (pl.) lest the enemies of our fellowship kill you. 15. No one shall we worship except the true God only. 16. Did not your children believe in Christ and were baptized in his name? 17. How often did I exhort you not to cause grief (to) the Holy Spirit? 18. And it came to pass after three days, they found him in the temple. 19. No one ever saw God except the (one) who came down (participle) from the heaven. 20. He called the twelve in front of him. 21. No one thoroughly knows the Son, except the father. 22. To no one have we ever spoken something except the truth. 23. Do not be fearing (pl.) anyone except the (one) who can (participle) kill both the body and the soul. 24. The Lord sent in front of him other seventy disciples. 25. From no one have I received anything (double negative).

Lesson Thirty-Six

*The "**μι**" Verbs:*
1. δίδωμι

1. The "μι" Verbs: General Rules. Besides the verbs which end in **ω** in the 1st person singular, present indicative active, there is a group of verbs called the "**μι**" verbs from the ending of the first person singular in the present active indicative. These verbs are not numerous, but some of them are very common in the NT, especially in a compound form.

2. The chief characteristic features of this group of verbs are the following:

(i) Their conjugation differs from that of the "**ω**" verbs only in the present and imperfect indicatives, and a few of the present and second aorist forms outside the indicative. In the indicative, most have a first aorist active with **κ** replacing **σ** as the characteristic consonant; outside the indicative, most have a second aorist active. In the other tenses, their conjugation is identical or very similar to that of the "**ω**" verbs, so that once you know the principal parts, you can reconstruct the conjugation.

(ii) In the present and imperfect of all three voices they reduplicate the stem, the reduplication consisting in the repetition of the initial consonant plus **ι**. With the exception of the verbs δίδωμι and τίθημι, the reduplication is not easily recognizable because it is effected on earlier forms of the verbs. In the reduplication of τίθημι, just as in that of the perfect of "**ω**" verbs, the hard dental is used.

(iii) They lengthen the vowel of the stem before the consonantal ending in all three persons of the singular in the present and imperfect active, and in both numbers of the other tenses in a way similar to that which takes place in the contract verbs (see **21 § 1**). Thus, δίδωμι: from the stem δο, τίθημι: from the stem θε (notice the harder dental for the reduplication), ἵστημι: from the stem στα (the original form was σίστημι and the place of **σ**, which was dropped, was taken by the rough breathing).

(iv) The endings of the present active indicative are:

–μι	–μεν
–ς	–τε
–σι	–ασι

The endings of the imperfect active indicative are:

–ν	–μεν
–ς	–τε
–	–σαν

3. The conjugation of the subjunctive is quite similar to that of a contract verb in the "**ω**" verbs. Note the circumflex accent on the ultima in the active singular and the antepenult in the plurals, reflecting the contraction.

4. In the conjugation of the "**μι**" verbs, as this is given in each of the following lessons, only the present, imperfect and aorist tenses are given fully. The remaining tenses are given only in the first person singular or in the person(s) found in the NT text, unless some tense presents a certain peculiarity, in which case that tense is given in all the persons which are found in the NT text.

5. The Verb δίδωμι. One of the most common verbs of this group is δίδωμι: *I give*. The principal parts of δίδωμι are as follows:

δίδωμι, δώσω, ἔδωκα, δέδωκα, δέδομαι, ἐδόθην

Notice the ***–κα*** ending on the first aorist form, as indicated in section 2 (i).

6. The conjugation of δίδωμι is as follows. The verb forms in **bold** type occur in the Greek NT. A genitive singular participle in **bold** type may indicate either the genitive singular or any other form outside the nominative singular.

NOTE: The imperfect in the active singular is identical in conjugation with δηλόω, a contraction taking place ἐδίδο—ον—ἐδίδουν.

ACTIVE VOICE

Indicative Mood

Present	Imperfect	1st Aorist	Perfect
δίδωμι or **διδῶ**	ἐδίδουν	**ἔδωκα**	**δ΄εδωκα**
δίδως	ἐδίδους	**ἔδωκας**	**δ΄εδωκας**
δίδωσι(ν)	**ἐδίδου**	**ἔδωκε(ν)**	**δ΄εδωκε (ν)**
δίδομεν	ἐδίδομεν	**ἐδώκαμεν**	δεδώκαμεν
δίδοτε	ἐδίδοτε	**ἐδώκατε**	δεδωκατε
διδόασι(ν) or **δίδωσιν**	**ἐδίδοσαν** or **ἐδίδουν**	**ἔδωκαν**	δεδωκαν

Subjunctive Mood

Present	2d Aorist
διδῶ	δῶ
διδῷς or διδοῖς	**δῷς**
διδῷ or διδοῖ	**δῷ** or **δοῖ** also **δώσῃ**, and **δώῃ**
διδῶμεν	**δῶμεν** or **δώσωμεν**
διδῶτε	**δῶτε**
διδῶσι(ν)	**δῶσι(ν)** or **δώσωσιν**

Imperative

Present	2nd Aorist
δίδου	**δός**
διδότω	**δότω**
δίδοτε	**δότε**
διδότωσαν	δότωσαν

Infinitive

Present	2nd Aorist
διδόναι	**δοῦναι**

Participle

	Present			2d Aorist	
M	**F**	**N**	**M**	**F**	**N**
διδούς	διδοῦσα	διδόν,	**δούς**	δοῦσα	δόν
διδόντος	διδούσης	**διδόντος**	**δόντος**	δούσης	**δόντος**

MIDDLE AND PASSIVE VOICE

Indicative Mood

Present Mid/pass	Imperfect Mid/pass	2d Aorist Middle	Aorist Passive
δίδομαι	ἐδιδόμην	ἐδόμην	ἐδόθην
δίδοσαι	ἐδίδοσο	ἔδου	ἐδόθης
δίδοται	ἐδίδοτο or ἐδίδετο	ἔδοτο or ἔδετο	**ἐδόθη**
διδόμεθα	ἐδιδόμεθα	ἐδόμεθα	ἐδόθημεν
δίδοσθε	ἐδίδοσθε	ἔδοσθε	ἐδόθητε
δίδονται	ἐδίδοντο	ἔδοντο	**ἐδόθησαν**

Subjunctive

διδῶμαι		δῶμαι	δοθῶ
διδῶ		δῶ	δοθῇς
διδῶται		δῶται	**δοθῇ**
διδώμεθα		δώμεθα	δοθῶμεν
διδῶσθε		δῶσθε	δοθῆτε
διδῶνται		δῶνται	δοθῶσι(ν)

Imperative

δίδοσο		δοῦ	δόθητι
διδόσθω		δόσθω	δοθήτω
δίδοσθε		δόσθε	δόθητε
διδόσθωσαν		δόσθωσαν	δοθήτωσαν

Infinitive

δίδοσθαι		δόσθαι	**δοθῆναι**

Participle

Present Passive

M	F	N
διδόμενος	διδομένη	**διδόμενον**
διδομένου	διδομένης	διδομένου

Aorist Middle

M	F	N
δόμενος	δομένη	δόμενον
δομένου	δομένης	δομένου

Aorist Passive

M	F	N
δοθείς	**δοθεῖσα**	δοθὲν
δοθέντος	**δοθείσης**	**δοθέντος**

7. Hints for Indentifying Forms of δίδωμι:

(i) διδ	Any voice or mood of the present tense
(ii) έδιδ	Any voice of imperfect indicative
(iii) ἔδο, ἐδω	Any voice of aorist indicative
(iv) διδ	Any mood of perfect or pluperfect

VOCABULARY:

ἀνταποδίδωμι:	I give back, I repay
ἀποδίδωμι:	I return, I render, I give back, I reward
μεταδίδωμι:	I share with someone, I impart
παραδίδωμι:	I give over, I deliver, I betray

EXERCISES

I.

Translate into English:

1. καὶ ἐσθιόντων αὐτῶν λαβὼν ἄρτον εὐλογήσας ἔκλασε καὶ ἔδωκεν αὐτοῖς. 2. ὁ πατὴρ ἡμῶν ὁ ἐν τοῖς οὐρανοῖς δώσει ἀγαθὰ

τοῖς αἰτοῦσιν αὐτόν. 3. δίδοτε καὶ δοθήσεται ὑμῖν. 4. δεδώκει δὲ ὁ παραδιδοὺς αὐτὸν σημεῖον αὐτοῖς. 5. πάντα μοι παρεδόθη ὑπὸ τοῦ πατρός μου. 6. ὁ πατήρ σου ὁ βλέπων ἐν τῷ κρυπτῷ ἀποδώσει σοι. 7. καὶ εἶπε δοθῆναι αὐτῇ φαγεῖν. 8. σοὶ δώσω τὴν ἐξουσίαν ταύτην ἅπασαν ὅτι ἐμοὶ παραδέδοται. 9. τὸ ποτήριον ὃ δέδωκέ μοι ὁ πατήρ, οὐ μὴ πίω αὐτό; 10. μακάριος ἔσῃ, ὅτι οὐκ ἔχουσιν ἀνταποδοῦναί σοι· ἀνταποδοθήσεται γάρ σοι ἐν τῇ ἀναστάσει τῶν δικαίων. 11. εἰ δέ τις λείπεται σοφίας αἰτείτω παρὰ τοῦ διδόντος θεοῦ πᾶσιν εὐθέως καὶ δοθήσεται αὐτῷ. 12. μακάριόν ἐστι μᾶλλον διδόναι ἢ λαμβάνειν. 13. ἔξεστι δοῦναι κῆνσον (tribute) Καίσαρι ἢ οὐ; δῶμεν ἢ μὴ δῶμεν; 14. ἐὰν δῶτε τὸν ἄρτον τῆς ζωῆς τοῖς πεινῶσι, καὶ αὐτοὶ μεταδώσουσιν αὐτὸν ἄλλοις. 15. ὁ ἔχων δύο χιτῶνας (shirts) μεταδότω τῷ μὴ ἔχοντι. 16. κάλεσον τοὺς ἐργάτας καὶ ἀπόδος τὸν μισθόν. 17. ἐγὼ δὲ παρέλαβον παρὰ τοῦ κυρίου, ὃ καὶ παρέδωκα ὑμῖν. 18. ἰδοὺ ἡ χεὶρ τοῦ παραδιδόντος με μετ᾽ ἐμοῦ ἐπὶ τῆς τραπέζης. 19. ὁ δὲ θεὸς δίδωσιν αὐτῷ σῶμα καθὼς ἠθέλησεν, καὶ ἑκάστῳ τῶν σπερμάτων ἴδιον σῶμα. 20. ᾧ μὲν ἔδωκε πέντε τάλαντα, ᾧ δὲ δύο, ᾧ δὲ ἕν, κατὰ τὴν ἰδίαν δύναμιν. 21. ὁ γὰρ ἄρτος τοῦ θεοῦ ἐστιν ὁ καταβαίνων ἐκ τοῦ οὐρανοῦ καὶ ζωὴν διδοὺς τῷ κόσμῳ. 22. δωρεὰν (freely) ἐλάβετε, δωρεὰν δότε. 23. βούλομαι γὰρ ἰδεῖν ὑμᾶς, ἵνα τι μεταδῶ χάρισμα ὑμῖν πνευματικόν. 24. μέλλει ὁ υἱὸς τοῦ ἀνθρώπου παραδίδοσθαι εἰς χεῖρας ἀνθρώπων, καὶ ἀποκτενοῦσιν αὐτόν. 25. ὅταν δὲ παραδῶσιν ὑμᾶς, μὴ μεριμνήσητε πῶς ἢ τί λαλήσητε· δοθήσεται γὰρ ὑμῖν ἐν ἐκείνῃ τῇ ὥρᾳ τί λαλήσητε.

II.

Translate into Greek:

1. These all (things) I shall give to thee if having fallen thou wilt worship me. 2. I made manifest thy name to the men whom thou gavest to me out of the world. 3. Ask and (it) will be given to you. 4. Give (pl.) glory to God. 5. God will render to each according to his works. 6. Brother will deliver brother to death. 7. This is my body which is being given (participle) in behalf of you. 8. The Father loves the Son and has given all (things) into (lit., in) his hand. 9. What is the wisdom

which was given (participle) to this (man)? 10. Give (pl.) to them to eat. 11. (There) was given to me all authority in heaven and upon the earth. 12. And he healed the child and gave it back to its father. 13. What do you want to give me, and I shall betray him to you. 14. And the glory which thou hast given me I gave to them. 15. The son of man will be given over to the high priests and the scribes. 16. Verily verily I say to you that one of you will betray me. 17. And he began to send (liquid) them, and he was giving them authority over unclean spirits. 18. To you (it) has been given to know the mysteries of the kingdom of the heavens, but to those (it) has not been given. 19. After he went away (participle) he cast him into prison until he should pay back (subjunctive) (that) which was being owed. 20. For I was hungered and you gave to me to eat. 21. God our Father, who loved us and gave us (participles) eternal comfort and good hope in grace, will comfort you. 22. Give (s.) to others out of the (things) which were given (participle) to thee. 23. If thy child should ask (for) bread, wilt thou give to it a stone? 24. Who is he who gave (participle) to thee this authority? 25. Many will betray each other and will hate each other.

Lesson Thirty-Seven

The "**μι**" *Verbs:*
2. ἵημι, ἀφίημι, συνίημι

1. The Verb ἵημι. This verb, "to send," is found only in compound forms in the NT, with a verbal stem of **ἑ**. The reduplication for the present and imperfect tenses is **ἱ**. The most important compound verb formed from ἵημι is ἀφίημι; and the only other significant verb is συνίημι. Both are discussed below.

2. The Verb ἀφίημι. This verb has a variety of meanings, such as: *to leave something behind, to forgive, to permit, to send away.* The context will help to determine the proper meaning in a particular text. The principal parts of ἀφίημι are:

ἀφίημι, ἀφήσω, ἀφῆκα, ἀφεῖκα, ἀφεῖμαι, ἀφέθην

3. The Conjugation of ἀφίημι. The verb forms in **bold** type occur in the Greek NT. The most unusual feature in the whole conjugation is the augmenting of the preposition itself in the imperfect act, which occurs twice in the book of Mark in the 3rd person singular form ἤφιε (ν).

ACTIVE VOICE

Indicative Mood

Present	**Imperfect**	**Future**	**1st Aorist**
ἀφίημι	ἤφιον	**ἀφήσω**	**ἀφῆκα**
ἀφεῖς	ἤφιες	**ἀφήσεις**	**ἀφῆκας** or **ἀφῆκες**
ἀφίησι(ν)	**ἤφιε(ν)**	**ἀφήσει**	**ἀφῆκε(ν)**
ἀφίεμεν or **ἀφίομεν**	ἠφίομεν	ἀφήσομεν	**ἀφήκαμεν**

ἀφίετε	ἠφίετε	ἀφήσετε	**ἀφήκατε**
ἀφίουσι(ν)	ἤφιον	**ἀφήσουσι(ν)**	**ἀφῆκαν**

Subjunctive Mood

Present	2d Aorist
ἀφιῶ	ἀφῶ
ἀφιῇς	ἀφῇς
ἀφιῇ	**ἀφῇ**
ἀφιῶμεν	**ἀφῶμεν**
ἀφιῆτε	**ἀφῆτε**
ἀφιῶσι(ν)	ἀφῶσι

Imperative Mood

Present	2d Aorist
ἀφίει	**ἄφες**
ἀφιέτω	ἀφέτω
ἀφίετε	**ἄφετε** or ἀφίετε
ἀφιέτωσαν	ἀφέτωσαν

Infinitive

ἀφιέναι	**ἀφεῖναι**

Participle

ἀφιείς, -εῖσα, έν	**ἀφείς,** -εῖσα, έν
	ἀφέντες n. m. pl.

MIDDLE OR PASSIVE

Indicative

Present Mid/Pass	Future Passive	Perfect Mid/Pass	Aorist Passive
ἀφίεμαι	**ἀφεθήσομαι**		
ἀφίεσαι			
ἀφίεται	**ἀφεθήσεται**		
ἀφιέμεθα			
ἀφίεσθε			
ἀφίενται	**ἀφεθήσονται**	**ἀφέωνται**	**ἀφέθησαν**
or **ἀφίονται** 3d pl.			

Subjunctive

Present		**Aorist Passive**	
ἀφιῶνται	3d pl.	**ἀφεθῇ**	3d sg.

4. Hints for Identifying Forms of ἀφίημι

(i) ἀφι: Any voice or mood of the present tense (ἀφεις, present active indicative, second person singular being the only exception).

(ii) ἀφησ: Future active indicative

(iii) ἀφηκ: First aorist indicative

(iv) ἠφι: Imperfect active indicative

(v) ἀφεθ: Any mood of active passive or aorist passive

(vi) Shortest forms tend to be second aorist outside the indicative.

5. The Verb συνίημι. This verb occurs only in the active voice of the present, future and aorist tenses. Its principal parts are as follows:

συνίημι, συνήσω, συνῆκα, _________, _________, ________.

All the forms appearing in the Greek NT are identical to their counterparts given in the conjugation of ἀφίημι but one: The present active indicative, 3p, uses the **–ασι**(ν) ending, which is more typical of the other **-μι** verbs: συνιᾶσι.

6. Shortest forms tend to be in the second aorist outside the indicative.

VOCABULARY

ἀφίημι: I leave something behind, I forgive, I permit, I send away

συνίημι: I understand

EXERCISES

I.

Translate into English

1. τότε ἀφίησιν αὐτὸν ὁ διάβολος, καὶ ἰδοὺ ἄγγελοι προσῆλθον καὶ διηκόνουν αὐτῷ. 2. καὶ ἄφες ἡμῖν τὰ ὀφειλήματα (debts)

ἡμῶν, ὡς καὶ ἡμεῖς ἀφήκαμεν τοῖς ὀφειλέταις (debtors) ἡμῶν. 3. οἱ δὲ εὐθέως ἀφέντες τὸ πλοῖον καὶ τὸν πατέρα αὐτῶν ἠκολούθησαν αὐτῷ. 4. ὁ δὲ Ἰησοῦς πάλιν κράξας φωνῇ μεγάλῃ ἀφῆκε τὸ πνεῦμα. 5. συνήκατε ταῦτα πάντα; 6. καὶ εἴ γυνή τις ἔχει ἄνδρα ἄπιστον, καὶ οὗτος συνευδοκεῖ (is willing) οἰκεῖν (to dwell) μετ᾽ αὐτῆς, μὴ ἀφιέτω τὸν ἄνδρα. 7. τότε διήνοιξεν (he opened) αὐτῶν τὸν νοῦν τοῦ συνιέναι τὰς γραφάς. 8. ἀφίετε εἴ τι ἔχετε κατά τινος, ἵνα καὶ ὁ πατὴρ ὑμῶν ὁ ἐν τοῖς οὐρανοῖς ἀφῇ ὑμῖν τὰ παραπτώματα (transgressions) ὑμῶν. 9. ἀφέντες τὴν ἐντολὴν τοῦ θεοῦ κρατεῖτε τὴν παράδοσιν τῶν ἀνθρώπων. 10. πᾶσα ἁμαρτία καὶ βλασφημία ἀφεθήσεται τοῖς ἀνθρώποις. 11. ἀκούσατέ μου πάντες καὶ σύνετε. 12. οὐχὶ ἀφήσει τὰ ἐνενήκοντα ἐννέα ἐπὶ τὰ ὄρη καὶ πορευθεὶς ζητεῖ τὸ πλανώμενον; 13. καὶ οὐκ ἤφιεν λαλεῖν τὰ δαιμόνια, ὅτι ᾔδεισαν αὐτόν. 14. ἐὰν ἀφῶμεν αὐτὸν οὕτως, πάντες πιστεύσουσιν εἰς αὐτόν. 15. ποσάκις ἁμαρτήσει ἐμὲ ὁ ἀδελφός μου καὶ ἀφήσω αὐτῷ; 16. καθὼς γέγραπται, οἷς οὐκ ἀνηγγέλη περὶ αὐτοῦ ὄψονται καὶ οἳ οὐκ ἀκηκόασι συνήσουσιν. 17. ἄφετε τὰ παιδία ἐλθεῖν πρός με. 18. οὗτός ἐστιν ὁ τὸν λόγον ἀκούων καὶ συνιείς. 19. ἀμὴν λέγω ὑμῖν, οὐ μὴ ἀφεθῇ ὧδε λίθος ἐπὶ λίθον. 20. οἱ υἱοὶ τῆς νυκτὸς οὐ συνιᾶσι τὴν ἐλπίδα τῆς ἀναστάσεως. 21. ἄφες ἐκεῖ τὸ δῶρόν σου ἐπὶ τὸ θυσιαστήριον (altar).

II.

Translate into Greek:

1. Man, thy sins have been forgiven to thee. 2. If we confess our sins, he is faithful and just in order that he should forgive the sins. 3. Behold we left all (things) and followed thee. 4. And they did not understand the word which he spoke to them. 5. Who can forgive sins, except God? 6. Peace I am leaving to you, my (possessive pro.) peace I give to you. 7. And he was saying to them, are you not yet understanding? 8. Then having left the multitudes he came into the house. 9. Yield up to him also thy garment. 10. I shall not leave you alone. 11. You (yoursives) are not entering, neither others are you permitting to enter. 12. In order that you should know that the Son of Man has

authority to be forgiving sins on the earth. 13. He was hoping that his brothers would understand (infinitive) that God, through His hand was giving salvation to them, but they did not understand. 14. If you will forgive the sins of certain (men), they have been forgiven. 15. You will hear and you will not understand. 16. Then they understood what he told them concerning the teaching of the Pharisees. 17. After the father understood (a. genitive absolute; b. articular infinitive) the (things) which have been written (participle) in the books of the new revelation, his children began to be giving good gifts to the poor ones according to the need of each. 18. If someone's brother will die and does not leave a child. 19. The one will be received and the other (one) will be left. 20. When their friends forsook them (genitive absolute) they were not left alone.

Lesson Thirty-Eight

*The "**μι**" Verbs:*
3. τίθημι

1. The Principal Parts of τίθημι. The verb τίθημι: *I place, I lay,* is built on the stem **θε**, and is conjugated in a way similar to that of ἵημι. The principal parts of τίθημι are as follows:

τίθημι, θήσω, ἔθηκα, τέθεικα, τέθειμαι, ἐτέθην

2. The Conjugation of τίθημι. Below is the major part of the conjugation of τίθημι. The verbs forms in **bold** type occur in the Greek NT.

A gentive singular participle in **bold** type may indicate the genitive singular or any other form outside the nominative singular.

Notice the lack of connecting vowels in the middle and passive for the present and imperfect. The endings are added directly to the **θε** stem. The aorist passive looks very strange until you realize that the **θ** you see is not part of the stem but the first part of the **θε** suffix of the aorist passive tense. Just as with the reduplication of the perfect, where they changed the **θ** of the reduplication to a **τ**, here they have changed the **θ** of the stem to the hard dental, **τ**. Thus, the aorist passive form, ἐτέθην, is a modification of the original form, ἐθέθην, and can be analyzed as: augment: **ε**; stem: **τε**; aorist passive suffix: **θ**(**ε**); active ending on a lengthened vowel: **ν**.

ACTIVE VOICE

Indicative Mood

Present	Imperfect	1st Aorist
τίθημι	ἐτίθην	**ἔθηκα**
τίθης	ἐτίθεις	**ἔθηκας**
τίθησι(ν)	**ἐτίθει**	**ἔθηκε(ν)**

τίθεμεν	ἐτίθεμεν	ἐθήκαμεν
τίθετε	ἐτίθετε	ἐθήκατε
τιθέασι(ν)	**ἐτίθεσαν**	**ἔθηκαν**
	or **ἐτίθουν**	

Subjunctive Mood

Present	2d Aorist
τιθῶ	**θῶ**
τιθῇς	θῇς
τιθῇ	**θῇ**
τιθῶμεν	**θῶμεν**
τιθῆτε	θῆτε
τιθῶσι(ν)	θῶσι(ν)

Imperative Mood

Present	2d Aorist
τίθει	θές
τιθέτω	θέτω
τίθετε	**θέτε**
τιθέτωσαν	θέτωσαν

Infinitive

Present	2d Aorist
τιθέναι	**θεῖναι**

Participle

	Present Active			Aorist Active		
	M	F	N	M	F	N
N.	**τιθείς**	τιθεῖσα	τιθέν	**θείς**	θεῖσα	θέν
G.	**τιθέντος**	τιθείσης	τιθέντος	**θέντος**	θείσης	θέντος

MIDDLE AND PASSIVE VOICE

Indicative Mood

Present Midd/Pass	Imperfect Midd/Pass	2d Aorist Middle	1st Aorist Passive
τίθεμαι	ἐτιθέμην	ἐθέμην	**ἐτέθην**
τίθεσαι	ἐτίθεσο	**ἔθου**	ἐτέθης
τίθεται	**ἐτίθετο**	**ἔθετο**	**ἐτέθη**
τιθέμεθα	ἐτιθέμεθα	ἐθέμεθα	ἐτέθημεν
τίθεσθε	ἐτίθεσθε	**ἔθεσθε**	ἐτέθητε
τίθενται	**ἐτίθεντο**	**ἔθεντο**	**ἐτέθησαν**

Subjunctive

		2d Aorist Middle	Aorist Passive
τιθῶμαι		θῶμαι	τεθῶ
τιθῇ		θῇ	τεθῇς
τιθῆται		θῆται	**τεθῇ**
τιθώμεθα		θώμεθα	τεθῶμεν
τιθῆσθε		θῆσθε	τεθῆτε
τιθῶνται		θῶνται	**τεθῶσιν**

Imperative

		2d Aorist
τίθεσο		θοῦ 2d sg.
τιθέσθω		θέσθω 3d sg.
τίθεσθε		**θέσθε** 2d pl.
τιθέσθωσαν		θέσθωσαν 3d pl.

Infinitive

τίθεσθαι		θέσθαι	**τεθῆναι**

Participle

Present Middle/Passive	Aorist Middle	Aorist Passive		
τιθέμενος, η, ον	**θέμενος**, η, ον	τεθείς	τεθεῖσα	τεθέν
τιθέμενου, ης, ου		**τεθέντος**	τεθείσης	τεθέντος

3. Hints for Identifying Forms of τίθημι:

(i) τιθ: Any voice or mood of the present tense
(ii) ἐτιθ: Any voice of the imperfect indicative
(iii) θησ: Active or middle of the future indicative
(iv) ἐθηκ: First aorist active indicative
(v) ἐτεθ: Aorist passive indicative
(vi) τεθ: Any voice or mood of the perfect tense or the aorist passive outside the indicative

(vii) Shorter forms tend to be second aorist outside the indicative.

VOCABULARY:

The most common compounds of τίθημι are given below, with those occurring more than 15 times listed in bold print. Use all of these words for the exercises, then add the bolded entries to your memorization vocabulary:

ἀποτίθημι:	(in the middle only): I put off
διατίθημι:	(in the middle only): I appoint, I make a will or covenant
ἐπιτίθημι:	(active): I put upon (middle): I put upon, I attack
μετατίθημι:	I transpose, I transfer
παρατίθημι:	I set before
περιτίθημι:	I put around
προστίθημι:	I add
τίθημι:	I place, I lay (foundation)

EXERCISES

I.

Translate into English:

1. ἐν τούτῳ ἐγνώκαμεν τὴν ἀγάπην, ὅτι ἐκεῖνος ὑπὲρ ἡμῶν τὴν ψυχὴν αὐτοῦ ἔθηκεν. 2. ἀποθώμεθα οὖν τὰ ἔργα τοῦ σκότους,

ἐνδυσώμεθα (put on) δὲ τὰ ὅπλα (armor) τοῦ φωτός. 3. καὶ ἔθεντο πάντες οἱ ἀκούσαντες ἐν τῇ καρδίᾳ αὐτῶν πάντα τὰ ῥήματα ταῦτα. 4. ἐλθὼν ἐπίθες τὴν χεῖρά σου ἐπ᾽ αὐτὴν καὶ ζήσεται. 5. πᾶς ἄνθρωπος πρῶτον τὸν καλὸν οἶνον τίθησιν. 6. τὴν ψυχήν σου ὑπὲρ ἐμοῦ θήσεις; 7. θεμέλιον (foundation) γὰρ ἄλλον οὐδεὶς δύναται θεῖναι. 8. λαβόμενοι Σίμωνά τινα Κυρηναῖον ἐρχόμενον απ᾽ ἀγροῦ ἐπέθηκαν αὐτῷ τὸν σταυρὸν φέρειν ὄπισθεν τοῦ Ἰησοῦ. 9. θέσθε ὑμεῖς εἰς τὰ ὦτα ὑμῶν τοὺς λόγους τούτους. 10. ὁ δὲ ἑνὶ ἑκάστῳ αὐτῶν τὰς χεῖρας ἐπιτιθεὶς ἐθεράπευεν αὐτούς. 11. ἀποθέμενοι τὸ ψεῦδος λαλεῖτε ἀλήθειαν ἕκαστος μετὰ τοῦ πλησίον αὐτοῦ. 12. ἐπιθέντος αὐτοῖς τοῦ Παύλου χεῖρας ἦλθε τὸ πνεῦμα τὸ ἅγιον ἐπ᾽ αὐτούς. 13. μείζονα ταύτης ἀγάπην οὐδεὶς ἔχει, ἵνα τις τὴν ψυχὴν αὐτοῦ θῇ ὑπὲρ τῶν φίλων αὐτοῦ. 14. χεῖρας ταχέως μηδενὶ ἐπιτίθει. 15. μνημεῖον καινὸν ἐν ᾧ οὔπω οὐδεὶς ἦν τεθειμένος. 16. τότε προσηνέχθησαν αὐτῷ παιδία, ἵνα τὰς χεῖρας ἐπιθῇ αὐτοῖς. 17. πρὸς τίνα δὲ τῶν ἀγγέλων εἴρηκέν ποτε, Κάθου ἐκ δεξιῶν (right side) μου, ἕως ἂν θῶ τοὺς ἐχθρούς σου ὑποπόδιον (footstool) τῶν ποδῶν σου; 18. καὶ εἶπον οἱ ἀπόστολοι τῷ κυρίῳ, Πρόσθες ἡμῖν πίστιν. 19. ὁ δὲ εἶπεν αὐτοῖς, Πηλὸν (clay) ἐπέθηκέν μου ἐπὶ τοὺς ὀφθαλμούς, καὶ ἐνιψάμην, καὶ βλέπω. 20. καὶ ἃ ἤκουσας παρ᾽ ἐμοῦ διὰ πολλῶν μαρτύρων, ταῦτα παράθου πιστοῖς ἀνθρώποις.

II.

Translate into Greek:

1. Then (those) who received (participle) his word were baptized and (there) were added that day three thousand souls. 2. Having taken the body he laid it in a new tomb. 3. And they besought him that he should put his hands upon him. 4. I marvel that thus quickly you are transposed from (him) who called (participle) you in grace into another gospel. 5. And he said, where have you laid him? 6. And these all (things) shall be added to you. 7. The good shepherd lays (down) his life on behalf of the sheep. 8. He was transferred and he was not being found for God transferred him. 9. He will lay his hands on your children and will heal them. 10. And the Lord was adding (those) who

were believing to the church. 11. After he took (participle) the five loaves he was giving them to his disciples in order that they should set them before them. 12. And the witnesses put off their garments by the feet of a certain man. 13. The priests who were in our city (prepositional phrase with possessive pronoun) were beseeching him that he should put ([a] infinitive, [b] subjunctive) his hands upon the sick ones. 14. Add (pl.) the peace of God to the grace which is in you (prepositional phrase). 15. If the Lord laid (down) his life in our behalf it is necessary that we should be loving (infinitive) him.

Lesson Thirty-Nine

*The "**μι**" Verbs:*
4. ἵστημι

1. Distinctive Features of ἵστημι. In the present active, future active and 1st aorist active voice, ἵστημι has a transitive meaning, *I cause to stand, I set, set up, I establish;* in the middle and passive and the active of the 2nd aorist and all other tenses it has an intransitive meaning: *I stand.* The same feature applies to the numerous compounds of this verb, the most common of which are listed in the vocabulary.

2. The Principlal Parts of ἵστημι are as follows:

ἵστημι, στήσω, ἔστησα or, ἔστηκα, ______, ἐστάθην
ἔστην

All breathing marks are rough, except for the aorist indicatives. Notice that, unlike the other **–μι** verbs that we have studied, ἵστημι has both 1st aorist active forms and 2nd aorist active forms in the indicative mood and outside the indicative mood. This is because of the distinction mentioned in **§ 1** concerning the transitive and intransitive forms. Notice also that, unlike the other three **–μι** verbs, the lst aorist active has the regular **σα** endings rather than the **κα** endings.

3. As with the verb οἶδα (**27 § 15**), ἔστηκα, the perfect of ἵστημι, has a present time meaning, "*I stand,*" rather than a perfect meaning, "*I have stood.*" Similarly the pluperfect, εἱστήκειν, has a past time idea: *"I stood."*

4. This verb is occasionally found in the NT text in the present indicative, participle and infinitive in the form ἱστάνω and is conjugated as a regular **ω** verb.

5. Conjugation of ἵστημι. The conjugation of the verb is as follows. The verb forms in **bold** type occur in the Greek NT. A genitive singular participle in **bold** type may indicate either the genitive singular or any other form outside the nominative singular.

ACTIVE VOICE

Indicative Mood

Present	Imperfect	1st Aorist	2nd Aorist
ἵστημι	ἵστην	ἔστησα	ἔστην
ἵστης	ἵστης	ἔστησας	ἔστης
ἵστησι(ν)	ἵστη	**ἔστησε(ν)** or **ἔστησεν**	**ἔστη**
ἵσταμεν	ἵσταμεν	ἐστήσαμεν	ἔστημεν
ἵστατε	ἵστατε	**ἐστήσατε**	ἔστητε
ἱστᾶσι(ν)	ἵστασαν	**ἔστησαν**	**ἔστησαν**

Subjunctive Mood

ἱστῶ		στήσω	στῶ
ἱστῇς		**στήσῃς**	στῇς
ἱστῇ		**στήσῃ**	στῇ
ἱστῶμεν		στήσωμεν	στῶμεν
ἱστῆτε		**στήσητε**	**στῆτε**
ἱστῶσι(ν)		στήσωσι(ν)	στῶσι(ν)

Imperative Mood

ἵστη		στῆσον	**στῆθι**
ἱστάτω		στησάτω	στήτω
ἵστατε		**στήσατε**	**στῆτε**
ἱστάτωσαν		στησάτωσαν	στήτωσαν

Infinitive

ἱστάναι or ἱστάνειν		**στῆσαι**	**στῆναι**

Participle

M. ἱστάς, **–άντος**	στήσας, –αντος	**στάς, -αντος**

F. ἱστάσα, –άσης	στήσασα, –άσης	**στᾶσα,** –άσης
N. ἱστάν, –άντος	στήσαν, –αντος	**στάν**, –αντος

MIDDLE & PASSIVE

Indicative Mood

Present Mid/Pass.	Imperfect Mid/Pass.	Aorist Passive
ἵσταμαι	ἱστάμην	**ἐστάθην**
ἵστασαι	**ἵστασο**	ἐστάθης
ἵσταται	**ἵστατο**	**ἐστάθη**
ἱστάμεθα	ἱστάμεθα	ἐστάθημεν
ἵστασθε	ἵστασθε	ἐστάθητε
ἵστανται	**ἵσταντο**	**ἐστάθησαν**

Subjunctive Mood

ἱστῶμαι		σταθῶ
ἱστῇ		
ἱστῆται		**σταθῇ** or σταθῇ 3d sg.
ἱστώμεθα		σταθῶμεν
ἱστῆσθε		**σταθῆτε**
ἱστῶνται		σταθῶσι (ν)

Imperative Mood

ἵστασο		στάθητι
ἱστάσθω		σταθήτω
ἵστασθε		**στάθητε**
ἱστάσθωσαν		σταθήτωσαν

Infinitive

ἵστασθαι		**σταθῆναι**

Participle

M. **ἱστάμενος–η**–ον		**σταθείς,** εῖσα, έν

6. Hints for Identifying Forms of ἵστημι:

(i) ἱστ: Any voice or mood of the present or any voice of the imperfect indicative.

(ii) ἑστ: Any voice of the aorist indicative

(iii) ἑστ: Any voice or mood of the perfect

(iv) στησ: Future active or middle indicative; or first aorist active outside the indicative

(v) σταθ: Aorist passive outside the indicative

(vi) Shorter forms (στ) other than (iv) and (v) tend to be second aorist outside the indicative.

VOCABULARY

The most common compounds of ἵστημι are given below, with those occurring 15 times or more listed in bold print. Use all of these words for the exercises, then add the bolded entries to your memorization vocabulary.

ἀνθίστημι	(tr., with dat.): *I set myself against*; *I withstand, I oppose*
ἀνίστημι	(tr.): *I raise up;* (intr.): *I rise*
ἀποκαθίστημι	(tr.): *I restore*
ἀφίστημι	(tr.): *I lead others to revolt*; (intr.): *I desert* (someone), *I go away* (from someone).
ἐξίστημι	(tr.): *I astonish*; (intr.): *I am astonished, I am out of my senses*
ἐφίστημι	(tr.): *I come up to, I approach*; (intr.): *I stand by, I am present*
ἵστημι	(tr.): *I cause to stand, I set, I set up, I establish; (intr.) I stand*
καθίστημι	(tr.): *I appoint*; (pass.): *I am appointed, I become*
παρίστημι	(tr.): *I place beside, I bring into someone's presence*; (intr.): *I stand beside, I am present*

EXERCISES

I.

Translate into English:

1. τί ἑστήκατε βλέποντες εἰς τὸν οὐρανόν; 2. λαβὼν παιδίον ἔστησεν αὐτὸ ἐν μέσῳ αὐτῶν. 3. εἰ ὁ Σατανᾶς ἀνέστη ἐφ' ἑαυτόν, οὐ δύναται στῆναι. 4. οὕτως γέγραπται παθεῖν τὸν Χριστὸν καὶ ἀναστῆναι ἐκ νεκρῶν τῇ τρίτῃ ἡμέρᾳ. 5. ἔγειρε καὶ στῆθι εἰς τὸ μέσον καὶ ἀναστὰς ἔστη. 6. καὶ οὐκ ἐδύναντο ἀντιστῆναι τῇ σοφίᾳ καὶ τῷ πνεύματι ᾧ ἐλάλει. 7. ἐν τῷ χρόνῳ τούτῳ ἀποκαθιστάνεις τὴν βασιλείαν τῷ Ἰσραήλ; 8. ἐπὶ ὀλίγα ἦς πιστός, ἐπὶ πολλῶν σε καταστήσω. 9. καὶ συντελέσας πάντα πειρασμὸν ὁ διάβολος ἀπέστη ἀπ' αὐτοῦ ἄχρι (until) καιροῦ. 10. ἄνδρες Νινευῖται ἀναστήσονται ἐν τῇ κρίσει μετὰ τῆς γενεᾶς ταύτης καὶ κατακρινοῦσιν αὐτήν. 11. καὶ ἐξῆλθον κρατῆσαι αὐτόν, ἔλεγον γὰρ ὅτι ἐξέστη. 12. καὶ ἄγγελος κυρίου ἐπέστη αὐτοῖς. 13. καὶ ὡς ἀναβλέποντες ἦσαν εἰς τὸν οὐρανόν, ἰδοὺ ἄνδρες δύο παρειστήκεισαν αὐτοῖς. 14. τὸ δὲ πνεῦμα ῥητῶς (explicitly) λέγει ὅτι ἐν ἐσχάτοις καιροῖς ἀποστήσονταί τινες τῆς πίστεως. 15. οἶδα ὅτι ἀναστήσεται ἐν τῇ ἀναστάσει ἐν τῇ ἐσχάτῃ ἡμέρᾳ. 16. ἐξελθὼν εὗρεν ἄλλους ἑστῶτας καὶ λέγει αὐτοῖς, Τί ὧδε ἑστήκατε ὅλην τὴν ἡμέραν ἀργοί (idle); 17. προσεῖχον (give attention) δὲ αὐτῷ διὰ τὸ ἱκανῷ χρόνῳ ταῖς μαγείαις ἐξεστακέναι αὐτούς. 18. ἀνάστηθι καὶ εἴσελθε εἰς τὴν πόλιν. 19. ἔγειρε ὁ καθεύδων, καὶ ἀνάστα ἐκ τῶν νεκρῶν. 20. ὥσπερ (just as) γὰρ παρεστήσατε τὰ μέλη ὑμῶν δοῦλα τῇ ἀνομίᾳ (lawlessness), οὕτως νῦν παραστήσατε τὰ μέλη ὑμῶν δοῦλα τῇ δικαιοσύνῃ. 21. εἰ Μωϋσέως καὶ τῶν προφητῶν οὐκ ἀκούουσιν, οὐδ' ἐάν τις ἐκ νεκρῶν ἀναστῇ πεισθήσονται. 22. καί τινες τῶν παρεστώτων ἀκούσαντες ἔλεγον, Ἴδε Ἠλίαν φωνεῖ. 23. ἤρξατο πάλιν λέγειν τοῖς παρεστῶσιν ὅτι, Οὗτος ἐξ αὐτῶν ἐστιν. 24. ἰδού, μακάριοί εἰσιν ἐκεῖνοι οἱ ἄνδρες οἱ ἑστῶτες ἐν τῷ ἱερῷ καὶ διδάσκοντες τὸν λαόν. 25. Τίς ἐστιν ὁ πιστὸς δοῦλος καὶ φρόνιμος ὃν κατέστησεν ὁ κύριος ἐπὶ τῆς οἰκετείας (household) αὐτοῦ τοῦ δοῦναι ἄρτον αὐτοῖς ἐν καιρῷ.

II.

Translate into English:

1. He stood in their midst and said to them, Peace to you. 2. The man having stood, Jesus commanded that he should be led (infinitive) to him. 3. And having risen he was baptized. 4. This Jesus, God raised up, of whom we all are witnesses. 5. And all the multitudes were amazed and were saying, "Is not this the Son of David?" 6. Man, who appointed me a judge upon (over)? 7. For this night there stood by me an angel of God whom I worship. 8. Oppose the devil and he himself will go away from you. 9. Go away from me, all the workers of injustice. 10. Having risen go down (s.) with them. 11. Elijah comes and he will restore all (things). 12. And, behold, three men came up to the house where we were. 13. Let every believer go away from injustice. 14. (There) are certain of (those) standing (present part.) here who will see the kingdom of God in its whole glory. 15. Two men stood by them (fem.). 16. The prophet said to the priests, "Rise and command all your slaves to rise."

Lesson Forty

*The "**μι**" Verbs:*

5. δείκνυμι, ἀπόλλυμι, φημί

The Optative Mood

1. δείκνυμι. The verb δείκνυμι: *I show,* which we have already found in its "**ω**" form (Lesson 8), instead of the normal reduplication in the present and imperfect, has **νυ** inserted between the stem **δεικ** and the ending in those two tenses. δείκνυμι always occurs in the active voice.

2. The present indicative is conjugated as follows:

δείκνυμι	δείκνυμεν
δείκνυς	δείκνυτε
δείκνυσι(ν)	δεικνύασι(ν)

The present in the other moods is formed by adding the proper endings of the "**ω**" verb to the stem δεικνύ–. The other tenses are formed by adding the proper endings of the "**ω**" verb to the stem **δεικ-**.

The following forms occur in the Greek NT. Three are from the **(ω)** group (see **lesson 8).** This verb happens to use both **ω** and **μι** endings.

δεικνύεις pres. act. ind. 2d sg. of **(ω)** group
δείξω fut. act. ind. (or aor. act. subj.) 1st sg.
δείξει fut. act. ind. 3d sg.
ἔδειξα aor. act. ind. 1st sg.
ἔδειξεν aor. act. ind. 3d sg.
δείξω aor. act. subj. 1st sg.
δεῖξον aor.act. imper. 2d sg.
δειξάτω aor. act. imper. 3d sg.
δείξατε aor. act. imper. 2d pl.

δεικνύντος gen. masc. sg. pres. act. part.
δεικνύοντος gen. masc. sg. pres. act. part. of (**ω**) group
δειχθέντα acc. mas. sg. aor. pass. part.
δεικνύειν pres. act. inf. of (**ω**) group
δεῖξαι aor. act. inf.

3. Hints for Identifying Forms of δείκνυμι:

(i) δεικν: Any mood of the present active tense.
(ii) ἐδειξ: Aorist active indicative
(iii) δειξ: Future active indicative or any aorist active outside the indicative.

4. ἀπόλλυμι. The verb(act.): I destroy, I loose; (pass.): I perish, I am lost is found in the NT in the following tenses: The principal parts of ἀπόλλυμι are as follows:

ἀπόλλυμι, ἀπολέσω, ἀπώλεσα, ἀπολώλεκα or (ἀπόλωλα).

ACTIVE VOICE

Indicative Mood

Present:	**Future:**	**Aorist:**
ἀπόλλυμι	ἀπολέσω or **ἀπολῶ** (1st sg.)	**ἀπώλεσα** (1st sg.)
ἀπολλύει (3d sg.)	**ἀπολέσει** (3d sg.)	**ἀπώλεσεν** (3d sg.)

Subjunctive Mood

ἀπολέσω (1st sg.)
ἀπολέσῃ (2d sg.)

ἀπολέσωμεν (1st pl.)
ἀπολέσητε (2d pl.)
ἀπολέσωσιν (3d pl.)

Imperative Mood

ἀπόλλυε (2d sg.)

Infinitive

Present:	Future:	Aorist:
		ἀπολέσαι

Participle

Aorist:	2nd Perfect:
ἀπολέσας (nom. masc. sg.)	**ἀπολωλώς** (nom. masc. sg.)
ἀπολέσασα (nom. fem. sg.)	**ἀπολωλός** (acc. neut. sg.)
	ἀπολωλότα (acc. neut. pl.)

MIDDLE & PASSIVE

Indicative

Present:	Imperfect	Future Middle	2nd Aorist Middle
ἀπόλλυμαι (1st sg.)		ἀπολοῦμαι	ἀπωλόμην
ἀπόλλυται (3d sg.)		**ἀπολεῖται** (3d sg.)	**ἀπώλετο** (3d sg.)
ἀπολλύμεθα (1st pl.)		**ἀπολεῖσθε** (2d pl.)	
ἀπόλλυνται (3d pl.)	**ἀπώλλυντο** (3d pl.)	**ἀπολοῦνται** (3d pl.)	**ἀπώλοντο** (3d pl.)

Subjunctive Aorist

ἀπόληται (3d sg.)
ἀπόλησθε (2d pl.)
ἀπόλωνται (3d pl.)

Infinitive

2nd Aorist middle
ἀπολέσθαι

Participle

Present:	2nd Aorist
ἀπολλύμενος	ἀπολόμενος
	ἀπολομένου (gen. masc. sg.)

ἀπολλυμένου gen. neu. sg.
ἀπολλυμένην acc. fem. sg.
ἀπολλύμενοι nom. mas. pl.
ἀπολλυμένοις dat. mas. pl.

5. Hints for Identifying Forms of ἀπόλλυμι

(i) ἀπόλλ: Any voice or mood of the present tense
(ii) ἀπόλ: Any future active or middle indicative, or aorist active or middle outside the indicative.
(iii) ἀπωλλ: Imperfect middle passive indicative
(iv) ἀπωλ: Aorist active or middle indicative
(v) ἀπολωλ: Perfect active participle

6. φημί. The verb φημί: *I say* is found in the NT only in the 1st and 3rd singular and 3rd plural persons of the present indicative: φημί, φησί (ν), φασί (ν) and in the 3rd singular person of the imperfect indicative: ἔφη. For the other tenses the corresponding tenses of λέγω are used. In the present this verb is enclitic.

7. The Optative Mood. The optative mood is much less frequently used in the NT than the other moods. As its name (from the Latin "opto": *I wish*) suggests, this mood is used to express a wish. It is also used to introduce indirect questions.

8. The optative is found in the NT in the present and 1st and 2nd aorist tenses. The distinguishing vowels (diphthongs) of the mood are:

(i) **οι** for the present in all voices and for the 2nd aorist active and middle.
(ii) **αι** for the 1st aorist active and middle tenses.
(iii) **ει** for the aorist passive tense.

The "**οι**" tenses:

Active		**Middle & Passive**	**Middle**
Present	**2nd Aorist**	**Present**	**2nd Aorist**
λύ – οιμι	λάβ – οιμι	λυ – οίμην	γεν – οίμην
λύ – οις	λάβ – οις	λύ – οιο	γέν – οιο
λύ – οι	λάβ – οι	λύ – οιτο	γέν – οιτο
λύ – οιμεν	λάβ – οιμεν	λυ – οίμεθα	γεν – οίμεθα
λύ – οιτε	λάβ – οιτε	λύ – οισθε	γέν – οισθε
λύ – οιεν	λάβ – οιεν	λύ – οιντο	γέν – οιντο

The "**αι**" tenses: The "**ει**" tenses:

Aorist Active	Aorist Middle	Aorist Passive
λύ – σαιμι	λυ – σαίμην	λυ – θείην
λύ – σαις	λύ – σαιο	λυ – θείης
λύ – σαι	λύ – σαιτο	λυ – θείη
λύ – σαιμεν	λυ – σαίμεθα	λυ – θείημεν
λύ – σαιτε	λύ – σαισθε	λυ – θείητε
λύ – σαιεν	λύ – σαιντο	λυ – θείησαν

9. The most important exceptions to the above rules are εἴη, present of εἰμί (found only in the 3rd person singular) and δῴη, 2nd aorist active 3rd person singular of δίδωμι.

10. The optative is negated through the use of μή. The most common negative optative found in the NT is μὴ γένοιτο: *may it not happen* (rendered in the KJV as *God forbid*).

VOCABULARY

ἀπόλλυμι:	(act.): I destroy, I lose; (pass.): I am lost
ἄρα:	therefore, then
ἀργύριον, ου, τό:	silver, money
δείκνυμι or δεικνύω:	I show
φημί:	I say

EXERCISES

I.

Translate into English:

1. καὶ δείκνυσιν αὐτῷ πάσας τὰς βασιλείας τοῦ κόσμου. 2. καὶ μείζονα τούτων δείξει αὐτῷ ἔργα. 3. καθὼς φασίν τινες ἡμᾶς λέγειν. 4. πάντες οἱ λαβόντες μάχαιραν ἐν μαχαίρῃ ἀπολοῦνται. 5. τὸ ἀργύριόν σου σὺν σοὶ εἴη εἰς ἀπώλειαν (destruction). 6. καὶ μετὰ βραχὺ (short time) ἕτερος ἰδὼν αὐτὸν ἔφη, Καὶ σὺ ἐξ αὐτῶν

εἶ. 7. ἔπεσα προσκυνῆσαι ἔμπροσθεν τῶν ποδῶν τοῦ ἀγγέλου τοῦ δεικνύοντός μοι ταῦτα. 8. κύριε, δεῖξον ἡμῖν τὸν πατέρα καὶ ἀρκεῖ (it is sufficient) ἡμῖν. 9. συγχάρητέ (συν χαίρω) μοι, ὅτι εὗρον τὸ πρόβατόν μου τὸ ἀπολωλός. 10. τοῦτο εἰπὼν ἔδειξεν τὰς χεῖρας καὶ τὴν πλευρὰν (side) αὐτοῖς. 11. ὁ θεὸς τῆς εἰρήνης ἁγιάσαι ὑμᾶς καὶ ὑμῶν τὸ πνεῦμα ἀμέμπτως (blamelessly) ἐν τῇ παρουσίᾳ τοῦ κυρίου ἡμῶν Ἰησοῦ Χριστοῦ τηρηθείη. 12. ἀπολῶ τὴν σοφίαν τῶν σοφῶν. 13. ὁ εὑρὼν τὴν ψυχὴν αὐτοῦ ἀπολέσει αὐτήν. 14. καὶ ἦλθεν ὁ κατακλυσμὸς (flood) καὶ ἀπώλεσεν πάντας. 15. ὁ πατὴρ τῆς δόξης δῴη ὑμῖν πνεῦμα σοφίας καὶ ἀποκαλύψεως. 16. ἄρα καὶ οἱ κοιμηθέντες ἐν Χριστῷ ἀπώλοντο. 17. τὸν υἱὸν τὸν μονογενῆ ἔδωκε, ἵνα πᾶς ὁ πιστεύων εἰς αὐτὸν μὴ ἀπόληται. 18. ἀπέρχεσθε πρός τὰ πρόβατα τὰ ἀπολωλότα τοῦ οἴκου Ἰσραήλ. 19. ἔφη αὐτῷ ὁ κύριος αὐτοῦ, Εὖ, δοῦλε ἀγαθὲ καὶ πιστέ, ἐπὶ ὀλίγα ἦς πιστός, ἐπὶ πολλῶν σε καταστήσω, εἴσελθε εἰς τὴν χαρὰν τοῦ κυρίου σου. 20. ὁ λόγος τοῦ σταυροῦ τοῖς ἀπολλυμένοις μωρία ἐστίν.

II.

Translate into Greek:

1. Lord, save, we are being lost. 2. Show me thy faith, and I shall show to thee my faith out of the works. 3. The Son of Man came to seek and save (that) which has been lost (participle). 4. He does not want that some should be lost (infinitive). 5. Jesus began to show to his disciples that he must go away to Jerusalem. 6. The high priests and the scribes heard and were seeking how they might destroy him. 7. Many good works I showed to you. 8. This is the will of (him) who sent me that I should not lose (that) which he has given me. 9. If you do not repent, you all likewise will be lost. 10. And he showed to me a river of life. 11. Do not be destroying (s) him in behalf of whom Christ died. 12. Didst thou come to destroy us? 13. Depart and show thyself to the priest. 14. What therefore? Shall we sin, because we are not under law, but under grace? God forbid (may it never happen)! 15. Verily I say to you, he will by no means lose his reward.

Summary of Morphology

The Noun

	First Declension				Second Declension	
Singular						
N. ἐκκλησία	γλῶσσα	γραφή	τελώνης	νεανίας	λόγος	δῶρον
G. ἐκκλησίας	γλώσσης	γραφῆς	τελώνου	νεανίου	λόγου	δώρου
D. ἐκκλησίᾳ	γλώσσῃ	γραφῇ	τελώνῃ	νεανίᾳ	λόγῳ	δώρῳ
A. ἐκκλησίαν	γλῶσσαν	γραφήν	τελώνην	νεανίαν	λόγον	δῶρον
V. ἐκκλησία	γλῶσσα	γραφή	τελῶνα	νεανία	λόγε	δῶρον
Plural						
N. ἐκκλησίαι	γλῶσσαι	γραφαί	τελῶναι	νεανίαι	λόγοι	δῶρα
G. ἐκκλησιῶν	γλωσσῶν	γραφῶν	τελωνῶν	νεανιῶν	λόγων	δώρων
D. ἐκκλησίαις	γλώσσαις	γραφαῖς	τελώναις	νεανίαις	λόγοις	δώροις
A. ἐκκλησίας	γλώσσας	γραφάς	τελώνας	νεανίας	λόγους	δῶρα
V. ἐκκλησίαι	γλῶσσαι	γραφαί	τελῶναι	νεανίαι	λόγοι	δῶρα

Third Declension

Singular						
N. φύλαξ	ἱερεύς	πόλις	ἄρχων	ἔθνος	αἷμα	πατήρ
G. φύλακος	ἱερέως	πόλεως	ἄρχοντος	ἔθνους	αἵματος	πατρός
D. φύλακι	ἱερεῖ	πόλει	ἄρχοντι	ἔθνει	αἵματι	πατρί
A. φύλακα	ἱερέα	πόλιν	ἄρχοντα	ἔθνος	αἷμα	πατέρα
V. φύλαξ	ἱερεῦ	πόλι	ἄρχων	ἔθνος	αἷμα	πάτερ
Plural						
N. φύλακες	ἱερεῖς	πόλεις	ἄρχοντες	ἔθνη	αἵματα	πατέρες
G. φυλάκων	ἱερέων	πόλεων	ἀρχόντων	ἐθνῶν	αἱμάτων	πατέρων
D. φύλαξι(ν)	ἱερεῦσι(ν)	πόλεσι(ν)	ἄρχουσι(ν)	ἔθνεσι(ν)	αἵμασι(ν)	πατράσι(ν)
A. φύλακας	ἱερεῖς	πόλεις	ἄρχοντας	ἔθνη	αἵματα	πατέρας
V. φύλακες	ἱερεῖς	πόλεις	ἄρχοντες	ἔθνη	αἵματα	πατέρες

The Adjective

First-Second Declension Adjectives

Singular

M.	F.	N.
N. ἅγιος,	–α,	–ον
G. ἁγίου,	–ας,	–ου
D. ἁγίῳ,	–ᾳ,	–ῳ
A. ἅγιον,	–αν,	–ον
V. ἅγιε,	–α,	–ον

Plural

M.	F.	N.
N. ἅγιοι,	–αι,	–α
G. ἁγίων,	–ων,	–ων
D. ἁγίοις,	–αις,	–οις
A. ἁγίους,	–ας,	–α
V. ἅγιοι,	–αι,	–α

M.	F.	N.
μικρός,	–ά,	–όν
μικροῦ,	–ᾶς,	–οῦ
μικρῷ,	–ᾷ,	–ῷ
μικρόν,	–άν,	–όν
μικρέ,	–ά,	–όν
μικροί,	–αί,	–ά
μικρῶν,	–ῶν,	–ῶν
μικροῖς,	–αῖς,	–οῖς
μικρούς,	–άς,	–ά
μικροί,	–αί,–	–ά

M.	F.	N.
σοφός,	–ή,	–όν
σοφοῦ,	–ῆς,	–οῦ
σοφῷ,	–ῇ,	–ῷ
σοφόν,	–ήν,	–όν
σοφέ,	–ή,	–όν
σοφοί,	–αί,	–ά
σοφῶν,	–ῶν,	–ῶν
σοφοῖς,	–αῖς,	–οῖς
σοφούς,	–άς,	–ά
σοφοί,	–αί,	–ά

M. & F.	N.
αἰώνιος,	–ον
αἰωνίου,	–ου
αἰωνίῳ,	–ῳ
αἰώνιον,	–ον
αἰώνιε,	–ον
αἰώνιοι,	–α
αἰωνίων,	–ων
αἰωνίοις,	–οις
αἰωνίους,	–α
αἰώνιοι,	–α

Third Declension Adjectives

Singular

M.& F.	N.
N. ἀληθής,	–ές
G. ἀληθοῦς,	–οῦς
D. ἀληθεῖ,	–εῖ
A. ἀληθῆ,	–ές
V. ἀληθές,	–ές

Plural

M.& F.	N.
N. ἀληθεῖς,	–ῆ
G. ἀληθῶν,	–ῶν
D. ἀληθέσι(ν),	–έσι(ν)
A. ἀληθεῖς,	–ῆ
V. ἀληθεῖς,	–ῆ

M.	F.	N.
πολύς,	πολλή,	πολύ
πολλοῦ,	πολλῆς,	πολλοῦ
πολλῷ,	πολλῇ,	πολλῷ
πολύν,	πολλήν,	πολύ
πολύς,	πολλή,	πολύ
πολλοί,	πολλαί,	πολλά
πολλῶν,	πολλῶν,	πολλῶν
πολλοῖς,	πολλαῖς,	πολλοῖς
πολλούς,	πολλάς,	πολλά
πολλοί,	πολλαί,	πολλά

M.	F.	N.
πᾶς,	πᾶσα,	πᾶν
πανδός,	πάσης,	παντός
παντί,	πάσῃ,	παντί
πάντα,	πᾶσαν,	πᾶν
πᾶς,	πᾶσα,	πᾶν
πάντες,	πᾶσαι,	πάντα
πάντων,	πασῶν,	πάντων
πᾶσι(ν),	πάσαις,	πᾶσι(ν)
πάντας,	πάσας,	πάντα
πάντες,	πᾶσαι,	πάντα

The Pronoun

	Personal					Demonstrative					
Singular		**M.**	**F.**	**N.**	**M.**	**F.**	**N.**	**M.**	**F.**	**N.**
N. ἐγώ	σύ	αὐτός,	–ή,	–ό	οὗτος	αὕτη	τοῦτο	ἐκεῖνος,	–η,	–ο
G. ἐμοῦ, μου	σοῦ	αὐτοῦ,	–ῆς,	–οῦ	τούτου	ταύτης	τούτου	ἐκείνου,	–ης,	–ου
D. ἐμοί, μοι	σοί	αὐτῷ,	–ῇ,	–ῷ	τούτῳ	ταύτῃ	τούτῳ	ἐκείνῳ,	–ῃ,	–ῳ
A. ἐμέ, με	σέ	αὐτόν,	–ήν,	–ό	τοῦτον	ταύτην	τοῦτο	ἐκεῖνον,	–ην,	–ο
Plural		**M.**	**F.**	**N.**	**M.**	**F.**	**N.**	**M.**	**F.**	**N.**
N. ἡμεῖς	ὑμεῖς	αὐτοί,	–αί,	–ά	οὗτοι	αὗται	ταῦτα	ἐκεῖνοι,	–αι,	–α
G. ἡμῶν	ὑμῶν	αὐτῶν,	–ῶν,	–ῶν	τούτων	τούτων	τούτων	ἐκείνων,	–ων,	–ων
D. ἡμῖν	ὑμῖν	αὐτοῖς,	–αῖς,	οῖς	τούτοις	ταύταις	τούτοις	ἐκείνοις,	–αις,	–οις
A. ἡμᾶς	ὑμᾶς	αὐτούς,	–άς,	–ά	τούτους	ταύτας	ταῦτα	ἐκείνους,	–ας,	–α

Relative			Interrogative		Indefinite		Relative – –Indefinite		
Singular									
M.,	**F.,**	**N.**	**M., & F., N.**		**M., & F., N.**		**M.**	**F.**	**N.**
N. ὅς	ἥ	ὅ	τίς	τί	τις	τι	ὅστις	ἥτις	ὅ, τι
G. οὗ	ἧς	οὗ	τίνος	τίνος	τινος	τινος			ὅτου
D. ᾧ	ᾗ	ᾧ	τίνι	τίνι	τινι	τινι			
A. ὅν	ἥν	ὅ	τίνα	τί	τινα	τι			
Plural									
M,	**F.**	**N.**	**M. & F. N.**		**M. & F., N.**		**M.**	**F.**	**N.**
N. οἵ	αἵ	ἅ	τίνες	τίνα	τινες	τινα	οἵτινες	αἵτινες	ἅτινα
G. ὧν	ὧν	ὧν	τίνων	τίνων	τινων	τινων			
D. οἷς	αἷς	οἷς	τίσι (ν)	τίσι (ν)	τισι (ν)	τισι (ν)			
A. οὕς	ἅς	ἅ	τίνας	τίνα	τινας	τινα			

The Pronoun

	Reflexive			Reciprocal
Singular				
G. ἐμαυτοῦ	σεαυτοῦ	ἑαυτοῦ		ἀλλήλων
D. ἐμαυτῷ	σεαυτῷ	ἑαυτῷ		ἀλλήλοις
A. ἐμαυτόν	σεαυτόν	ἑαυτόν		ἀλλήλους
Plural				
G. ἑαυτῶν	ἑαυτῶν	ἑαυτῶν		
D. ἑαυτοῖς	ἑαυταῖς	ἑαυτοῖς		
A. ἑαυτούς	ἑαυτάς	ἑαυτά		

The Article

	M.	F.	N.
N.	ὁ	ἡ	τό
G.	τοῦ	τῆς	τοῦ
D.	τῷ	τῇ	τῷ
A.	τόν	τήν	τό
N.	οἱ	αἱ	τά
G.	τῶν	τῶν	τῶν
D.	τοῖς	ταῖς	τοῖς
A.	τούς	τάς	τά

The Verb

ACTIVE VOICE

Indicative Mood

Present	Imperfect	Future	Aorist	Perfect	Pluperfect
λύω	ἔλυον	λύσω	ἔλυσα	λέλυκα	(ἐ) λελύκειν
λύεις	ἔλυες	λύσεις	ἔλυσας	λέλυκας	(ἐ) λελύκεις
λύει	ἔλυε (ν)	λύσει	ἔλυσε (ν)	λέλυκε (ν)	(ἐ) λελύκει
λύομεν	ἐλύομεν	λύσομεν	ἐλύσαμεν	λελύκαμεν	(ἐ) λελύκειμεν
λύετε	ἐλύετε	λύσετε	ἐλύσατε	λελύκατε	(ἐ) λελύκειτε
λύουσι(ν)	ἔλυον	λύσουσι(ν)	ἔλυσαν	λελύκασι(ν)	(ἐ) λελύκεισαν

Subjunctive

Present	1st Aorist	2d Aorist*	Perfect
λύω	λύσω	λίπω*	λελύκω
λύῃς	λύσῃς	λίπῃς	λελύκῃς
λύῃ	λύσῃ	λίπῃ	λελύκῃ
λύωμεν	λύσωμεν	λίπωμεν	λελύκωμεν
λύητε	λύσητε	λίπητε	λελύκητε
λύωσι(ν)	λύσωσι(ν)	λίπωσι(ν)	λελύκωσι(ν)

Imperative

Present	1st Aorist	2d Aorist*	
λῦε	λῦσον	λίπε*	
λυέτω	λυσάτω	λιπέτω	
λύετε	λύσατε	λίπετε	
λυέτωσαν	λυσάτωσαν	λιπόντωω or	
λυέοντων	λυσάντων	λιπόντων	λιπέτωσαν

* There are no 2nd aorist examples of λύω in the New Testament; therefore, λείπω has been used to demonstrate the paradigms.

The Verb

ACTIVE VOICE

Indicative Mood

(continued from p. 263)

Infinitive

Present:	Future:	Aorist:	Perfect:
λύειν	λύσειν	λῦσαι	λελυκέναι

Participle

Present:	Future:	Aorist:	Perfect:
λύων, λύουσα, λῦον	λύσων, λύσουσα, λῦσον	λύσας, λύσασα, λῦσαν	λελυκώς, λελυκυῖα, λελυκός

MIDDLE AND PASSIVE VOICE

Indicative

Present Mid/Pass.	Imperfect Mid/Pass.	Future Middle	Future Passive	Aorist Middle	Aorist Passive	Perfect Mid/Pass.	Pluperfect Mid/Pass.
λύομαι	ἐλυόμην	λύσομαι	λυθήσομαι	ἐλυσάμην	ἐλύθην	λέλυμαι	(ἐ) λελύμην
λύῃ	ἐλύου	λύσῃ	λυθήσῃ	ἐλύσω	ἐλύθης	λέλυσαι	(ἐ) λέλυσο
λύεται	ἐλύετο	λύσεται	λυθήσεται	ἐλύσατο	ἐλύθη	λέλυται	(ἐ) λέλυτο
λυόμεθα	ἐλυόμεθα	λυσόμεθα	λυθησόμεθα	ἐλυσάμεθα	ἐλύθημεν	λελύμεθα	(ἐ) λελύμεθα
λύεσθε	ἐλύεσθε	λύσεσθε	λυθήσεσθε	ἐλύσαθε	ἐλύθητε	λέλυσθε	(ἐ) λέλυσθε
λύονται	ἐλύοντο	λύσονται	λυθήσονται	ἐλύσαντο	ἐλύθησαν	λέλυνται	(ἐ) λέλυντο

Subjunctive

Present	Aorist Middle	Aorist Passive
λύωμαι	λύσωμαι	λυθῶ
λύῃ	λύσῃ	λυθῇς
λύηται	λύσηται	λυθῇ
λυώμεθα	λυσώμεθα	λυθῶμεν
λύησθε	λύσησθε	λυθῆτε
λύωνται	λύσωνται	λυθῶσι(ν)

Imperative

Present	Aorist Middle	Aorist Passive
λύου	λῦσαι	λύθητι
λυέσθω	λυσάσθω	λυθήτω
λύεσθε	λύσασθε	λύθητε
λυέσθωσαν	λυσάθωσαν	λυθήτωσαν

Infinitive

Present	Aorist Middle	Aorist Passive	Perfect
λύεσθαι	λύσασθαι	λυθῆναι	λελύσθαι

Participle

Present	Aorist Middle	Aorist Passive	Perfect
λυόμενος, –η, –ον	λυσάμενος, –η, –ον	λυθείς, λυθεῖσα, λυθέν	λελυμένος, –η, –ον

The Verb

List of verbs with one or more tenses formed irregularly, including liquid/nasal verbs. Only verbs which are dealt with in this book are contained in this list.

Present	Future	Aorist	Perfect	Perf. M/P	Aorist
–ἀγγέλλω	–ἀγγελῶ	–ἤγγειλα	–ἤγγελκα	ἤγγελμαι	–ἠγγέλην
ἄγω	ἄξω	ἤγαγον		ἦγμαι	ἤχθην
αἴρω	ἀρῶ	ἦρα	ἦρκα	ἦρμαι	ἤρθην
ἀκούω	ἀκούσω or ἀκούσομαι	ἤκουσα	ἀκήκοα		ἠκούσθην
ἁμαρτάνω	ἁμαρτήσω	ἡμάρτησα or ἥμαρτον	ἡμάρτηκα		
ἀνατέλλω		ἀνέτειλα	ἀνατέταλκα		
ἀνοίγω	ἀνοίξω	ἤνοιξα or ἀνέῳξα or ἠνέῳξα	ἀνέῳγα	ἀνέῳγμαι	ἠνοίχθην or ἀνεῴχθην
ἀποκτείνω	ἀποκτενῶ	ἀπέκτεινα			ἀπεκτάνθην
ἀπόλλυμι	ἀπολέσω or ἀπολῶ	ἀπώλεσα	ἀπολώλεκα or ἀπόλωλα		
ἀφίημι	ἀφήσω	ἀφῆκα		ἀφέωμαι	ἀφέθην
–βαίνω	–βήσομαι	–έβην	–βέβηκα		
βάλλω	βαλῶ	ἔβαλον or ἔβαλα	βέβληκα	βέβλημαι	ἐβλήθην
βλαστάνω		ἐβλάστησα			
γράφω	γράψω	ἔγραψα	γέγραφα	γέγραμμαι	ἐγράφην
γίνομαι	γενήσομαι	ἐγενόμην	γέγονα	γεγένημαι	ἐγενήθην
γινώσκω	γνώσομαι	ἔγνων	ἔγνωκα	ἔγνωσμαι	ἐγνώσθην
δείκνυμι or δεικνύω	δείξω	ἔδειξα	δέδειχα	δέδειγμαι	ἐδείχθην

Present	Future	Aorist	Perfect	Perf. M/P	Aorist
δέχομαι	δέξομαι	ἐδεξάμην		δέδεγμαι	ἐδέχθην
δέω	δήσω	ἔδησα	δέδεκα	δέδεμαι	ἐδέθην
διδάσκω	διδάξω	ἐδίδαξα			ἐδιδάχθην
δίδωμι	δώσω	ἔδωκα	δέδωκα	δέδομαι	ἐδόθην
δύναμαι	δυνήσομαι				ἠδυνήθην
ἐγείρω	ἐγερῶ	ἤγειρα		ἐγήγερμαι	ἠγέρθην
εἰμὶ	ἔσομαι				
ἔρχομαι	ἐλεύσομαι	ἦλθον	ἐλήλυθα		
ἐσθίω	φάγομαι	ἔφαγον			
εὑρίσκω	εὑρήσω	εὗρον	εὕρηκα		εὑρέθην
ἔχω	ἕξω	ἔσχον	ἔσχηκα		
θέλω	θελήσω	ἠθέλησα			
–θνήσκω	–θανοῦμαι	–ἔθανον	τέθνηκα		
ἵστημι	στήσω	ἔστησα or ἔστην	ἕστηκα		ἐστάθην
καλέω	καλέσω	ἐκάλεσα	κέκληκα	κέκλημαι	ἐκλήθην
κλαίω	κλαύσω	ἔκλαυσα			
κλείω	κλείσω	ἔκλεισα		κέκλεισμαι	ἐκλείσθην
κράζω	κράξω	ἔκραξα	κέκραγα		
κρίνω	κρινῶ	ἔκρινα	κέκρικα	κέκριμαι	ἐκρίθην
κρύπτω	κρύψω	ἔκρυψα		κέκρυμμαι	ἐκρύβην
λαμβάνω	λήμψομαι	ἔλαβον	εἴληφα	εἴλημμαι	ἐλήμφθην
λέγω	ἐρῶ	εἶπον	εἴρηκα	εἴρημαι	ἐρρέθην or ἐρρήθην
λείπω	λείψω	ἔλιπον		λέλειμμαι	ἐλείφθην
μανθάνω		ἔμαθον	μεμάθηκα		

Present	Future	Aorist	Perfect	Perf. M/P	Aorist
μένω	μενῶ	ἔμεινα	μεμένηκα		
ξηραίνω		ἐξήρανα		ἐξήραμμαι	ἐξηράνθην
ὁράω	ὄψομαι	εἶδον	ἑώρακα		ὤφθην
πάσχω		ἔπαθον	πέπονθα		
πείθω	πείσω	ἔπεισα	πέποιθα	πέπεισμαι	ἐπείσθην
πίνω	πίομαι	ἔπιον	πέπωκα		ἐπόθην
πίπτω	πεσοῦμαι	ἔπεσα, ἔπεσον	πέπτωκα		
ποιμαίνω	ποιμανῶ	ἐποίμανα			
σπείρω		ἔσπειρα		ἔσπαρμαι	ἐσπάρην
–στέλλω	–στελῶ	–ἔστειλα	–ἔσταλκα	ἔσταλμαι	–ἐστάλην
στρέφω	στρέψω	ἔστρεψα		ἔστραμμαι	ἐστράφην
τελέω	τελέσω	ἐτέλεσα	τετέλεκα	τετέλεσμαι	ἐτελέσθην
τίθημι	θήσω	ἔθηκα	τέθεικα	τέθειμαι	ἐτέθην
τίκτω	τέξομαι	ἔτεκον			ἐτέχθην
φαίνω	φανοῦμαι φανήσομαι	ἔφανα			ἐφάνην
φέρω	οἴσω	ἤνεγκα or ἤνεγκον	ἐνήνοχα		ἠνέχθην
φεύγω	φεύξομαι	ἐφυγον	πέφευγα		
χαίρω	χαρήσομαι	ἐχάρην			

Greek—English Vocabulary

The numerals in parenthesis refer to the lessons in which each word is dealt with. Certain verbs are given in tenses other than the present indicative, in addition to that, because these are formed on an entirely different stem. All verbs which present some irregularity in the formation of one or more tenses are listed in a special table in pp. **268–270**. Bold numbers (**26**, 31) in parenthesis refer to the vocabulary words found at the end of the chapter. Plain-text numbers refer to words found in the text of the lesson.

A

Ἀβραάμ, ὁ (**31**):	Abraham.
ἀγαθός, ή, όν (**7**):	good.
ἀγαπάω (**20**):	I love.
ἀγάπη, ης, ἡ (**6,** 10):	love.
ἀγαπητός, ή, όν (**7**):	beloved.
ἄγγελος, ου, ὁ (**4**):	angel, messenger.
ἄγειν (31):	to lead.
ἁγιάζω (**8**):	I sanctify.
ἅγιος, α, ον (**7**):	holy, saint.
ἀγνοέω (**21**):	I am ignorant.
ἀγρός, οῦ, ὁ (**9**):	field.
ἄγω (**11**):	I lead.
ἀδελφή, ῆς, ἡ (**31**):	sister.
ἀδελφός, οῦ, ὁ (**4**):	brother.
ἀδικέω (**21**):	I act unjustly, I wrong someone.
ἄδικος, ον (**7**):	unrighteous, unjust.
ἀδύνατος, ον (**24**):	weak, unable.
ἀθετέω (**21**):	I reject, I nullify.
αἷμα, ατος, τό (**25**):	blood.

αἴρω (**17**, 22):	I take up, I take away.
αἰτέω (**20**):	I ask, I make a request.
αἰών, αἰῶνος, ὁ (**23**):	age.
αἰῶνα, εἰς τόν:	forever.
αἰώνων, εἰς τούς αἰῶνας τῶν:	forever and ever.
αἰώνιος, ον (**7**, 29):	eternal.
ἀκάθαρτος, ον (**10**):	unclean.
ἄκανθα, ης, ἡ (22):	thorn, a thornbush.
ἀκολουθέω (**20**):	I follow (with dat.).
ἀκούω (**3**):	I hear (with acc. or gen.).
ἅλας, ἅλατος, τό (**25**):	salt.
ἀλήθεια, ἡ (**5**):	truth.
ἀληθής, ές (**29**):	true, truthful.
ἀληθινός, ή, όν (**10**):	true, genuine.
ἀληθῶς (34):	truly (adverb).
ἁλιεύς, ἁλιέως, ὁ (**24**):	fisherman.
ἀλλά (**6**):	but.
ἀλλήλων, οις (33):	of one another.
ἄλλος, η, ο (**7**):	another; preceded by the article: the other.
ἁμαρτάνω (**15**):	I sin.
ἁμαρτία, ας, ἡ (**5**):	sin.
ἁμαρτωλός, όν (**7**):	sinful, sinner.
ἀμήν (**34**):	amen, truly, verily.
ἄν (**32**):	a particle introducing an element of generalization or uncertainty into the sentence.
ἀνά (9):	(with acc.) among; used distributively, ἀνὰ δύο, "two by two."
ἀναβαίνω (**11**):	I go up.
ἀναβλέπω (**11**):	I look up, I recover my sight.
ἀναγγέλλω (**22**):	I make known, I announce.
ἀναγινώσκω (**11**):	I read.
ἀνάστασις, εως, ἡ (24):	resurrection.

ἀνατέλλω (**22**):	(trans.) I cause to rise; (intr.): I rise (usually of the sun).
ἀνέρχομαι (**14**):	I come or go up (deponent).
ἀνήρ, ἀνδρός, ὁ (**23**):	male, husband, man (as distinct from woman, compare ἄνθρωπος).
ἀνθίστημι (**39**):	(trans. with dat.) I set against; (intr.) I oppose.
ἄνθρωπος, ου, ὁ (**4**, 2, 29):	man (mankind, not in distinction to woman, but "human being").
ἀνίστημι (**39**):	(trans.) I raise up; (intr.) I rise.
ἀνοίγω (**8**):	I open.
ἀνταποδίδωμι (**36**):	I give back, I repay.
ἀντί (9):	(with gen.) instead of.
ἄνω (34):	above; ἄνωθεν: from above, from the beginning (adverb).
ἄξιος, α, ον (**13**):	worthy (adverb).
ἀπαγγέλλω (**17**):	I announce, I proclaim.
ἀπάγω (**11**):	I lead away.
ἀπαιτέω (**29**):	I demand.
ἅπαξ (35):	once (an adverbial number).
ἅπας, ἅπασα, ἅπαν (**29**):	whole; (pl) all.
ἀπέρχομαι (**14**):	I go away, I depart (deponent).
ἄπιστος, ον (**7**):	unfaithful, unbelieving, unbeliever.
ἁπλοῦς, ῆ, οῦν (**21**):	single, clear, sincere, good.
ἀπό (**9**,**14**):	(with gen.) from, away from.
ἀποδίδωμι (**36**):	I render, I return, I give back.
ἀποθνῄσκω (**11**,16):	I die.
ἀποκαθίστημι (**39**):	I restore.
ἀποκαλύπτω (**12**):	I uncover, I reveal.
ἀποκάλυψις, εως, ἡ (**24**):	revelation.
ἀποκρίνομαι (**14**,16):	I answer (deponent; with dat.).
ἀποκτείνω (**11**):	I kill.
ἀπόλλυμι (**40**):	(act.) I destroy, I lose; (mid.) I perish, I am lost.
ἀπολύω (**11**):	I release.

ἀποπλανάω (**21**):	I lead astray.
ἀποστέλλω (**11**, 22):	I send (usually on a mission, in distinction to the more general πέμπω.).
ἀπόστολος, ου, ὁ (2,**4**,7):	apostle.
ἀποτίθημι **(38)**:	(in the middle voice only) I put off.
ἅπτομαι (**14**):	I touch (with gen.).
ἄρα **(40)**:	therefore.
ἀργύριον, ου, τό (**40**):	silver, money.
ἀργυροῦς, ᾶ, οῦν (21):	silver.
ἀρνέομαι (**20**):	I deny (deponent).
ἄρτι (34):	now, just now (adverb).
ἄρτος, ου, ὁ (**6**):	bread; (pl.) loaves.
ἀρχή, ῆς, ἡ (**8**,**14**):	beginning.
ἀρχιερεύς, έως, ὁ (**24**):	high priest.
ἄρχομαι (**14**):	I begin.
ἄρχω (**14**):	I rule (with gen.).
ἄρχων, ἄρχοντος, ὁ (**23**):	ruler.
ἀσθένεια, ας, ἡ (**32**,5):	weakness, illness.
ἀσθενέω (**21**):	I am weak, sick.
ἀσθενής, ές (**29**):	weak, sick.
ἀσπάζομαι (**19**):	I salute, I greet (deponent).
ἀστήρ, έρος, ὁ (**23**):	star.
αὔριον (**32**,34):	tomorrow.
αὐτός, αὐτή, αὐτό (**12**):	(personal pronoun) he, she, it, also in predicate position: intensive pronoun, himself, herself, itself **(12 § 11, ii)**.
ἄφεσις, ἀφέσεως, ἡ (**24**):	release, forgiveness.
ἀφίημι **(37)**:	I leave, I leave something behind, I forgive, I permit, I send away.
ἀφίστημι (39):	(trans.) I lead others to revolt; (intr.) I depart.
ἄφρων, ον (**29**):	foolish.

B

βαίνω (**11**,18,32):	I go (In the NT only as part of a compound verb).
βάλλω (**6**,18, 22):	I cast, I throw.
βαπτίζω (**3**):	I baptize.
βάπτισμα, ατος, τό (**25**):	baptism.
βαπτιστής, οῦ, ὁ (**17**):	Baptist (used only as title for John).
βασιλεία, ας, ἡ (**5**,7):	kingdom.
βασιλεύς, έως, ὁ (**24**):	king.
βαστάζω (**15**):	I carry, I bear.
Βηθλεέμ, ἡ (**28**):	Bethlehem (indecl.).
βιβλίον, ου, τό (**9**,**11**,**12**):	book.
βλαστάνω (**17**, **22**):	I sprout.
βλασφημέω (**21**):	I blaspheme, I speak reproachfully.
βλέπω (**3**):	I see, I watch, (as an imperative: beware of).
βούλομαι (**31**):	I am willing, I wish (deponent).
βοῦς, βοός, ὁ, ἡ(24):	ox, cow.

Γ

Γαλιλαία, ας, ἡ (**27**):	Galilee.
γάμος, ου, ὁ (**19**):	marriage, wedding; pl. wedding festivities.
γάϱ (**7**):	for, (postpositive).
γενεά, ᾶς, ἡ (**19**):	generation, race.
γεννάω (**25**):	I beget; (pass.) I am born.
γένος, γένους, τό (**25**):	offspring, race.
γεύομαι (**14**):	I taste (deponent; with gen.).
γῆ, γῆς, ἡ (**29**):	ground, earth.
γίνομαι (10,**14**,16,19):	I become; it comes to pass (deponent).
γινώσκω (**3**, 11):	I know.
γλῶσσα, ης, ἡ (**5**):	tongue.
γνῶσις, εως, ἡ (**24**):	knowledge.
γονεύς, έως, ὁ (**24**):	parent.
γόνυ, γόνατος, τό (25):	knee.
γϱαμματεύς, έως, ὁ (**24**):	scribe.

γραφή, ῆς, ἡ (**6**,7):	writing, Scripture.
γράφω (**3**,6,12):	I write.
γυνή, γυναικός, ἡ (**23**):	woman, wife.

Δ

δαιμόνιον, ου, τό (**11**):	demon, evil spirit.
Δαυίδ, ὁ (**28**):	David (indecl.).
δὲ (6,7,12):	and, but, now, then (postpositive).
δέησις, εως, ἡ (**24**):	prayer, supplication.
δεῖ (**31**):	it is necessary (an impersonal verb; cf. 31 § 12.).
δείκνυμι or δεικνύω (**8,40**):	I show.
δεῖπνον, ου, τό (**22**):	supper.
δέκα **(35)**:	ten.
δέκα ὀκτώ (35):	eighteen.
δέκαπέντε (35):	fifteen.
δέκατέσσαρες (35):	fourteen.
δέκατος, η, ον (35):	tenth.
δέκα χιλιάδες (35):	ten thousand.
δένδρον, ου, τό (**9**):	tree.
δεῦτε (**32**):	come here, come (addressed to more than one person an imperative).
δεύτερος, α, ον **(35)**:	second.
δέχομαι (**14**):	I receive (deponent).
δέω (**26**):	I bind.
δηλόω (**20**):	I declare, I signify.
διά (9,12):	(with gen.) through, throughout; (with acc.) on account of, because of.
διάβολος, ου, ὁ (**10**):	devil.
διαθήκη, ης, ἡ (**12**):	covenant, testament.
διακονέω (**21**):	I serve, I minister (with dat.).
διάκονος, ου, ὁ (**13**):	servant, deacon.
διακόσιοι, αι, α (35):	two hundred.
διατίθημι **(38)**:	(in the middle voice only) I appoint, I make a will or covenant.

διαφέρω (**23**):	I differ.
διδασκαλία, ας, ἡ, (**12**):	teaching, instruction.
διδάσκαλος, ου, ὁ (**4**,12):	teacher.
διδάσκω (**3**,12):	I teach.
διδαχή, ῆς, ἡ (**12**):	teaching, instruction.
δίδωμι (36,40):	I give.
διέρχομαι (**14**):	I go through (deponent).
δίκαιος, α, ον (**7**):	righteous, just.
δικαιοσύνη, ης, ἡ (**12**):	righteousness.
δικαιόω (**21**):	justify.
διπλοῦς, ῆ, οῦν (21):	double.
δίς (**35**):	twice.
δισχίλιοι, αι, α (35):	two thousand.
διψάω (**20**):	I thirst.
διώκω (**10**):	I pursue, I persecute.
δοκεῖ (**31**):	It seems good (an impersonal verb; cf. 31 § 12.)
δοκέω (**21**, 31):	I suppose, I seem (It is also used as an impersonal verb; see δοκεῖ.).
δόξα, ης, ἡ (**5**):	glory.
δοξάζω (**6**):	I glorify.
δουλεύω (**25**,29):	I serve (with dat.).
δοῦλος, ου, ὁ (**4**,6,12):	slave.
δύναμαι (**31**):	I can, I am able (deponent).
δύναμις, εως, ἡ (**24**):	power, miracle.
δύο (**35**):	two.
δώδεκα, δωδέκατος, η, ον (**35**):	twelve, twelfth.
δώδεκα χιλιάδες (35):	twelve thousand.
δῴη (40):	He may give (optative of the verb δίδωμι).
δωρεά, ᾶς, ἡ (**32**):	gift.
δῶρον, ου, τό (**4**):	gift.

E

ἐάν (**32**):	if.
ἐὰν μή, εἰ μὴ (35 § 10):	except, unless.

ἑαυτοῦ, ῆς, οῦ(33):	(refl. pron.) of himself, herself, itself.
ἑβδομήκοντα, (35):	seventy.
ἑβδομηκοντάκις, (35):	seventy times.
ἕβδομος, η, ον (35):	seventh.
ἐγγίζω (**9**):	I approach (usually with the dat.).
ἐγγύς **(34)**:	near (adverb).
ἐγείρω (**3**):	I raise.
ἐγκαταλείπω (**11**):	I forsake.
ἐγνώσθην (19):	I was known (aor. pass. of γινώσκω).
ἐγώ (12):	I.
ἔδει (31):	It was necessary (an impersonal verb; the imperfect of δεῖ, cf. 31 § 12).
ἔθνος, ους, τό (**25**):	nation; in the pl. usually "gentiles."
εἰ (10,**26**):	if.
εἶδον (18):	I saw; 2nd aor. act. of ὁράω (βλέπω).
εἰδῶ (27, 32):	I may know; perf. subj. of οἶδα.
εἰδώς, εἰδυῖα, εἰδός (27):	perf. participle of οἶδα.
εἴκοσι (ν) (35):	twenty.
εἰκών, εἰκόνος, ἡ (**30**):	image.
εἰμί (10,12,14,16,40):	I am.
εἶπον (18):	I said; 2nd aor. act. of λέγω (**3**).
εἴρηκα, εἴρημαι (3, 26):	I have said, perf. act. and pass. of λέγω.
εἰρήνη, ης, ἡ (**5**,12):	peace.
εἰς (9):	(with acc.) into.
εἷς, ἑνός (**35**):	one (masc.).
εἰσέρχομαι (**14**):	I come or go in, I enter. (deponent).
εἶτα (**34**)	then, next
ἐκ, ἐξ (9,10,11):	(with gen.) out of; (ἐξ, 14)
ἕκαστος, η, ον (**15**):	each, every.
ἑκατόν (**35**):	hundred.
ἑκατοντάρχης, ου, ὁ (**34**):	centurion.
ἐκβάλλω (**11**):	I cast out.
ἐκεῖ, ἐκεῖθεν (**32**,34):	there, from there (adverb).
ἐκεῖνος, η, ο (**13**):	(demonstr. pron.) that.
ἐκέλευσεν (31):	He commanded.
ἐκκλησία, ας, ἡ (**5**):	church.

ἐκκόπτω (**29**):	I cut down.
ἐκλεκτός, ή, όν (**13**):	chosen, elect.
ἐκπορεύομαι (**16**):	I go out (deponent).
ἕκτος, η, ον (35):	sixth.
ἐλάσσων, ον (29):	smaller: comparative degree of μικρός.
ἐλάχιστος, η, ον (29):	smallest: superlative degree of μικρός.
ἐλέγχω (**8**):	I reprove, I rebuke, I convict.
ἐλεέω (**21**):	I have mercy on, I pity.
ἔλεος, ους, τό (**25**):	mercy.
ἐλεύθερος, α, ον (**19**):	free, free person.
ἐλευθερόω (**21**):	I set free.
ἐλεύσομαι (16):	I will go; fut. (deponent) of ἔρχομαι (**14**).
ἐλήλυθα (26):	I have gone; perf. act. of ἔρχομαι (**14**).
Ἕλλην, Ἕλληνος, ὁ (**23**):	Greek.
ἐλπίζω (**15**,16):	I hope, I trust in.
ἐλπίς, ἐλπίδος, ἡ (**23**):	hope.
ἔμαθον (18):	I learned; 2nd aor. of μανθάνω.
ἐμαυτοῦ, ῆς, (33):	(refl. pron.) of myself.
ἐμβαίνω (**22**):	I go into, I embark.
εμβλεπω (11)	I look at.
ἐμός, ή, όν (22):	(poss. pron.) my, my own.
ἐμπαίζω (**16**):	I mock.
ἐμπίπτω (**31**):	I fall in.
ἔμπροσθεν (**34**):	(with gen.) before, in front of, ahead, in front (adverb).
ἐν (9,10,11):	(with dat.) in, on (as in on the eighth day), by in an instrumental sense.
ἕν, ἑνός (35):	one (neut.).
ἕνδεκα, ἑνδέκατος, η, ον (35):	eleven, eleventh.
ἐνενήκοντα (35):	ninety.
ἐννέα, ἔνατος, η, ον (35):	nine, ninth.
ἐντελλομαι (**14**):	I command (deponent).
ἐντολή, ῆς, ἡ (**5**):	commandment.
ἐξ, ἐκ (9,11,**14**):	out of.
ἕξ, ἑξήκοντα (35):	six, sixty.

ἐξέρχομαι (**14**):	I come or go out (deponent).
ἔξεστι (ν) (**31**):	it is lawful (with dat.) (an impersonal verb).
ἐξίστημι (**39**):	(trans.) I astonish; (intr.) I am astonished, I am out of my senses.
ἐξουσία, ας, ἡ (**15**):	authority.
ἔξω (**19**, 34):	outside (an adverb, sometimes used as a preposition with gen.).
ἐπαγγελία, ας, ἡ (**6**):	promise.
ἐπάγω (**31**):	I bring upon.
ἔπαθον (18):	2nd aor. of πάσχω (**9**). I suffer.
ἐπαινέω (**32**):	I approve, I praise.
ἐπαίρω (**22**):	I lift up; (pass.) I exalt myself.
ἐπάνω (34):	above
επείσθην (19):	aorist passive of πείθω (**16**). I obeyed.
ἔπειτα (34):	afterwards (adverb).
ἐπερωτάω (**27**):	I ask, I question.
ἔπεσα, ἔπεσον (18):	1st and 2nd aor. of πίπτω (**9**). I fell.
ἐπί (10):	(with gen.) upon, in the time of; (with dat.) upon, indicates the authority on which an act is done, at (indicating the reason); (with acc.) upon, towards, against.
ἐπιβάλλω (**22**):	I lay upon, I beat upon.
ἐπιγινώσκω (**11**):	I know thoroughly, I acknowledge.
ἐπιμένω (**22**):	I continue, I persevere.
ἐπιπίπτω (**28**):	I fall upon.
ἐπιστολή, ῆς, ἡ (**5**,12):	letter.
ἐπιστρέφω (**11**):	I return.
ἐπιτίθημι (38):	(act.) I put upon; (mid.) I attack.
ἐπιτιμάω (**21**):	I rebuke, I warn (with dat.).
ἐπορεύθην (19):	aorist passive of πορεύομαι (**14**) I went.
ἐπράχθην (19):	aorist passive of πράσσω (**15**). I did, I finished.
ἑπτά, ἑπτάκις (**35**):	seven, seven times.

ἐργάζομαι (**14**):	I work (deponent).
ἐργάτης, ου, ὁ (**13**):	worker.
ἔργον, ου, τό (**6**):	work.
ἔρημος, ου, ἡ (**9**):	desert.
ἐρρέθην or ἐρρήθην, (19):	aor. pass. act. of λέγω (**3**). It was said.
ἔρχομαι (**14**,16):	I come, I go (deponent).
ἐρῶ (22):	I will say; fut. act. of λέγω (**3**).
ἐρωτάω (**20**):	I ask a question, I inquire, I beseech.
ἐσθίω (**6**):	I eat.
ἔσομαι (**16**):	fut, of εἰμί (12 § 13). I shall be.
ἔσχατος, η, ον (**7**):	last.
ἔσω, ἔσωθεν (34):	within, from within (adverb).
ἕτερος, α, ον (**10**):	another, different.
ἔτι (**28**,34):	still, yet (adverb).
ἑτοιμάζω (**9**):	I prepare.
ἔτοσ, ους, τό (**35**):	year
εὖ (34):	well (adverb).
εὐαγγελίζομαι (**14**):	I bring good news, I evangelize (deponent).
εὐαγγέλιον, ου, τό (**8**):	gospel.
εὐάρεστος, ον (7):	acceptable, well pleased.
εὐθέως, εὐθύς (**28**, 34):	immediately (adverb).
εὐθύς, εῖα, ες (**29**):	straight (an adjective).
εὐλογέω (8,**20**):	I bless.
εὐλογία, ας, ἡ (**12**):	blessing.
εὑρίσκω (**6**):	I find.
εὐσέβεια, ας, ἡ (5):	godliness, reverence.
εὐχαριστέω (**21**):	I give thanks (with dat.).
ἔφαγον (18):	I ate, 2nd aor. of ἐσθίω (**6**).
ἔφην (40):	imperf. of φημί, I was saying.
ἐφίστημι (**39**):	(trans.) I approach; (intrans.) I stand by, I am present.
ἐχθρός, ά, όν (**9**):	enemy.
ἔχω (**3**,**8**):	I have.
ἑώρακα (**20**):	perf. of ὁράω, I have seen.
ἑώρων (**20**):	imperf. of ὁράω, I was seeing.

ἕως (34):	until (adverb).
ἕως ὅτου (30):	until.

Z

ζάω (**21**):	I live.
ζητέω (**20**):	I seek.
ζωή, ῆς, ἡ (**5**):	life.

H

Ἡ, ἡ (5):	the; (def. article, fem.).
ἤ (**13**):	either, or; in comparisons, than (disjunctive particle).
ἥ (17):	who (rel. pron., fem.).
ἡγεμών, όνος, ὁ (**23**):	governor, king.
ᾔδειν (27):	pluperf. of οἶδα, I knew.
ἤδη (**17**,34):	already (adverb).
ἦλθον (18):	2nd aor. of ἔρχομαι (**14**). I came, I went.
Ἠλίας, ου, ὁ (**32**):	Elijah.
ἥλιος, ου, ὁ (**18**):	sun.
ἡμεῖς, ῶν (12):	we (pers. pron.).
ἡμέρα, ας, ἡ (**5**):	day.
ἡμέτερος, α, ον (22):	our, our own (poss. pron.).
ἤμην (14 § 11):	imperf. of εἰμὶ (12 § 13) I was.
ἤνεγκα, ἤνεγκον, ἠνέχθην (17, 19):	1st and 2nd aor. act. and aor. pass. of φέρω (**3**) I brought, I was brought.
Ἡρῴδης, ου, ὁ (**31**):	Herod.
ἥτις (30):	whoever (indefin.-rel. pron., fem.).

Θ

θάλασσα, ης, ἡ (1, **18**):	sea.
θάνατος, ου, ὁ (**6**):	death.
θανατόω (**20**):	I put to death.
θαυμάζω (**15**):	I wonder at.

θεάομαι (**21**):	I behold (deponent).
θέλημα, ατος, τό (**25**):	will, desire.
θέλω (**31**):	I am willing, I wish.
θεός, οῦ, ὁ (**4**,10,12):	God.
θεραπεύω (**13**):	I heal.
θεωρέω (**27**):	I look at, I observe.
θησαυρός, οῦ, ὁ (**10**):	treasure.
θλῖψις, εως, ἡ (**24**):	affliction, tribulation.
θνῄσκω (11):	I am dead, used in the NT only in the compound ἀποθνῄσκω with the exception of the perfect τέθνηκα.
θρίξ, τριχός, ἡ (**23**):	hair.
θρόνος, ου, ὁ (**12**):	throne.
θυγάτηρ, τρός, ἡ (**23**):	daughter.
θύρα, ας, ἡ (**8**,10):	door.
θυσία, ας, ἡ (**12**):	sacrifice.

I

Ἰάκωβος, ὁ (**31**):	James.
ἰάομαι (**21**):	I heal (deponent).
ἴδιος, α, ον (**16**):	one's own.
κατ᾽ ἰδίαν	privately, apart.
ἰδού (**28**):	behold (adverb).
ἰδών, –οῦσα, –όν (27):	2nd aor. act. part. of ὁράω (**20**). Having seen.
ἱερεύς, έως, ὁ (**24**):	priest.
ἱερόν, οῦ, τό (**4**):	temple (See also ναός.).
Ἰερουσαλήμ, ἡ (**26**):	Jerusalem (indeclinable).
Ἱεροσόλυμα, -ων, τά (**26**):	Jerusalem.
Ἰησοῦς, οῦ, ὁ (**8**):	Jesus.
ἱκανός, ή, όν (**15**):	sufficient, able, large; pl. enough, many.
ἱμάτιον, ου, τό (**17**):	garment.
ἵνα(32):	in order that, so that (with subj.).
Ἰουδαία, ας, ἡ (**28**):	Judea.

Ἰουδαῖος, α, ον (**9**):	Jewish, Jew.
ἵστημι (**39**):	(trans.) I cause to stand, I place, I establish; (intr.) I stand.
ἰσχυρός, ά, όν (**29**):	mighty, strong, powerful.
ἰσχύς, ἰσχύος, ἡ (24):	strength, power, strong.
ἰχθύς, ἰχθύος, ὁ (**24**):	fish.
Ἰωάννης, ου, ὁ (**17**):	John.

K

καθαρίζω (**8**, 16, 22):	I cleanse.
καθαρός, ά, όν (**7**,**10**):	clean, pure.
καθεύδω (**30**):	I sleep.
κάθημαι (**28**):	I sit, I am seated.
καθίζω (**15**):	(intrans.) I sit, (trans.) I cause to sit.
καθίστημι (**39**):	(act.) I appoint; (pass.) I am appointed, I become.
καθώς (**31**):	just as (adverb).
καί (**3**, 6):	and, even, also; καὶ . . . καὶ; both . . . and; (cf. τέ).
καινός, ή, όν (**7**):	new (See also νέος.).
καιρός, οῦ, ὁ (**17**):	time, due time, appointed time, opportunity (See also χρόνος).
κακός, ή, όν (**18**):	evil, bad.
καλέω(**20**,26):	I call.
καλός, ή, όν (**7**,1):	good, beautiful.
καλύπτω (**16**):	I cover.
καλῶς (34):	well (adverb).
καρδία, ας, ἡ (**5**):	heart.
καρπός, οῦ, ὁ (**9**):	fruit.
κατά (9,14):	(with gen.): down from, against; (with acc.): according to, throughout, towards.
κατ᾽ ἰδίαν (**16**):	privately, apart.
καταβαίνω (**11**):	I go down.
κατακρίνω (**11**):	I condemn.

καταλείπω (**11**):	I leave behind, I forsake.
καταράομαι (21):	I curse (deponent).
κατέρχομαι (**14**):	I come down (deponent).
κατηγορέω (**21**):	I accuse (with gen.).
κατοικέω (**22**):	I dwell.
κελεύω (**31**):	I command.
κενός, ή, όν (**12**):	empty; without effect.
κέρδος, κέρδους, τό (**31**):	gain.
κεφαλή, ῆς, ἡ (**12**):	head.
κηρύσσω (**6**):	I preach, I proclaim.
κλαίω (**8**):	I weep, I cry.
κλάω (**21**):	I break.
κλείω (**8**,26):	I close.
κλέπτω (**30**):	I steal.
κληρονομέω (**29**):	I inherit.
κληρονομία, ας, ἡ (**32**):	inheritance.
κληρονόμος, ου, ὁ (**32**):	heir.
κλίνη, ης, ἡ (**28**):	bed.
κοιλία, ας, ἡ (**35**):	womb, belly.
κοιμάομαι (**30**):	I sleep I fall asleep.
κοινωνία, ας, ἡ (**12**):	fellowship, communion.
κοπιάω (**26**):	I toil, I work hard, I get tired.
κόπος, ου, ὁ (**26**):	labor, work.
κόσμος, ου, ὁ (**4**):	world.
κράζω (**15**):	I cry out.
κρατέω (**26**):	I take hold of, I hold.
κραυγή, ῆς, ἡ (**30**):	shout.
κρέας, ατος, τό (25):	meat.
κράτιστος, η, ον (29):	best; superlative degree of ἀγαθός.
κρείσσων, ον (29):	better; comparative degree of ἀγαθός.
κρίνω (**6**):	I judge.
κρίσις, εως, ἡ (**24**):	judgment.
κριτής, οῦ, ὁ (**12**,5):	judge.
κρούω (**27**):	I knock.
κρυπτός, ή, όν (**13**):	secret, hidden, concealed.
κρύπτω (**10**):	I hide, I conceal.

κτίσις, κτίσεως, ἡ (**24**):	creation, creature.
κύριος, ου, ὁ (**4**,12):	the Lord, master.
κώμη, ης, ἡ (**18**):	village.
κωφός, ή, όν (**26**):	deaf, dumb.

Λ

λάθρᾳ (34):	secretly (adverb).
λαῖλαψ, απος, ἡ (23):	storm, tempest.
λαλέω (**20**):	I speak.
λαμβάνω (1,2,**3**):	I take, I receive.
λαός, οῦ, ὁ (**17**):	people.
λέγω (**3**,31,40):	I say.
λείπω (**11**, 19):	I leave, I lack.
λεπρός, ά, όν (**8**):	leper.
λευκός, ή, όν (**13**):	white.
λίθος, ου, ὁ (**6**):	stone.
λόγος, ου, ὁ (**4**,10):	word.
λοιπός, ή, όν (**13**):	remaining.
τό λοιπόν or τοῦ λοιποῦ:	henceforth, from now on.
λυπέω (**21**):	I cause grief.
λύω (**3**):	I loose, I destroy.

Μ

μαθητής, οῦ, ὁ (**5**,10):	disciple.
μακάριος, α, ον (**7**):	blessed.
μακράν (34):	far (adverb).
μακρόθεν (34):	far off (adverb).
μᾶλλον (34):	more, rather (adverb).
μανθάνω (**3**):	I learn.
Μάρθα, ας, ἡ (18):	Martha.
μαρτυρέω (**20**):	I witness, I bear witness (with dat.).
μαρτυρία, ας, ἡ (**13**):	testimony.
μάρτυς, μάρτυρος, ὁ (**23**):	witness.
μέγας, μεγάλη, μέγα (**16**,29):	great, large.
μέγιστος, η, ον (29):	greatest; superlative degree of μέγας.
μείζων, ον (29,35):	greater comparative degree of μέγας.

μελλω (**31**)	I am about to (+ infinitive), I am going to (+ infinitive)
μέλει (**31**):	it matters (with dat.) it is a concern, (an impersonal verb; cf. 31 § 12.).
μέλος, μέλους, τό (**25**):	member.
μέν . . . δέ (**6**):	on the one hand . . . on the other.
μένω (**9**):	I remain, I abide.
μεριμνάω (**21**):	I am anxious.
μέρος, ους, τό (**25**):	part.
μέσος, η, ον (**12**):	middle;
ἐκ μέσου:	from among.
ἐν μέσῳ:	in the midst.
Μεσσίας, ου, ὁ (**5**):	Messiah.
μετά (9):	(with gen.) with; (with acc.) after.
μεταδίδωμι (**36**):	I share with someone, I impart.
μετανοέω (**20**):	I repent.
μετάνοια, ας, ἡ (5, **13**):	repentance.
μεταξύ (**30**):	of time: meanwhile, in the meantime (adverb); prep. (with gen.) of place: between.
μετατίθημι (**38**):	I transpose, I transfer.
μή (**6**,33, 35):	not.
μὴ γένοιτο (40):	God forbid, may it never be.
μηδείς, μηδεμία, μηδέν (35):	no one, nothing (used with a verb in moods other than the indicative.).
μηκέτι (34):	no longer (used with moods other than the indicative.) (adverb).
μὴν, μηνός, ἡ (**35**)	month.
μήποτε (35):	whether, perhaps.
μήπω (34):	not yet (used with moods other than the indicative) (adverb).
μήτε . . . μήτε (**32**):	neither . . . nor (used with moods other than the indicative).
μήτηρ, μητρός, ἡ (**23**):	mother.

μήτι (35):	not (in questions expecting a negative answer).
μία, ας (35):	one (fem.).
μικρός, ά, όν (**7**):	small.
μισέω (**21**):	I hate.
μισθός, οῦ, ὁ (**12**,30):	reward, wages.
μνημεῖον, ου, τό (**19**):	grave, tomb.
μονογενής, ές (**29**):	only begotten (lit. one of a kind).
μόνον (34):	only (adverb).
μόνος, η, ον (**9**):	alone, only.
μυριάς, μυριάδος, ἡ (35):	ten thousand.
μύριοι, αι, α (35):	ten thousand.
μυστήριον, ου, τό (**12**):	mystery.
μωρός, ά, όν (**12**):	foolish.

N

ναός, οῦ, ὁ (**4**):	temple, sanctuary (See also ἱερόν.).
νεκρός, ά, όν (**7**):	dead.
νέος, α, ον (**7**):	new, young (See also καινός.).
νεφέλη, ης, ἡ (**19**):	cloud.
νηστεύω (**8**):	I fast.
νικάω (**32**):	I overcome.
νίπτω (**32**):	I wash.
νόμος, ου, ὁ (**12**):	law.
νοῦς, νοός, ὁ (**24**):	mind.
νύμφη, ης, ἡ (**19**):	bride.
νυμφίος, ου, ὁ (**19**):	bridegroom.
νῦν (**34**):	now (adverb).
νύξ, νυκτός, ἡ (**23**):	night.

Ξ

ξηραίνω (**22**):	I dry; (pass.) I become dry, I wither.

O

ὁ (ὁ, ἡ, τό) (5 § 17):	the (def. art., masc.).

ὅ (17):	which (rel. pron., neut.).
ὀγδοήκοντα (35):	eighty.
ὄγδοος, η, ον (35):	eighth.
ὅδε, ἥδε, τόδε (13):	this (demonstr. pron.).
ὁδός, οῦ, ἡ (**4**,5):	road, way.
οἶδα (**27**):	I know (perf. with present meaning).
οἰκία, ας, ἡ (**28**):	house.
οἰκοδομέω (**21**):	I build, I build up, I edify.
οἶκος, ου, ὁ (**6**):	house.
οἶνος, ου, ὁ (**10**,2):	wine.
οἴσω (15):	fut. of φέρω (**3**). I shall bear, I shall carry.
ὀκτώ (35):	eight.
ὀλίγος, η, ον (**9**):	little; pl. few.
ὅλος, η, ον (**10**):	whole.
ὅμοιος, α, ον (**15**):	like (with dat.), resembling to.
ὁμοιόω (**28**):	I liken, I compare
ὁμολογέω (**20**):	I confess, I declare publicly.
ὁμοῦ (34):	together.
ὅμως (34):	nevertheless.
ὄνομα, ατος, τό (**25**):	name.
ὄντως (34):	really (adverb).
ὄπισθεν (34):	from behind (adverb).
ὀπίσω (**34**):	(with gen.) after, behind (also as an adverb).
ὅπου (**34**):	where (adverb).
ὅπως (32):	in order that, so that.
ὁράω (**20**):	I see.
ὅραμα, ατος, τό (**35**)	vision.
ὀργή, ῆς, ἡ (**18**):	anger, wrath.
ὄρος, ὄρους, τό (**25**):	mountain.
ὅς (17 § 7):	who (rel. pron., masc.).
ὁσάκις (35):	as often as (adverb).
ὅσος, η, ον (**29**,35):	as much as; (pl.) as many as (adverb).
ὅστις (30):	whoever (indef. rel. pron., masc.).
ὀσφύς, ύος, ἡ (24):	waist, loins.

ὅταν (**32**,34):	whenever, when, at the time that (conj.).
ὅτε (**13**,**22**,34):	when.
ὅτι (8):	that, because.
ὅ, τι (30):	whichever (indef. rel. pron., neut.).
οὐ, οὐκ, οὐχ (**6**,10,35):	not, no.
οὐδέ (**6**,35):	and not, but not, not even; οὐδέ . . . οὐδέ: neither . . . nor (only with the indicative).
οὐδείς, οὐδεμία, οὐδέν (35):	no one, nothing. (only with the indicative.)
οὐκέτι (**8**, 34):	no longer (only with the indicative.) (adverb).
οὖν (**17**):	therefore, accordingly (postpositive).
οὔπω (μήπω) (**14**, 34):	not yet (only with the indicative).
οὐρανός, οῦ, ὁ (**10**):	heaven, sky.
οὖς, ὠτός, τό (**25**):	ear.
οὔτε . . . οὔτε (**32**):	neither . . . nor (only with the indicative).
οὗτος, αὕτη, τοῦτο (13):	(demonstr. pron.) this.
οὕτως (**34**):	so, thus, in this manner (adverb).
οὐχί (6,35):	no, not (used in questions expecting an affirmative answer).
ὀφθαλμός, οῦ, ὁ (**15**):	eye.
ὀφείλω (18,**32**):	I owe.
ὄχλος, ου, ὁ (**15**):	people, multitude, crowd.
ὄψομαι (15):	fut. of ὁράω (**20**). I shall see (deponent).

Π

παιδίον, ου, τό (**19**):	child, little child, infant.
παῖς, παιδός, ὁ, ἡ (**23**):	servant, child (boy or girl).
παλαιός, ά, όν (**12**):	old (never of persons).
πάλιν (**31**,34):	again (adverb).
πάντοτε (34):	always (adverb).

παρά (2,10):	(with gen.) motion from, seeking or taking from (always of persons); (with dat.) beside, nearby; (with acc.) at, beside, along, contrary to.
παραβολή, ῆς, ἡ (**5**):	parable.
παραγγέλλω (**27**):	I command, I charge (with dat. of the person).
παραγίνομαι (**28**):	I arrive, I come.
παραδίδωμι (**36**):	I deliver, I betray, I give over.
παράδοσις, εως, ἡ (**24**):	tradition.
παρακαλέω (**21**):	I exhort, I beseech, I comfort.
παράκλησις, εως ἡ (**24**):	consolation, exhortation.
παραλαμβάνω (**11**):	I receive.
παραλυτικός, ή, όν (**18**):	paralytic, palsied.
παρατίθημι (**38**):	I place before.
παρθένος, ου, ἡ (**18**):	virgin.
παρίστημι (**39**):	(trans.) I set beside; (intr.) I stand beside, I am present.
παρουσία, ας, ἡ (**16**):	coming, the second coming of Christ, presence.
πᾶς, πᾶσα, πᾶν (**29**):	every; pl. all.
πάσχα, τό (**32**):	Passover (indecl.).
πάσχω (**9**):	I suffer.
πατήρ, πατρός, ὁ (**23**):	father.
Παῦλος, ου, ὁ (**17**):	Paul.
πείθω (**16**,19,26):	I persuade (passive; I obey).
πεινάω (**20**):	I hunger.
πειράζω (**15**):	I tempt, I test.
πειρασμός, οῦ, ὁ (**18**):	temptation.
πέμπτος, η, ον (35):	fifth.
πέμπω (**6**):	I send.
πενθέω (**27**):	I mourn.
πεντάκις (35):	five times.
πεντακισχίλιοι, αι, α (35):	five thousand.
πεντακόσιοι, αι, α (35):	five hundred.
πέντε (**35**):	five.

πεντεκαιδέκατος, η, ον (35): fifteenth.
πεντήκοντα (35): fifty.
πεντηκοστή, ῆς, ἡ (35): Pentecost.
πέποιθα (**27**): (perfect of πείθω), I put trust in, have confidence in.
πέπονθα (26): perf. of πάσχω (**9**). I suffered.
πέπτωκα (26): perf. of πίπτω (**9**). I fell.
πέπραχα—γμαι (26): I did. I accomplished; perf. of πράσσω (**15**).
πέραν (34): on the other side, beyond (adverb).
περί (9,11,12): (with gen.) about, concerning; (with acc.) around.
περίλυπος, ον (7): exceedingly sorrowful.
περιπατέω (**21**): I walk.
περισσεύω (**27**): I exceed a certain number, I abound.
περιτίθημι (**38**): I put around.
πέτρα, ας, ἡ (**30**): rock.
Πέτρος, ου, ὁ (**17**): Peter.
πίνω (**10**,16): I drink.
πίπτω (**9**,16): I fall.
πιστεύω (**10**): I believe (with dat. or with εἰς . . .).
πίστις, εως, ἡ (**24**): faith, belief.
πιστός, ή, όν (**7**): faithful, believer.
πλανάω (**21**): I lead astray.
πλεῖστος, η, ον (**16**,29): most: superlative degree of πολύς.
πλείων, ον (**16**,29): more: comparative degree of πολύς.
πλῆθος, θους, τό (**25**): multitude, company.
πλήρης, ες (**29**): full.
πληρόω (**21**): I fill, I fulfill.
πλησίον (34): near (adverb).
πλοῖον, ου, τό (**9**): ship, boat.
πλοῦς, πλοός, ὁ (24): voyage.
πλούσιος, α, ον (**13**): rich.
πλουτέω (**31**): I become rich.
πνεῦμα, ατος, τό (10,12,**25**): spirit.
πόθεν (10,34): whence? (adverb).

ποιέω (**20**):	I make, I do.
ποιμαίνω (**22**):	I feed, I tend sheep.
ποιμήν, μένος, ὁ (**23**):	shepherd.
πόλις, εως, ἡ (**24**):	city.
πολλάκις, (34):	often (adverb).
πολύ (34):	much, greatly (adverb).
πολύς, πολλή, πολύ (**16**,29):	much; pl. many.
πονηρός, ά, όν (**7**):	evil, wicked, bad.
πορεύομαι (**14**,19):	I go (deponent).
ποσάκις (35):	how often? (adverb).
πόσος, η, ον (35):	how great?; (pl.), how many? (adverb).
ποταμός, οῦ, ὁ (**18**):	river.
πότε (**30**,34):	when? (adverb).
ποτέ (10,**30**,34):	at some time, ever (enclitic) (adverb).
ποτήριον, ου, τό (**16**):	cup.
ποῦ (10,34):	where? (adverb).
πούς, ποδός, ὁ (**23**):	foot.
πρᾶγμα, ατος, τό (**27**):	thing, matter.
πράσσω (**15**):	I do, I accomplish.
πραΰς, –εῖα, ύ (**29**):	meek.
πρεσβύτερος, α, ον (**8**):	elder.
πρίν, (34):	before (adverb).
πρό (9,11,12):	with gen.) before (of place or time).
προάγω (**28**):	(trans.) I lead forward; (intr.) I go before hand.
πρόβατον, ου, τό (**12**):	sheep.
πρόνοια, ας, ἡ (5):	providence.
πρός (9,10,12,14):	(with dat.) near, at; (with acc.) to, towards.
προσδοκάω (**29**):	I expect, I look for.
προσέρχομαι (**14**):	I come to (with dat., deponent).
προσευχή, ῆς, ἡ (**5**):	prayer.
προσεύχομαι (**14**):	I pray (deponent).
προσκυνέω (**21**):	I worship (usually with dat.).
προστίθημι (**38**):	I add, I give more.
προσφέρω (**11**):	I bring to, I offer.
πρόσωπον, ου, τό (**6**):	face.

προφήτης, ου, ὁ (**5**):	prophet.
πρῶτος, η, ον (**7, 35**):	first.
πτωχός, ή, όν (**13**):	poor.
πῦρ, πυρός, τό (**25**):	fire.
πῶς (10,**26**,34):	how? (adverb).

Ρ

ῥηθείς, –εῖσα, έν (28):	aor. pass. participle of λέγω (**3**). spoken.
ῥῆμα, ῥήματος, τό (2,**25**)	word.
ῥίζα, ης, ἡ (**22**):	root.
ῥύομαι (**30**):	I deliver, I rescue (dep.).

Σ

σάββατον, ου, τό (**8**):	Sabbath.
Σαδδουκαῖος, ου, ὁ (**31**):	Sadducee.
σάρξ, σαρκός, ἡ (**23**):	flesh.
Σατανᾶς, ᾶ, ὁ (**5**):	Satan.
σεαυτοῦ (33):	of thyself (refl. pron.).
σημεῖον, ου, τό (**15**):	sign, miracle.
σήμερον (**30**,34):	today (adverb).
σιωπάω (**21**):	I am silent.
σκανδαλίζω (**8**):	I offend, I cause one to stumble.
σκάνδαλον, ου, τό (**22**):	offense, stumbling block.
σκεῦος, ους, τό (**25**):	vessel.
σκότος, ους, τό (**25**): (also σκοτία, ας, ἡ)	darkness.
σός, σή, σόν (22):	thine (poss. pron.).
σοφία, ας, ἡ (**10**):	wisdom.
σοφίζω (26):	I make wise, I enlighten.
σοφός, ή, όν (**12**):	wise.
σπείρω (**9**):	I sow.
σπέρμα, ατος, τό (**25**):	seed.
σταυρός, οῦ, ὁ (**11**):	cross.
σταυρόω (**20**):	I crucify.
στάχυς, χυος, ὁ (24):	ear of grain.

στέφανος, ου, ὁ (**16**):	crown.
στόμα, ατος, τό (**25**):	mouth.
στρατιώτης, ου, ὁ (**30**):	soldier.
στρέφω (**19**,26):	I turn.
συγχαίρω (11):	I rejoice with.
σύ (12):	(pers. pron.): thou.
συλλαμβάνω (**11**):	I seize, I conceive (of a woman).
συμφωνέω (11):	I agree with.
σύν (9,11,12,**14**):	(with dat.), with.
συνάγω (**11**):	I gather together.
συναγωγή, ῆς, ἡ (**8**):	synagogue.
συνείδησις, εως, ἡ (**24**):	conscience.
συνέρχομαι (**14**):	I come together (deponent).
συνεσθίω (**31**):	I eat with.
συνίημι (**37**):	I understand.
συντελέω (**21**):	I accomplish.
σφόδρα (34):	exceedingly (adverb).
σῴζω (**3**):	I save.
σῶμα, ατος, τό (**25**):	body.
σωτήρ, σωτῆρος, ὁ (**23**):	savior.
σωτηρία, ας, ἡ (**18**):	salvation.

T

ταλαίπωρος, ον (**30**):	miserable, wretched.
τάλαντον, ου, τό (**19**):	talent (sum of money).
ταπεινός, ή, όν (**8**):	humble.
ταπεινόω (**30**):	I humble, I humiliate.
ταράσσω (**16**):	I disturb, I trouble.
ταχέως (34):	quickly, at once (adverb).
τέ (10,**18**):	and, both and (often followed by . . . καί or another τέ) (enclitic).
τέκνον, ου, τό (**4**):	child (in relation to the parent).
τέλειος, α, ον (**12**):	perfect, complete.
τελέω (**21**):	I finish.
τέλος, ους, τό (**25**):	end.
τελώνης, ου, ὁ (**5**,6):	tax-collector.

τέξομαι (16):	fut. of τίκτω, I shall give birth (deponent).
τεσσαράκοντα (**35**):	forty.
τέσσαρες, α (**35**):	four.
τέταρτος, η, ον (35):	fourth.
τετρακισχίλιοι, αι, α (35):	four thousand.
τετραπλοῦς, ῆ, οῦν (21,35):	fourth, fourfold.
τετρακόσιοι, αι, α (35):	four hundred.
τηρέω (**20**):	I keep, I observe.
τίθημι (**38**):	I put, I place, I lay.
τίκτω (**16**):	I give birth.
τιμάω (**20**):	I honor.
τιμή, ῆς, ἡ (**19**):	honor, price.
τις, τι (10,30):	a certain; (pl.) some (enclitic) (indefin. pron.).
τίς, τί (30):	who? which? (interrog. pron.).
τό (5):	the (def. art., neut.).
τόπος, ου, ὁ (10):	place.
τότε (**8**,34):	then (adverb).
τράπεζα, ης, ἡ (**16**):	table.
τρεῖς, τρία (**35**):	three.
τριάκοντα (35):	thirty.
τρίς (35):	three times (adverb).
τρίτος, η, ον (**35**):	third.
τυφλός, ή, όν (10):	blind.

Y

ὑγιής, –ές (**29**):	whole, sound, healthy.
ὕδωρ, ὕδατος, τό (**25**):	water.
υἱός, οῦ, ὁ (2,**8**):	son.
ὑμεῖς (12):	you (pl.) (pers. pron.).
ὑμέτερος, α, ον (22):	your (pl.) (poss. pron.).
ὑπάγω (**28**):	I go, I depart.
ὑπακούω (**11**):	I obey (with dat.).
ὑπέρ (9):	(with gen.) in behalf of, instead of, in favor of, in place of; (with acc.) above.

ὑπό (9):	(with gen.) by; (with acc.) under.
ὑποκριτής, οῦ, ὁ (**13**):	hypocrite.
ὑπομένω (**22**):	I endure.
ὑπομονή, ῆς, ἡ (**10**):	patience.
ὑποστρέφω (**11**):	I return.
ὑποτάσσω (**17**):	I subject, I bring into subjection.

Φ

φάγομαι (16):	(deponent) fut. of ἐσθίω (**6**). I shall eat.
φαίνω (**22**):	I shine; (pass.). I appear.
φανερός, ά, όν (**13**):	manifest, in public.
φανερόω (**20**):	I make manifest, I show, I make clear.
Φαρισαῖος, ου, ὁ (**13**):	Pharisee.
φέρω (**3**):	I carry, I bring, I bear (fruit).
φεύγω (**9**,16,18):	I flee.
φημί (10,**40**):	I say.
φιλέω (**20**,25):	I love.
φίλος, η, ον (**8**):	friendly, friend.
φοβέομαι (**20**):	I fear, I am afraid (deponent).
φόβος, ου, ὁ (**9**):	fear.
φονεύω (**17**):	I kill, I murder.
φρέαρ, φρέατος, τό (25):	well, pit.
φρόνιμος, ον (**12**):	prudent.
φυλακή, ῆς, ἡ (**19**):	prison, a time of watch.
φυλάσσω (**12**,25):	I keep, I guard.
φύσις, εως, ἡ (**24**):	nature, natural condition.
φωνέω (**31**):	I call.
φωνή, ῆς, ἡ (**5**):	voice.
φῶς, φωτός, τό (**25**):	light.

X

χαίρω (**8**,16,18):	I rejoice.
χαρά, ᾶς, ἡ (**13**):	joy.
χάρις, ιτος, ἡ (**23**):	grace.
χάρισμα, τος, τό (**25**):	spiritual gift
χείρ, χειρός, ἡ (1,**23**):	hand.

χείρων, ον (29): comparative degree of κακός (**18**): worse.

χήρα, ας, ἡ (1,**29**): widow.
χιλιάς, χιλιάδος, ἡ (35): one thousand.
χίλιοι, αι, α (35): one thousand.
χορτάζω (**27**): I feed, I satisfy one with food.
χοῦς, χοός, ὁ (24): dust.
χρεία, ας, ἡ (**17**): need, necessity.
Χριστός, οῦ, ὁ (**4**): Christ, Messiah.
χρόνος, ου, ὁ: time (See also καιρός).
χρυσοῦς, ῆ, οῦν (21): golden.
χωλός, ή, όν (**13**): lame.
χωρίς (34): without, separately, apart from (adverb).

Ψ

ψυχή, ῆς, ἡ (**6**): soul, life.

Ω

ὦ (**5**): O, (particle with vocative).
ὧδε (**34**): here, hither (adverb).
ὥρα, ας, ἡ (**6**): hour.
ὡς (10,18,**23**): as, how, about, like.
ὡσεί (**31**): as, like.
ὥστε (**31**): so that, therefore.
ὦτα, ων, τά (25): ears, pl. of οὖς.
ὠφέλιμος, ον (7): useful, profitable.
ὤφθην (19): aor. pass. of ὁράω (**20**). I was seen.

English—Greek Vocabulary

A

abide:	μένω
able, many, sufficient:	ἱκανός
able, am:	δύναμαι
abound:	περισσεύω
about:	περί (with gen.)
above:	ἄνω, ἐπάνω, ἐπί (with acc.), ὑπέρ (with acc.).
Abraham:	Ἀβραάμ
accomplish:	συντελέω, πράσσω
according to:	κατά (with acc.)
accordingly:	οὖν
accuse:	κατηγορέω (with gen.)
add:	προστίθημι
affliction:	θλῖψις
afraid, am:	φοβέομαι
after:	μετά (with acc.)
again:	πάλιν
against:	ατά (with gen.) ἐπί (with acc.).
age:	αἰών
all:	πᾶς, ἅπας (pl.)
alone:	μόνος

alongside:	παρά (with acc.)
already:	ἤδη
also:	καί
always:	πάντοτε
am:	εἰμί
and:	καί, δέ, τέ
and not:	οὐδέ, μηδέ
angel:	ἄγγελος
anger:	ὀργή
announce:	ἀγγέλλω, ἀναγγέλλω, ἀπαγγέλλω
another:	ἄλλος, ἕτερος
(one) another:	ἀλλήλων
answer:	ἀποκρίνομαι
anyone:	τις
anything:	τι
anxious, am:	μεριμνάω
apart:	κατ᾽ ἰδίαν
apart from:	χωρίς
apostle:	ἀπόστολος
appear:	φαίνομαι
appoint:	καθίστημι
approach:	ἐγγίζω
approve:	ἐπαινέω
around:	περί (with acc.)
arrive:	παραγίνομαι
as:	ὡς, ὡσεί; just as: καθώς
as much as, as many as:	ὅσος
as often as:	ὁσάκις
ask (inquire):	ἐρωτάω, ἐπερωτάω
ask (make a request):	αἰτέω, ἐρωτάω
astray, lead:	πλανάω, ἀποπλανάω
at:	παρά (with acc.)
at some time:	ποτέ
authority:	ἐξουσία
away from:	ἀπό (with gen.)

B

bad:	κακός, πονηρός
baptize:	βαπτίζω
baptism:	βάπτισμα
bear (a burden):	φέρω, βαστάζω
bear (children):	γεννάω, τίκτω
bear (fruit):	φέρω
bear witness:	μαρτυρέω (with dat.)
because:	ὅτι
because of:	διά (with acc.)
become:	γίνομαι
bed:	κλίνη
before:	πρό (with gen.) ἔμπροσθεν (with gen.)
beget:	γεννάω
begin:	ἄρχομαι
beginning:	ἀρχή
beginning, from the:	ἄνωθεν
behind:	ὀπίσω
behind, from:	ὄπισθεν
behold (v.):	θεωρέω
behold!:	ἰδού!
believe:	πιστεύω
believer:	πιστός
beloved:	ἀγαπητός
beseech:	παρακαλέω, ἐρωτάω
beside:	παρά (with dat. & acc.)
betray:	παραδίδωμι
better:	κρείσσων (a comp. of ἀγαθός)
beware of:	βλέπω, προσέχω.
bind:	δέω
birth, give:	τίκτω
blaspheme:	βλασφημέω
bless:	εὐλογέω
blessed:	μακάριος
blessing:	εὐλογία

blind:	τυφλός
blood:	αἷμα
boat:	πλοῖον
body:	σῶμα
book:	βιβλίον
both . . . and:	καί . . . καί; τε . . . καί
boy, child:	παῖς
bread:	ἄρτος
break:	κλάω
bride:	νύμφη
bridegroom:	νυμφίος
bring:	φέρω
bring to:	προσφέρω
bring upon:	ἐπάγω
brother:	ἀδελφός
build:	οἰκοδομέω
but:	ἀλλά, δέ
but not:	οὐδέ, μηδέ
by:	ὑπό (with gen.)
by means of:	ἐπί (also expressed by the noun itself in the dative)

C

call:	καλέω, φωνέω
can, (able):	δύναμαι
care about:	μέλει (with dative)
carry:	φέρω
cast, throw:	βάλλω
cast out:	ἐκβάλλω
centurion:	ἑκατατοντάρχης
certain:	τις
charge, command:	παραγγέλλω
chief priest:	ἀρχιερεύς
child:	παῖς
little child:	παιδίον
in relation to the parent:	τέκνον

chosen:	ἐκλεκτός
Christ:	Χριστός
church:	ἐκκλησία
city:	πόλις
cleanse:	καθαρίζω
clean:	καθαρός
clear, make:	φανερόω
close:	κλείω
cloud:	νεφέλη
come:	ἔρχομαι, παραγίνομαι
come down:	κατέρχομαι
come in, into:	εἰσέρχομαι
come to:	προσέρχομαι
come together:	συνέρχομαι
come to pass:	γίνομαι
come up:	ἀνέρχομαι
comfort:	παρακαλέω
coming, second:	παρουσία
command:	κελεύω, παραγγέλλω
commandment:	ἐντολή
communion:	κοινωνία
concealed:	κρυπτός
conceive (of a woman):	συλλαμβάνω
concerning:	περί
condemn:	κατακρίνω
confess:	ὁμολογέω
conscience:	συνείδησις
consolation:	παράκλησις
continue:	ἐπιμένω
contrary to:	παρά (with acc.)
convict:	ἐλέγχω
covenant:	διαθήκη
cover:	καλύπτω
creation:	κτίσις
cross:	σταυρός
crowd:	ὄχλος

crown: στέφανος
crucify: σταυρόω
cry out: κράζω
cup: ποτήριον
curse: καταράομαι
cut down: ἐκκόπτω

D

darkness: σκότος, σκοτία
daughter: θυγάτηρ
David: Δαυίδ
day: ἡμέρα
deacon: διάκονος
dead: νεκρός
deaf: κωφός
death: θάνατος
declare: δηλόω
declare publicly: ὁμολογέω
deliver: παραδίδωμι
deliver (rescue): ῥύομαι
demand: ἀπαιτέω
demon: δαιμόνιον
deny: ἀρνέομαι
depart: ὑπάγω, ἀπέρχομαι, ἀφίστημι
desert: ἔρημος
destroy: λύω, ἀπόλλυμι
devil: διάβολος
die: ἀποθνῄσκω
differ: διαφέρω
different: ἕτερος
disciple: μαθητής
disturb: ταράσσω
do: ποιέω, πράσσω
door: θύρα
drink: πίνω

dry: ξηραίνω
dumb: κωφός
dwell: κατοικέω

E

each: ἕκαστος
each other: ἀλλήλων
ear: οὖς
earth: γῆ
eat: ἐσθίω
elder: πρεσβύτερος
elect: ἐκλεκτός
Elijah: Ἠλίας
end: τέλος
endure: ὑπομένω
enemy: ἐχθρός
inquire: ἐρωτάω, ἐπερωτάω
enter: εἰσέρχομαι
eternal: αἰώνιος
evangelize: εὐαγγελίζομαι
even: καί
ever: ποτέ (enclitic)
every: ἕκαστος, πᾶς
evil: κακός, πονηρός
exalt oneself: ἐπαίρομαι
exceed a certain number: περισσεύω
exceedingly: σφόδρα
except: εἰ μή, ἐάν μή
exhort: παρακαλέω
exhortation: παράκλησις
expect: προσδοκάω
eye: ὀφθαλμός

F

face: πρόσωπον
faith: πίστις

faithful: πιστός
fall: πίπτω
far: μακράν; afar, from; μακρόθεν
fast: νηστεύω
father: πατήρ
fear (n.): φόβος
fear (v): φοβέομαι
feed, satisfy one with food: χορτάζω
fellowship: κοινωνία
few: ὀλίγοι
field: ἀγρός
find: εὑρίσκω
finish: τελέω
fire: πῦρ
fish: ἰχθύς
fisherman: ἁλιεύς
flee: φεύγω
flesh: σάρξ
follow: ἀκολουθέω (with dat.)
foolish: μωρός, ἄφρων
foot: ποῦς
forever: εἰς τόν αἰῶνα
forgive: ἀφίημι
forgiveness: ἄφεσις
forsake: ἐγκαταλείπω
free: ἐλεύθερος
free, set: ἐλευθερόω
friend: φίλος
from: ἀπό, παρά, ἐκ (all with gen.)
fruit: καρπός
fulfill: πληρόω
full: πλήρης

G

gain: κέρδος
Galilee: Γαλιλαία

gather together:	συνάγω
generation:	γενεά
gentiles:	ἔθνος (pl.)
gift:	δῶρον, δωρεά
girl, child:	παῖς
give:	δίδωμι
give back:	ἀποδίδωμι, ἀνταποδίδωμι
give over:	παραδίδωμι
give thanks:	εὐχαριστέω (with dat.)
glorify:	δοξάζω
glory:	δόξα
go:	πορεύομαι, ὑπάγω
go away:	ὑπάγω, ἀπέρχομαι
go down:	καταβαίνω
go in:	εἰσέρχομαι, ἐμβαίνω
go out:	ἐξέρχομαι, ἐκπορεύομαι
go through:	διέρχομαι
go to:	προσέρχομαι
go up:	ἀναβαίνω, ἀνέρχομαι
God:	Θεός
golden:	χρυσοῦς
good:	ἀγαθός, καλός
good news, bring:	εὐαγγελίζομαι
gospel:	εὐαγγέλιον
gospel, preach the:	εὐαγγελίζομαι
governor:	ἡγεμών
grace:	χάρις
greater:	μείζων (comparative degree of μέγας.)
Greek:	Ἕλλην
greet:	ἀσπάζομαι
guard (n.):	φύλαξ
guard (v):	φυλάσσω

H

hair:	θρίξ
hallow:	ἁγιάζω

hand:	χείρ
hate:	μισέω
have:	ἔχω
he:	αὐτός
head:	κεφαλή
heal:	θεραπεύω, ἰάομαι
healthy:	ὑγιής
hear:	ἀκούω
heart:	καρδία
heaven:	οὐρανός
heir:	κληρονόμος
here, hither:	ὧδε
hide:	κρύπτω
hidden:	κρυπτός
high priest:	ἀρχιερεύς
himself, herself, itself:	αὐτός, –ή, –ό
hold, take hold of:	κρατέω
holy:	ἅγιος
honor (n.):	τιμή
honor (v.):	τιμάω
hope (n.):	ἐλπίς
hope (v.):	ἐλπίζω
hour:	ὥρα
house:	οἶκος, οἰκία
how?:	πῶς;
how many?:	πόσοι;
how often?:	ποσάκις;
humble (adj.):	ταπεινός
humble (v.):	ταπεινόω
hunger, to be hunger:	πεινάω
husband:	ἀνήρ
hypocrite:	ὑποκριτής

I

I:	ἐγώ
if:	εἰ, ἐάν

ignorant, am:	ἀγνοέω
ill:	ἀσθενής
illness:	ἀσθένεια
image:	εἰκών
immediately:	εὐθέως, εὐθύς
in:	ἐν (with dat.)
in favor of, in place of:	ὑπέρ (with gen.)
in front of:	ἔμπροσθεν (with gen.)
in order that:	ἵνα, ὅπως
in order that not:	ἵνα μή
in the time of:	ἐπί (with gen.)
in this manner:	οὕτως
infant:	νήπιος, παιδίον
inherit:	κληρονομέω
inheritance:	κληρονομία
instead of:	ἀντί (with gen.)
into:	εἰς (with acc.)

J

James:	Ἰάκωβος
Jerusalem:	Ἱερουσαλήμ, Ἱεροσόλυμα
Jesus:	Ἰησοῦς
Jew:	Ἰουδαῖος
John:	Ἰωάννης
joy:	χαρά
Judea:	Ἰουδαία
judge (n.):	κριτής
judge (v.):	κρίνω
judgment:	κρίσις
just (adj.):	δίκαιος
justify:	δικαιόω

K

keep:	τηρέω, φυλάσσω
kill:	ἀποκτείνω
king:	βασιλεύς, ἡγεμών

kingdom:	βασιλεία
knee:	γόνυ
knock:	κρούω
know:	γινώσκω, οἶδα
know thoroughly:	ἐπιγινώσκω
knowledge:	γνῶσις

L

labor:	κόπος
lack:	λείπω
lame:	χωλός
land:	γῆ
large:	ἱκανός
last (adj.):	ἔσχατος
law:	νόμος
lawful, it is:	ἔξεστι (ν)
lay upon:	ἐπιτίθημι
lead:	ἄγω
lead astray:	πλανάω, ἀποπλανάω
lead away:	ἀπάγω
lead forward:	προάγω
learn:	μανθάνω
least:	ἐλάχιστος (superlative of μικρός.)
leave behind:	καταλείπω, ἀφίημι
leper:	λεπρός
lest:	ἵνα μή, μή
letter:	ἐπιστολή
life:	ζωή, ψυχή
lift up:	ἐπαίρω
light:	φῶς
like (adj.):	ὅμοιος (with dat.)
liken:	ὁμοιόω
little:	ὀλίγος, μικρός
live:	ζάω
loaf of bread:	ἄρτος
look at:	θεωρέω

look up: ἀναβλέπω
loose: λύω
lord, Lord: κύριος, Κύριος
lose: ἀπόλλυμι
lost, I am: ἀπόλλυμαι
love (n.): ἀγάπη
love (v.): ἀγαπάω, φιλέω

M

make: ποιέω
man: ἄνθρωπος; ἀνήρ (in distinction to woman)
manifest, in public: φανερός
manifest, make: φανερόω
many: πολλοί
marriage: γάμος
marvel: θαυμάζω
meat: κρέας
meek: πραΰς
member: μέλος
mercy: ἔλεος
mercy on, have: ἐλεέω
messenger: ἄγγελος
Messiah: Μεσσίας
middle: μέσος
midst, in the: ἐν (τῷ) μέσῳ
mind: νοῦς
mind, am in right: σωφρονέω
minister: διακονέω (with dat.)
miracle: δύναμις, σημεῖον
miserable: ταλαίπωρος
more (adj.): πλείων
more (adv.): μᾶλλον
Moses: Μωϋσῆς
mother: μήτηρ
mountain: ὄρος

mourn:	πενθέω
mouth:	στόμα
much:	πολύς
multitude:	πλῆθος, ὄχλος
must:	δεῖ
my:	ἐμός, μου
myself:	ἐμαυτοῦ
mystery:	μυστήριον

N

name:	ὄνομα
nation:	ἔθνος
nature:	φύσις
near:	ἐγγύς, πλησίον
nearby:	παρά (with dat.)
near, draw:	ἐγγίζω
necessary, it is:	δεῖ
necessity, need:	χρεία
neither . . . nor:	οὐδέ . . . οὐδέ; μηδ . . . μηδέ; οὔτε . . . οὔτε
nevertheless:	ὅμως
new:	καινός, νέος
night:	νύξ
no:	οὐ, οὐκ, οὐχ
no longer:	οὐκέτι, μηκέτι
no one, nothing:	οὐδείς, εμία, έν, μηδείς, εμία, έν
not even:	οὐδέ, μηδέ
not yet:	οὔπω, μήπω
now:	νῦν, ἄρτι
nullify:	ἀθετέω

O

O (with the vocative):	ὦ
obey:	ὑπακούω (with dat.), πείθω (in passive).
observe:	θεωρέω

offend:	σκανδαλίζω
offer:	προσφέρω
offspring:	γένος
often:	πολλάκις
old:	παλαιός (never of persons)
on a particular day:	ἐν
on account of:	διά (with acc.)
one another:	ἀλλήλων
only (adv.):	μόνον
only (adj.):	μόνος
only begotten:	μονογενής
open:	ἀνοίγω
opportunity:	καιρός
or:	ἤ
other:	ἄλλος, ἕτερος
ought:	δεῖ, ὀφείλω
our:	ἡμέτερος, ἡμῶν
out of:	ἐκ (with gen.)
outside:	ἔξω
outside, from the:	ἔξωθεν
overcome:	νικάω
own, one's:	ἴδιος

P

parable:	παραβολή
paralytic:	παραλυτικός
parent:	γονεύς
part:	μέρος
Passover:	πάσχα
patience:	ὑπομονή
Paul:	Παῦλος
peace:	εἰρήνη
people:	λαός
perfect:	τέλειος
perish:	ἀπόλλυμαι
permit:	ἀφίημι

persecute: διώκω
persevere: ἐπιμένω
persuade: πείθω
Peter: Πέτρος
Pharisee: Φαρισαῖος
pity: ἐλεέω
place: τίθημι
poor: πτωχός
power: δύναμις
powerful: ἰσχυρός
praise: ἐπαινέω
pray: προσεύχομαι
prayer: προσευχή, δέησις
preach: κηρύσσω
preach the gospel: εὐαγγελίζομαι
precede (go before): προάγω
prepare: ἑτοιμάζω
presence: παρουσία
present, am: παρίστημι
price: τιμή
priest: ἱερεύς
prison: φυλακή
privately: κατ' ἰδίαν
proclaim: κηρύσσω, ἀπαγγέλλω
promise (n.): ἐπαγγελία
promise (v.): ἐπαγγέλλω
prophet: προφήτης
prudent: φρόνιμος
pure: καθαρός
pursue: διώκω
put around: περιτίθημι
put off: ἀποτίθημι
put on: ἐπιτίθημι
put trust in: πέποιθα

Q

question, ask a:	ἐρωτάω, ἐπερωτάω
quickly:	ταχέως

R

race:	γενεά, γένος
raise, raise up:	ἐγείρω, ἀνίστημι
read:	ἀναγινώσκω
really:	ὄντως
rebuke:	ἐπιτιμάω (with dat.), ἐλέγχω
receive:	δέχομαι, λαμβάνω, παραλαμβάνω
reject:	ἀθετέω
rejoice:	χαίρω
release (n.):	ἄφεσις
release (v.):	ἀπολύω
remain:	μένω
remaining:	λοιπός
render:	ἀποδίδωμι
repent:	μετανοέω
repentance:	μετάνοια
reprove:	ἐλέγχω
resembling:	ὅμοιος
resurrection:	ἀνάστασις
return (v. intrans.):	ἐπιστρέφω, ὑποστρέφω (trans.): ἀποδίδωμι
reveal:	ἀποκαλύπτω
revelation:	ἀποκάλυψις
reward:	μισθός
rich:	πλούσιος
righteous:	δίκαιος
righteousness:	δικαιοσύνη
rise: (v. intrans.):	ἀνίστημι, ἐγείρομαι of the sun: ἀνατέλλω
river:	ποταμός
road:	ὁδός

rock: πέτρα
root: ῥίζα
rule: ἄρχω
ruler: ἄρχων

S

Sabbath: σάββατον
sacrifice: θυσία
Sadducee: Σαδδουκαῖος
saint: ἅγιος
sake of, for the: διά (with acc.)
salt: ἅλας
salvation: σωτηρία
same: αὐτός (after the article)
sanctify: ἁγιάζω
Satan: Σατανᾶς
save: σῴζω
savior: σωτήρ
say: λέγω, φημί
scribe: γραμματεύς
Scripture: γραφή
sea: θάλασσα
see: βλέπω, ὁράω
seed: σπέρμα
seek: ζητέω
seem: δοκέω
send: πέμπω, ἀποστέλλω
separately: χωρίς
servant: διάκονος, παῖς
serve: διακονέω, δουλεύω
set before: παρατίθημι
she: αὐτή
sheep: πρόβατον
sheep, tend: ποιμαίνω
shepherd: ποιμήν
shine: φαίνω

ship:	πλοῖον
shout:	κραυγή
show:	δείκνυμι, δεικνύω, φανερόω
sight, recover one's:	ἀναβλέπω
sign:	σημεῖον
signify:	δηλόω
silver (adj.):	ἀργυροῦς
similar:	ὅμοιος (with dat.)
sin (n.):	ἁμαρτία
sin (v.):	ἁμαρτάνω
sincere:	ἁπλοῦς
sinful, sinner:	ἁμαρτωλός
sister:	ἀδελφή
sit:	κάθημαι, καθίζω
sky:	οὐρανός
slave:	δοῦλος
sleep:	καθεύδω, κοιμάομαι
small:	μικρός
smallest:	ἐλάχιστος (the superlative degree of μικρός)
so:	οὕτως
so that:	ὥστε, ἵνα
soldier:	στρατιώτης
someone, something:	τις, τι
son:	υἱός
sorrow, cause:	λυπέω
soul:	ψυχή
sow:	σπείρω
speak:	λαλέω
spirit:	πνεῦμα
sprout:	βλαστάνω
stand (v. intrans.):	ἵστημι
stand beside:	παρίστημι, ἐφίστημι
stand, cause to:	ἵστημι
star:	ἀστήρ
still:	ἔτι

stone: λίθος
straight: εὐθύς
strength ἰσχύς
strong: ἰσχύς
stumble, cause to: σκανδαλίζω
stumbling block: σκάνδαλον
subject: ὑποτάσσω
suffer: πάσχω
sufficient: ἱκανός
sun: ἥλιος
supper: δεῖπνον
supplication: δέησις
suppose: δοκέω
synagogue: συναγωγή

T

table: τράπεζα
take: λαμβάνω
take away, take up: αἴρω
talent: τάλαντον
taste: γεύομαι (with gen.)
tax-collector: τελώνης
teach: διδάσκω
teacher: διδάσκαλος
teaching: διδασκαλία, διδαχή
temple: ἱερόν, ναός
tempt: πειράζω
temptation: πειρασμός
test: πειράζω
than: ἤ
thanks, give: εὐχαριστέω (with dat.)
that (demonstr.): ἐκεῖνος
that (conj.): ὅτι
the: ὁ, ἡ, τό
then: τότε
thence: ἐκεῖθεν

there:	ἐκεῖ
therefore:	ἄρα, οὖν, ὥστε
thing:	πρᾶγμα
think:	δοκέω
thirst:	διψάω
this:	οὗτος, αὕτη, τοῦτο
thou:	σύ
throne:	θρόνος
through:	διά (with gen.) κατά (with acc.)
throughout:	διά (with gen.), κατά (with acc.)
throw:	βάλλω
throw out:	ἐκβάλλω
thus:	οὕτως
thy:	σός
time:	χρόνος
appointed time:	καιρός
tired, get:	κοπιάω
to:	εἰς, πρός (with acc.)
today:	σήμερον
together:	ὁμοῦ
toil:	κοπιάω
tomb:	μνημεῖον
tomorrow:	αὔριον
tongue:	γλῶσσα
touch:	ἅπτομαι (with gen.)
towards:	πρός, κατά, ἐπί (with acc.)
tradition:	παράδοσις
treasure:	θησαυρός
tree:	δένδρον
tribulation:	θλῖψις
trouble:	ταράσσω
true:	ἀληθής, ἀληθινός
truly:	ἀληθῶς
trust:	πέποιθα (perfect of πείθω)
truth:	ἀλήθεια
turn:	στρέφω, ἐπιστρέφω

U

unbeliever, unfaithful:	ἄπιστος
unclean:	ἀκάθαρτος
uncover:	ἀποκαλύπτω
under:	ὑπό (with acc.)
understand:	συνίημι
unjust:	ἄδικος
unjustly, act:	ἀδικέω
until:	ἕως, ἕως ὅτου
upon:	ἐπί (with gen. and dat.)

V

vessel:	σκεῦος
village:	κώμη
virgin:	παρθένος
voice:	φωνή

W

wages:	μισθός
walk:	περιπατέω
warn:	ἐπιτιμάω
wash:	νίπτω
watch, a time of (n.):	φυλακή
watch (v.):	βλέπω
water:	ὕδωρ
way:	ὁδός
we:	ἡμεῖς
weak:	ἀσθενής
weak, am:	ἀσθενέω
weakness:	ἀσθένεια
wedding:	γάμος
weep:	κλαίω
well (n.):	φρέαρ
well (adv.):	εὖ, καλῶς
what?:	τί;
when:	ὅτε

when?:	πότε;
whenever:	ὅταν
where:	ὅπου
where?:	ποῦ;
white:	λευκός
who, which:	ὅς, ἥ, ὅ
who?, which?:	τίς; τί;
whoever, whichever:	ὅστις, ἥτις, ὅ, τι
whole:	ὅλος, ἅπας
why?:	τί, διὰ τί
widow:	χήρα
wife:	γυνή
will (n.):	θέλημα
willing, am; wish:	βούλομαι, θέλω
wine:	οἶνος
wisdom:	σοφία
wise:	σοφός
with:	μετά (with gen.) σύν (with dat.)
wither:	ξηραίνομαι
within:	ἔσω; within, from: ἔσωθεν
witness (n.):	μαρτυρία, μάρτυς
witness (v.):	μαρτυρέω
woman:	γυνή
womb:	κοιλία
wonder at:	θαυμάζω
word:	λόγος, ῥῆμα
work (n.):	ἔργον
work (v.):	ἐργάζομαι
work hard:	κοπιάω
worker:	ἐργάτης
world:	κόσμος
worship:	προσκυνέω (usually with dat.)
worthy:	ἄξιος
wrath:	ὀργή
write:	γράφω

writing:	γραφή
wrong someone:	ἀδικέω

Y

yet:	ἔτι
you:	ὑμεῖς (pl.)
your:	ὑμέτερος
yourselves:	ἑαυτῶν

New Testament Scripture Index

General Index

A

Q

R

S